The Psychology of Genocide
and Violent Oppression

The Psychology of Genocide and Violent Oppression

A Study of Mass Cruelty from Nazi Germany to Rwanda

RICHARD MORROCK

McFarland & Company, Inc., Publishers

Jefferson, North Carolina, and London

LIBRARY OF CONGRESS CATALOGUING-IN-PUBLICATION DATA

Morrock, Richard.
The psychology of genocide and violent oppression : a study of mass
cruelty from Nazi Germany to Rwanda / Richard Morrock.
p.   cm.
Includes bibliographical references and index.

ISBN 978-0-7864-4776-3
softcover : 50# alkaline paper ∞

1. Genocide — History.
2. Genocide — Psychological aspects.
3. Political violence — Psychological aspects.
4. Psychohistory.
I. Title.
HV6322.7.M67   2010   304.6'63 — dc22   2010010464

British Library cataloguing data are available

Cover image ©2010 Shutterstock

Manufactured in the United States of America

McFarland & Company, Inc., Publishers
Box 611, Jefferson, North Carolina 28640
www.mcfarlandpub.com

To the memory of
Jean Jackson,
primal therapist

Acknowledgments

Many psychohistorians have assisted me in this long project, with information or encouragement, or by allowing themselves to serve as sounding boards. In no particular order, they include Lloyd deMause, Allan Mohl, Jacques Szaluta, Gerrold Atlas, Evan Malachowsky, Geraldine Pauling and Dennis King, Robert Young and Barbara LaMonica, David Beisel, Harriet Fraad, Joan Lachkar, Peter Berton, Joe Reilly, Jay Sherry, Don Nelson, Landon Dowdey, Henry Lawton, Robert Schaeffer, Barbara Legutko, Deborah Tanzer, David Lotto, Helen Gallant, Aurelio Torres, Jay Gonen, Mary Coleman, Marvin Goldwert, Mel Kalfus, Mel Goldstein, Daniel Dervin, Herbert Barry, Eli Sagan, Rudolph Binion, and James Villareal.

Hannah Lessinger, Fred Mackey, and Robert Kearney gave me invaluable assistance with my research on Sri Lanka, as did Jennifer Davis on South Africa, and Warren Weinstein on Africa in general. I had the good fortune to be able to discuss Iranian politics with Dr. Jack Moadel in the delightful ambience of Club Med Martinique. My cousin Mel Weiselberg gave a useful critique of the chapter on Cambodia.

Thanks, of course, to Arthur Janov and Vivian Janov for coming up with primal therapy. And thanks to the incredibly effective crew of therapists at the New York Primal Institute: Jean, Tracy, Skip, Alix, Scott, Ditto, Cindy, John, Ann F., and G.P.

Thanks also to Joel Carlinsky for his insights into the Reichian movement.

And a special thanks to my buddy John Leicmon for his insights during the early stages of my research.

Needless to say, none of these friends and colleagues should be held responsible for any factual errors in the text, or for my conclusions, which are entirely my responsibility.

Table of Contents

Preface

As an undergraduate, studying history and political science during the early 1960s, I came to believe that no full understanding of politics — particularly the rise of fascism during the previous generation — was possible without comprehending the crucial role of psychology. The problem was that academic psychology was then dominated by Skinnerian behaviorism, which struck me as a refined form of sophistry having nothing to add to our understanding of the human mind. The behaviorists brooked no opposition. If Sigmund Freud made an appearance in the classroom, it was typically in the literature department.

Over the next few decades, I witnessed, among other events, the Chinese Cultural Revolution, the continued conflict in Northern Ireland, the ethnic war in Sri Lanka, Pol Pot's bizarre revolution in Cambodia, and the transformation of modernizing, secular Iran into a theocracy. It seemed that a new way of looking at political extremism was necessary. It wasn't even a question of the old approach being outdated — there *was* no old approach. Conventional historians and political scientists were attributing these horrors, along with earlier ones like the Holocaust, to the evil impulses of a few leaders. But it was clear to me that something was going on with the *masses* who were eagerly following these leaders. Whatever Ayatollah Khomeini's personal grudges against the world, millions of Iranians stood behind him against both the Shah and rival anti-royalist movements. The enthusiasm of many Germans for Hitler was almost orgasmic. Likewise, the anti–Catholic bigot the Rev. Ian Paisley won enough popular support among Northern Ireland's Protestants to supplant the existing Unionist establishment, which had held power for generations. A new paradigm for the understanding of political extremism was necessary, and the horrors of Cambodia during the 1970s, and Rwanda during the 1990s — not to mention al-Qaeda's attack on the United States on September 11, 2001 — were making it all the more urgent. Not to understand history, it has been often said, is to risk repeating it.

In the following pages, I discuss events in sixteen countries in various regions of the world during roughly the past century, looking at them as expressions of neurotic symptoms which were widely shared by members of that society. Other countries, such as Russia, France, or Japan, might also lend themselves to such an approach, but will have to wait for other authors. And having been trained in history and political science, I have emphasized political developments, perhaps to the detriment of the study of childhood. But in putting the "history" back in psychohistory, I believe I have avoided the trap of reductionism.

Like many activist intellectuals who came of age during the 1960s, I developed an interest in the theories of Wilhelm Reich, the brilliant but eccentric psychoanalyst whose works sometimes appear to have been written about some alternate universe. Reich's *Sex-Pol Essays*, and even more his *Mass Psychology of Fascism*, took an approach that cast the rise of fascism in Germany (and particularly his native Austria) in a new light. He was, aside from the more conventional Erich Fromm, the only one who was interpreting *mass* delusions in a psychological manner, instead of merely focusing on the pathology of individuals like Hitler. Yet there still seemed to be something lacking in Reich's theories. Did sexual repression *cause* the right-wing political extremism Reich was describing? Or was sexual repression merely the *consequence* of class oppression — a consequence that made it possible for the masses to tolerate their oppression without rebelling? Reich appeared to be taking both positions, and it was never clear whether he thought that the answer to fascism was on the barricades or in the psychoanalyst's office. While he noted that the sexual repression that followed the Bolshevik victory in Russia soon reversed itself, turning into a strange form of sexually repressed "Red Fascism," Reich seemed unable to explain why. He never answered the question of why millions of people, having been liberated from both social and sexual repression, should have decided to put themselves back into the straitjackets from which they had just been freed. The short answer is that they were suffering from repression of *feelings*, not just their sexuality.

The psychological theorist who put feelings at the center was Arthur Janov, founder of primal therapy, first developed in California in the 1960s. Basic to Janov's approach is that defenses are bad. Instead of protecting us from Pain (he prefers to capitalize the word), they prevent past traumas from being felt, causing them to remain in our unconscious and keeping us neurotic. Most other psychological approaches — the Reichians are a bit ambivalent on this question — believe in building up the patient's defenses. In primal therapy they are rendered inoperative, one at a time.

To simplify things, the human mind has four functions: Memory, Consciousness, Repression, and Pain. For thousands of years, only the first two had been recognized. Freud made the next step at the end of the nineteenth century, when he identified Repression. But without an understanding of Pain, Freud's psychoanalysis remained flawed, with many patients failing to improve.

Developments in psychotherapy since Freud have represented, in my judgment, retreats rather than advances. Alfred Adler's "individual psychotherapy" dropped Freud's concept of Repression, and reverted to the sort of ineffective common sense approach that long predated psychoanalysis. Karen Horney proceeded along the same lines, as did Anna Freud and the pioneers of "ego psychology," essentially cognitive therapy in psychoanalytic garb. Freud's onetime follower Carl Gustav Jung dropped Memory from the repertoire of his "analytical psychology," replacing it with *myth*. This led him to welcome the rise of Nazism, although he soon grew disenchanted. Reich, in contrast, substituted *energy* for Consciousness. He became increasingly unconscious of his own repressed anger, and started imagining that the government was spying on him from airplanes. Eventually, he believed that he was shooting down hostile UFOs (the lights in the sky may have been the effects of nearby nuclear tests) with orgone rays. Ironically, while psychoanalysts continue to read his work on character analysis, flying saucer buffs, taking umbrage at Reich's notion that hostile space aliens could be defeated by mere humans, dismiss him as a crackpot.

Janov's development of primal therapy in the 1960s made an advance over Freud, adding the function of Pain to the trio of Memory, Consciousness, and Repression. Janov postulated that emotional Pain is processed the same way as physical, and that repression of Pain causes reverberating circuits in the brain, which produce neurotic symptoms. Feel the Pain, he showed, and the symptoms go away. In primal therapy, the patient experienced maximum possible reactions to emotional stimuli. The patient moved from talking about some incident in the present, to reliving earlier events that felt much the same way. This was often accompanied by pounding a padded wall or a pillow. Patients had dramatic results: adults began sobbing like small children; black-and-blue marks reappeared from injuries suffered at birth. I began primal therapy in 1979, in part to clear up the damage from a previous Reichian therapy, and in my own case I re-experienced a "charley horse" from a basketball game I had played *twenty-one years earlier*, after reliving a painful event that followed the game. This primal experience resulted in a major, permanent improvement in my overall state of mind. Clearly, I realized, Janov was on to something. And if his theories could apply to my personal problems, could they not be applied to the study of political extremism as well?

Over the next twenty years and more, I was involved with the International Psychohistorical Association (IPA), presenting at their annual conventions and helping to put out their newsletter. Founded by Lloyd deMause, who was influenced by both Freud and Janov, the IPA is one of the few places where social scientists and clinical therapists can exchange ideas and help illuminate each other's work. Many IPA members are eclectic in their perspective, like deMause himself, while others tend to be more orthodox Freudians; occasionally a Jungian or Adlerian shows up, but I appear to be the only veteran of genuine (beware of imitations) primal therapy. The chapters that follow are revised versions of papers most of which were presented at IPA conventions since the 1980s. My approach was to immerse myself in books on each country, note what was particularly irrational in its politics, and then ask myself, "What would I be feeling if I were to act like that?"

This is not the first work to attempt to draw comparisons between the various acts of genocide we have seen over the last hundred years. DeMause's own *Foundations of Psychohistory* was seminal, and Neil Kressel's *Mass Hate* and Stuart J. Kaufman's *Modern Hatreds* also cover the psychological roots of political violence. But I differ from deMause in my rejection of the reductionist paradigm, while Kressel and Kaufman have not familiarized themselves with Janov's theories. Other books that cover some of the same countries, such as Sumantra Bose's *Contested Lands*, are not psychohistorical works at all. In treating such tragedies as Bosnia or Sri Lanka as if their causes were entirely historical, many authors have overlooked the effects of child-reading, birth trauma, miseducation, and drugs. Without such understanding, the promise of "Never Again" each after catastrophe remains sadly empty, as we can see from the current slaughter in Sudan's Darfur region.

1

A Psychohistorical Perspective on a Violent Century

Throughout the twentieth century, phenomenal advances occurred in all fields of human endeavor. Radio, television, and ultimately the personal computer and the internet changed the way we communicate, while the automobile and airplane revolutionized transportation. Humans walked on the moon, and unmanned spacecraft sent photographs back to Earth from Mars and beyond. Diseases such as diphtheria, polio and smallpox were wiped out, while significant progress was made in the struggle against cancer. The energy of the atom was harnessed, new elements were discovered, and the secrets of the unconscious mind began to give way to the persistent probing of psychotherapists.

The world's population increased approximately four-fold, and there was an even more massive growth of major cities, in both the developed and underdeveloped nations. Illiteracy was all but eliminated in many countries, and reduced substantially in others. Universities expanded and multiplied. Women gained the right to vote and obtained access to careers and political power to a degree unprecedented in history.

At the start of the twentieth century, about a third of the world's population lived under colonial rule, including many European nations, but by the century's end, colonialism was dead, and the number of sovereign states had nearly quadrupled. In 1901, most countries outside the Western hemisphere were absolute monarchies, but by 2000 this form of government had largely disappeared.

Massive land reforms — some more successful than others — were carried out as a result of revolutions in many countries. Electrification spread to the countryside, and draft animals were increasingly replaced by tractors. In the cities of the more developed nations, the horse — still the primary mode of transportation in 1901 — had all but vanished from the streets by mid-century. The six billion people of 2000, in many cases, lived lives that would have been nearly unrecognizable to their great-grandparents.

And yet it would be a mistake to say that the twentieth century, with all its progress, represented an era of sweetness and light. Even allowing for the increased world population, it may well have been the bloodiest hundred years in history. Compared to the nineteenth century — no stranger to war itself — the twentieth century looks almost like a reversion to the Dark Ages.

Three cases of full-fledged genocide occurred during the nineteenth century — the Native Americans in parts of the Western Hemisphere, the Armenians in Turkey, and the

Congo under the Belgians — the last two continuing into the early twentieth century, indicating things to come. In the twentieth century, on the other hand, cases of genocide included the Jews, Gypsies, Poles and Russians at the hands of the Nazis, the Serbs in the short-lived Ustashi state of Croatia, the Chinese under Japanese occupation, Bangladesh in 1970, East Timor in 1973 and after, the southern Sudan, and Rwanda in 1994, not to mention Cambodia's horrific auto-genocide and numerous other cases. There were from fifteen to twenty conflicts in the twentieth century in which at least a million people died — including World War II, the largest in all history, with an estimated 75 million victims. And if that conflict had ended with the victory of the Axis, rather than the Allies, as it might have, the death toll could have easily run into the billions, with numerous nations completely exterminated.

Throughout the twentieth century, psychopaths, mountebanks and greedy thugs seized power in nations great and small. Some of these dictators, like Hitler, Pol Pot, or François Duvalier, were clearly deranged; others, like Chiang Kai-Shek, Mobuto Sese Seko, or Saddam Hussein, were merely corrupt and power-hungry sociopaths. Military coups were a frequent occurrence; Syria alone experienced at least a dozen of them, and several Latin American countries were not far behind. Torture, largely eliminated during the nineteenth century, became widespread. The latter part of the twentieth century saw the emergence of the "failed state," one which — like Somalia or Afghanistan — proved unable to perform the most basic functions of government.

What caused this curious juxtaposition of political, social, economic and technological progress with world wars, totalitarian dictatorships, and massive ethnic and political violence? It would be tempting to blame it all on the world's greatly increased population. Obviously, wars are likely to kill more people if there are more people to kill. Yet, in percentage terms, one would have to search long and hard to find any other nation in history that slaughtered fully ten percent of its population in a matter of a few weeks, as Rwanda did during 1994 in the name of "Hutu Power," or which murdered a quarter of its own people in three years as did Cambodia under Pol Pot. Likewise, Jewish history is filled with pogroms and massacres, but at no point in two thousand years of dispersion, prior to World War II, did the Jews ever lose one-third of their entire number to anti–Semitic persecution, as happened during the Nazi Holocaust.

Another overly simple explanation is that the technology of warfare has made massacres and genocide easier; 150,000 people, after all, were slain in a split second when the United States dropped an atomic bomb on Hiroshima. Yet the total number of victims of nuclear bombs amounts to barely one tenth of one percent of the twentieth century's war dead. In Bangladesh in 1970, three million people were killed by the same kind of weapons that existed during the nineteenth century. In Cambodia, the Khmer Rouge slit the throats of their victims with sharp-edged palm-leaf stems, while in Rwanda, Hutu militants used clubs to kill Tutsis and other enemies. Weapons like these were available even in the Stone Age.

A major ideology during the twentieth century was Marxism, largely discredited by the turn of the millennium. Marxism would explain the intensity of the world's violence in terms of the class struggle. But what characterized many cases of mass slaughter over the past hundred years was precisely the *absence* of any economic conflict between the perpetrators and victims. Jewish capitalists were murdered by Hitler along with Jewish workers;

Croats killed Serbs under the Ustashi regardless of class; Chinese workers fought other Chinese workers during the Cultural Revolution.

In contrast, psychohistory — as pioneered by the eclectic thinker Lloyd deMause — has long postulated that the development of better child-rearing practices is the main force behind political and social development; this *psychogenic theory of history*, as he terms it, is a challenge to Marxism, which has always attributed such development to class struggle and technological innovation, not to mention conventional history, which generally fails to even ask the question of *why* things happen the way they do. It also raises the questions about the cultural determination advocated by such figures as Margaret Mead; from the psychohistorical point of view, culture is a *dependent* rather than independent variable, caused by the same psychological factors as history itself. Yet if deMause's explanation is accurate, the healthier child-rearing practices now increasingly common in the West should have resulted in *less* violence as compared to previous ages. DeMause, in response to this dilemma, has proposed that political development often gets ahead of psychological development, promoting a form of anxiety — Erich Fromm, thinking along similar lines, called it "fear of freedom" — which takes the form of political repression, genocide, and military aggression. To be sure, Nazi Germany, following in the wake of the Weimar Republic, fits this model well, as do Fascist Italy and Rwanda under the Hutu extremists. But the slaughter in Pol Pot's Cambodia did not follow any meaningful democratization, and the triumph of Khomeini's theocratic followers in Iran came on the heels of the Shah's installation of a totalitarian regime in place of an authoritarian one. In addition, one might question how political development could outspace psychological development if the latter alone is the cause of the former.

Marxists might respond to deMause by arguing that fascist movements do not result from "fear of freedom," so much as from the ruling class's concern that long-oppressed social classes might take advantage of this freedom to advance their own interests. Nazism, from this perspective, represented less a reaction to the freedom of Weimar democracy than to the rapid growth of the German Communist Party in the wake of the Great Depression. That this fails to account for the auto-genocide in Cambodia should be self-evident. Nor does it begin to explain why movements which clearly oppose the interests of the oppressed have managed to recruit so many of them.

Both deMause and the Marxists take a *reductionist* view of history, each explaining the turmoil of the twentieth century as a result of a single factor — either child-rearing, or the ruling class's fear of revolution. Reductionism, in the words of philosopher Walter Kaufman, is the notion that "something is *nothing but* something else." When put that way, its fallacy is self-evident. My own approach rejects reductionism in favor of what I call *interactionism*. In my view, many factors interact to product the violent events we have been seeing throughout history, particularly in the last century. These include birth trauma, child-rearing practices, the educational system, and — in a number of cases — drugs of one kind or another, as well as the political, social, and economic factors which conventional historians are already familiar with. Reductionist paradigms are overly simplistic, and have, in fact, been partially responsible for many of our recent horrors, such as Nazi genocide, informed by biological reductionism, as well as Stalin's purges, rationalized by the economic reductionism of Soviet Marxism. To fully understand the political madness of the twentieth century, it is not enough to focus exclusively on childhood or economics; one must look at everything.

We now live in a world where little can be taken for granted. Our system of government might change suddenly through war or revolution; our nation's boundaries might shrink or expand; the province we live in might become a sovereign nation almost overnight, or even part of a former enemy nation; our familiar home town might double in population in a few years, with its old neighborhoods filling up with immigrants from strange and distant lands. New inventions change the way we live and the way we relate to others. Technological change occurs at such a speed that parents may find it difficult to communicate with their computer-savvy, text-messaging children. Even scientific truths may be swiftly overturned by new discoveries or interpretations. The "miracle drugs" of one decade can be all but useless in the next. And the plagues they were expected to treat may spread like wildfire because of the increased ease of worldwide transportation.

While some welcome change, there are also those who fear it. One such group is what Theodore Adorno described as "authoritarian personalities," people who have a rigid commitment to their political and religious beliefs, are intolerant of differences, and prefer to live in a hierarchical society in which everyone knows their place. Another group, yet to be recognized by social scientists unfamiliar with the world of psychologist Arthur Janov, are those who suffered intense birth trauma, memories of which can be activated by unsettling events on either the personal or social level. It is one of the many ironies of the twentieth century that even as *child-rearing* has become more humane and empathetic in the developed nations, the medical management of the *birth process*— with its excessive use of anesthesia and its scheduled feeding of the newborn — has increased the amount of birth trauma in these same societies. To complicate matters, people with less childhood trauma tend to have easier access to their buried birth memories, a fact that goes far to explain the rise of Fascism in Italy, a country where child-rearing has generally been fairly lenient.

Another distinguishing characteristic of the twentieth century was the ease with which ideas could spread — through the increasing number of schools and universities, through newspapers and magazines which reached vastly more people as a result of the spread of literacy and less expensive printing, and through the electronic media. This made it possible for what psychohistorians call *group fantasies* to develop to an unprecedented degree. For example, the medieval-minded Ayatollah Khomeini made use of tape cassettes to spread his ideas, while the pan–Islamists of Ayman al-Zawahiri and Osama bin Laden became adept with the internet. Likewise, both Germany's Nazis and Rwanda's Hutu extremists made extensive use of the radio, while television played a major role in the rise of ethnic separatist movements in Yugoslavia. Mass communication — especially, in recent years, the Internet — has created a *group mind*, and sometimes this mind, like that of an individual, can break down under stress.

It has been an axiom of psychohistory that "nations are like people." Some are large, and some small; some weak, and some strong; some rich, and some poor; some healthy, and some dysfunctional. One can, to be sure, exaggerate the similarities. No one has ever seen his left leg secede from the rest of his body to strike out on its own as a separate individual, as Ireland broke away from Great Britain, or as the Southern region has been trying to break away from Sudan. But the nations that social scientists study are made up of individuals whose personal traumas, if shared in common, inevitably influence the directions that their countries take, just as the nation itself — through its schools, laws, holidays, patriotic pageants, armed forces, public speeches, political parties and other institutions —

affects the lives of its citizens. And whereas many observers have insisted that "the personal is the political," psychohistory has emphasized that the reverse is also true: the political is the personal.

The failure of reductionist paradigms led, tragically, to a dimming of the Enlightenment at century's end, as fundamentalists promoted Biblical literalism as "science," astrologers and "spiritual advisors" undercut costlier but often equally ineffective psychotherapies, and ultra-nationalists and mystics sprouted like mushrooms in the soil fertilized by the decay of Communism. Yet the human spirit has long resisted attempts to bind it, and it may only be a matter of time before a Second Enlightenment arrives to free us from reductionism as the first freed us, however incompletely, from belief in the supernatural.

The following is my attempt to reinvent psychohistory on an interactionist basis, using Janov's primal theory to explain the political madness which has created so much havoc in the twentieth century.

The Two-Self Model

Arthur Janov holds that we have two selves: one is our *real* self, what we really are; the other is the *unreal* self that we had to invent in order to gain the love and acceptance of those — our parents, in most cases — who raised us. Withdrawal of this love creates Pain, which is unbearable for the child, whose life depends on the caretakers' efforts. This withdrawal may take the form of neglect, or emotional, physical, or even sexual abuse. Or it may take the form of subtle pressure on the child to become what the parent wants, rather than what the child wants: a soldier, a "gentleman," a "lady," an athlete, a genius, or even a child of the opposite sex.[1] Whereas psychoanalysis has tended to focus on particularly bizarre traumas as the cause of neurosis — severe beatings, sexual abuse, and the like, as witness Alfred Hitchcock's Freudian-influenced film *Marnie*— most of the material that came up for the patients in primal therapy involved everyday events such as scoldings, cross looks, unfair punishments, being left at school when too young, lack of attention, overprotection, or unrealistic expectations on the part of parents. In the course of primal therapy, the unreal self simply dissolves, and the patient becomes real.

The two-self model can also be applied to psychohistory. Nations, like people, may function in a real or unreal manner. On the social level, the real self responds to economic interests; people in their real selves vote according to their interests as workers, businessmen, peasants, landowners, pensioners, civil servants, or members of ethnic minorities. It is the unreal self which falls prey to demagogues, who symbolically express buried feelings stemming from childhood traumas, including birth. To understand the appeal of a Hitler, or a Pol Pot, or an Ayatollah Khomeini, one must look at how they make us feel.

In primal therapy, a feeling is distinct from an emotion, much as a song is distinct from the key in which it is played. There are only a few basic emotions, expressed in single words such s "joy," "anger," "fear," "need," "hurt," or "grief." Feelings are more specific: "I need you, daddy," "I am angry with you, mommy," "I can't be what you want," "I am afraid you won't love me," "Please don't hurt me." On the social level, we are looking primarily at the effects of repressed *anger, fear, hurt, need,* and *grief.* Repressed anger is common in countries like Cambodia, where the Buddhist religion emphasized remaining calm and unemotional under all circumstances, but it also shows up in Europe, where children were not allowed to express anger against parents. Repressed fear turns up primarily in militaristic nations, which cannot allow even children to experience legitimate fear, or in nations like the United States, which experienced unexpected defeats in war. America has yet to come to terms with its defeat in Vietnam, as witness the black POW flags still flying over our public buildings; we are fantasizing that since Americans are still being held prisoner in Vietnam, the war is not over, and we haven't lost yet.

Repressed need is most common in countries like Rwanda where children are raised in extreme economic deprivation, but it also appeared in Germany, where the deprivation was primarily emotional. The Iranians repressed their grief during the Iran-Iraq War, only to have it burst open when the United States shot down an Iran Air passenger plane in 1988. And Germany's response to the war guilt clause of the Treaty of Versailles was repressed hurt.

Among the feelings which have led to political madness in the twentieth century are: I am angry at daddy and mommy; I am angry at myself; I am afraid of someone weak (or someone strong); I am afraid of humiliation; I am afraid of annihilation (birth feeling); I am being poisoned (also birth); I am afraid of chaos (again birth); I need to be nourished (physically or intellectually); I need to break out of confinement (once again, birth). We will meet all of them as we examine sixteen nations in the chapters that follow.

All neurosis, as I learned in primal therapy, is based on repressed feelings — not on instinct, conditioned reflexes, or wrong information, as other therapies would have it. This is equally true of the irrationality we have seen for the past hundred years in politics. Some have maintained that "obedience to authority" is the key factor in genocidal outbursts.[2] Others have proposed that ethnic persecution results primarily from the desire of the killers to steal the property of the victims. Both of these factors are involved, to be sure, but mindless obedience and greed are relative constants in the human condition. Events like the Holocaust, the genocide in Rwanda, Argentina's "dirty war," or the post–1991 conflicts in Yugoslavia, on the other hand, are episodic. Something on the social level triggers them; and that something may be an event in the nation's immediate past, or, as we shall see, even one that happened years earlier, producing a delayed reaction.

Politics and Brain Structure

Anger and fear are controlled by an organ in the brain called the amygdala, part of the limbic system, which deals with the emotions. Repressed fear, and even more so repressed anger, can cause all sorts of symptoms ranging from mental illness to heart attacks and back problems. Frequently, when anger is repressed, it takes the form of paranoia, with the patient experiencing his own unfelt anger as that of others directed at him. The amygdala turns this anger into pseudo-fear; the patient imagines that people are out to get him. But this pseudo-fear can easily be distinguished from the genuine fear felt by people facing real threats; the paranoid may think that the CIA, space aliens, or the Mafia are planning to kill him, but considering the alleged danger, he seems noticeably unconcerned about it.

Repressed fear, likewise, may be turned by the amygdala into pseudo-anger. Children brought up in homes where they are in constant fear are more likely to become criminals or terrorists, taking out their pseudo-anger on society. One of the most effective ways in which people deal with repressed fear is by making others afraid of them. Persecution of ethnic or religious minorities is the result of repressed fear operating at the social level, sometimes coupled with repressed anger. Often, the nature of the minority chosen for persecution — while other minorities remain unaffected — gives us a clue as to what specific feeling is behind the political madness.

Identification with the Aggressor

This concept was first promulgated by Anna Freud, to describe how neurotics attempt to cope with their dysfunctional families of origin. Unloved for who they are, and unable to express their anger about it, neurotics begin regarding themselves as "the enemy." This mechanism also occurs on the social level, usually within nations, as subordinated ethnic groups begin identifying with the dominant group, but usually without gaining any degree of equality. People of Indian descent in Latin America, for example, remain oppressed, as part of a subordinate social class, even after they have adopted the language, religion and identity of their Spanish conquerors.

Sometimes, an entire nation may identify in some respect with an outside aggressor. Cambodia's belligerent attitude toward Vietnam after 1975 appears to have resulted from the substitution of Vietnam, a fellow victim of American aggression, for the United States itself, which had bombed and invaded Cambodia for years, resulting in vast destruction. In attacking Vietnam, which had been the enemy of the United States, Pol Pot's Cambodia was unconsciously identifying with America.[3] Another example was India's 1962 conflict with China over the virtually uninhabited Aksai Chin. The previous year, India's annexation of the Portuguese colony of Goa had been bitterly denounced by Britain and the United States, notwithstanding the fact that Goa's population was nearly all Indian, and wanted liberation from the Portuguese. In provoking a war the following year with China, India was seeking to regain the support of the Western powers, much as a child might engage in self-destructive acts in order to regain the love of his or her parents.

The Origin Folk

Often, the group chosen for persecution is what may be termed an "Origin Folk." This is an ethnic group, typically a large minority or even a majority, from which the dominant ethnic group is derived. An example would be the Africans in southern Sudan, who share much the same biological ancestry as the "Arabs" who waged brutal war against them for nearly 40 years.[4] Both ethnic groups were African, or course, and Sudanese "Arabs" are often simply Muslim pastoralists with little or no Arab ancestry. A similar case would be the Indians in Guatemala, slaughtered by the hundreds of thousands by death squads organized by the U.S.–backed government, whose members were typically "Ladinos" — that is, Spanish-speaking Guatemalans of largely Indian ancestry. The Tamils in Sri Lanka also constitute an Origin Folk, since the dominant Sinhalese are derived from them; the latter evolved into a separate ethnic group as a result of their conversion to Buddhism, followed by their adoption of a new language based on the Buddhist scriptures. The Ulster Catholics are an Origin Folk in relation to the Protestants, who adopted the identity of the British conquerors. The same is true of Hindus in regard to South Asian Muslims; Pakistan's Muslims can be provoked to hate Hindus became they used to *be* Hindus.

Collective neurosis, like individual neurosis, often involves denial of one's past. The Sinhalese, following Western historians, believe that they migrated to Sri Lanka from northern India to subjugate the local Tamil population, although the two groups are indistinguishable in appearance. Argentina classifies itself as 97 percent European, denying the considerable American Indian element in its population. The Ulster Protestants have invented a myth linking themselves to the Cruthin (or Picts) of ancient times, although this long-vanished people never occupied more than a fraction of Northern Ireland and, around the time of the fall of Rome, was forced out by the Gaels, from whom most of the Irish — Catholic and Protestant alike — are descended.

The relationship between the dominant group and the Origin Folk is isomorphic (i.e., shares a common structure) to that between the unreal and the real self. Neurotics seek to repress their real selves in order to gain love from their parents — and, later, acceptance from authority figures. Nations may do much the same thing with their Origin Folk, leading to civil war and even genocide.

The Catalytic Community

Some nations contain minorities which are more urbanized and better educated than the dominant group. In times of social stress, these minorities are prone to being singled out for persecution. Attributing their persecution to their countries' unjust social structure, not without reason, these ethnic groups — which I term Catalytic Communities — tend to become supporters of social change and leftist politics, which only results in even more persecution by the majority.

The classic example of a Catalytic Community are the Jews in Europe, who were the intellectual pioneers in many fields, and provided a disproportionate number of leaders on the left. Many factors combined to put the Jews in this position, including Judaism's ethics of truth — in contrast to Christianity's ethics of love — and its sharp distinction between what is human and what is divine. There was also, prior to Israel's creation, the universal minority status of the Jews, and, of course, the prohibition in many countries on Jewish ownership of land, which drove them into the cities where a good many managed to prosper.

Other Catalytic Communities include the Vietnamese minority in Cambodia, the Chinese in Indonesia, and the Indians in South Africa under apartheid. All were better off than the majority group in terms of income and education; all were heavily involved in movements for radical change; and all suffered persecution as a result. The Tamils in Sri Lanka and the Armenians in Ottoman Turkey had the unfortunate distinction of being both Origin Folk and Catalytic Communities at the same time, which goes a long way toward explaining their fate.

Catalytic Communities may serve as "poison containers" — a psychohistorical term — during times of social stress. When elites call upon the masses to turn on Catalytic Communities, they are acting on their own legitimate fear of social and political change; but the masses who respond to this call are often acting on their own repressed anger against their parents. The concept of the poison container helps to explain the paranoid delusion of so many Germans in the Third Reich that the Jews — at the time a homeless and persecuted people — secretly ruled the world.

Enablers and Delegates

Enablers and delegates exist in politics just as they do in dysfunctional families. A demagogic leader typically serves as an enabler, selecting the poison containers and providing the rationalization for their persecution. The delegates are those who actually engage in the persecution — perhaps some downtrodden group which finds psychological satisfaction in persecuting an even worse-off group; think of poor white racists in the American South, or Cossacks in Czarist Russia. After the enablers lose power and the nation must come to terms with its actions, the delegates may then become poison containers in their own right, as the rest of the nation blames them for everything that went wrong.

Entitlement Fantasies

Sometimes people who suffer abuse in childhood entertain the notion that, "Because I have been deprived, I am now entitled to get anything I want." In an individual, this Entitlement Fantasy is likely to lead to ridicule and isolation. In a nation with an army to back up its demands, it can be particularly dangerous.

Long before Hitler invaded the Soviet Union, he endorsed the notion that since Germany had a large population which it needed to feed, it had the right to colonize countries to the east, exterminate or enslave their "inferior" inhabitants, and use their land and other resources for its own purposes. England and France had, of course, used similar arguments during their colonization of Africa, but it was coupled with the notion of "civilizing the natives," rather than exterminating them.

American racism is a form of Entitlement Fantasy. White supremacists do not merely feel morally or intellectually superior to African Americans; they also believe that they have the *right* to do them harm. Lynching blacks who violated social mores was seen not as a crime, as W.E.B. DuBois pointed out, but as a perfectly legitimate way of keeping the social order intact. Photographs of lynch mobs show the whites evidently unashamed of their actions, and some of them are dressed in suits and ties, indicating that they were not all from "the wrong side of the tracks."

The pan–Islamist terrorists of the World Islamic Jihad and al-Qaeda also have an Entitlement Fantasy. They believe that they have the God-given right to kill members of other religions — along with any of their fellow Muslims who either get in their way or disagree with their goals. In the Muslim world, the widespread sexual abuse of young boys may be a long-overlooked factor in the rise of terrorism. Not only does it fill the victim with rage and rob him of his innocence, but it may also make the victim feel "special," an essential element of the Entitlement Fantasy.

Mnemonism

Mnemonism is the collective desire on the part of a society to return to a largely fantasized past; it appears repeatedly in the case studies that follow. The "Marxist" Angkar (Khmer Rouge) longed for the days of the Angkor Empire, when Cambodia was a powerful nation. Mussolini spoke of restoring the Roman Empire, while the Nazis celebrated Germany's tribal and pagan past. South Africa's Afrikaner Nationalists echoed the politics of the two Boer Republics whose independence was extinguished by the British. The Argentine Nationalists regarded the Spanish colonial regime as a lost paradise. Northern Ireland's Loyalists appear to be stuck in a time warp where the religious conflicts of centuries past never ended. Serb and Croat extremists in Yugoslavia revived their long-submerged homelands by tearing their country apart. Even Mao's Red Guards, with their messianic hopes of communizing the world, sometimes appeared nostalgic for a distant past where China was the "Central Kingdom," and other lands looked toward it for guidance; Mao became a god-king in the latter stages of the Cultural Revolution, with people kow-towing to his busts, exchanging mantras, and doing "loyalty dances." And, in the United States, the Religious Right — actually a political movement — longs for the time when male and female roles were clearly defined, homosexuals stayed in the closet, people lived in small and homogenous communities, and America was the dominant power in the world.

Nationalist movements which seek to restore their nation's independence after hundreds, or even thousands, of years, are not necessary mnemonist, although they may include some unreal factions. For the most part, nationalism — at least until it takes power — is a legitimate response to oppression. But when an already independent country seeks to restore an era of bygone glory, or when a group of people are ready to sacrifice their own welfare in order to break away from a larger nation, psychohistorians can then diagnose the development as a form of political madness.

Mnemonism is the political equivalent of regressive behavior on the individual level. The neurotic represses feelings from the past, which are then stored in his brain, influencing his behavior when events in his life become painful. Just as an alcoholic may revert to an infantile state when all he needed to be content was to suck on a bottle, so a nation may come to function politically and militarily in the real world, while functioning psychologically in a fantasy world made up partially of memories and partially of wishful thinking.

Inferiority Complexes

The inferiority complex, probably the most common neurotic syndrome, operates on a variety of levels. First, there are the private feelings of inadequacy that many of us try to keep to ourselves. Second, there are the feelings of low self-esteem which affect our personal relationships with others. Third, there are collective feelings of inferiority held by one group in regard to another within a given nation. And finally, there are feelings of inferiority held by one nation in regard to others.

A number of political movements can be interpreted as attempts to overcome the last two kinds of inferiority complex. Black nationalism, in the United States, Haiti, and South Africa, was a response to the low self-esteem exacerbated by white supremacy. Much of the violence of the Chinese Cultural Revolution stemmed from certain social groups feeling inferior to others. And as some have already noted, German anti–Semitism derived at least in part from German feelings of inferiority toward the Jews. Hitler's claims that Jews were an "inferior race" were nothing more than a defense mechanism; if Jews were "inferior," how could they have ruled the world, as he also believed?

Political movements, unfortunately, are no cure for feelings of inferiority, which originate in the family dynamic. This is the reason that movements which seek to counteract low self-esteem tend to grow ever more irrational as they gain power and influence.

Shrinking Boundary Syndrome

One important trigger for political madness is the loss of territory. Aside from the legitimate problem faced by any government trying to subsidize its activities with a reduced base of taxes and resources, territorial loss also evokes prenatal memories of contractions in the womb. These memories produce fears of annihilation, notions of being polluted (from the toxins entering the neonate's bloodstream through the umbilical cord as the mother goes into labor), and feelings of needing to be delivered, which can lead to support dictators or — in somewhat less troubled times — join cults. Fear of annihilation on the part of the Turks during World War I, when there was a possibility of being overrun by Czarist Russia, led to their own genocide against the Armenians; along with the real concern that the Christian Armenians might have sided with their Russian co-religionists, the Turks were also affected by more than a century of territorial loss in the Balkans and North Africa, which had already reduced the size of their empire by more than half.

Germany's violent anti–Semitism in the aftermath of World War I, which prepared the way for Hitler some years later, may be partly attributed to the post–World War I loss of several of its provinces to Poland, France, and Denmark, as well as its colonial empire in Africa and the Pacific. Hungary, which became vehemently anti–Semitic after losing two-thirds of its original territory in 1918, is another example; in each case, of course, anti–Semitism was also a response to the prominent role played by Jewish leaders in failed left-wing revolutions.

In both the Pakistani and Indian parts of the Punjab, the division of the province in 1947 led to purification campaigns directed against small religious minorities: the Ahmaddiyas in Pakistan, and — following a second partition within India, which created a Sikh-majority Punjabi state — the Nirankari sect, an offshoot of the Sikhs. Both of these small groups were targeted became they were regarded as "impure" by the orthodox majority.

In another case from India, the long conflict between the Assamese majority and the large Bengali minority in the state of Assam might be attributed to the continued reduction in its size as various tribal territories were sliced off to form new states.[5]

Territorial expansionism may be one consequence of Shrinking Boundary Syndrome, as in the case of Germany under Hitler, or Hungary during the period from 1919 to 1944. Both countries annexed large parts of neighboring nations from 1938 on — Germany through military conquest, and Hungary largely through diplomatic maneuvering as a member of the Axis. Fascist Italy was also highly expansionist, but this was not caused by any loss of territory after World War I; Italy had actually gained territory, although not nearly as much as it had hoped for. Yet even though the catalyst for territorial expansion on the *historical* level might not have been the same for Italy as for the two other countries, the *psychological* roots in all three cases were the product of birth trauma, when the neonate must deal with the feeling of "I need to get out."

The Adowa Cycle

One of the more curious phenomena of the 20th century is the fact that traumas to nations seem to produce delayed reactions, typically after 15 years. The first example of this was Italy, which suffered a defeat in 1895 at the hands of Ethiopia at the Battle of Adowa. This drubbing by a backward African empire was not only humiliating, but also — at least as important — quite unexpected. Fifteen years later, the currents in popular sentiment emerged which soon led to Fascism.

The Adowa Cycle has appeared in a number of countries, but it has taken a variety of forms. An unexpected defeat, an unexpected victory, or a revolution leads to a major change in the public mood. But the passage of 15 years leads to a turnover in both the population and leadership. A new mood arises, which responds to the original trauma in a different way. China's Cultural Revolution came 15 years after the Communist victory over the Kuomintang; Stalin's purges peaked 15 years after the end of the Russian Civil War; Hitler took over nearly 15 years after Germany's defeat in World War I; 15 years separated the Munich Pact from the paranoia of the Slansky trials in Czechoslovakia; and it was 15 years from the French defeat at Dien Bien Phu in 1953 to the 1968 revolt by the students and workers; these dates also correspond to Cambodia's independence and the beginning of the left-wing insurgency against the royalist government. Yet, as we shall see in Chapters 10 and 11, there was a foreshortened Adowa Cycle in Pakistan, because of the effects of partition, and prolonged 30-year cycles in Algeria and Iran, in part because of the slow turnover in the leadership.

Psycho-geography

Psycho-geography is a subfield of psychohistory which focuses on the relationship between geography and the mind. In my own approach to psychohistory, it refers to projections onto the map of unfelt feelings. For example, some Sinhalese nationalists have noted that their homeland of Sri Lanka resembles a teardrop; indeed it does, but only someone with a good deal to cry about would be likely to mention this. Croatian nationalists have described their country as resembling a spread pair of legs. To others, it might look like the gaping jaws of a crocodile, but if one regards the map as a Rorschach test, the "spread legs" response might give us some idea of the kind of childhood trauma that gave rise to the Ustashi and their ideological successors of the 1990s.

Two related phenomena, which were widespread during the late 20th century, were what we might term *orientophobia* and *occidentophobia*, each an outgrowth of fear of change. The orientophobe — like Hitler, the Kaiser, or Neville Chamberlain — sees change coming by way of violent revolution, from the East, however that may be defined. Orientophobia became a virtual mass delusion in the United States during the Cold War, and was chiefly responsible for America's interminable intervention in Vietnam, in the vain hope of stemming the spread of revolution. Its counterpart, occidentophobia, is likewise a form of fear of change, but occidentophobes see change coming from the West, in the form of cultural contamination. The Chinese Cultural Revolution was informed by occidentophobia, as were Khomeini's Islamic Revolution in Iran and the pan–Islamist terrorist campaign of Osama bin Laden and Ayman al-Zawahiri.

Other aspects of psycho-geography, which merit further investigation, include the effects of urbanization on psychological development, and the relationship of terrain to psychology — how mountain dwellers differ from plains dwellers, for example, or how the work ethic of people from arid terrains differs from those from well-watered areas.

The Structure of Reality

The popularity of reductionism stems from the weakness of what I call *compartmentalism*—the treatment of each field of knowledge as separate from all other fields, as if the biology of the brain had no effect on psychology, and the "brain" and the "mind" were separate phenomena, or as if culture, child-rearing practices, or even economics had nothing to do with political events. To those educated in universities where compartmentalism reigns, reductionism comes almost as a revelation. But it is a false dawn, as we can now see from its practice in countries like the USSR, Nazi Germany, or "Democratic Kampuchea."

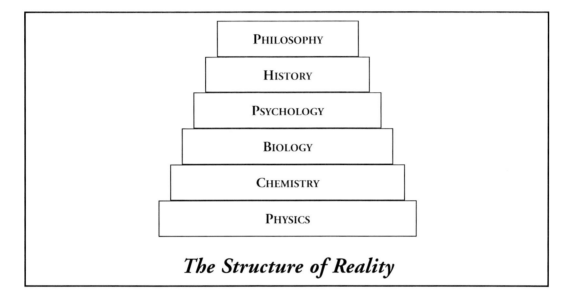

The Structure of Reality

Holistic thought, which was briefly popular during the late 20th century, flourished as a response to reductionism. Holists see no distinction between any two fields of knowledge, as if they all operated according to the same laws, or perhaps none at all. In the final analysis, holism — which all but denied the possibility of science — was a non-starter.

Interactionism is yet another approach to the interrelationship between events, and I will elaborate on the interactionist approach to psychohistory in the following chapters. According to the interactionist perspective, all events may be said to operate on one of six levels of reality, stacked atop one another like the layers of a wedding cake. These levels are physics, chemistry, biology, psychology, history (including the other social sciences), and, at the top, philosophy (see illustration).

An event which occurs at any of these levels must follow the laws applicable at this level, as well as those of all the levels below. A football game, for example — a social event — occurs at the historical level, and must follow the rules of football. But the game could not be played if the players and spectators were not aroused by it (psychological level). This psychological arousal must involve the brain and nervous system (biological level), which involves chemicals, which in turn are composed of atoms. Yet the event can only be understood at the highest level at which it operates; trying to understand what is going on only by monitoring the adrenaline levels of the fans and players would obviously be an exercise in futility.

The *cause* of any event may be a set of circumstances which operate on the same level, or it may be those operating at one or two levels below or above. While a football game may be caused by the profit motive on the part of the team owners, or the desire of the fans for a distraction from their everyday lives, an event such as a war may be caused by psychological as well as social factors. Germany's desire to overturn the painful war guilt clause of the Versailles Treaty appears to have been at least as important in its seduction by Hitler as the fear of Bolshevism. Likewise, America sought to reverse the effects of the Vietnam War by fighting another war on the banks of the Tigris; the need for oil could not have been the only reason for George W. Bush's 2003 invasion of Iraq, as it would have been easy enough to work out a deal with Saddam Hussein to end his isolation in exchange for his selling us Iraqi oil at low cost.

Psychohistory is not, as some of my colleagues in the Freudian school would have it, the study of the "whys" of history, since many of these "whys" operate at the historical level in the form of economic, military, or political forces — many, to be sure, but not quite all. Unconscious factors also operate on historical events, distorting their "normal" course as nations begin acting like disturbed individuals. In the chapters that follow, the focus is not on the normal events of history, but on events that should be considered quite abnormal, or *unreal* in primal terms: millions slaughtered in Europe because of a paranoid delusion that they ruled the world; tens of thousands tortured and killed in Argentina in order to suppress a guerrilla insurrection that had already ceased to be any kind of threat; white supremacists in South Africa managing to recruit non-white movements to their cause; hundreds of thousands butchered in Cambodia in the name of "revolution" because they were in some way connected with Vietnam, the same country which had virtually made Cambodia's revolution through its own efforts; a one-time juvenile delinquent and intellectual poseur raised to the level of a deity in Italy, a country with thousands of years of civilization to its name; religious violence raging in a remote corner of the United Kingdom centuries after it had been resolved elsewhere in Europe; functioning nations like Sri Lanka, Rwanda, or Yugoslavia tearing themselves apart in ethnic conflicts that had already been resolved at the political level; Ottoman Turkey moving from enlightened reform to genocide and ethnic cleansing in less than a decade; Pakistani political/religious leaders seeing a threat from a sect numbering little more than one tenth of one percent of their country's population; a political revolution in Iran which led the nation backward into the Dark Ages; a civil war in Algeria in which one side hoped to do the same; Chinese youths attacking the authority of the Communist Party in the name of Communism; a regime in the Sudan promoting genocide and slavery in the name of a religion that originally championed equality; a Haitian dictatorship whose corrupt and demented leader was worshipped as a god. This is the political madness that cries out for explanation through psychohistory.

2

Germany

The Complex Roots of National Socialism

More than half a century after the final collapse of the Nazi dictatorship, its meteoric rise and brief, bloody procession across the stage of history remains an enigma. Attempts to explain National Socialism have usually focused on the personality of Adolf Hitler, but here too, a full explanation still evades us. Did Hitler launch World War II and instigate the Holocaust, as some have maintained, because he was afflicted with sexual deformities or perversions? If this is so, why did no others with the same difficulties stain the history books with similar atrocities? And could Hitler's likely monorchidism or coprophilia possibly explain why he gained millions of followers?

Are we on more solid ground when we consider the brutal manner in which Hitler was treated by his violent, alcoholic father? Such abuse was not all that uncommon in the Europe of the late 19th century, as Erich Fromm has observed, and it was undoubtedly a factor in the rise of fascist movements during the following generation. At the same time, similar family situations have existed in countries like Ireland without producing anything resembling a mass-based Nazi-type party. Even in Russia, where alcoholism and domestic violence were common, Soviet Stalinism, notwithstanding its frequent brutality, appears to have lacked the sadistic element typical of German Nazism.

Some historians have suggested a *Sonderweg*, or "special path," of German history, leading from the anti–Jewish massacres of Friedrich Barbarossa during the Crusades, through Martin Luther's anti–Semitic rantings, directly to Hitler's Final Solution. Daniel Goldhagen speaks for this point of view in his controversial work, *Hitler's Willing Executioners*—excoriated by some, but curiously embraced by many younger German readers. Referring to the Holocaust as a "national project," Goldhagen disproves the claim that Germans who participated in it were "only following orders." He refers to the perpetrators as "Germans" throughout his book, rather than "Nazis," as if previous writers had avoided the obvious. Goldhagen may have said little that was not familiar to students of the subject, but the way he said it was provocative. He gives us an account of the Holocaust in which Hitler is all but absent.

Medieval persecution of Jews was not limited to Germany, nor was Martin Luther the only figure in Church history who dreamt of spilling Jewish blood. But if the horrors of World War II seem a bit more banal when viewed in the light of European history, they should also be regarded in the context of the enlightened 19th century, when the torture chambers and religious frenzies of the past were abandoned. What happened in Germany between 1933 and 1945 represented an extreme case of mnemonism, when the country began reliving all of its past traumas at once; this is what needs to be explained.

The Psychological Roots of Authoritarianism

Three themes have been neglected in the study of the rise of the Nazi movement, without which it makes little sense. These are (1) the role of *birth trauma*; (2) Germany's *harsh educational system*, itself an outgrowth of its rigidly stratified social system; and (3) the notion of the *search for hidden knowledge*, partly a result of the educational system. These factors, correctly understood, permit us to understand which groups Hitler chose to victimize.

Anyone familiar with birth symbolism will recognize it in the following dream related by Chancellor Otto von Bismarck:

> ...I was riding on a narrow Alpine path, a precipice on the right, rocks on the left. The path grew narrower, so that the horse refused to proceed, and it was impossible to turn round or dismount, owing to the lack of space. Then, with my whip in my left hand, I struck the smooth rock and called on God. The whip grew to an endless length, the rocky wall dropped like a piece of stage scenery and opened out a broad path, with a view over hills and forests, like a landscape in Bohemia....[1]

Fear of falling, being trapped in a narrow space, and suddenly making a breakthrough all symbolize memories dating back to birth. The elongated whip represents the umbilical cord; both Hitler and his long-time follower Julius Streicher, editor of the anti–Semitic scandal sheet *Der Sturmer*, liked to carry whips. It is particularly significant that the final image is of a province outside the German Empire with a mostly Slav population.

Hitler himself had a "lifelong fear of strangulation and loss of breath,"[2] an unconscious memory of birth trauma, when the neonate runs the risk of losing his oxygen supply as the umbilical cord is choked off before his head has emerged from the womb and he is able to breathe. Some of the odd metaphors which illustrate *Mein Kampf* might best be seen in the context of perinatal imagery. Hitler's reference to "the flag of the Reich" springing "from the womb of war" sounds like a placental symbol; and when he says about poverty, "He who has not himself been gripped in the clutches of the strangulating viper will never come to know its poisoned fangs,"[3] we should perhaps focus less on his confusion about different kinds of snakes, and more on the likelihood that he had difficulty getting out of his mother's womb.

Even Hitler's speeches seemed to echo the birth experience. He would engage in "long-winded narrative abounding with endless historical or pseudo-philosophical disquisitions designed to tire his listeners and, like hypnosis, break down their mental resistance." Then he would switch to an emotional harangue which would leave his listeners in rapture and himself in a state of exhaustion.[4]

Following the defeat of Germany in World War I, the bizarre "Hollow Earth" theory became popular. It held that the world was a spherical bubble, and that we all lived on the inside. Failing to account for where the sun and moon go when they set, this theory was an unconscious birth memory if ever there was one. It won adherents even among high-ranking Nazi leaders, to the point where German naval vessels were actually sent to the Baltic Sea during the war in order to take photographs of England.[5] Not surprisingly, it didn't work.

The *Lebensraum* doctrine became the dominant world-view of German foreign policy toward the end of World War I.[6] It maintained that Germany's large population gave it the moral right to occupy Russia, drive its inhabitants across the Urals into Siberia, and colonize the country with German settlers. Hitler was an avid supporter of this rationalization for imperialism. "[W]hat is the reason for all our economic troubles?" he inquired in January 1939. "Simply the overpopulation of our *Lebensraum!*"[7] Closely parallel to Fascist Italy's dream of making the Mediterranean an "Italian lake," *Lebensraum* was an expression of repressed memories of struggling to escape from a contracting womb.

Authoritarian movements tend to thrive in societies where neonates experience severe birth trauma. The psychodynamic involved here is that conflict on the social/historical level arouses repressed birth memories, particularly those associated with feelings of anxiety and confusion. The anxiety evokes the fear of dying, which is typical of birth, where the likely outcome is unclear to the infant. The confusion echoes the feelings of the neonate when the mother's womb starts contracting. At that point, people begin searching for an infallible leader — as with Bismarck calling on God in his dream — who will make decisions for them and protect them from unknown dangers. In their minds, they imagine that this leader will "deliver" them, although, in practice, dictators usually get their nations into even greater difficulties.

Traumatic birth practices go well together with rigid societies, each contributing to the other. Germans were raised in authoritarian families, attended authoritarian schools, served — if male — in an authoritarian military, and worshipped in authoritarian churches (Roman Catholic or Lutheran). These factors were all interdependent, since the churches received government support, military veterans staffed the schools, and the churches, with their official status, endorsed the government's "spiritual" policies of militarism and ultra-nationalism. Although Germany, prior to 1918, had been divided into numerous states, each with their own dynasties, and countless emperors, kings, dukes and princes had ruled over all or part of its territory, there had hardly been a single incident of tyrannicide in all of German history.[8] But assassinations soon became common after the establishment of the short-lived Weimar democracy, and Rosa Luxemburg, Karl Leibknecht, and Walter Rathenau all met their deaths at the hands of right-wing conspirators.

Germans' unwillingness to countenance the murder of even their worst monarchs — an insane Bavarian ruler, done in by nobles, is the sole exception — is the obverse of Germany's long history of anti–Semitism. Unwilling to kill bad rulers, Germans have historically turned on Jews instead, after imputing superhuman power to them. The tale of the "Jew Suss," which figured prominently in Nazi propaganda, with a popular film being made of it, was based on an actual event. A financier who loaned money to a hated local ruler, the historical Suss was murdered by nobles who could not bring themselves to turn on their king, the actual cause of their rage.

Hitler's vehement Jew-hatred, judging by his own account in *Mein Kampf*, stemmed from late in World War I, when he spotted a clerk he thought was Jewish serving in the German Army in Berlin. "Every Jew a clerk," he ranted in his book, "and every clerk a Jew," making a broad double generalization from a single instance. His reaction should be seen in its proper context. A few months before, an American pilot died in combat — Quentin Roosevelt, son of Theodore Roosevelt. The German public learned that Teddy Roosevelt had three other sons serving in the front lines, two of whom were wounded. The Kaiser's six sons were all serving as generals, all but two of them safely in the rear. This was the moment when the average German began comparing monarchism with democracy, to the distinct advantage of the latter. Hitler, however, preferred to direct his rage against the Jews, rather than against the royal family.

Writes Joachim Fest:

> The German mind accords unusual respect to the categories of order, discipline, and self-restraint. Idolization of the state as a court of last resort and bulwark against evil, and even faith in a leader, have their origin in such historical experiences.[9]

Nazi propagandists spoke a great deal of "the will," but they had a unique definition of this concept. Army psychologists in the Third Reich considered it to be the "habit of voluntary response to the command of a superior leader."[10] So ingrained was this culture of blind obedience that Hitler could "fall significantly short of Nazifying the armed forces, the state bureaucracy, the courts, and the school system,"[11] since these institutions quickly conformed to his regime with little resistance. This was particularly true of the school system, and it is worth noting that two of the most brutal Nazi leaders, Heinrich Himmler and Julius Streicher, both worked as teachers during their pre–Nazi years.

Nazism's Historical Antecedents

Historically, Germany might best be understood as a country colonized by its own aristocracy. This process had its origin in Prussia, an area along the Baltic between Lithuania and Poland, originally inhabited by a pagan people related to the Lithuanians. They were conquered by Germany's Teutonic Knights — whose heritage was later evoked by the SS — during the 13th century.[12] The Knights converted the Prussians, Germanized them, and reduced them to abject servitude. The conquered region remained separate from Germany itself until it was purchased in 1618 by the Hohenzollerns,[13] a Protestant dynasty from mostly Catholic Swabia, which had already acquired extensive holdings in Brandenburg and Pomerania. With the acquisition of Prussia, the Hohenzollern domains took the name "Kingdom of Prussia," and the former domain of the Knights was renamed "East Prussia." The rigid system of master-serf relations was carried over into the Hohenzollern army, and the heirs of the Knights, known as Junkers, soon acquired a monopoly of all civil and military offices in the expanded kingdom.[14]

In an example of mnemonism, Heinrich Himmler planned to settle SS "soldier-farmers" in parts of the Ukraine after World War II had been won. Like the Teutonic Knights, they would "till the earth, sow ancient grains, tend antique cattle breeds, live in medieval-style houses, heal the sick with traditional plant remedies and age-old magical incantations, play time-honored musical instruments such as the *lur*, practice the old Germanic religion, and generally follow the traditions of their ancestors...."[15]

One major source of Nazi racism was *biological determinism*. In the German context, the doctrine of superior Teutonic blood rationalized the subjugation of the indigenous Baltic Prussians. The doctrine spread with Prussian state power, and was reinforced during the scramble for Africa at the end of the 19th century, when Germany managed to acquire a colonial empire in Africa and the Pacific. Nazism, a doctrine which contained not a single original element, used the same justification for the conquest of Europe.

Also stemming from Prussia's early past was the German tendency known as *Staats-frömmigkeit*, "a quasi-religious reverence toward the state."[16] Friedrich the Great, who first made Prussia a military power, originated this when he substituted the state for God in his concept of royalty.[17] A possible insight into this ruler's mentality is provided by the story that, while still Crown Prince, he was forced to watch the beheading of his close friend on his father's orders, as punishment for one of his own transgressions.[18] Not surprisingly, when Friedrich became king, sadomasochism was the cornerstone of Prussian military training. Soldiers were taught to be as immobile as statues, and were punished for speaking, coughing or sneezing.[19] The officers were trained so harshly that people said "that a man who had been through the *Kriegsakademie* never looked happy again."[20] Under Bismarck, the army "was virtually a state within a state.... Officers enjoyed many social and other privileges and expected the deference of civilians when they met on the street."[21] The common use of monocles by German officers — as late as World War II — illustrated the control they were supposed to have over their emotions; only by keeping a rigid expression could they avoid dropping their eyepieces and looking ridiculous. Militarism spread from the army into Prussian society through many routes, including the state bureaucracy, which under Friedrich was part of the army.[22] School teachers, typically army veterans,[23] preached Prussian virtues of obedience and discipline in their classrooms. Most important, the youths trained in the army eventually returned to civilian life to raise their own families in a disciplinarian fashion.

Spartan-style militarism succeeded in making Prussia a major European power, particularly as a result of the 18th-century partition of Poland, and the subsequent defeat of Napoleon early in the 19th century. As a result of Napoleon's defeat, Prussia made major territorial acquisitions in western Germany, although the new possessions, such as the Catholic Rhineland, did not always take well to Protestant Hohenzollern rule. Power in the kingdom remained in the hands of the landowning Junkers east of the Elbe River. After the wars of 1866–1870 — against Denmark, Austria and France — Prussia emerged as the supreme power in Germany. Some of the lesser states, such as Hanover, were incorporated as Prussian provinces, while the others ultimately recognized Prussia's king as Germany's emperor. Retaining political autonomy, they typically permitted Prussian officers to drill and command their own armies.[24]

Militarized Germany promoted what would have been considered pathological masochism in any other country. German military cadets practiced vicious forms of torture on their compliant juniors; when the practice was revealed, as late as 1920, it caused much concern.[25] At that time, German army psychologists were involved in the careful study of body language and vocal tone among the country's soldiers, as they searched for leadership material for a future, rearmed nation. "Monotone, hard timbre and staccato accentuation were considered indicative of calm and determined will power."[26] Others might have regarded these characteristics as early warnings of emotional distress.

German youth were taught to consider war not as an opportunity for a boy to prove his manhood, as in the United States, but as a chance to avoid reaching it. "Gentlemen," ran the standard talk given to ten-year-olds entering the Prussian military academy, "you are here to learn that which gives your life its ultimate meaning. You are here in order to learn how to die."[27] This had its echo in the Hitler Youth slogan, "We are born to die for Germany."[28] Concludes Fest, "Hitler was not exaggerating when he asserted, as he regularly did, that he had asked his followers for nothing but sacrifices."[29]

German unification was followed by a wave of overseas colonial expansion, but there was stiff competition from other industrialized nations, some of whom had an earlier start. The most valuable colonies had already been acquired by other powers before Germany began its colonial venture, and what Berlin was able to acquire had little economic value.[30] Its empire included four colonies in Africa and a number of islands in the Pacific. Few Germans settled there, and their limited resources, such as coconuts, made little contribution to the German economy. Nonetheless, their loss was felt keenly after 1918, and Hitler's demand for their return was popular. Colonies gave ordinary Germans a chance to lord it over other peoples, even vicariously, as their own aristocracy lorded it over them at home.

In 1945, the German aristocracy was quick to assure the Allies that they had been "against Hitler all along." They were a small group, only three-quarters of one percent of the population.[31] Yet this stratum included five of the 22 people who occupied cabinet posts during the Third Reich.[32] They dominated the Army officer corps and the diplomatic service, and made up nine percent of the leadership of the SS[33] and more than a fourth of the leadership of the Nazi Farmers' Association.[34] They included the head of the Hitler Youth for much of the Nazi period. Generals and aristocrats stood at Hitler's side on March 21, 1933, when the army, SS and SA marched by to salute the new chancellor. "[A]n unwitting member of the audience that day might have thought that the restoration of the monarchy and the feudal state was imminent."[35] Many aristocrats sympathized with the failed July 1944 coup against Hitler, but this was late in the war, and their defection from the Nazi cause was often more a matter of opportunism than of stalwart anti-fascism. Even at this date, not all the aristocrats deserted Hitler. They were numerous among the plotters because they made up such a large contingent of Nazi cadres to begin with.

At the same time, according to Peter Padfield, Himmler was keeping an eye on the Goerdeler-Beck group, the cabal of army officers that plotted the 1944 anti–Nazi coup. Since this group never issued any proclamations or literature, and lacked even a formal name, it would seem that Himmler must have had an informer inside it. This means that he was most likely aware that, encouraged by the dissident colonel Klaus von Stauffenberg, the Goerdeler-Beck group was planning to kill Hitler with a bomb at a high-ranking meeting in East Prussia. Curiously, Himmler failed to attend. Could Hitler's most loyal associate have been hoping to see the Führer assassinated, perhaps expecting to take over Germany himself in the wake of Hitler's death?

The German army stood behind Hitler from the beginning. He was recruited by their secret service in 1919, trained as a speaker and propagandist, and used to scout out extremist organizations in Munich to see which ones could be of use to the General Staff.[36] It was in this capacity that he showed up at a meeting of the tiny German Workers Party, the group he took over while adding "National Socialist" to its name. Throughout his steady rise to power, Hitler "received protection from the Reichswehr and the paramilitary organizations."[37]

German Anti-Semitism

While nothing in German history equals the horrors of the Third Reich, signs of pathology in the culture go back for centuries. Robert Waite recounts typical themes from the German fairy tales collected by the famous Brothers Grimm: children are eaten by their mother; a child is dismembered by bears; a girl's tongue and eyes are torn out; a boy is cooked and eaten by his father; a girl is beheaded.[38] These are grim fairy tales indeed, and those who regard the Holocaust as an aberration might do well to reflect on the ultimate fate of the witch in "Hansel and Gretel."

Given the aristocratic domination of Germany, which survived the incomplete revolution of 1918, it should be evident that the Weimar period, rather than the Nazi era, was more of an aberration. Anti–Semitism has a long and intense history in Germany, not least in the modern era. German Jews lived in ghettoes until they were freed by the French during the Napoleonic conquest, only to be returned there once the French had been expelled. They were not granted formal equality until after unification in 1870, and that initiated the very period when rabid anti–Semitic parties flourished. A popular folk legend blamed venereal disease on the "Wandering Jew" Ahasuerus,[39] and even such thinkers as Kant and Goethe — not to mention composer Richard Wagner — were influenced by anti–Semitic ideas.[40]

Discrimination against Jews was widespread in the *Kaiserreich*,[41] although this tends to be overlooked by Jews and Germans alike. There was also widespread anti–Semitism in France at the time, a result of the Dreyfus case — caused by the 1870 defeat of France by Prussia and the loss of Alsace-Lorraine — but even so, there were more than 700 Jewish officers in the French army upon the outbreak of World War I, compared to none in Germany.[42] Anti-Jewish parties were able to elect their leaders to the Reichstag. The importance of these extremist groups should be measured less by their popular support, which was modest, than by the influence they had on major parties such as the Conservatives. In 1893, this governing party adopted the anti–Semitic program to "combat the manifold upsurging and decomposing Jewish influence in our national life."[43] A decade later, "the anti–Semites in parliament had been all but absorbed by the Conservative government...."[44]

Even as barriers to equality fell during the Weimar period, some allegedly middle-of-the-road parties competed with one another in denouncing the Jews, long before Hitler and his brownshirts came along. In 1921, the anti–Semitic attacks on Foreign Minister Walther Rathenau — a Jew, but intensely proud of being German — were led by the German National People's Party (DNVP), which described itself as "the only party that opposes the Jews...."[45] This was not even true at the time. The more moderate German People's Party (DVP) and even the liberal German Democratic Party (DDP) also flirted with anti–Semitism, although the latter invariably won most of the Jewish vote.

The Jews were only a symbol for Germany's ultra-nationalists. Prior to 1918, the largest minority in Germany were the Poles, most of whom then became citizens of Poland. The Jews were only about one percent of Germany's population, and were assimilated to the point where even a portion of *them* were anti–Semitic, like Heidelberg professor Walter Jellinek, who justified Hitler's anti–Semitic laws and was then fired under them.[46] Rightwing claims that Jews made up most of the leadership of the radical left during the post–1918 period were true; but it was also true that the Communists and Socialists would have gotten nowhere unless millions of ordinary German workers supported them. Repeatedly, the Nazis attributed their own sinister plans for world conquest to the "international Jewish conspiracy," borrowing their delusions from pro–Czarist Russian exiles who had fled to Western Europe.

Anti-Semitism came naturally to the German radical right because the Jews were perceived, not without justification, as the beneficiaries of the social revolutions brought about by military defeat — both during Napoleonic times, and a century later in the wake of World War I and the Treaty of Versailles. Coupled with the ideology of biological determinism that prevailed in Germany (and elsewhere), and the threat of Bolshevism after the Russian Revolution, German history permits us to make some sense of the Holocaust, the most irrational act of mass murder even in the violent 20th century. The Nazis perceived themselves as engaging in a preemptive strike against a group that was *biologically predisposed* to support and lead radical social movements.

At the same time, even leading figures in Nazi Germany sometimes behaved as if they didn't believe a word of their own propaganda. All during World War II, the Nazis declared that Jews controlled England, the United States, and the Soviet Union. This was repeated in speeches, books, articles, and editorial cartoons *ad infinitum*. Typically, Nazi wartime cartoons showed squat, plump, hook-nosed characters sporting tell-tale Stars of David on their chests, sitting triumphantly on the shoulders of John Bull, Uncle Sam, and Ivan. Yet some top Nazis were secretly working for a separate peace with the Western Allies while hoping to continue the war against Communist Russia, while others were intriguing for peace with the USSR at the expense of the West; neither of these outcomes would have been conceivable had there been any truth to the fantasy of Jewish world domination.

Choosing the Victims

The Jews were not the only group that faced persecution at Nazi hands. It would seem that the persecutors were motivated by three separate repressed feelings: the first was a generalized feeling of infantile need — for food, warmth, and love — coupled with a sense of being unworthy of getting them; the second was the search for hidden knowledge, common to both Nazism and the occult; the third and perhaps most important was the fear of someone weak, essentially the Nazis' own fathers who were generally impotent figures within Germany's rigid, caste-ridden society.

In the first two cases, the Nazis projected these feelings onto groups which they then sought to enslave or exterminate. Groups onto which Germans projected repressed need included Slavs, the disabled, the mentally ill, and the retarded. The last three were characterized as "useless eaters," who took from society without giving anything back — like small children in the family. Nazis considered Slavs suitable only for the most menial labor, and during the occupation of Poland, the Polish intelligentsia were singled out for elimination. There were long-standing conflicts between the Germans and their Slav neighbors, leading to Orientophobia — the *Drang nach Osten* — as a consistent theme in German foreign policy. Heinrich Himmler liked to imagine himself as the literal incarnation of King Heinrich I, a tenth-century ruler who crusaded against the Slavs.[47] A small and virtually unknown group in ancient times, the Slavs ultimately came to occupy lands stretching from Central Europe eastward to the Pacific. World War I resulted in the independence of the Poles, Czechoslovaks and Yugoslavs, although pan–Slav ideology was eclipsed as a result of the fall of the Czarist regime in Russia.

The resurgence of the smaller Slavic nations awakened a *starvation fantasy* among the Germans, who imagined the Slavs consuming Europe's resources and leaving nothing for them. This fantasy is also expressed in the "Hansel and Gretel" tale. The two children are exiled from their home by their wicked stepmother, who fears that they might eat her out of house and home. They then attempt to do precisely that to the witch who lives in the forest, nibbling away at her gingerbread house, but the witch nearly turns the tables on the pair, caging Hansel and fattening him up with the intention of making a meal out of him. As Bruno Bettelheim observed in *The Uses of Enchantment*, the entire "Hansel and Gretel" story is suffused with images of hunger and food. (There are also hints of sexual abuse, when the witch repeatedly feels Hansel's "thumb" to see if it is big enough.) Unable to contribute to the upkeep of their families, children are the quintessential "useless eaters," a term used by the Nazis to describe all sorts of groups they hoped to exterminate.

Another source of anti–Slav feeling was the fact that many Germans in the eastern provinces were themselves of Polish ancestry. Polish place-names are found in the outskirts of Berlin, and an entire Slav ethnic group — the Sorbs — still live in the heart of Saxony. To a degree, the Slavs were an Origin Folk in relation to the Germans. Hitler himself came from a Slav-German borderland, where the Germans had been gradually replacing the Czechs through assimilation. His own surname may have been of Czech origin,[48] and his father's second wife, the mother of his older half-brother, Alois, and half-sister, Angela, was partly Czech. But Nazi animosity toward the Slavs was hardly consistent. Bulgaria, Croatia and Slovakia were Axis members, and Ukrainian and Russian anti–Communists served as SS auxiliaries.

Two other groups which faced persecution at Nazi hands were the Gypsies (Roma and Sinti) and the Masons. They shared with the Jews the image of possessing hidden knowledge. Like the Jews, the Gypsies were seen as outsiders who had migrated into Europe from the east, and were regarded as permanent aliens by many of the peoples among whom they resided. Often earning their living as fortune-tellers, the Gypsies shared with the Jews the reputation of being "particularly adept at the arcane arts."[49] So widespread was the belief that Jews held the key to hidden knowledge that German occult societies used mock Hebrew in their rituals during the 1920s.[50]

Like the Jews, the Masons were identified with an international movement — in their case it was real — and were also blamed for plotting the spread of the enlightenment. The Masons had been in fact strong supporters of the radical ideas of the French Revolution, but by the 20th century they had already evolved into an apolitical fraternity of comfortable bourgeoisie. This did not dissuade the Nazis from outlawing their organization.

Nietzsche anticipated Hitler when he defined reality as "the will to power."[51] Since knowledge can be translated into power, it has always been held in high regard in Germany, whose universities have served as models for the rest of the world. But genuine knowledge can lead to consciousness — defined here as *awareness of meaning*—and that is something that repressed and traumatized people, not to mention those who repress them, would rather avoid. Avoidance of painful truth coupled with hunger for knowledge leads people to the occult, which offers the trappings of knowledge minus the content; mumbo-jumbo replaces information, and even the possibility of making sense of the universe is denied. In reifying its adherents' defenses, the occult turns personal neurosis into collective pseudo-history.

"In the years preceding World War I," writes Dusty Sklar, "German anti–Semitism was fed by an underground stream of secret cults running like a sewer beneath Vienna and other cultural centers. Hitler dipped into this stream."[52] Two leading occultists who influenced the young Hitler (exactly to what degree is still in dispute) were Jorg Lanz von Liebenfels, publisher of *Ostara* magazine — which called itself "The Newspaper for Blond People"[53]— and the racist pamphleteer Guido von List. Von Liebenfels wrote of the eternal struggle between blond, blue-eyed "Heldings" and ape-like dwarfs he called "Schrattlings," whom he proposed to exterminate or deport to Africa.[54] Interestingly, the latter group were not specifically identified with Jews, even though their description is echoed by Nazi stereotypes in *Der Stürmer* and elsewhere. It appears that the genocidal impulse expressed during the Holocaust existed in German culture even before it had settled on a definite target. Von Liebenfels believed that the ancient Aryans had "electric organs" in their brains, which had been lost through intermarriage with inferior races. Eugenics, he hoped, would allow the Aryans to "rekindle their electromagnetic-radiological organs and become all-knowing, all-wise, and all-powerful."[55]

Von List, from whom Hitler borrowed the term "Gauleiter," the swastika, and the runic SS symbol, argued as early as 1911 for a world war to destroy the "hydra-headed international Jewish conspiracy."[56] Along with many other occultists, he believed that Germany's pagan forefathers had access to secret sources of knowledge, which had been passed on through various occult orders.[57] They believed that the reacquisition of these doctrines through the purification of the Aryan race would allow the latter to live again as godlike beings.[58] Images of the Aryan race being polluted by intermarriage with non–Aryans are simultaneously memories of toxins reaching the newborn through the umbilical cord, and revulsion at one's own sexual drives after they are repressed through religious indoctrination; in primal terms, they are both first-line and second-line. The godlike Aryan ancestors are primarily symbolic of the real self, but also idealized representations of the country's all-powerful rulers, as well as the believer's parents.

Defeat in World War I — after a quick victory had been promised by the Kaiser — followed by economic collapse, brought about an upsurge in the irrational in Germany. "Charlatans, astrologers, clairvoyants, numerologists and mediums flourished,"[59] not unlike in the United States after its own unexpected defeat in Vietnam. The "Stab-in-the-Back" myth, borrowed from the plot of Wagner's *Götterdämmerung*, in which the hero Siegfried is betrayed,[60] became widespread; it bears comparison with the American belief that the "politicians" betrayed the army in Vietnam. In Ernst Otto Montanus' novel, *Salvation of the West* (1921), defeated Germany finds a savior — an ex-officer who rediscovers his Aryan roots, leads his fellow veterans to power in Germany, and destroys the world created by Versailles.[61] This turned out to be chillingly prophetic.

The Great Depression was not the only factor which led millions of Germans to Nazism; Fest believes that Hitler fully understood this.[62] Peter Merkl's intensive study of the autobiographies of early Nazi recruits indicates that most victims of the depression among the hundreds of respondents were already Nazis before the stock market collapsed in 1929. And those who joined after 1929 were either in economic difficulty when times were good, or came from affluent social strata only marginally affected by the depression.[63] Similarly, William Sheridan Allen's detailed account of the Nazi rise to power in a small central German town notes that "[t]he middle classes were hardly touched by the depression,"[64] although they formed the core of Hitler's support.

What concerned the middle class, and drove it into Hitler's arms, was the possibility that the depression would drive the workers toward Communism, as was already beginning to happen, not only in Germany. The German middle class was not bothered by the total-itarian aspects of Communism; they eagerly embraced another totalitarian ideology them-selves. They were far more concerned about protecting their social privileges from any Marxist revolution, even one which might have tolerated some degree of personal freedom. Communism was also identified with "chaos," notwithstanding Stalin's own iron-fisted dic-tatorship in the USSR. To an authoritarian personality, regardless of nationality, "chaos" is the most terrifying threat; it represents not only the threat of physical violence, but the loss of one's social identity due to the breakdown of society, the ultimate source of the unreal self. Militarists are prone to perceiving "chaos" in the countries they intend to invade.

Flawed Supermen

The top Nazi leaders were quite a sorry lot. Hitler had numerous symptoms of emo-tional disturbance, whatever the truth about his alleged genital deficiencies. Himmler was overweight, myopic, and a hypochondriac. Martin Bormann and Robert Ley were severely alcoholic, and Göring was a drug addict and obese. Goebbels was a compulsive lecher. Rudolf Hess had signs of schizophrenia, while Streicher's sexual deviance was so repulsive that even his fellow Nazis ultimately eliminated him from the Party leadership. Most Nazi leaders despised one another: Goebbels hated Göring; Göring toppled Streicher; Himm-ler and Göring plotted against SA leader Ernst Roehm, even as Himmler intrigued against the corpulent Reichsmarshall; Ley and Ribbentrop were considered hopeless dimwits by their colleagues; and virtually every Nazi leader except Hitler himself hated Goebbels, whom they referred to as a "spiteful dwarf" and a "devil." Only Hitler's charisma kept the Nazi Party from ripping apart at the seams.

It is well known that Hitler was the product of an abusive home. His father, Alois — an Austrian customs official — was a brutal bully who once caned little Adolf more than two hundred times, and stopped only when his son showed he could take it without crying.[65] Echoing this event, Hitler told a Youth rally in 1935 that the German ideal was the "tough young man, impervious to wind and weather," as measured by "how many blows he can withstand...."[66] But we lack evidence of similar abuse in the childhood homes of other Nazi leaders. Göring was abandoned by his parents for years while they lived abroad, and was raised by an aunt, which perhaps explaining his drug addiction and his fondness for steal-ing art treasures; he had massive buried pain from the abandonment, and may have been trying to steal back what he had lost. Goebbels, the most intelligent of the Third Reich's leaders, appears to have been brought up in a normal, loving family. Himmler's father was far too strict and intrusive, leading the son to develop an early interest in spying on others (he started with his brother); but even so, the Himmler home was not one which we would expect to produce a mass murderer. The most powerful Nazis, individually responsible for tens of millions of deaths, were not recruited in the prisons, insane asylums, or the crimi-nal underworld. Had their party not come to power, they would probably have gone on to lead fairly conventional lives.

The two exceptions are Hitler himself and Streicher. There is little about Hitler's early life, before he joined the Nazis, that one might consider normal. Unable to form healthy relationships, he was also unsuccessful as an artist, and it is hard to conceive of him being content with an ordinary job. In a world at peace, Hitler probably would have grown increasingly bitter about his lack of success until he finally killed himself during a mid-life crisis. Devoid of any real creative talent, Hitler could not have found a calling outside the ranks of right-wing extremist politics.

Streicher, like Goebbels, came from what appeared to have been a normal home. Born in a Bavarian village, he moved to Nuremberg at age 24, where he became the leader of a local extremist group that later merged with Hitler's NSDAP. Streicher's Nuremberg became the spiritual Mecca for the Nazi movement, the annual scene of its largest rallies. His own newspaper, *Der Stürmer*, preached a primitive anti–Semitism distinct from the "scientific" racism Hitler claimed to prefer. *Der Stürmer* was promoted by the Nazis, who placed it in public display cases throughout Germany. Appointed Gauleiter of Franconia (northern Bavaria), Streicher was removed in early 1940 after he was overheard making a disparaging remark about Göring's manhood, and he spent the rest of the war under a lenient form of house arrest on his estate.[67] A clue to Streicher's psychological makeup may be his shaven head; as with Mussolini, this was most likely a symbol of birth trauma.

The authoritarian school system in Germany appears to have been an important factor in the development of the Nazi mentality, both among the leaders and followers. The classic German film, Heinrich Mann's *The Blue Angel*, should best be seen in this context. In the film, Rath, an inoffensive middle-aged fellow who teaches English to adolescent boys, first loses control of his classroom. Later, he develops an improbable infatuation with a young nightclub singer, played by Marlene Dietrich, who humiliates him on stage until he goes mad. This is less a tale of unrequited love than a revenge fantasy in which the teacher is the victim of humiliation, instead of the perpetrator.

Goebbels, Göring and Himmler were all humiliated by their teachers. When the club-footed Goebbels developed a schoolboy crush on the mother of another student and wrote love poems to her, his teacher found them and "read them aloud to the entire class, with sarcastic allusions to his defect."[68] Young Heinrich Himmler — pudgy, nearsighted, and hopeless at athletics — was humiliated in front of his class by his physical education instructor, who "was a source of terror to him."[69] Göring's experience resulted from an essay he wrote about "the man I most admire in the world," his wealthy, aristocratic godfather, a man named Epenstein, who lived in a castle surrounded by servants in medieval dress. Epenstein was the lover of Göring's mother — having literally rented her from her husband — and was probably the biological father of Göring's younger brother.

> The next day Hermann was called in by the headmaster and told that boys at this school were not meant to write papers praising Jews.... When Hermann indignantly identified his godfather as a Catholic, the headmaster showed him a copy of a type of German Social Register in which titled German families of Jewish origin were listed, and there was Epenstein's name.[70]

Hermann was punished by the headmaster, got into a fight with other boys over the incident, and then "was forced to march around the school grounds with a placard around his neck saying, 'My Godfather Is a Jew.'"[71] It should not come as a surprise that nearly a third of the Nazi leadership had served as schoolteachers during the Weimar period.[72] In the universities, the Nazis were obliged to eliminate a bit more than a tenth of the professors, whereas postwar denazification had to purge fully one-third.[73]

We have no direct evidence that Hitler himself suffered any humiliation at the hands of his teachers, but given his poor academic record, it would seem likely. There is plenty of evidence, though, that he was humiliated by his father. Fritz Redlich relates the story, which came from the wife of Hitler's friend Ernst Hanfstangl, via John Toland:

> In a show of rebellion, Adolf decided to run away from home. Somehow, father Alois learned of these plans and locked the boy in an upstairs room. During the night, Adolf tried to squeeze through the barred window. He couldn't quite make it, so he took off his clothes. As he wriggled his way to freedom, he heard his father's footsteps on the stairs and hastily withdrew, draping his nakedness with a tablecloth.... Alois ... burst into laughter and shouted to Clara [Hitler's mother] that she should come up and look at the "toga boy."[74]

There is little reason to believe that the traumatic childhood humiliations of the top Nazi leaders were atypical of what a great many German boys experienced. It was no wonder that the humiliation of defeat in World War I, followed by the "war guilt" clause inserted into the Versailles Treaty, resonated so strongly with the German people.

In her investigations of the Holocaust, historian Lucy Davidowicz thought it significant that during the early stages of World War II, Hitler made repeated references to a speech he had delivered in January, 1939. But he misremembered the date as September 1, the outbreak of war with Poland, when the actual date was seven months earlier. In that speech, to which Hitler constantly alluded during the war years, when the Jews of Europe were being exterminated, he made the following revealing statement:

> And one more thing I would like now to state on this day memorable perhaps not only for us Germans. I have often been a prophet in my life and was generally *laughed at*. During my struggle for power, the Jews primarily received *with laughter* my prophecies that I would someday assume the leadership of the state and thereby of the entire Volk and then, among many other things, achieve a solution of the Jewish problem. I suppose ... the then *resounding laughter* of Jewry in Germany is now choking in their throats.
>
> Today I will be a prophet again: If international finance Jewry within Europe and abroad should succeed once more in plunging the peoples into a world war, then the consequences will be not the Bolshevization of the world and therewith a victory of Jewry, but on the contrary, the destruction of the Jewish race in Europe.[75] [*Emphasis added*]

It is unfortunate that so many historians, and even psychohistorians, have accepted that something actually done by the Jews to Hitler, at some point in his life, led him to become history's greatest anti–Semite. Could it have been a Jewish prostitute who gave him syphilis during his youth in Vienna? Or the Jewish doctor who unsuccessfully treated his mother for cancer? The first tale appears to be nothing but an unsubstantiated rumor; there is no evidence that Hitler ever had syphilis, and the incessant references to the dreaded disease in *Mein Kampf* probably stemmed from his neurotic fear of intimacy, along with the fact that no cure for the disease existed then. As for the second theory, Hitler was sincerely grateful to his family doctor for doing everything he could to save his mother's life, and even gave him special privileges when the latter had to flee Vienna after the *Anschluss*. In actuality, the very speech in which Hitler promises the annihilation of the Jews contains references, only slightly obscured, to the humiliating experience mentioned above at the hands of his father. The link between his father and the Jews, in Hitler's mind, was merely that they were both people he didn't like. The Jews, long the scapegoat in German history, were an acceptable target for Hitler's repressed hatred and fear of his father.

Nazism and the German People

To what degree was Hitler's pathology reflected in the German public? From Goldhagen's perspective, the Holocaust was not the work of terrified Germans following the orders of a handful of psychopaths, but the expression of long-standing and deep-seated hatred of Jews by the vast majority of the German people. Hitler, one could conclude from reading Goldhagen, was less of a tyrant imposing his will upon a reluctant public, than an enabler, permitting the Germans to engage in crimes they could only commit with official permission.

One might remember that Hitler came to power with less than half of the vote, but is there any reason to assume that his fast-rising party failed to recruit any more followers *after* it seized control of Germany? There is no evidence that the masses of Nazi supporters became disillusioned with the regime during its early years, although a few were clearly disenchanted — some because of the widespread lawlessness, and others, particularly among the SA and the lower middle class, because they regarded Hitler's economic policies as insufficiently radical. Clearly, no authentic test of public opinion could take place under the Nazi dictatorship; but the 1935 Saar plebiscite and the elections in the Free City of Danzig may be good indications of what was going on the minds of most Germans. The plebiscite in the Saar went for Germany by a ten-to-one margin, and around the same time, the Danzigers chose a Nazi government in a free election.

Goldhagen, however, fails to ask why the Germans did not massacre the Jews in Eastern Europe when they occupied the area during World War I. The obvious difference between the two conflicts was that in the second, the Germans recognized the possibility that they could be defeated. This concern evoked the birth-related feeling of fear of annihilation, which was defended against by persecuting groups that had already been reduced to helplessness — Jews and Gypsies. Hitler was constantly harping on this fear in his speeches: Germany was being strangled by the West, threatened by subhuman Bolsheviks led by evil Jews, and facing starvation due to lack of *Lebensraum*. Coupled with the birth-related fear of annihilation was the childhood feeling of *I am afraid of someone weak*, which could refer to the mother or the father in the German family, either one of whom could punish the even weaker child. This may explain why Nazi persecution of the Jews increased as the latter became increasingly powerless. In connection with fear of annihilation, it should not surprise us that the very social classes that gave the strongest support to the rising Nazi party — the army, the peasantry, the lower middle class, and the aristocracy — were the same groups that faced social annihilation during the Weimar period as a consequence of demilitarization, urbanization, economic depression, and popular pressure for social reform. Little wonder that the German states in which the Nazis won local elections prior to Hitler's appointment as Chancellor — Mecklenburg-Schwerin, Mecklenburg-Strelitz, Oldenburg, Brunswick, Anhalt, and Lippe-Detmold — were heavily rural, while the NSDAP's growth in urban Berlin and Hamburg lagged behind the rest of the country.

The enigma that an advanced nation like Germany could have reverted to such barbarism between 1933 and 1945 may be explained when one distinguishes between conscious and unconscious motivations — between the real and the unreal selves. Western education cultivates the intellect, but ignores the emotions. Although highly educated, the Germans were emotionally repressed. The "war guilt" clause in the Versailles Treaty was more than many Germans could handle, and this led them to support Hitler's endeavor to shift all the guilt to the Jews. It was ironic that this treaty should have had such a powerful effect on the German psyche; only a few years before, the Kaiser had dismissed another treaty, protecting Belgium's neutrality, as just "a scrap of paper." But the guilt which Versailles triggered had already been planted in the German unconscious by years of harsh child-rearing. Films of Hitler's speeches show him reaching out to his audience, appearing to take something from them, and stuffing it in his pants; he is telling them, through non-verbal communication, to *give him their guilt.*

The Allies established a stable democracy in West Germany, where most of the shortcomings of Weimar were corrected. Proportional representation, which had encouraged the proliferation of political parties, was eliminated, and those with less than five percent of the vote were excluded from the Bundestag. Prussia disappeared from the map, with much of it being ceded to Poland and the USSR and the German population expelled westward. Junkers' estates, if they were not in the ceded provinces, became collective farms in East Germany (there were fewer estates in the West). The universities were denazified, and the aristocracy no longer played a significant role in the leadership of the armed forces. Most important, the standard of living in West Germany rose dramatically; business cycles no longer threatened to impoverish German families, since foreign workers — who came to make up a large portion of the labor force — simply returned to their homes when unemployment rose. Yet these changes did not affect child-rearing practices, and some German couples continued to treat their children in a harsh manner.

Neo-Nazi and skinhead movements still have a following in the reunited Germany, particularly in the East, and have engaged in numerous acts of violence reminiscent of the Nazi days. No one seriously anticipates their rise to power, but the victory of Jorg Haider's far-right Freedom Party in Austria, in 2000, was also unexpected. All it took to bring this group to power was a sudden influx of refugees from the Balkans — although the previous scandal over Kurt Waldheim's wartime record, years earlier, may have helped set the stage.

Unlike Japan, whose leaders still sometimes deny their country's unspeakable behavior in occupied China — or the United States, which has yet to admit wrongdoing in Vietnam — Germany has made serious attempts to come to terms with its past. German leaders have acknowledged their country's responsibility for the murder of six million Jews, along with millions of other victims; enormous reparations were paid by the Federal Republic, and anti–Semitism was outlawed officially in both German states.

One may still wonder, however, just how much has changed on the unconscious level. During the 1980s, a successful film, *Sugarbaby*, was produced in West Germany. The title character is a lonely, obese woman approaching middle age. Deciding that she wants to have a romantic relationship, she makes a play for a handsome, married man several years her junior and, against the odds, manages to land him as a lover. Their tryst comes to an abrupt end when the wife catches up to the couple as they are dancing together in a disco. In full view of the other patrons, she pummels the blubbering Sugarbaby to the floor, while the errant husband stands by, looking embarrassed, but doing nothing to stop her.

In any other country, even the most callous philanderer would have tried to restrain his wife from beating up his girlfriend. But not this lothario. As long as Sugarbaby takes the punishment for their shared transgression, the husband can avoid feeling the burden of his own guilt. It is all too reminiscent of the millions of ordinary Germans who blamed the Jews or the Communists for the loss of World War I, and then placed the exclusive blame on Hitler and his Nazis for World War II and its unprecedented atrocities. One can almost imagine the unfaithful husband, back in his apartment, explaining to his wife: "I was just following orders!" "I didn't *know* I was having an affair with her!" "I was against Sugarbaby all along!"

3

Northern Ireland

The Politics of Fear

British Home Secretary Reginald Maudling, drink in hand, put it bluntly as his plane left Belfast for London in 1972, following yet another unsuccessful attempt by Great Britain to solve the problems of Northern Ireland. "What a bloody awful country!" he exclaimed.[1]

It may not have been entirely clear whether Maudling's reference was to the six-county Northern Irish state or to the whole of Ireland. In either case, his remark epitomizes a common British attitude toward the Irish problem: after centuries of attempting to absorb all or part of their smaller neighbor, the British regard the resulting fiasco — a consequence of their own policies of economic exploitation and divide and rule — as proof that the Irish cannot manage their own affairs, and therefore require even more British intervention.

At a time when virtually all colonial territories have gained their independence, a colonial regime continues to rule over 1.5 million people in — of all places — Western Europe. And whereas most colonized peoples welcomed the end of colonial rule, much of the Northern Irish population is prepared to take up arms to defend their right to remain colonized.

The essence of the Northern Ireland problem is that the Protestants oppose unification because it would make them a minority. Northern Ireland's Catholics, however, support unification in the hope of becoming part of the majority. Unionist James Molyneaux has maintained: "It's not a question of whether you're a Catholic or a Protestant, it's a question of which nation you want to belong to...."[2] But only the Protestants are prepared to fight to remain part of the British Empire, even against the British themselves. As Sinn Fein leader Gerry Adams points out, Northern Ireland's Protestants "have a desperate identity crisis."[3] They are not sure which nation they belong to in the first place. A poll on national identity in the six counties showed that only 30 percent of the Protestants regarded themselves as British by nationality, another 32 percent as Ulstermen, and 20 percent as Irish (comparable figures among Catholics were 15 percent, 5 percent and 76 percent).[4] Almost a fifth of the Protestants were apparently unable to give any answer at all to the question of what nation they belonged to. Complicating matters further, these identities were somewhat fluid,[5] and by no means mutually exclusive.

The Irish, during their fight for independence, had their share of renegades — called "Shoneens" — who supported the colonial power, but the Protestant loyalists are another phenomenon altogether. The more fanatical among them regard Catholics as their enemies

35

by definition. This antagonism can be traced back to the seventeenth-century Westminster Confession of Faith, in which the Presbyterians — now the largest Protestant denomination in Northern Ireland — designated the Pope as the Antichrist.[6] It continues to the present day, as extremist groups such as Tara, a quasi-military loyalist cult, argue for "eliminating all Catholics within the Ulster state, and ... eventually taking over the south."[7] As even the IRA finally concluded, the first task of the Irish nationalist movement was not the expulsion of the British, but rather the awakening of Irish consciousness among the Ulster Protestants. This may be difficult, because the Protestants have their own inverted version of Irish nationalism; whereas the Catholics project negative feelings about their parents onto the Queen and Empire, the Protestants project them onto the Catholic Church and Irish nationalism. Protestant loyalism is *inverted Irish nationalism*, and not — as the loyalists often maintain — the expression of a separate "Ulster" nationalism.

If churches and nations are the repositories of feelings about our parents, Ireland is somewhat unique in the degree of splitting one finds; one set of authority symbols is seen as totally good, the other as totally evil. This may be connected with the high degree of alcoholism in the country, north and south. Alcoholic parents may be in radically different moods, depending upon whether they are drunk or sober. To the child of an alcoholic, it is almost like having two fathers or mothers — one loving, and one ill-tempered and mean.

Irish Protestant Identity

Who are the Northern Irish Protestants, and why have they been so unalterably opposed to Irish unification? The Ulster Defense Association, a Protestant paramilitary group, replies:

> We are a hybrid race descended from men who colonized Scotland from Ireland in the fifth century and who then colonized Northern Ireland from Scotland in the seventeenth century.... For 400 years we have known nothing but uprising, murder, destruction and repression. We ourselves have repeatedly come to the support of the British Crown only to be betrayed within another 20 years or so by a fresh government of that Crown.[8]

Historically, the Scots — whose own Gaelic language is much the same as Irish Gaelic[9] — crossed from Ireland into Scotland after the fall of the Roman Empire, forcing out the indigenous Picts, who migrated eastward. As early as 1400, there was a reverse migration of Gaelic Scots back to County Antrim, around Belfast,[10] but the most important wave of Scottish settlement came after 1603, when the English conquerors "planted" thousands of Scottish ex-soldiers in Antrim and Down.[11] Ironically, the strongest resistance to the English invaders was in Ulster, the last of Ireland's four provinces to surrender.[12] So many local Irish men were killed that the Scottish settlers had their pick of the local women, and plenty of farmland was there for the taking. While Scots and English continued to settle Ulster in later years, the province's "hybrid" character stems from the events of 1603.

The British regime promoted the myth that the Scottish settlers brought civilization to the Irish wilderness, driving out the savage natives. As Rev. Ian Paisley, a leading Protestant militant, put it in 1981, "[O]ur ancestors cut a civilization out of the bogs and meadows of this country while [Irish Prime Minister] Mr. [Charles] Haughey's ancestors were wearing pig-skins and living in caves."[13] Historian Edmund Curtis observes that this is a "rhetorical exaggeration," noting that some local Irish joined the immigrants in becoming landholders under the English.[14] And Ireland had its own civilization — although it was never unified under a single monarch — long before England even emerged as a nation.

English rule in Ireland was characterized by what is termed the "Protestant Ascendency"— a collection of anti–Catholic laws and policies which continued, in spirit if not in letter, during the fifty years of Unionist Party rule in Northern Ireland. As early as 1642, following a bloody uprising in which thousands of Protestant settlers were killed,[15] Catholics were categorically excluded from the Irish Parliament.[16] By the early eighteenth century, Catholics were prohibited from voting, serving on grand juries, or practicing law; and — except in linen-weaving, a major part of the economy — they were not permitted to employ more than two apprentices.[17] Derry — Northern Ireland's second city — had walls, within which Catholics were not permitted to live.[18] A visitor to the city today will find the walls still in place, and no Catholics living inside them. Unlike in the United States, it is the *dominant* group in Northern Ireland which lives in ghettoes.

Under the British, there was massive alienation of land from the Catholics. According to R.F. Foster, "...Catholics held about 60 per cent of Irish land in 1641; about 9 per cent in 1660; and about 20 per cent after the Restoration settlement."[19] In 1697, England went so far as to outlaw Catholicism in Ireland altogether.[20]

Ironically, for a long time, the Scottish-descended Presbyterians also faced discrimination at the hands of the dominant Anglicans. Many were consequently recruited into Irish nationalist organizations such as the United Irishmen, whose founder, Wolfe Tone, was himself a Protestant. But this situation changed during the nineteenth century, following the 1800 Act of Union, which abolished the separate Irish Parliament and created the United Kingdom. With the help of semi-secret societies such as the Orange Order, the Presbyterians were split away from the Irish cause and persuaded to align themselves with England.[21] By the middle of the century, secular Irish nationalism was nearly extinct. "Catholicism had been securely identified as the national experience.... [N]ationalism was almost entirely Catholic; and Unionism was principally, if less exclusively, Protestant."[22]

The English did not rely entirely on Protestant loyalism to keep the Catholic majority in check. In 1792, as revolutions swept continental Europe, the British government began subsidizing Maynooth College, a Catholic seminary near Dublin. The purpose was to replace Ireland's traditionally nationalist brand of Catholicism with a tamer, more conservative variety, with stronger ties to both the Vatican and the British Crown. It was "an attempt to ensure a loyal clergy not 'contaminated' by the ideas of republicanism."[23] British policy was thus responsible for creating two antagonistic political cultures in Ireland: a "Green" culture torn between its longings for national self-determination and its adherence to a socially conservative clergy; and an "Orange" culture equally torn between its theological pluralism and its political loyalty to the hierarchical institutions of the British Empire.

Orange Power

The First World War was a powerful catalyst for Irish nationalism. England was not only compelled to commit itself to independence for the small subject nations of Europe, but it became indebted to the United States, where the large Irish-American community had been actively supporting the nationalist cause for generations. Although the 1916 Easter

Rising failed, it nonetheless sowed the seeds of the 1920–1921 war which led to the creation of the Irish Free State.

While the Free State was a Dominion within the Commonwealth, and British military bases remained on Irish soil, the most galling shortcoming of independence from the Nationalist perspective was the continued British rule over the predominantly Protestant North. Fearful of being a minority in even a semi-autonomous Ireland, the Ulster Protestants had begun arming themselves against Home Rule as early as 1913.[24] "Home Rule," they loudly proclaimed, "is Rome Rule." Sir Edward Carson, a Protestant lawyer from Dublin, emerged as the leader of the Protestant resistance, and obtained 200,000 signatures on a petition which opposed any kind of self-government for Ireland.[25] There was already a division between the largely English-descended Protestants in Dublin, who opposed partition, and the predominantly Scottish-descended Protestants of the North, who soon came to favor it,[26] and dominated the loyalist movement by sheer force of numbers. While Carson is honored as the founder of the Northern Irish state, he chose not to lead it, and resigned as head of the Unionist Party.[27]

Nine of Ireland's thirty-two counties were in Ulster, but Cavan, Monaghan and Donegal had large Catholic majorities; had they been included in the separate Northern state, its Protestant majority would have been diluted. As it was, the Protestants constituted no more than two-thirds of the six counties' population. The Catholics were actually in a majority, by a modest margin, in Fermanagh and Tyrone, and were almost half the population in Derry and Armagh; only in the two easternmost counties were there large Protestant majorities: 68 percent in Down, and 77 percent in Antrim.[28] Even in Down, the southern portion around Newry was predominantly Catholic.

The Northern Catholics were unhappy with partition, and elected Nationalists to office in areas where they dominated the electorate. These local governments were disbanded by the Unionists, and replaced by commissioners appointed from Belfast. The same thing happened to the county governments in Fermanagh and Tyrone. In Derry City, where Catholics were a large majority, the police and armed Protestant paramilitaries were sent in to overthrow the city council by force, leaving 18 dead.[29]

The six counties were given their own parliament, Stormont, with extensive powers, including control over the police and education. Northern Ireland was also represented in the British Parliament, although not in proportion to its population. But it was understood that even though the six counties were part of the United Kingdom, the Parliament at Westminster would generally refrain from concerning itself with Northern Irish affairs.[30]

The Unionist Party — formally affiliated with the British Conservatives — virtually monopolized Northern Ireland's politics from 1922, when the country was partitioned, until Stormont was abolished fifty years later. During this time, no one other than Unionists ever served in a cabinet post in Northern Ireland. Often, the Nationalist opposition refused to take its seats in Stormont, leaving the small Northern Irish Labor party, which included members of both the Catholic and Protestant communities, as the only official opposition.

The Unionist Party, on the other hand, was not open to Catholics. A suggestion in 1959 that Catholics be admitted to membership was adamantly rejected.[31] The Unionist Minister for Education justified this stand by stating: "All the minority are traitors and have always been traitors to the government of Northern Ireland."[32] The Unionists do, however, admit Jews and members of other religions, as well as atheists.

Within the Unionist Party, the Orange Order holds immense influence. This sectarian fraternity is the direct descendant of a Protestant terrorist outfit founded in the 1780s, the Peep O'Day Boys, which murdered Catholics "in a protracted struggle for domination of the linen trade," and became the Orange Order in 1795.[33] It has been known to expel members for attending a Catholic mass, and sends a large bloc of delegates to the Unionist Party's ruling council.[34] The term "boys," incidentally, is commonly used by both Catholics and Protestants to describe their armed fighters; it is an enabling device, reassuring the fighters that they will not be held responsible for their violence, since, after all, "boys will be boys."

"Until very recently membership [in] the Orange Order was obligatory for political advancement."[35] Unionist MPs are almost always members,[36] as were nearly all Cabinet Members at Stormont.[37] The Orange Order's semi-secret nature[38] counteracted the effect of the province's seemingly open and democratic political institutions.

The Orange state had two police forces. The Royal Ulster Constabulary (RUC), a descendant of the Royal Irish Constabulary, admitted Catholics, although they never constituted more than 17 percent of the RUC's ranks, in 1936,[39] and had dropped to 12 percent by 1961.[40] The second, and much larger, police force were the B-Specials. These were part-time militiamen, exclusively Protestant, who were recruited directly from among the most extreme elements of the community. "[T]he notorious 'B-Specials' absorbed not only the remnants of the [paramilitary] Ulster Volunteer Force, but also unsavory murder gangs like the United Protestant League...."[41] Sometimes they were recruited right out of the Orange Lodges.[42] The B-Specials, far more than the RUC, were used to terrorize the Catholic population.

To its supporters, Northern Ireland was "a Protestant state for a Protestant people," and this meant a parochialism like that of the Free State after Catholicism was declared the national religion in 1937.[43] Pubs and movie theaters are closed on Sunday, "the Lord's day,"[44] and the Protestant version of history is taught in the schools.[45] Evangelicals preach their gospel everywhere: a couple strolling in lovers' lane might even be approached by a missionary with a tract on "What God Says About Kissing."[46] Ironically, while Northern Protestants point to the Republic's Church-inspired laws against abortion as an argument against reunification,[47] the Unionists outlawed it themselves in the North,[48] and, like the Church in the South, opposed the legalization of divorce.[49]

The Unionists ruled Northern Ireland for fifty years through a combination of appeals to religious bigotry, political repression, and legally rigged elections. They were assisted by the fact that Northern Ireland had its own court system, separate from the English courts; while the House of Lords in London served as the final court of appeals for the Six Counties, few cases ever reached that body.[50] There were property qualifications for voting rights which excluded the poor — disproportionately Catholic — from the rolls, while business owners, mostly Protestant, were permitted extra votes. The gerrymandering of the electoral boundaries to ensure Protestant control of Catholic-majority towns such as Derry City[51] was notorious.

Stormont regularly banned publications by "subversive" groups, lumping together the Communists, the Irish Republicans, and even Catholic religious orders[52]; and opposition demonstrations were outlawed during the 1950s.[53] Under the Special Powers Act, which was superseded only in 1973, the government could arrest people without warrants, try them without juries, and imprison them without trial. People could be arrested for making false statements, and the government was allowed to seize people's bank accounts.[54] The act also provided for "flogging and the death penalty for arms and explosives offenses; and allowed for the total suspension of civil liberties."[55] Of course, this could all be argued for in the name of fighting IRA terrorism.

Religious discrimination was official government policy under the Unionists, and it was extended to the private sector with the avid encouragement of leading Unionist politicians.[56] In 1933, Sir Basil Brooke—later Northern Ireland's Prime Minister for two decades—fired all 125 of the Catholic employees on his Fermanagh estate, boasting publicly of his deed.[57] Two years later, "the Orange Order began an official boycott of Catholic pubs, while an unofficial boycott of Catholic shops and businesses had been going on for some time."[58] Most of the six counties' pubs are Catholic-owned, although some of them cater to a Protestant clientele. In Northern Ireland, it can be fatal to wander into the wrong pub.

While anti–Catholic discrimination created a few marginal benefits for Protestant workers, it simultaneously prevented unity among the poor on both sides of the religious divide. The Unionists' "economic record ... by all normal rules of political behavior would have resulted in that party's cremation a long time ago," states one observer.[59] There have been, in fact, numerous working-class Protestant revolts against Unionist policies — but they have been invariably co-opted by sectarian forces.

In 1969, following his resignation as Northern Irish Prime Minister, the reformist Terence O'Neill made a curious statement:

> It is frightfully hard to explain to Protestants that if you give Roman Catholics a good job and a good house they will live like Protestants, because they will see neighbors with cars and television sets.
> They will refuse to have eighteen children, but if a Roman Catholic is jobless and lives in the most ghastly hovel, he will rear eighteen children on National Assistance.
> If you treat Roman Catholics with due consideration and kindness, they will live like Protestants, in spite of the authoritative [sic] nature of their Church.[60]

O'Neill seemed to be oblivious to the existence of many impoverished Protestants who also lived in hovels, faced unemployment, and didn't own cars. It was these poor Protestants who flocked into the extremist organizations that brought a halt to O'Neill's modest reform program and forced him to step down.

Repressed Fear and National Identity

The loyalism of Ulster's poor Protestants is a paradox. On tenement walls in Belfast's Protestant slums, one can see the slogan, "This We Shall Maintain"— referring to the Union with Great Britain, not the slums themselves, "although the connection between the two is more than accidental."[61] Protestant loyalists have often maintained that the distinction between Northern and Southern Ireland is national, rather than religious; they define themselves as Ulstermen, rather than Irishmen. As a senior Unionist leader stated, "I'm an Ulsterman, not an Irishman — I don't jig at crossroads or play Gaelic football. We've got two races on this island...."[62] Nonetheless, this man's country's official name remains the United Kingdom of Great Britain and *Northern Ireland*, and the local branch of the Anglican Church which many of his fellow Ulstermen attend is still called the Church of Ireland.

Protestant loyalism is not an example of nationalism, although it shares many of its characteristics: Irish Protestants, notwithstanding loyalist mythology, do not constitute a nation, but a religious minority, and even here, the differences in the forms of worship between Protestant Anglicans and Roman Catholics are less than those between Anglicans and Baptists. If Irish Protestants were legitimately entitled to separate from the Catholic majority, why wouldn't Methodists, Presbyterians, and other denominations have the right to set up their own states? Likewise, if the Scottish-descended Protestants of Northern Ireland can claim the right to remain within the United Kingdom, wouldn't the right of secession also apply to the Irish-descended Scottish Catholics who make up much of the population of Glasgow? Shouldn't they be permitted to join the Irish Republic?

And yet, given the not always felicitous conditions of non–Catholic minorities in some European Catholic countries — such as the Jews in interwar Poland, or the Protestants in Spain under Franco — it is not too hard to see why the Protestants were leery of a united Ireland. Irish nationalism has long been closely linked with Catholicism, and had the Catholic Church been stamped out by the English as effectively as was the Gaelic language, to survive only in remote corners of the Emerald Isle, it is likely that the Union Jack would still be flying over Dublin and Cork.

Fear of minority status is all but universal among dominant ethnic groups, which typically fight to the bitter end to keep from losing their power: one need only think of the French in Algeria or the whites in South Africa and Zimbabwe. Yet minorities have been known to survive and even prosper, and it would be hard to imagine a unified Irish state carrying out pogroms against its Protestant minority, which would constitute about 25 percent. The now-flourishing Irish economy would be wrecked, and other powers would surely intervene. Protestant fear of unification stems less from the likelihood of religious persecution in a future 32-county Ireland, than from repressed fear carried forward from a traumatic childhood. This explains why Northern Ireland's working-class Protestants are more eager to maintain partition than their middle-class counterparts who actually benefit most from it; their childhoods were more likely to be traumatic.

Children growing up in working-class neighborhoods in Belfast or Derry, Catholic or Protestant, have a great deal to be afraid of. Their families are financially insecure; there are nervous English troops patrolling the streets; terrorists bomb pubs; mobs burn down houses; criminal gangs take advantage of the disorder to kill people at random.

Among the Protestants, the fathers had probably served in the British Army, perhaps as officers; the discipline imposed on them is often reflected in the way they raised their children. They might have been B-Specials, or members of anti–Catholic paramilitary groups, or both; in either case, there would be guns in the house. There might have been loose talk about "Fenians" being killed in the line of duty. The notion that his father might have killed someone for being "bad," that is disobedient to the established order of Queen and Country, would be sufficient to create anxiety in any child.

These fears could not be expressed, either in the family or outside. In an empire where the navy had the highest prestige, Northern Ireland was a major source of recruits for the army. Northern Ireland's Protestants, in fact, take immense pride in the sacrifices they made for Britain at the battle of the Somme in World War I, where more than 5,000 soldiers from Ulster perished.[63] Some of the slogans favored by loyalists seem to reflect the trench warfare of this long-past conflict: "No Surrender!" "Not One Inch!" "Ulster Will Fight, and Ulster Will be Right!"

A soldier cannot be allowed to display fear, and children raised to be soldiers are denied the right to feel their normal childhood fears from a very early age. Denied fear does not go away; it may be displaced onto other objects, causing phobias, or if even more completely repressed, produce bullying, psychopathic behavior, as the individual seeks to allay his own unconscious terror by inflicting it on someone else.

How does this work in practice in Northern Ireland? Listen to extremist leader Rev. Ian Paisley's response to the claim that his fellow Protestants are motivated primarily by fear:

> I don't know what they mean by Protestant fears.... I don't think Protestants are walk-
> ing about in fear. I think the only thing Protestants are legitimately afraid of is a dirty,
> underhanded deal done behind their backs, because while we have the majority we have
> absolutely no political power whatsoever. We're in the hands of our English masters.
> And we understand they are not our friends. They would like to destroy us. So that's
> our only fear, but we're not wandering about in fear of anybody.[64]

Paisley, in other words, denies that Protestants are afraid, even as he maintains that they are completely subordinate to treacherous "English masters" bent on their destruction.

Internal Partition

For more than 40 years, Northern Ireland's politics were largely based on sectarianism, although economic divisions between rich and poor were also important. Each of the two religious communities had its own political parties, lived in its own neighborhoods, attended its own pubs and social clubs, and read its own newspapers. Factories, shops and banks were associated with one or the other group.[65] Schools were segregated in practice, and even pastimes were divided along religious lines, with Protestants playing English games while Catholics leaned more toward traditional Gaelic sports.[66] The two religious communities even tended to regard each other as separate races. In Derry, William Kelleher noted that Catholics thought they could spot Protestants because their eyes were close together, while Protestants believed the same thing about Catholics.[67]

Protestant voters, regardless of class, usually supported the Unionist Party, except from time to time in Belfast, where either Labor or extremely sectarian "Independent Unionists" sometimes showed strength. The Catholics usually voted for the abstentionist Nationalist Party, led by the Catholic middle class and backed by the Church.[68] Partition between North and South was echoed by an internal divide between Catholics and Protestants in the North.

This system, notwithstanding its intrinsic injustice, remained remarkably stable for decades. Only six men held the office of Prime Minister of Northern Ireland in the half century from 1922 to 1972, when Stormont was suspended; two of these remained in power for about 20 years each. Except in Belfast, Protestants were afraid to defect from the Unionists for fear of splitting the Protestant vote and handing elections to the Catholics; the same process worked in reverse where Catholics were the majority. In the towns where Catholics were numerous enough to take office, they discriminated against Protestants in turn.[69] This was virtually inevitable, since Catholics had few other jobs available for them, and, as elsewhere, one has to take care of one's own. But this discrimination, along with the violence of the Irish Republican Army, only drove the Protestants even deeper into the loyalist camp.

What undermined Northern Ireland's political system was a series of unrelated events which began eroding the long-standing religious antagonism, starting in the late 1950s. A liberal Pope, John XXIII, was chosen in 1959; the following year, John F. Kennedy was elected the first Catholic president of the United States; in 1962, the IRA halted its violent "border campaign,"[70] which had taken a total of only 16 lives — 6 Ulster policemen and 10 IRA militants — in six years,[71] compared to roughly 3,500 who died in the conflict which began in the mid–1960s and continued until early in the next century. In 1963, Terence O'Neill, a reform-minded Unionist, became Prime Minister of Northern Ireland; Labor came to power in Great Britain in 1964, with the votes of Irish immigrants playing a large role in Harold Wilson's victory; and finally, in 1965, the Irish Republic recognized the legality of the border when its Prime Minister, Sean Lemass, visited O'Neill in Belfast — the first official contact between the two Irish governments since partition.

For a while, the sectarian bitterness appeared to be turning into a thing of the past. "The overall look and mood of Northern Ireland proclaimed that it was actually changing for the better, and that the Paisley phenomenon was a desperate reaction by extremists to the liberalization of Ulster life which had been under way since 1963."[72] But as it turned out, the sectarian barriers which were coming down were also the pillars of Northern Ireland's stability; the wall between the two communities, in other words, was holding up the roof. As a result of the decline in sectarian hatred, Catholics began pressing for equal rights *within* the six-county state, and — along with some sympathetic Protestants — organized the Northern Ireland Civil Rights Association (NICRA). Rank-and-file Protestants, in response, began moving into the extremist camp.

Ironically, in persuading Catholics to accept partition in return for equal treatment, it would appear that NICRA might have guaranteed the survival of the six-country state. But since the northern state was predicated on the inability of Catholics and Protestants to live together in harmony, anything that proved that the two groups could cooperate was automatically a threat to the status quo. As an artificial entity, Northern Ireland was strengthened by the IRA's armed struggle against it, but was undermined by a movement which sought to make the state more responsive to its population.

NICRA's emergence was also divisive within the Catholic community, as the IRA had to rearm to protect Catholics against both Protestant extremists and the police. The Catholics are now split into two camps. The first includes NICRA; the now largely moribund Official IRA; its political arm known as the Workers' Party, which is influenced by Trotskyism; and the moderate Social Democratic and Labor Party. The other camp includes the Provisional IRA; its political affiliate the Sinn Fein; the leftist People's Democracy movement, stemming from the student movement of the 1960s; and the conservative Irish Independence Party. The first camp favors working within the system, building alliances between Catholic and Protestant workers, and postponing reunification to some later date. The second camp prefers to work for Irish reunification first, with social and economic reforms coming afterward, if at all. This means that leftists in the six counties are generally less opposed to British rule than nationalists. One small group, the British and Irish Communist Organization (BICO), even combines a Marxist economic program with loyalty to England, a stand which more or less follows logically from the assumption that Irish Protestants constitute a separate nation.

There are also bitter conflicts among the Protestants, who are now divided into five hostile camps:

1. Moderates — the Alliance Party, Northern Irish Labor, and BICO — who support continued British rule, but with no sectarian discrimination;
2. The Official Unionist Party, which favors the restoration of extensive self-government for Northern Ireland within the United Kingdom, with continued discrimination against Catholics;
3. Secular extremists, such as the Ulster Defense Association, who tend to favor independence for the six-county state[73];
4. The parochial extremists, such as Ian Paisley's Democratic Unionist Party, who tend to favor complete integration of the six counties into the United Kingdom,[74] which would mean abandonment of Northern Ireland's self-government, but increased representation at Westminster.
5. A few secular Unionists who favor Paisley's strategy of full integration into the U.K.

Although the extremists — or loyalists — are often lumped together by outsiders, there are significant differences between the third and fourth camps.

Secular Protestants

The Ulster Defense Association (UDA) began as the armed wing of Vanguard, led by William Craig, a hard-line Unionist cabinet minister.[75] Fearful that the Unionist leadership might agree to Irish unification some day, Craig declared in 1972: "We are determined ... to preserve our British traditions and way of life. And God help those who get in our way."[76] When asked whether his program would entail "killing all Catholics in Ulster," Craig replied: "It might not go so far as that but it could go as far as killing...."[77] Oddly, his followers "were often educated, articulate and ambitious [Unionist] Party members and officials, rather than the stereotyped backwoodsmen."[78] When Vanguard fell apart after Craig uncharacteristically came out in favor of sharing power with moderate Catholics[79] — seriously misjudging the mood of his supporters — the UDA, led by Andy Tyrie, inherited its niche in the political spectrum. Later, the UDA founded its own political arm, the Ulster Loyalist Democratic Party.

The UDA is nationalist and militarist, but there are occasional overtones of social radicalism. It publicly repudiates Paisley's overt Protestant sectarianism, preferring to interpret the struggle for Ulster in more secular terms:

> [F]or four centuries by murder, boycott, bombing and every means possible with no holds barred the Gaelic Irish have endeavoured to oust from Ireland those who favored a broader outlook with political, religious and economic ties with the outside world — the Ulster people.[80]

There is a curious parallel here with the Provisional IRA, which also sees the Irish struggle in terms of the conflict "between two civilizations: Catholic, Gaelic values — non-material, spiritual, sharing, altruistic, other-directed — and Protestant, English values — permissive, material, consumer-oriented, self-directed."[81] Yet these "two civilizations" share the same language, have a common history, and are strongly puritanical, but with a fondness for violence.

Paisleyism

The Paisleyites — themselves firm champions of spiritual, if not quite altruistic, values — see the conflict in very different terms. On one hand, they perceive Ulster's Protestants as locked in a struggle with diabolical "papists," ready to bring the horrors of the Inquisition to the villages of County Down; on the other hand, they are equally fearful of the forces the ecumenism and modernism, now dominant among mainstream Protestants in the English-speaking countries. By arguing for Christian unity, liberal Protestants threaten to take away the loyalists' poison containers, leaving the latter without defenses against their own repressed fear. Without the Pope and the Catholic Church to hate, Paisley's followers might have to face their feelings about their own parents.

Paisley himself is quite explicit in describing the effects of his own pain:

> If God gave me the due reward for my deeds, he would send me to hell. I am a sinner.
> There is nothing good about me. From the sole of the foot to the crown of the head
> there is no soundness in man, but wounds and bruises and putrifying sores.[82]

Paisley's father was a Protestant minister, and his mother was a member of an extremely devout sect in her native Scotland. He was born in Ballymena, "the most devoutly Protestant town in the North...."[83] As an adolescent, "he had a reputation as something of a bully."[84] His parents, however, seem to have regarded Ian as the "good boy" of the family; the "bad boy" was his brother Harold, who was kicked out of the RUC for public drunkenness. Harold later became a minister of the Plymouth Brethren sect, and emigrated to Canada. This church is so devout that Ian's own Free Presbyterians look almost like agnostics by comparison. Harold is fond of criticizing the "Romish" clerical collar Ian wears in the course of his duties.[85]

With little formal training, Ian became a Presbyterian minister, and eventually started his own breakaway denomination. The Free Presbyterian Church's social conservatism, opposition to liberal sexual mores, lack of internal democracy, and intolerance of other churches are reminiscent of the Catholic Church itself during its worst moments.[86] In fact, it would be helpful to regard many of the more fanatical Protestant denominations in Ulster as reaction formations against an underlying identification with Irish Catholicism.

In Paisleyite ideology, the Catholic Church is not only demonized, but sexualized as well. In 1986, Paisley accused Cardinal Suenens of Belgium of presiding over an atavistic fertility rite: he related details of plastic penises being inflated at the altar, as young girls screamed with delight and priests smeared their bodies with semen — all this supposedly happening at a theological congress in Brussels.[87] This story surely tells us more about the inner workings of Paisley's own mind than anything else. Paisley was motivated to enter politics by Terence O'Neill's attempt to reform the political system. While O'Neill's policies were far from radical, they caused a loyalist backlash among the poor Protestants. Particularly in the rural areas, many of them flocked to Paisley's extremist Protestant Unionist Party, later renamed the Democratic Unionist Party, although it remains dominated by Free Presbyterians.[88]

Many of the Protestant paramilitary groups overlap with the Democratic Unionists — although this is not true of the UDA, whose members are not generally churchgoing types. The Ulster Protestant Volunteers (UPV) was Paisley's own creation, and while the UPV engaged in no armed action, many of its members were also in the Ulster Volunteer Force (UVF).[89] The UVF was known for its random killings of Catholics, particularly in Belfast.

One of its gunmen, Billy Mitchell, who was also a founder of Paisley's UPV, originally taught Sunday school at a Free Presbyterian church.[90] This raises questions about Paisley's claim in 1969 that even though he hated the Catholic Church, "God being my judge, I love the poor dupes who are ground down under that system."[91]

Repressed pain underlies the fanaticism of Ulster's Protestant extremists, who — unlike the Catholics — are not responding to actual social repression. From repressed *fear*, we see the desire to bully those in a subordinate position. Repressed *anger* leads to paranoid belief systems; loyalists perceive the entire world ganging up against them, although most of it is obviously indifferent to events in Northern Ireland. Repressed *hurt* leads to notions that one is superior to some other group. And Repressed *need* leads people to blindly follow some authoritarian political or religious leader.

The Transformation of Protestant Extremism

By the beginning of the twenty-first century, the Northern Irish situation appeared to be somewhat settled, as the violence died down and the Sinn Fein entered the Stormont cabinet, even though the Provisional IRA stubbornly — but understandably — continued to hold on to its weapons, and the breakaway "Real IRA" engaged in occasional acts of violence. In 1997, a Catholic nationalist was elected Lord Mayor of Belfast, and removed the Union Jack from his office.[92] The Orange Order lost more than a third of its members, having come under the control of increasingly unpopular extremists.[93]

Protestant extremism may contain within it the seeds of its own destruction. Fear of betrayal by England has led the loyalists to take up arms, but the act of arming themselves tends to relieve the fear which distorted their perceptions in the first place. It is hard to be afraid when you belong to a well-armed and organized group. Sinn Fein's Gerry Adams noted during the mid–1990s that the political spokesmen of the UDA and UVF were more open to talks with his movement than the official Ulster Unionist Party and Paisley's Democratic Unionist Party.[94]

At the same time, the loyalist paramilitaries have clashed repeatedly with the British, with many of their leaders tossed in jails where they, ironically, come under the influence of IRA activists. The notorious UVF leader Gusty Spence became an anti-sectarian socialist while in prison, through his contacts with the leftist Official IRA, but he had already lost control of his paramilitary group to more extremist figures.[95] And the clashes and jailings have left a legacy of bitterness among the Protestant masses, who could conceivably align themselves with Catholic militants in opposition to the common British enemy.

In 1995, a group of Protestants, including some prominent loyalist paramilitaries, issued a statement entitled *A New Beginning*. It said:

> [W]e challenge Loyalists and Republicans to acknowledge that over the centuries each community has imbued many of the other's attributes, to the extent that the heritage of both traditions has increasingly become a shared one. We challenge Loyalists to acknowledge the "Irish" component of their heritage, and Nationalists to acknowledge the "British" component of theirs."[96]

As the degree of fear declines, the extremism which feeds on it also begins to fade. The loyalist decision to arm against the forces of Irish nationalism may, ironically, ultimately lead them into a reunified Ireland.

4

Yugoslavia

Prisoners of Myth and History

The disintegration in 1991 of the multi-ethnic state of Yugoslavia, and the eruption of ethnic violence in its successor states, represent a tragedy of epic proportions. The Marxist notion that social systems unilaterally determine our culture and psychology falls apart as bearded Chetniks and black-uniformed Ustashi, long vanished from the scene, reappear with a vengeance in a curious parallel to the Freudian "return of the repressed." The one-time Communist leader, Milovan Djilas, said: "We proceeded from the view that national minorities and national ambitions would weaken with the development of socialism, and that they are chiefly a product of capitalist development."[1] Two generations of socialism were unable to prevent the re-emergence of the most virulent forms of nationalism following Tito's demise. Looking at a map of the Balkans at the century's end, and comparing it with a map of partitioned Yugoslavia during the Nazi occupation, one might almost think that Hitler had won the war.

At the same time, we cannot settle for psychologically reductionist approaches which focus exclusively on family pathology and fail to explain why the Yugoslav peoples formed their unified state in 1918, why they chose to rebuild it after the bloodletting of World War II, or how the country survived for nearly half a century after that. When psychiatrist Jovan Raskovich, once the leader of the now largely expelled Serb minority in Croatia, tells us that "the Croats are characterized by castration anxiety, the Muslims by anal frustration, and the Serbs by Oedipal conflicts,"[2] he raises more questions than he answers.

I would propose, rather, the application of a two-self psychohistorical model to the Yugoslav situation. While the real self is simply motivated by a healthy desire for peace and prosperity, the unreal self responds to buried pain from past traumas. In Yugoslavia, the unreal self is engaged in a *struggle to be the victim*. Each player in this struggle — Serbs, Croats, Bosnian Muslims, Macedonians, Albanians — seeks to rewrite history to portray itself as the victim of some other player. Earning victim status absolves one of a sense of sin, itself nothing but buried pain. Past atrocities are wiped off the slate, and one may even commit a few more on credit, as it were. Victims become the beloved favorites of the West, which takes on the role of the parent. The ethnic conflict becomes less a battle for territory than for the approval of Western — particularly American — public opinion.

The problem is that only those who *lose* wars get to be perceived as victims. But those

47

who *win* wars get to write the official history. Each side has to lose in order to win. Little wonder that the fighting continued for so long.

The Yugoslav Peoples

Slavs first began migrating to the Balkans only a century or so after the fall of the Roman Empire. The current distinctions of the Balkan Slavs into Slovenes, Croats, Bosniaks (Bosnian Muslims), Serbs, Macedonians, and Bulgarians is more than a bit arbitrary. Bulgarians and Macedonians speak different dialects of the same language. Slovene is similar to the Croatian spoken in Zagreb, but Croatians living in most other regions speak the Serbian dialect, while those in Istria speak their own. Orthodox Serbs and Roman Catholic Croats are divided by religion, but the Serbs almost became Catholics when they first adopted Christianity; if they had, the two hostile nations would most likely be one today.

The central myth of Serbian history is that their nation was subjected to a Christ-like martyrdom as a result of its defeat in the battle of Kosovo at the hands of the Turks in 1389. This martyrdom, in which the Serbs voluntarily chose the "heavenly kingdom" of Christianity over the "earthly kingdom" of vassalage under the Muslim invaders, granted the Serbs — in their own estimation — the right to lead the other Yugoslav peoples. They were able to impose their myths on the other Yugoslavs after 1918 because they were the largest of the country's many component groups, although this was, in part, because Macedonians were counted as "South Serbs." The Serbs also had experience in self-government, which the Slovenes, Bosniaks, and some of the Croats lacked. And, not least, they also controlled the new country's army.

The corresponding Croat myth is that their nation defended its independence while standing guard at the border of Europe to protect Western civilization from Oriental barbarism. While the Serbs adhere to a "hero culture," ultimately derived from the ancient Greeks, the Croats follow a "paladin culture," based on absolute loyalty to the ruler, whomever it might be; this was absorbed from their German and Hungarian overlords. Yugoslavia's tragedy, both under the Karadjorgevich dynasty (1918–1941) and Tito's federated socialist state, was that the authoritarian political structure created to maintain the unity of the country, in the face of separatist pressure, led to the obliteration of the Serb hero culture.

Both the Serb and Croat national myths are based on fantasies. It has long been "a mystery to the rest of humanity"[3] that the Serbs should have chosen to celebrate a *defeat* at Turkish hands as their national holiday. The Turks supposedly won the battle, but the legends deriving from it were passed on in song and verse, and inspired later resistance to Turkish rule.[4] Consequently, "every Serb feels himself an actor in a great drama that is being played out across the centuries."[5] Ironically, the Christian alliance that fought the Turks at Kosovo included Bosnians, Albanians, and other Balkan peoples,[6] while some Serbs fought on the Turkish side. Even more odd, the battle appears to have been a victory of sorts for the Christian alliance. Although the Serb leader, Prince Lazar, was slain, the Turkish Sultan was also killed — by a "Serb" hero who may have actually been an Albanian or a Hungarian, if indeed he even existed. The Turkish troops retreated,[7] and Serbia did not fall until many decades afterward.

The Croats were invited into the Balkans by the Byzantine Emperor, who needed them "to fight the Avars and their Slavic dependents."[8] They shed Byzantine rule and adopted Roman Catholicism in 880, but remained independent for little more than two centuries. In 1102, Croatia became part of Hungary,[9] retaining its own legislative assembly with considerable autonomy; the Dalmatian region, ethnically Croat, came first under Venice, and then became part of Austria. This situation prevailed until the end of World War I.[10]

Bosnia (technically, Bosnia-Herzegovina) is nearly surrounded by Montenegro, Serbia and Croatia, but contains a large Muslim community of Slav origin. Typically, these Muslims have identified with whomever rules them: in Ottoman times they considered themselves Turks; in the interwar period they tended to regard themselves as Serbs; during the Nazi occupation, when Bosnia was part of the puppet Croat state, the Muslims declared themselves Croats; under Tito, they sometimes called themselves "Yugoslavs," and sometimes just "Muslims." Today, they call themselves "Bosniaks." At no time, however, did Muslims ever constitute a majority of the population of Bosnia. During the interwar period, Serbs were nearly half of the Bosnian population, with Muslims constituting about one third and Croats the rest. Under Tito and afterwards, due to wartime massacres and post-war migration, the proportions of Serbs and Muslims were reversed.[11]

The Slavs of Macedonia — some of whom live in Bulgaria and Greece — received recognition as a distinct ethnic group only under Tito. Previously, many had regarded themselves as Bulgarians, but the experience of being ruled by Bulgaria during the Axis occupation disenchanted them. In the north, the Slovenes have their own distinct language, and are mostly Catholics. During the interwar period, they allied with the Serbs, perhaps out of fear of being gobbled up by fascist Italy, which had annexed some Slovene territory; but under the Communists, the Slovenes became the foremost champions of Yugoslavia's decentralization, typically in opposition to the Serbs.

In addition, non–Yugoslav ethnic groups were found in the country. The largest of these were the Albanians, in Kosovo and western Macedonia. Germans, Hungarians, Romanians, and Slovaks formed important communities in Voivodina, and there were also Jews, Gypsies, Turks, and Italians in various parts of the country.

The Illyrian Heritage

During the nineteenth century, the Illyrian movement, named after the people who lived in the area in ancient times, fostered unity among the Yugoslav peoples. The Croats were more likely to identify themselves as Illyrians than the Serbs, although the Albanians probably had the best claim of all. Croat journalist Branka Magaš found that the "common Illyrian origins" she shared with the Albanians of Kosovo explained "why I felt so much at home with these people,"[12] although mutual resentment of the Serbs might be an equally valid explanation. Serbs identify far more strongly with Slavdom, notwithstanding their perennial quarrels with the Croats and Bulgarians. To the Serbs, the Illyrians are literally ancient history. As for their Albanian neighbors, the Serbs regard them as subhuman, saying — quite seriously — that they only lost their tails during the nineteenth century.[13]

The Illyrians, as it happens, were savage warriors, whose "blood-thirsty ways ... are mentioned with disgust by Greek writers, notably the custom of using the skull of an enemy as a drinking tankard."[14] Illyrians were known to practice human sacrifice, and reportedly "killed their own weak and wounded, so that they did not fall into the hands of the enemy live and edible."[15]

The Illyrians owned their land collectively,[16] which may have been the origin of the extended family system known in Yugoslavia as the *zadruga*. Slovene psychohistorian Alenka Puhar has detailed the conditions in the *zadruga* in the pages of *The Journal of Psychohistory*.[17] While economically useful for the efficient cultivation of Yugoslavia's often poor-quality farmland, the *zadruga* was also the source of considerable oppression of women and children. Just as women were subordinate to men, so younger members were considered little more than the servants of their elders.[18] Young men remained in a position of dependence, as they continued to reside within the *zadruga*, married to a bride chosen by their parents, who was herself expected to do the most menial chores.[19] The *zadruga* system disappeared among the Yugoslavs under Tito, but can still be found among the Kosovo Albanians.[20]

Rival Political Cultures

Following the Napoleonic Wars, the Yugoslav peoples were mostly divided between the Habsburg and Ottoman Empires, with only tiny Montenegro — smaller than its present modest size — enjoying independence. Serbia had been self-governing within the Turkish state since 1804, and gained full independence in 1830. Slovenia was part of the Austrian Empire, along with Dalmatia. The rest of Croatia belonged to Hungary, along with Voivodina, with its ethnically mixed population. Bosnia remained Turkish until 1878, while Macedonia and Kosovo were under Turkish rule until the First Balkan War in 1912. While the Croatians retained some of their old autonomy, this benefited only the local nobility, itself largely of German or Hungarian ancestry, who, according to a Croat writer, "treated their subjects worse than cattle...."[21] Completely dominating the politics of the Croatian vassal state, these aristocrats were responsible for the "burning, indestructible devotion to the Habsburgs" which characterized the Croats during the nineteenth century,[22] as well as the "curious mythology ... in which the Goths were seen as the ancestors of the Croats," notwithstanding the fact that the Gothic occupation of the region was brief, and their Teutonic language unrelated to Serbo-Croat.[23]

In 1848, widespread social and national revolts nearly toppled the Habsburg Empire. The Vienna rulers appointed Baron Josip Jelachich as *ban* (governor) of Croatia.[24] When Hungary tried to break away from Habsburg rule, under Louis Kossuth, Jelachich invaded Hungary and saved the tottering empire.[25] The quintessential paladin, Jelachich became the Croat national hero; the statue of him in the main square, removed during the Communist regime, was restored after Croatia became independent. Curiously, about half of Jelachich's troops during his war against Kossuth and the workers of Vienna were ethnic Serbs who had settled in Croatia.[26] Following the defeat of the 1848 revolts, the autonomy of both Hungary and Croatia was severely restricted. Hungarians taunted the Croats by reminding then, "What you received as a reward, we got as a punishment."

During the nineteenth century, Serbia continued to expand its territory at the expense of the declining Turkish Empire. The once-large Turkish population in Serbia was brutally expelled, and the Albanian community in the city of Nish met a similar fate when that region became part of Serbia in 1878.[27] In Serb eyes, Christians who underwent conversion to Islam were traitors; that included both Slav Muslims and most Albanians. The Serbs perceived themselves as the nation which refused to bow down to the Islamic invaders. This conflation of the national struggle with Christianity has deep roots among the Serbs, some of whose kings were elevated to sainthood by the Serbian Orthodox Church.[28] This created difficulties with the Catholic Croats after 1918, since they didn't recognize Orthodox saints. In addition, Croats regarded Serbia as somewhat backward and uncivilized. Each of the two nationalities saw itself as the senior partner in the relationship, the Serbs because of their history, and the Croats because of their higher degree of modernization.

Serbs and Croats fought on opposite sides during World War I. Serbia experienced a brutal occupation, and the war cost the country half of its male population between the ages of 18 and 55.[29] Long forgotten by outsiders, but relevant to the recent conflict in Bosnia, was the organization of Muslim and Croat paramilitary units by the Habsburg regime to slaughter Bosnian Serb villagers, who resisted with guerrilla warfare. By late in the war, nearly 100,000 Bosnian Serbs had been jailed or deported.[30] Concentration camps were established in Hungary to accommodate them, and many never returned.[31] Similarly, the treatment of the population in occupied Serbia during World War I brings to mind events typically associated with the next conflict. In language similar to Hitler's, an Austrian commander instructed his troops:

> In dealing with a population of this kind all humanity and kindness of heart are out of place, they are even harmful.... I therefore give orders that, during the entire course of the war, an attitude of extreme severity, extreme harshness, and extreme distrust is to be observed towards everybody.[32]

While the suffering they experienced during the war strengthened the attachment of the Serbs to their monarchy and cultural traditions, other groups in the new Yugoslav state regarded the government in Belgrade as alien, corrupt, and inefficient. The former Habsburg territories — where the Croats, Slovenes and Bosniaks, as well as many Serbs, lived — were forced to pay higher taxes than the residents of the old Serbian kingdom.[33] This was rationalized by the Serbs on the grounds that their homeland had suffered so much devastation during the war. Slovene and Bosniak politicians cooperated with the Serb-dominated government during most of the interwar period; however, the leaders of the Serbs in the former Habsburg territories, the *prichanski* ("across the river") Serbs, tended to align themselves with their Croat neighbors in opposition to the politicians in Belgrade.

For more than a decade following its unification in 1918, Yugoslavia had a more or less freely-elected parliament; there were a great many parties, although few of them extended beyond a single ethnic group.[34] But instruments of repression existed alongside this democratic façade, and were dominated by the Serbs. Of the army's 165 generals, 161 were Serbs, two Croats, and two Slovenes.[35] There was also the paramilitary Chetnik organization. Half a million strong,[36] the Chetniks were originally irregulars used to fight the Turks and Bulgarians in Macedonia before 1913, when the Balkan Wars settled the fate of the disputed province. After 1918, the Chetniks were used to intimidate opponents of the Belgrade government.[37]

The largest Croat political party was the Croatian Peasant Party, which favored a federal, and preferably republican, Yugoslavia. The Party of Pure Right was an avowedly separatist group with mostly urban, lower-middle-class support. An extremist outgrowth of this party was the Ustashi ("Rebel") movement, headed by Ante Pavelich. From exile in Italy, Pavelich engineered the assassination of Yugoslavia's King Alexander in 1934.[38] The regime in Belgrade carried on under a Prince Regent and a prime minister who adopted Mussolini's outward style; but by 1939, a *modus vivendi* had been worked out between the Serbs and the Croatian Peasant Party. Croatia gained an extensive degree of self-government, and its territory was enlarged to include parts of Bosnia-Herzegovina.[39] Following this agreement, known as the *sporazum*, Yugoslavia seemed to be moving toward some sort of federal system, but Serb politicians from the dominant Radical Party raised objections to all decentralizing tendencies.[40] They were worried about local nationalism in Macedonia as well, which would have reduced Serb numbers in the kingdom if the Macedonians had been granted equal status as a nationality.

Yugoslavia Under Hitler

During the tragic Balkan conflicts of the 1990s, some were quick to equate the Serbs with the Nazis. They might remember that in 1941, the Serb-dominated government in Belgrade signed the Axis pact, but within two days, that government was overthrown in a coup,[41] and replaced by a pro–Allied junta,[42] as Serb crowds demonstrated in Belgrade shouting: "Rather war than the pact; rather death than slavery."[43] Given the fact that Yugoslavia was nearly surrounded by Axis nations, this stance was virtually suicidal. Of course, had the other peoples of Europe reacted the same way when their governments were about to sell out to Hitler — at the time of the Munich Pact, for example — World War II would never have happened.

In the wake of the Axis invasion, Ante Pavelich returned to Croatia with a handful of followers. Declaring himself the *poglavnik* (führer) of the "Independent State of Croatia," Pavelich began a genocidal campaign against Serbs, Jews, and Gypsies, who together numbered more than a third of the state's six million inhabitants. "The formula that was to be applied to the Serbian population was simple: about one-third would be expelled to Serbia, one-third would be converted to Roman Catholicism, and one third would be exterminated."[44] Reliable estimates of Serb deaths at Ustashi hands have ranged from 500,000 to 700,000.[45]

Many Bosniaks supported the Ustashi.[46] There was also an SS division, *Handzhar* (Scimitar), recruited among them, which was backed by the Grand Mufti of Jerusalem.[47] On the other hand, Tito's Partisans also gained a following among the poorer Bosniaks, concentrated in the Bihać region in western Bosnia — the only part of the province where the lowest strata of the peasantry was Muslim rather than Christian. Social class was as important as religion in determining Bosniak leanings during the occupation.

The Croatian Catholic Church, "well known as being the most conservative in Europe,"[48] had close relations with the Ustashi regime, and took advantage of its genocide to convert close to a quarter of a million Serbs to Catholicism.[49] Some priests may have been sincerely trying to save their Orthodox neighbors from massacre, but the presence of Franciscan clergy among the most bloodthirsty Ustashi units indicates that the Church's motives might not have been entirely humanitarian. At the war's end, there were cases where the Croatian Catholics refused to return converted orphans to their Serbian Orthodox relatives — similar to cases elsewhere in Europe involving rescued Jewish children. In addition, elements in the Catholic Church played a major role in setting up the escape route to Latin America for Ustashi war criminals, a route that was subsequently used by Nazi fugitives.[50]

Ustashi terror drove the Serb minority in the Croatian puppet state into the resistance. But the resistance was divided between the Communist Partisan movement and the royalist Chetniks. The latter, led by the Yugoslav army Col. Drazha Mikhailovich, were officially pro–Allied and loyal to the Yugoslav government-in-exile in London. Unofficially, they favored the creation of a Greater Serbia, and were in regular contact with the collaborationist regime of Gen. Milan Nedich in Belgrade.

Mikhailovich's Chetniks fought against the Nazis at the beginning, in alliance with Tito's Partisans, but soon decided that the Communists were a greater threat to their pan–Serbian aims than the Nazis. They withdrew from the armed anti-fascist struggle, rationalizing their move on the ground that resistance would encourage German reprisals and cost Serbian lives. At the same time, they conducted open warfare against the Partisans, notwithstanding the loss of lives which that entailed. And Mikhailovich knew that Serbs were being slaughtered by the Ustashi — as well as by Albanian and Hungarian fascists — even when they didn't resist. It was not concern over the loss of Serbian lives that caused the Chetniks to abandon the struggle against the Axis, but their opposition to the restoration of Yugoslavia, especially under Communist leadership; this was a goal they shared with the collaborationists in Belgrade. Although they never publicly endorsed the occupation and the partition, the Chetniks were in contact with the Germans as early as October, 1941, seeking an alliance against the Partisans.[51]

By 1943, Chetnik political director Stevan Moljevich was openly calling for "the cleansing of the land of all non–Serb elements," through the massive deportation of Croats from Bosnia and other mixed areas, and the resettlement of the Slav Muslims in Turkey.[52] A Chetnik manual proposed to "help the Croats rediscover their national soul" by eliminating a portion of the Croatian intelligentsia, which would have supposedly strengthened the unity of the two nations.[53] Given Ustashi outrages, this response might be understandable, even if the rationalization is absurd. Chetnik atrocities against Croats, Bosniaks and Albanians during the Axis occupation were widespread, and rivaled the crimes of the Ustashi.

Although they were originally backed by the British, the Chetniks lost Western support as their policy of non-resistance to the Germans and reprisals against non–Serbs increasingly compromised their claims to be a resistance movement. Despite their hostility to Communism, the British were obliged to switch their support to Tito, whose opposition to the Axis was both more effective and consistent. As the war progressed, the government-in-exile in London found itself bitterly divided along Serb-Croat lines, with the Croat members particularly opposed to any continued support for the Chetniks. Under pressure from the government-in-exile, Mikhailovich was forced to expel many of his subordinate commanders as their collaboration with the invaders was revealed. When the Partisans finally captured him at the end of the war, he was left with only two dozen men under his command.[54]

The New Yugoslavia

The Communist government that ruled Yugoslavia from the end of the war until 1991 was a one-party dictatorship, but except for the three years immediately after the war, there was generally less political repression than elsewhere in Eastern Europe. By the 1980s, the Yugoslavs were not only enjoying greater political liberty than their Communist neighbors, but had a higher standard of living as well — although there were serious discrepancies between the various republics and regions. Tito made a sincere attempt to resolve the vexing national question: six republics were given nominal self-government, including the right of secession; the Macedonians were granted recognition as a nation; and some limited autonomy was granted within Serbia to Kosovo and Voivodina. If this arrangement failed in the long run, it was less because of its inherent shortcomings than because too many Yugoslavs were raised in dysfunctional families, making it impossible for them to live in a multi-ethnic society except under a strong leader. Another factor in the collapse of Yugoslavia, it should be kept in mind, was the sudden and prolonged downturn in the economy, which began around the time of Tito's death in 1980.[55]

Serbs and Croats each perceived the Titoist system as unfairly partial to the other group. According to Serbian-American historian Alex Dragnich, the fact that "many Serbs were left in each of the other republics except Slovenia" was really "a way of weakening Serbia,"[56] although the geographical dispersal of the Serbs made their division inevitable. Furthermore, the existence of three regions with Serb majorities — Serbia itself, Voivodina, and Montenegro — gave the Serbs greater influence at the federal level. And finally, both the Croats and Muslims were also divided among different republics. Curiously, Dragnich argues that "the Yugoslav Communists after the war made Croatia larger than it had been in 1939,"[57] although Tito's Croatia was in fact *smaller* because a number of districts of pre-war Croatia had been returned to Bosnia.

At the same time, Croatian-American sociologist Stjepan Meštrović was arguing: "Communism in the former Yugoslavia was a disguised Serbian attempt to impose a Greater Serbia and was understood as such by the other republics in the former Yugoslavia."[58] This, oddly, is the same charge leveled by pro–Moscow loyalists after the Tito-Stalin split. Meštrović is not backed up by the statistics. They show that Serbs, Croats, Slovenes and Macedonians were all represented in the federal Yugoslav government more or less in proportion to their numbers. Montenegrins, however, were heavily overrepresented — with 3 percent of the population, but 15 percent of government jobs. The Muslims were underrepresented, with 9 percent of the population but just 5 percent of the jobs. This probably reflected their respective contribution to the Partisan movement, which was particularly strong in Montenegro. On the other hand, non–Yugoslav minorities — largely Albanians, Hungarians, Romanians and Turks — made up 18 percent of the population, but held only 3.5 percent of the government jobs.[59]

The Kosovo Question

The Serb-Albanian quarrel can be dated back at least to the 1912 annexation of Kosovo and Macedonia by Serbia as a result of the First Balkan War. The Serbs regarded the annexation as the redemption of Christian lands from Muslim rule, although a large part of the population was in fact Muslim, and was considered potentially disloyal by the Belgrade government.

Serb mistreatment of the Albanians after World War I led to a brief upsurge of guerrilla warfare by the Albanians, but they received no assistance from neighboring Albania.[60] This had its parallel in the 1990s, when the Kosovo Liberation Army (KLA) failed to win the backing of either the Albanian Communist government or its non–Communist successor. As the smallest and weakest country in the Balkans, Albania was wary of calling for the revision of borders, lest Greece raise the issue of its own disputed border with Albania.

Italy invaded and occupied Albania in 1939, and two years later, with the invasion and partition of Yugoslavia by the Axis, most of Kosovo, along with Albanian-inhabited western Macedonia, was merged with Albania. The Kosovo Albanians were happy to be rid of Serb rule, and while rival Communist Partisan and nationalist Chetnik resistance movements sprung up in Albania, the Kosovars leaned toward collaboration — although the Partisans were particularly strong in western Macedonia. In the fall of 1943, Germany occupied all of Albania in the wake of Italy's surrender. The nationalist Balli Kombetar, which had fought against Italy, made a deal with the German invaders, and formed a "neutral" government in Tirana which continued the war against the Communist-led National Liberation Movement together with the Germans. Meanwhile, in Kosovo, the Germans recruited thousands of Albanians into the "Skanderbeg" division of the SS,[61] which "carried on a campaign of expulsion and extermination against the Serbian population,"[62] and even assisted in the roundup of local Jews.[63] The Partisans had little support within Kosovo, except from the beleaguered Serb minority.

Kosovo's wartime history caused its Albanian majority to be viewed with suspicion after the Partisan victory. Although Kosovo had formal autonomy within the Serbian republic, Albanians were barely represented in the local Communist party, constituting only a fifth of one percent of local party membership.[64] Yugoslavia's leaders were divided on how to treat the Albanians, with Alexander Rankovich — a hard-liner and a Serb — distrusting them, while Tito and party theoretician Edvard Kardelj, a Slovene, favored concessions. The issue was complicated by the Tito-Stalin split, when Albania's ruler Enver Hoxha strongly supported Moscow. Later, when China and the USSR drifted apart and the latter became more friendly toward Yugoslavia, the Albanians became China's sole ally in Eastern Europe.

Genuine autonomy for Kosovo was not implemented until Rankovich's fall in 1966. Eventually, the Albanians in Yugoslavia had access to education in their own language up to the university level. Following the adoption of the 1974 constitution, Kosovo was granted all the prerogatives of the six Yugoslav republics except for the right to secede. This was far more than most minorities in the Balkans enjoyed.

In 1968, the Soviet invasion of Czechoslovakia saw Albania and Yugoslavia on the same side, backing the Czechs against Russian hegemony. Belgrade began to regard Albania as less of a threat. Ironically, it was just then that anti–Serb riots broke out in Kosovo.[65] Serbs began leaving the region, partly for economic reasons, but also because they felt threatened by the Albanians.[66] Serb representation in local government positions dropped steadily after 1969,[67] until they were significantly underrepresented. "Albanian language and culture became predominant in administration, education, and the media, aided by hundreds of teachers brought in from Albania."[68]

The 1974 constitution permitted extensive decentralization of the country, granting greater rights to the republics even as Yugoslavia remained under a single party system. Kosovo and Voivodina, still nominally parts of Serbia, functioned in practice as republics, exercising veto power over federal policy.[69] This had few consequences in Voivodina, where the Serbs were a majority of the ethnically-mixed population, but Kosovo was another matter. Not only were Albanians a large majority in the region, but their numbers were growing rapidly because of their higher birth rate. This was probably due to the unwillingness of the Albanians to allow their daughters to be educated, which lowered their age of marriage and shortened the average length of a generation. This may explain why the Serbs' belief that the Albanians were outbreeding them is not reflected in the statistics showing approximately the same number of children per household. Of course, Serb emigration from Kosovo was also a factor, as was immigration of Albanians from Macedonia who attended the Albanian-language university in Pristina and then stayed on.

The Yugoslav Communists made a major effort to reduce Kosovo's poverty. Between 1982 and 1985, Kosovo—the poorest of the country's eight units—was slated to receive about $4.5 billion from the rest of the country.[70] The money was apparently wasted. In 1984, Kosovo's unemployment rate reached 29 percent, more than twice the national average, and astonishingly high for a supposedly socialist society.[71] Journalist Robert Kaplan, visiting the province in 1989, described men holding up their pants with safety pins, and people living in wooden shacks with no electricity.[72] The region's economic problems, after 15 years of decentralization, could no longer be attributed to Belgrade's neglect. In fact, "[b]y 1980, Albanians constituted fully 92 percent of those employed in the social sector, with Serbs dramatically underrepresented at a mere 5 percent."[73] It was the local Albanian leadership which was promoting a policy of economic deterioration.

This self-impoverishment fed a growing nationalist movement among the Kosovo Albanians, beginning in the early 1980s. The separatists officially favored only the elevation of the Kosovo region to republic status within Yugoslavia, but this moderate stance masked an openly irredentist agenda which Albanian groups promoted in private.[74] At the same time, Albania, where living standards were even lower than Kosovo's, had little appeal to many of the separatist leaders. Like Slobodan Milosevich's Serbian chauvinist movement which arose in response, the Albanian nationalist movement in Kosovo was strong on emotional appeal but weak on program.

By 1986, Albanian nationalism in Kosovo had produced a strong Serb backlash. Interethnic tension was fueled by reports of rapes of Serb women, and even men, by Albanians,[75] Such interethnic crime was actually rare in Kosovo.[76] In one notorious case in 1985, a Serb farmer charged than he had been anally raped by an Albanian, using a bottle. It was never established whether the incident had actually happened; the Serbs believed the farmer, while the Albanians automatically supported the defendant.[77]

It was in this context that the Serbian Academy of Sciences (SANU) got involved, issuing a memorandum condemning the entire Yugoslav state for a consistent anti–Serb bias. The document was endorsed by many academics, including some dissidents with no previous record of pan–Serbian leanings.[78] Oddly disregarding the existence of Serb and Montenegrin republics in Yugoslavia, these neo-nationalists argued that "the Serbs were the only Yugoslav nation without a right to form their own state."[79]

In 1987, Milosevich, at the time head of the Serbian League of Communists, got an earful when he attended a party meeting in Kosovo. As 300 mostly Albanian delegates gathered inside a hall, 15,000 local Serbs gathered outside and attempted to enter to present their grievances. When police tried to push them back, Milosevich made his famous declaration: "Nobody, either now or in the future, has the right to beat you." From then on, he was a Serb hero.[80] Of course, he was perfectly content, some time later, to use force to suppress opposition demonstrations in Belgrade.

Milosevich and his allies inside the army pushed an "anti-bureaucratic revolution," whose ideology fused pan–Serbianism with a vaguely leftist critique of the increasingly stratified Yugoslav society. "Hundreds of meetings were organized throughout Serbia, demanding removal of the provinces' [Kosovo and Voivodina] autonomous status, the re-centralization of Serbia, and the re-centralization of Yugoslavia."[81] "Rallies for Truth" were sponsored throughout the country, and the Voivodina administration, itself mostly Serb, was toppled in 1989 by Milosevich's supporters in what was termed the "Yogurt Revolution."[82] Millions participated in the movement, and Milosevich became the spokesman for the Serb minorities in the other republics.[83] By 1990, Serbia had a new constitution which virtually abolished the autonomy of Kosovo and Voivodina.[84]

This naturally alienated the Croats and Slovenes, who were already deeply suspicious of Serb chauvinism. The breakup of Yugoslavia began when the Slovene government banned a "Truth" rally by Kosovo Serbs and their supporters which was scheduled to be held in Ljubljana, the Slovene capital. Milosevich, in reprisal, called for an economic boycott of Slovenia.[85] Slovenia then seceded, followed shortly after by Croatia. In July 1990, Albanian leaders in Kosovo declared their region a separate Yugoslav republic,[86] but the Serbs were by then in full control of Kosovo, while Yugoslavia was already in the process of disintegration. The Albanian lawmakers were unable to enter their legislature building, and had to meet in the street.[87] A shadow Albanian government emerged in Kosovo, coexisting uneasily with the Serb-dominated regime, while émigrés in other countries began forming the underground Kosovo Liberation Army (KLA).

The Disintegration of Yugoslavia

Developments in Yugoslavia — the war between Serbs and Croats in Croatia, the chaos in Bosnia, and the war in Kosovo — were inevitable once the central government collapsed and each ethnic group sought to grab whatever it could from the wreckage. The conflict was presented in the United States as one between Nazi-Stalinist Serb aggressors committing genocide against peace-loving, democratic Croats, Bosniaks, and Albanians, but this was a one-sided view at best.

To begin with, the Croat government of Franjo Tudjman, who died in 2000, was not exactly a paragon of democratic virtue. Tudjman himself, the youngest Partisan general during World War II, later stated, "I was on the wrong side when I was very young."[88] His book, *Horrors of War*, is a calculated attempt to whitewash the bloodthirsty Ustashi. He makes endless references to Serb writers who claim that 600,000 Serbs and other victims were slain during the war "in Jasenovac," the largest and most notorious of the Ustashi concentration camps. This, Tudjman maintains, is a "distortion," since only 40,000 victims died in that particular camp. Tudjman barely mentions that 90 percent of the Ustashi's victims were not killed in camps, but in their own villages; Jasenovac, like Auschwitz, was the tip of the iceberg.

Tudjman's Croatian Democratic Party (HDZ) swept the 1990 elections, but with only 42 percent of the total vote, running against a divided opposition.[89] The inevitable proliferation of Croat nationalist symbolism under the HDZ alarmed the republic's Serb minority (about a sixth of the population). The historical symbol of Croat statehood, the red-and-white checkered shield, the *shahovnitsa*, was displayed everywhere, as in the Ustashi state.[90] The Cyrillic alphabet was banned, and the Croat dialect of Serbo-Croat was imposed, although most of the country's people — Serb and Croat alike — spoke the Serbian variant.[91] Croatia's currency was called the *kuna*, as under Pavelich, and Tudjman even renamed a school after an Ustashi leader.[92] Meanwhile, the Croatian public was treated to a steady stream of propaganda minimizing Ustashi wartime atrocities, with the horrors of Jaseno-vac being blamed on Jewish inmates.

Worse than the symbolism was the blatant discrimination against the Serb minority. "Croatian-controlled enterprises dismissed thousands of Serbian workers.... Far from offer-ing any hope of reconciliation, Tudjman's Croatian nationalists mounted a concerted effort to alienate and disenfranchise the Serbs of Croatia."[93] A more sympathetic policy might have avoided the Serb insurrection that nearly destroyed the country, but that might have alienated wealthy Ustashi sympathizers in the West who were subsidizing the HDZ. Por-traying itself to the West as centrist and democratic, the HDZ was increasingly dominated by extremists the further one got from Zagreb.[94] The 1991 fighting in Vukovar, near the Serb-Croat border, which destroyed a city where several ethnic groups had previously lived together in harmony, was presented in the West as a classic case of Serb intolerance and barbarism. It actually began when the local assembly of the district, which had a small Serb majority, was disbanded by Tudjman's government, which then "appointed its own repre-sentative to govern the area."[95] For Tudjman, "democracy" was merely a code word for Ser-bophobia.[96]

Slovenia was little affected by ethnic violence, since it is relatively homogeneous. It has established a stable multi-party system, but there is evidence of mnemonist pathology there as well. The independence movement was preceded by the emergence of the multimedia artistic movement known as *Neue Slowenische Kunst* ("New Slovene Art"), whose name was always given in German. It included the rock group "Laibach" (the German name for Ljubl-jana), whose members "wear brown shirts and Nazi-style regalia, sing in German, and con-duct totalitarian-style ceremonies in their performances."[97] This was identification with the aggressor, carried to a degree rarely seen even in Eastern Europe.

The 1990 elections in Slovenia were won by DEMOS, a six-party coalition dominated by the conservative Catholics.[98] Campaigning under the slogan, "Who is not with us is against the nation,"[99] DEMOS supported the "abolition of special laws protecting the repub-lic's [Hungarian and Italian] ethnic minorities...."[100] In independent Slovenia, "philosophy students wishing to study Hegel, Marx or Freud are being tacitly encouraged to think again."[101] This might be nothing more than the growing pains of a country experiencing independence for the first time in its modern history. But the emergence of the Slovene National Party, a chauvinist group which won 12 percent of the assembly seats in 1992, should cause some concern.[102]

The independence of Bosnia-Herzegovina quickly became a *cause célèbre* for Ameri-can literati. *New York Times* columnist Anthony Lewis quoted the last U.S. ambassador to Yugoslavia, Warren Zimmerman, as comparing Bosnian Serb leader Radovan Karadžić to Heinrich Himmler.[103] Not to be outdone, Susan Sontag flew off to Sarajevo to put on *Wait-ing for Godot* for its residents, as if they hadn't suffered enough!

Lost in the rush to turn the Bosnian conflict into the moral equivalent of the Spanish

Civil War was the fact that the Bosnian state did not have the support of the majority of its own population. Only the Muslims — later termed Bosniaks — regarded the virtually landlocked republic as their nation, but the 1991 census put them at 44 percent of the population, with the Serbs at 31.5 percent and the Croats at 17; the remainder generally identified themselves as Yugoslavs.[104] Support for independence came from both the Bosniaks and Croats, but this was only because of their common opposition to remaining under Belgrade. "Once removed from Yugoslavia, [the Bosnian Croats] were going to remove themselves from BiH [Bosnia-Herzegovina] also and annex themselves to Croatia."[105]

Bosnian President Alija Izetbegovich authored an "Islamic Declaration" which was circulated in the 1970s — leading to his arrest — and reprinted in 1990. In this document, he stated, "There can be neither peace nor coexistence between the Islamic religion and non-Islamic social and political institutions."[106] It turned out to be a self-fulfilling prophecy.

The fighting began in Sarejevo when Muslim gunmen attacked a Serb wedding party, inflicting two casualties. "A few weeks later, in the town of Siekovas near Sarajevo, Muslims invaded the town, killed all the men and children, and burned down eighty homes."[107] It didn't take much, given Bosnia's history during World War II, to convince the large Serb minority that it had no future in the new state. The Serbs rebelled and established a "Bosnian Serb Republic," with its capital at the resort town of Pale in the hills east of Sarajevo, and soon put the Muslim government on the defensive. Most of the Bosnian territory "occupied" by Serb forces had been inhabited primarily by Serbs to begin with. As the Bosnian Serbs brought in volunteers from Serbia and Russia, the Bosniaks imported their own from the Middle East. Meanwhile, the Bosnian Croats set up their own state, with Zagreb's support, in western Herzegovina.[108]

Notwithstanding the supposedly ethnic nature of the conflict, there were some Bosnian Serbs who supported Izetbegovich's government, regarding it as a non-ethnic state. At the same time, a Muslim faction in western Bosnia, where the Partisans had originally gained widespread support among the poor Muslim peasants, sided with the Serb rebels against the Sarajevo government.

Serb and Croat Defense Mechanisms

The 1995 war by NATO against the Bosnian Serbs brought an end to the fighting, under a convoluted constitution, involving federations within federations. The West has denied for the Bosnian Serbs what it demanded for Serbia's Albanians. And the "ethnic cleansing" which the West righteously opposed when it was applied by the Serbs has now been applied to Kosovo's own minorities by the Albanian extremists.

The dominant defense mechanism among the Serbs today is paranoia, which is symptomatic of repressed anger. The Serbs feel themselves to be surrounded by enemies — which is largely the case. It is when they begin imagining that their enemies are *working together* that they depart from reality. "[W]e are sure that Tito was the extended hand of the Vatican," a Serbian government employee explained to an American journalist. "Everything he did here about the Serbs was absolutely in line with Vatican strategy, centuries old."[109] This notion of an improbable Communist-Vatican alliance reflects the state of mind which led to support of Slobodan Milosevich.

Coupled with this is the belief that they are "a nation that can't do anything unless it has a strong leader to follow," in the words of Montenegrin songwriter Antonio Pusic. His most popular song included the lyrics:

> Shepherd, come back
> Your sheep can't live without you
> We thought the grass was greener elsewhere
> We thought you wanted the grass for yourself.[110]

The Croats, in contrast, are characterized by borderline defense mechanisms — particularly denial, projection, loss of reality testing, and fear of annihilation. This is not new. In 1939, a rightist Croat student group argued for the inclusion of all of Bosnia-Herzegovina in the newly-autonomous Croatia, saying: "Without Bosnia and Herzegovina between the two *outstretched legs* of Croatia there would yawn a fatal abyss."[111] (Emphasis added.) This is evidently a disguised reference to childhood rape, the region's boundaries serving as a kind of Rohrschach test. And decades later in 1971, the Croat cultural society Matica hrvatska, criticized a Croat magazine for publishing in "impure language,"[112] an indication of pollution anxiety, which stems from memories of toxins entering the infant's bloodstream from the mother's placenta during the birth process.

The treatment of the Serb minority in post–1991 Croatia, whatever the responsibility of the minority's own leaders, appeared to have evoked guilt feelings among the Croats in regard to Ustashi genocide. Croatian priests began charging that "the Serbs carried out a genocide against the Jews" during the Nazi occupation.[113] The fact remains that, except for Lithuania — which was completely under German control — Croatia was the only country in Axis Europe where the majority of the Jews were killed by local fascists rather than the Germans. As for Serbia's role in the Holocaust, Raoul Hilberg's authoritative account indicates that none of the Jews in that country were killed by their Serb neighbors; the men were shot by the Germans in reprisal for attacks on the invaders by Serb resistance fighters, while the women and children were gassed in a German camp in the town of Zemun, in the Croatian puppet state. "The Croat government graciously gave its permission for the construction" of this camp, states Hilberg.[114]

Orientophobia and Mass Hysteria

From the outside, it seems strange that the Serbs and Croats, who speak the same language, should have become such bitter enemies. There have been debates over whether the Balkan antagonisms are "ancient" or "modern," but it is clear that the problem can be traced back at least to the nineteenth century, when Serb and Croat intellectuals argued over the question of whether "all Serbs are Croats," or, on the other hand, whether "all Croats are Serbs." On one level, this "debate" is preposterous, since both sides are saying the same thing; but on the psychohistorical level, the argument is over *which nation is the Origin Folk* — and, consequently, which nation is allowed to get away with more, the assumption being that Origin Folk are to be indulged like children.

It is the similarity between the Serbs and Croats which is at the root of much of the hostility, as with Ulster and Rwanda. The Serbs despise in the Croats the servility they fear to see in themselves, while the Croats hate the Serbs for their rebelliousness — even as the most fanatical Croats adopted the name Rebels (Ustashi). Both groups exhibit Orientophobia, the Croats seeing themselves as defenders of the West against Eastern pan–Slavism, while the Serbs see their own nation defending Christian civilization against the inroads of militant Islam.

The depth of pan–Serb pathology can be demonstrated by outrages against civilians in Vukovar, Serebrenica, and Kosovo — although the fighting in Mostar between the Croats and Bosniaks produced "some of the worst atrocities of the war," according to Louis Sell.[115] There is an equally bizarre pathology among the Croats. In 1981, the year after Tito's death, several children in the village of Medjugorje reported seeing a vision of the Virgin Mary. While neither the Vatican nor even the local Catholic hierarchy endorsed the visions, the alleged miracle was exploited by the Franciscan order, which had supported the Ustashi during the war. Medjugorje is actually in western Herzegovina, which has long been a stronghold of extreme Croat nationalism; the village itself was the scene of an Ustashi war crime in which a number of women and children had been killed.[116] The Virgin continued to appear before crowds of believers, speaking the "pure" dialect of Zagreb, rather than the local one. She was described as having blue eyes and a fair complexion, unlikely traits for the historical Mary, who was Middle Eastern; in fact, she looked suspiciously like a young woman whose picture was used in advertisements by a Sarajevo brewery.[117]

According to Meštrović, the appearance of the Virgin at Medjugorje — similar to events in Miami's Little Havana during the Elian Gonzalez affair — represents "the yearning of Slovenia and Croatia in the West for greater pluralism and democracy versus the Serbian leanings in the East for fascist-like nationalism and monolithic political systems."[118] It would be more appropriate to regard this event as proof of the powerful hold which the most backward elements of the Catholic Church, with their abysmal record on human rights, still have over the Croat and Slovene people. Meštrović's interpretation itself indicates the extent to which buried need for parental love is translated into a quest for Western approval.

5

Rwanda

Rage, Anxiety, and Genocide

In the space of roughly three months in the spring of 1994, an estimated 800,000 Rwandans were slaughtered, mostly members of the minority Tutsi tribe, victims of the extremists among the Hutu majority. They represented a tenth of the total population of the Maryland-sized country — the largest population loss suffered, in terms of percentage of people killed in such a short period of time, even in the bloody twentieth century.

Jared Diamond, who discusses the Rwandan catastrophe in his popular work *Collapse*, attributes the bloodbath to the country's high population density. Indeed, with 800 people per square mile prior to the genocide, Rwanda was the most densely populated country on the African continent, although peaceful Mauritius, in the Indian Ocean, is even more crowded. And given the ethnic conflict that has devastated such sparsely-populated nations as Sudan, Somalia and Chad, it would be difficult to argue that overcrowding is the only cause of conflict in Africa. In fact, Diamond's own evidence indicates that one particularly densely-populated district in northwest Rwanda — with almost no Tutsis — lost about 5 percent of its population in the violence, as Hutus turned on one another; but this was only half the death rate for the country as a whole.[1]

Political scientists have attributed fascist political movements to rapid industrialization taking place in nations where land reform has not been carried out; examples are Italy, Germany, Japan, and Perón's Argentina. Yet Rwanda had almost no industry at the time of the genocide, while the land was widely distributed, with no large estates to speak of.

Yet another explanation of such conflicts is the psychohistorical theory proposed by Lloyd deMause that economic growth produces anxiety, with a need for sacrifice. This may apply to some countries, but is hardly relevant to Rwanda, where the collapse of coffee prices in 1989 — affecting 75 percent of the country's export earnings[2] — created economic deprivation in the years preceding the genocide. The panic that provoked the mass slaughter of the Tutsis appears to have stemmed less from fear of growth than from the Hutu majority's fear of humiliation and annihilation at the hands of the Tutsi former rulers of the country, who were poised for a comeback, along with the legacy of anger towards the Belgian former colonists, displaced toward the Tutsis.

The violence in Rwanda may also have roots in the Flemish-Walloon rivalry in Belgium. Might it not be entirely accidental that Belgium's three former colonies (Rwanda,

Burundi, and Congo) all suffer from severe tribal strife, while two of Italy's former colonies (Libya and Somalia) have both pursued expansionist policies reminiscent of Fascist Italy?

Races, Tribes, or Castes?

Located far from the ocean, Rwanda was isolated from the outside world, and was not affected by the slave trade — a likely reason for its high population density. The first European arrived there only in 1892.[3] There are three indigenous ethnic groups in Rwanda: the agriculturalist Hutu, the pastoralist Tutsi, and the forest-dwelling Twa (Pygmies). Prior to independence, the Tutsi made up about 15 percent of the population, the Twa perhaps 1 percent, and the Hutu constituted the remainder. All three groups speak the same language, Kinyarwanda, which is also spoken in neighboring parts of Uganda and Congo, and is the most widely spoken language in East Africa.[4] The country — along with neighboring Burundi and the mainland portion of present-day Tanzania — fell under German rule during the "scramble for Africa" in the late nineteenth century. But Germany's defeat in World War I led to the loss of its colonial empire, and Rwanda and Burundi were awarded to Belgium by the Treaty of Versailles. For nearly half a century, the two small kingdoms were ruled together as Ruanda-Urundi. The two countries had identical social structures, with Tutsi monarchies ruling over largely Hutu populations, but they spoke different languages, and went their separate ways when they became independent in mid–1962.

The colonial rulers, German and Belgian alike, promoted the myth that the Tutsi-Hutu distinction was racial. The Tutsis were identified as "Semitic" or "Hamitic," the Hutus as "Negroes," and stereotyped accordingly. Shortly before World War I, the Duke of Mecklenburg wrote in a travel book that "The Watutsi are a tall, well-made people with an almost ideal physique....," while describing the "ungainly figures" of the Hutus, who "patiently bow themselves in abject bondage to the later arrived yet ruling race, the Watutsi."[5] Other European writers insisted that the Tutsi were lighter-skinned than the Hutus, and that their "love of money" proved their Semitic origin; they were alleged to have originally migrated from Ethiopia — or perhaps Asia Minor, or Melanesia, India, Tibet, Atlantis, or the Garden of Eden.[6] Missionaries followed suit, describing the Hutus as "childish in nature, both timid and lazy, and as often as not, extremely dirty."[7] Under the Belgians, the two groups were given different kinds of education, the Tutsis in French, and the Hutus in Swahili.[8] The effects of this discrimination were still being felt decades later.

The truth about the "racial" distinction is more complicated. BBC correspondent Fergal Keane observed: "I never saw any evidence in Rwanda or Burundi to support the proposition that Tutsis were lighter-skinned than Hutus. Like much else that has been written about the two groups, it appears to be fanciful nonsense, a carry-over from the colonial era."[9] During the genocide, Hutu extremists complained of Tutsis passing themselves off as Hutus, even while arguing that they were racially distinct immigrants from Ethiopia who had no right to live in Central Africa.[10] Scholar Michael Mann states that about a quarter of all Rwandans "have both Hutus and Tutsis among their eight great-grandparents,"[11] and the foreign minister of Burundi, speaking to a Sudanese visitor, admitted that while it was possible to tell a Tutsi from a Hutu, it was only "with a margin of error of 35 percent...."[12] One French physical anthropologist even claimed that the Tutsis were *darker* than the Hutus, and had *more* Negroid features.[13]

In fact, intermarriage between the two Rwandan groups has been extensive — although, since a wife automatically takes on the ethnic identity of her husband (and the children that of their father), mixed marriages might not always show up as such in census figures. The tall and slender figures of the Tutsi are concentrated among the old aristocracy and their progeny, and appear to result from a prolonged pattern of selective breeding. Tutsis with no aristocratic forebears are usually the same height as their Hutu neighbors.

At the same time, some non-local pastoralist groups may have migrated into Rwanda from the north in pre-colonial times, to be absorbed over time by the Tutsi. In the renowned film "Hotel Rwanda," the central character, hotel manager Paul Rusesabagina, has a Tutsi sister-in-law named Fedens; this appears to be a variation of the Ethiopian female name Fedenchu. Yet Tutsis in Rwanda speak the same language as Hutus, which raises serious doubts about the theory that they were a race of conquerors from Ethiopia or Asia. When have invaders adopted the language of subjugated natives? The strongest likelihood is that the two groups started out as hereditary occupation-linked castes, such as one finds in India, and that the Tutsi subsequently absorbed a number of cattle-raising migrants from Ethiopia. According to Alison Des Forges, the word "Tutsi" originally meant a person owning lots of cattle, while "Hutu" meant a subordinate of a more powerful person.[14] They were not, in other words, the names of distinct tribes. Largely as a result of Belgian colonial policy, the distinction between the two groups was hardened, as those defined as Hutus were excluded from positions of power and deprived of higher education, except for a few students at religious seminaries.[15]

Family and State

Rwandans, like most people elsewhere, bear two names. Their first names are nearly always French, because of the dominant French culture of their Belgian colonial rulers. Their second names are Kinyarwandan. But these second names are also given at birth, rather than inherited. A Rwandan does not bear a name linking him or her to either parent.[16] Families tend to be stable — at least compared to equally poor countries in the Caribbean — but they are not a source of personal identity. It would appear that this causes Rwandans to identify all the more with their political leaders, which may explain how the Tutsi minority was able to rule over the Hutu majority for so long, as well as why so many Rwandan Hutus were willing to follow orders to kill their Tutsi neighbors, and even relatives, during the carnage of 1994. Interestingly, during the regime of Juvenal Habyarimana, from 1973 to 1994, the dictator was referred to as *Umubyeyi*, or "the parent."[17]

Within the family, adults were considered more valuable than children, a pattern common to much of sub–Saharan Africa, where famine and war are frequent threats, and children are little use either as producers or fighters. Philip Gourevitch noted in 1997 that while children starved in Hutu refugee camps in the Congo, the adults were often well-fed. "'When we get food, I eat first,' a 'husky, thirty-five-year-old father of three starving children' told the [New York] Times, and 'aid workers said his situation was not uncommon.'"[18]

As in Burundi, Ethiopia, and parts of Uganda, the Rwandan political system was a territorially-based state, not a kinship-based tribe. The Tutsi monarchy emerged during the eighteenth century,[19] gradually annexing tiny Hutu principalities. The northern part of the country was not conquered until after the arrival of the Germans, when the latter helped the Tutsis defeat the local Hutus.[20] Even afterwards, some Hutu-ruled statelets maintained a semi-autonomous existence, while tributary to the Tutsis.[21] A symbol of the Rwandan state was the *Kalinga*, the sacred royal drum, which was decorated with the testicles of defeated Hutu chiefs; needless to say, this item was hardly fit to qualify as a symbol of national unity.[22]

For most of their rule, the Belgians sided with the Tutsis. In 1933, they introduced identity cards, making it difficult for Rwandans to change their tribal identification, which had been common previously.[23] In addition, a brutal system of forced labor was imposed on the Hutus; they worked under Tutsi supervisors, who could confiscate their crops.[24] Things began to change after World War II, partially in response to the rise of African nationalism, but also, it would seem, as a result of ethnic rivalry between Belgium's own two groups, the culturally dominant French-speaking Walloons and the Dutch-speaking Flemings — itself exacerbated as a result of the German occupation during World War II. Flemish missionaries who arrived in the country during the 1950s were quick to identify with the oppressed Hutus.[25]

Four political parties emerged as the end of Belgian colonial rule neared. The Rwandese National Union (UNAR) was a Tutsi monarchist party which received moral support from the Communist bloc,[26] less for its social policies than for its uncompromising support for independence. The rival Rwandese Democratic Union (RADER), made up mostly of liberal, pro–Western Tutsis, had limited support.[27] The Hutu parties were the Association for the Social Promotion of the Masses (APROSOMA), founded in 1957 by a "somewhat unbalanced" Hutu businessman, Joseph Gitera[28]; and the Party of the Movement for the Emancipation of the Hutu (PARMEHUTU), headed by Gregoire Kayibanda.[29] The two Hutu parties tended to be based in different regions of the country, with PARMEHUTU gaining the support of the northwest, which had come under the rule of the Tutsi monarchy only a few decades earlier. PARMEHUTU was the more explicitly tribalist, while APROSOMA reached out to the poorer sections of the Tutsi group. That it failed was probably due both to Gitera's inadequate leadership and the effects of the Belgian divide-and-rule policy.

A key catalytic event leading to the Hutu "revolution" of 1961 was the death of Rwanda's King Rudahigwa. Although he probably died of natural causes, rumors spread that he had been assassinated by the Belgians.[30] Traditionally, Rwandan kings did not appoint their successors, inevitably leading to struggles at the king's death.[31] Rudahigwa was succeeded by his 24-year-old half-brother, Kigeli V, who was just a figurehead.[32] In this context, PARMEHUTU gained widespread support for its policy of removing the monarchy and eliminating Tutsi privilege. Shortly after Kigeli's accession, an attack by Tutsi activists on a Hutu led to violence spreading throughout the country.[33] With Belgian encouragement, the Hutus killed at least 10,000 Tutsis,[34] and prepared for the overthrow of the weakened monarchy. Curiously, when UN observers arrived in Rwanda in 1962, they were met by demonstrators, presumably Hutus, who called for "No Immediate Independence." The UN, which by that time already had a sizeable bloc of African member states, supported independence nonetheless.[35]

PARMEHUTU preached the doctrine of the oppressed against the oppressors, but included all Tutsi, regardless of social class, in the latter category. This was despite the fact that a survey in the mid–1950s showed average Tutsi incomes only 5 percent higher than

Hutu, with the tiny Twa minority well below both.[36] The higher incomes of Tutsi aristocrats were evidently balanced by the lower incomes of poorer Tutsi cattle-herders. PARMEHUTU's ideology emphasized the "intrinsic worth of being Hutu," the "need to follow a moral Christian life," and the "uselessness of politics which should be replaced by hard work."[37] This sounds more like Vichy France than anything the revolutionary left was preaching during that period. In 1960, the Belgians began replacing local Tutsi chiefs and officials with Hutus, giving PARMEHUTU supporters control at that crucial level. Early in 1961, PARMEHUTU staged what became known as the "coup of Gitarama," assembling more than 3,000 local elected officials in a provincial town west of the capital. They were joined by tens of thousands of curious locals, and members of the provisional government, already dominated by PARMEHUTU. The monarchy was formally abolished, a president elected, and Kayibanda called upon to form a new government as prime minister.[38] In the 1961 elections, PARMEHUTU triumphed with nearly four-fifths of the total vote; the UNAR lagged far behind, and the other parties were nearly wiped out.[39] In 1962, Kayibanda formed a coalition government including two UNAR cabinet members.[40] But in response to Tutsi exile raids from Burundi in 1963, Tutsi political leaders were physically liquidated by the Kayibanda government.[41] Over the next few years, even Hutus from southern Rwanda found themselves increasingly excluded from political power.[42]

During the Kayibanda years, from 1961 to 1973, a system of affirmative action was set up in which Tutsis were declared to be 9 percent of the population, and were consequently restricted to 9 percent of all government jobs and school places. Of course, they had once been about 15 percent of the population, but this had been reduced by the emigration of 130,000 Tutsis to neighboring Uganda and Burundi[43]; in addition, some Tutsis were passing themselves off as Hutus. Under Kayibanda, Tutsis who scored poorly on entrance exams were favored over those who scored higher.[44] Philip Gourevitch writes, "A deep, almost mystical sense of inferiority persisted among Rwanda's new Hutu elite...."[45]

There was a consistent pattern of attacks against Rwanda by armed Tutsi exiles, referred to as *Inyenzi* ("cockroaches"), followed by reprisals against the Tutsis remaining in the country, thousands of whom fled, further strengthening the exile groups. The 1973 ethnic violence, which undermined the Kayibanda government, was triggered by the slaughter of 200,000 Hutus in Burundi, where a Tutsi dictatorship ruled.[46] Under Kayibanda, Tutsis remaining in Rwanda were largely excluded from politics, but many of them were able to prosper in business, or get good jobs working for foreign embassies. Curiously, the favoritism shown to Hutus under Kayibanda was never extended to the private sector, and it was unemployed Hutus who backed the Habyarimana coup in 1973,[47] as well as playing a major role in the genocide in 1994.

Structure of a Totalitarian Regime

Like the 1994 genocide, the 1973 coup by General Juvenal Habyarimana was provoked by an anti–Hutu bloodbath instigated by the Tutsi government of neighboring Burundi. Despite later claims, Habyarimana's coup was not bloodless, and involved the death of about 55 people. President Kayibanda and his wife were captured, and, because Habyarimana was unwilling to shed blood, "were starved to death in a secret location."[48] The new military government no longer officially defined Tutsis as a separate race,[49] but discrimination against them continued, and for a few years, even intermarriage between Hutus and Tutsis was prohibited.[50] PARMEHUTU was replaced by the National Revolutionary Movement for Development (MRND), which promoted obedience to authority. "[E]very single Rwandan citizen had to be a member, including babies and old people."[51] The military regime originally steered the country away from the anti–Tutsi violence of the Kayibanda years, but the pogroms soon returned — provoked, to be sure, by the continued incursions of Tutsi exiles from Uganda and Burundi. At the same time, a small number of Tutsis held important positions in the new government and its ruling party: as of 1990, there was one Tutsi cabinet member out of a total of 19, two Tutsi parliamentary deputies out of 70, one Tutsi prefect out of 10, and two Tutsi members of the MRND Central Committee out of 16. At the same time, the Rwandan army had only one Tutsi army officer, and the burgomasters, who played a key role in the political system, included no Tutsis at all.[52]

The burgomasters headed the 143 communes, which were subdivisions of the country's 10 prefectures, and were further divided into sectors and even smaller units. The burgomasters "held court once or twice a week to receive citizens and explain the latest news from the capital." The burgomaster "determined land use, mediated property conflicts, settled family disputes, placed children in secondary schools, and decided whether cases ought to go to a higher court."[53] Remarks Dina Temple-Raston, "The communities were so successfully hierarchical, so parsed and divided and subdivided again, that they were easily mobilized. The men ... listened to those in authority with bovine obedience."[54] An example of this is provided by American journalist Bill Berkeley, who visited the prisons where Hutu war criminals were kept after the RPF victory. Although the prisoners were kept in extremely overcrowded conditions, he noted that there appeared to be no fights among them. "It's forbidden to fight," he was told.[55]

The political system worked well enough in the small and homogenous country; roads were kept in good repair, and the telephones — unlike in the Congo — operated properly. Rwanda gained ground economically compared to its immediate neighbors, but this was probably the result of the ongoing civil conflict in three of the four neighboring states.

Behind the government was the *Akazu*, or "little house," a clique involving Habyarimana's wife, four brothers-in-law, a son-in-law, and several other key figures in the government, the army, military intelligence, and the private sector.[56] The *Akazu* was also known as the Zero Network, and "was composed mostly of the people of Habyarimana's home region," Gisenyi prefecture in the northwest,[57] the last Hutu area to be subjugated by the Tutsis.[58] Resembling the cliques that had existed during the Tutsi monarchy involving queens and queen mothers, the *Akazu* sometimes appeared to operate at cross-purposes to the dictator. For example, in April 1988, an army colonel, Stanislas Mayuza, who was being groomed by Habyarimana as his successor, was murdered. The alleged assassin was himself killed — in a scenario which might be familiar to Americans — along with the prosecutor investigating the case.[59] A key figure in the *Akazu* was Col. Theoneste Bagosora, later the strongman of the post–Habyarimana regime and chief architect of the genocide.[60]

This odd situation where the dictator played an almost moderate role, while his wife, in-laws, and immediate subordinates conspired to promote extremism, prevailed until Habyarimana's assassination. This might be attributed to the fact that Rwanda, unlike most other totalitarian states, was a small, impoverished country which was heavily dependent on foreign powers, particularly France, for its economic survival. With a potentially restive population, and Tutsi exiles launching invasions from north and south, Rwanda, by the 1990s, "became the third largest arms importer in Africa,"[61] as "the military consumed almost 70 percent of the Rwandan government's budget."[62] There was something in it for France too, since the major powers depend on foreign markets for their arms and military equipment in order to keep the per-unit price down.

One important figure involved in the arms trade was Jean-Christophe Mitterand,[63] son of the French president, and director of the French government's Africa Office.[64] He was the one who arranged for a private jet to be given to Habyarimana, the same plane the Rwandan president was killed in.[65] In addition, the declining value of coffee — Rwanda's main export — led to the growth of marijuana production, which enriched a number of army officers.[66] Holding on to a market for French arms, rather than the desire to promote French cultural influence in Africa — as some have it — was probably Paris' chief motive in backing the Rwandan regime even after its racist and genocidal nature became obvious. At the same time, the influence of his foreign protector may have caused Habyarimana to moderate his outward stance regarding the Tutsis.

His wife, Agathe Kanziga Habyarimana, was another matter. Together with wealthy businessman Felicien Kabuga, related to the presidential couple by marriage, she financed the notorious RTLM (Free Radio and Television of the Thousand Hills), whose transmitter was even connected by cable to the presidential mansion.[67] It was this station which preached the anti–Tutsi hatred which led to the genocide, and some journalists connected to it were ultimately charged with being war criminals. It used popular songs, off-color jokes, and chatty talk shows in the vernacular to get its message across, and had little trouble competing with the boring official station.[68]

Origins of a Revolution

Developments in neighboring Uganda during the 1970s and 1980s soon played a part in Rwandan politics. The collapse of the brutal regime of Idi Amin in 1979 was followed by Tanzanian occupation, instability, and tribal conflict, ultimately leading to the rise of Yoweri Museveni's National Resistance Army in 1986. Uganda was home to nearly two million people who spoke Kinyarwanda, both Tutsi and Hutu; they included political refugees, economic migrants who had escaped from forced labor under the Belgians, and indigenous Ugandan nationals.[69] Many of them, including refugees such as Paul Kagame, participated in Museveni's insurrection,[70] receiving valuable military training as a result. But when Museveni came to power, he sought to repatriate the Rwandans, fearing that his movement would lose popular support if it became too closely identified with foreigners. In 1990, Uganda's National Ruling Council removed the Rwandans from the army and barred them from owning land.[71] The Rwandan Patriotic Front (RPF), a largely Tutsi political organization — and its military affiliate, the Rwandan Patriotic Army (RPA)— served Museveni's purpose, and in addition shared his radical nationalist affinities.

As the Habyarimana regime became increasingly authoritarian and corrupt, the Tutsi exiles underwent a transformation in the opposite direction, moving to the left. Although he had trained at the U.S. Army General Staff College,[72] RPA commander Paul Kagame had leftist leanings.[73] While the exile army was virtually all Tutsi, its political wing managed to recruit some leading Hutu figures. Because of their role in bringing Museveni to power, their ultimately successful war against the Hutu extremists in Rwanda, and their subsequent part in bringing down the Mobutu dictatorship in the Congo, the Tutsis began playing the role of a *catalytic community*—an ethnic minority with relatively advanced ideas which promotes radical change.

During the mid–1980s, even before the collapse of coffee prices, Rwandans began having premonitions of a blood-bath, including visions of countless corpses and people being slain with machetes; images of the Virgin Mary began appearing on a hill in the center of the country.[74] Given the increasingly isolated position of the Habyarimana regime within Rwanda, its eagerness to scapegoat Tutsis, and the emergence of the RPF, it was certainly possible for some to foresee the outcome without any supernatural assistance.

In October, 1990, the RPA launched an invasion of Rwanda from Uganda, pushing to within 45 miles of Kigali, the capital.[75] The invasion received no support from the local population, even from the Tutsis, and caused 300,000 people to flee into refugee camps.[76] Despite two weeks of advance warning, Habyarimana failed to reinforce his troops on the frontier. Taking advantage of this opportunity to neutralize the opposition, the dictator faked an attack on Kigali, blaming it on the RPA.[77] A thousand troops from France and Belgium, along with helicopter gunships, were needed to rescue him from the rebels; they were accompanied by troops from Zaire (Congo) who did nothing but loot and rape.[78] At this time, increasingly dependent on aid from the World Bank and other donors, Habyarimana was under pressure to introduce democracy.[79]

Without popular support, the RPA invasion was a failure, but it led to Paul Kagame's rise to the leadership of the exile movement.[80] The Rwandan Patriotic Front met in Brussels with other opposition parties to condemn Habyarimana and his anti–Tutsi racism.[81] These parties originally took a centrist position between Habyarimana's ruling MRND and the Rwandan Patriotic Front. They included the Democratic Republican Movement (MRD), based on Kayibanda's old followers; the Liberal Party (PL); the Social Democratic Party (PSD); and the small Christian Democratic Party (PDC). To the right of the MRND was the Coalition for the Defense of the Republic (CDR), an extremist group which "forbade from its membership anyone with Tutsi grandparents."[82] The MRND and the CDR each maintained their own militias, the *Interahamwe* ("hunters") and the *Impuzamugambe* ("fanatics"). These loosely-organized bands of unemployed youths appear not to have clashed with each other at any time, and were all but indistinguishable in their methods and ideology. They had been trained by both Rwandan and French officers.[83] The CDR was, in fact, just another face of the MRND, reporting to the same behind-the-scenes leadership. As the MRND added the word "Democracy" to its official title, its supposed rival, the CDR, continued to preach rabid hatred of the Tutsis.

With his arm being twisted by foreign aid donors, Habyarimana initiated his democratic opening, legalizing the opposition. At the same time, strong-arm tactics were used against opposition parties, which sometimes replied in kind. Pogroms against Tutsis continued, particularly in the northwest, which was strongly loyal to the regime, and in the Bugesera region on the Burundi border, which had been settled by migrants from the northwest.[84] A broad-based transitional government was supposed to be installed in January 1993, but it was postponed repeatedly,[85] largely because of factional disputes within the centrist parties; it was also likely that the regime was reneging on the agreement. In February 1993, the RPA launched a second invasion, which was only halted by French military intervention; this new invasion displaced a further 1,000,000 people.[86]

By August of that year, the government and the opposition signed an agreement in Arusha, Tanzania, which reduced Habyarimana to figurehead status. Power was transferred to the Prime Minister, and the man originally chosen for that job was Faustin Twagiramunzu, a leader of the moderate wing of the MRD.[87] The Arusha accords permitted prosecution of officials for past crimes,[88] which did not sit well with corrupt MRND leaders. The Hutu extremists believed that they had been sold out by foreigners and opposition parties, which had been part of the government delegation at Arusha. The January 1993 agreement allowed the RPF to keep a strip of territory in the north, along the Uganda border,[89] and hold five positions in the cabinet, equal to the once-dominant MRND.[90] In addition, 600 RPA soldiers were allowed to be stationed in Kigali.[91] When they arrived, later that year, they were welcomed by "large and happy crowds of Hutus and Tutsis."[92]

Complicating matters was the coup in Burundi in October 1993, when Tutsi officers in the army assassinated the freely-elected Hutu president, Melchoir Ndadaye, a moderate who sought cooperation between the two ethnic groups.[93] In the wake of Ndadaye's death, fighting broke out between Tutsis and Hutus throughout Burundi, ultimately leading to the deaths of perhaps 50,000, and the flight of over a third of a million Burundian Hutu refugees into Rwanda. At a huge rally in Kigali, the RPF was implausibly blamed for the Burundi crisis, and it was argued that the Tutsis were out to enslave or exterminate Hutus throughout the entire region. "A politician called Froduald Karamira [from the extremist wing of the MRD] brought the crowd to fever pitch with a warning that 'the enemy' was everywhere, among them all. Everyone knew he meant Tutsi. 'We cannot sit down and think that what happened in Burundi will not happen here,' Karamira said."[94]

During this time, the "hate radio" of RTLM continued its barrage of anti–Tutsi propaganda. Its managers recruited the popular singer Simon Bikindi, who recorded a paean of hate directed against Hutu moderates: "I hate these Hutus, these arrogant Hutus, braggarts, who scorn other Hutus, dear comrades ... / I hate these Hutus, these de–Hutuized Hutus, who have disowned their identity, dear comrades..."[95] The corrupt political elite knew that democratization would mean that "the whole system of patronage and clientelism would collapse."[96] The moderate parties, with their potentially broad appeal, posed as much of a threat to the system as did the well-armed guerrillas of Kagame's RPA. But Hutu members of these parties were vulnerable to anti–Tutsi appeals.

Who Killed the President?

The trigger for the genocide was the death of President Habyarimana on April 6, 1994, along with the new Burundian president and several top Rwandan aides, as they flew back to the capital from Tanzania. Struck by two missiles,[97] Habyarimana's plane crashed on the grounds of his own mansion. Although attempts were made to blame the attack on the RPA, one authority writes that Theoneste Bagosora "appears to have been the principal architect of the assassination of Habyarimana."[98] Evidence implicating him is overwhelming. For a start, Bagosora was the commander of the Kanombe military base near the capital,[99] which appears to be where the missiles were launched. For another, with the death of Col. Elie Sagatwa, commander of the Presidential Guard, who was aboard the ill-fated plane, Bagosora was able to take control of this crucial military unit.[100] For two days after the president's murder, the Presidential Guard and the militia engaged in killings of Tutsis and Hutu moderates, while the regular units of the army tried to stop it; but the army started going along with the killings when the RPA launched their final offensive.[101]

Two days before the shoot-down, Bagosora had declared to UN officials that "the only plausible solution for Rwanda would be the elimination of the Tutsi...."[102] On the day after, Bagosora showed up at a party at the Hotel des Diplomates and stated that the Tutsis would be killed; the attendees celebrated Habyarimana's death with champagne.[103] Several days before the assassination, the extremist radio station RTLM predicted an incident which would trigger a conflict.[104] As early as February 1994, teachers in Rwandan schools "were registering the ethnic identities of their pupils and seating them according to who was Tutsi and who was Hutu."[105] On the day before the shoot-down, the *Interahamwe* were seen toting grenades and death lists[106]; needless to say, the government would not have permitted the undisciplined youths in the militia to carry grenades unless it was expected that they were going to be using them soon; and the death lists are an obvious indication of government intentions. And the murder of the moderate Hutu prime minister Agathe Uwilingiyamana and her family by the elite Recon Battalion, shortly after the president's death but obviously planned in advance, was ordered by Bagosora.[107]

To be sure, according to Linda Melvern, "Bagosora appeared genuinely shocked by the death of the President,"[108] but he may have only been concerned about the plot possibly misfiring — or, just as likely, he was putting on an act. Suggesting the latter, on the following day, Bagosora called for the quick implementation of the Arusha accords, which he had previously opposed.[109] At the same time he was calling for peace, however, he was taking full control of the government and ordering his troops to engage in wholesale genocide. He installed an aging physician, Theodore Sindikubwabo, as a figurehead president on April 8.[110]

Bagosora's coup was not only directed against President Habyarimana, who had postured as a moderate, but also against the *Akazu*, the backstage clique that ran the government. With Habyarimana dead, the First Lady and her relatives and in-laws no longer had influence over the government; they fled the country under French protection.[111] History repeated itself as the president's death triggered an outbreak of ethnic cleansing much as had the Tutsi king's in 1959.

Selecting the Victims

Who were the victims in the Rwandan genocide? The first to be killed, aside from Habyarimana and his aides, were leading Hutu political figures in the moderate camp. After that, the victims were Tutsis, from all walks of life and all political views; these constituted the large majority of those killed. Pygmies were also targeted,[112] since the Hutu extremists regarded them as having been allies of the Tutsis during the days of the monarchy. The RTLM also incited its listeners to kill all Belgians,[113] although Belgium tried to remain neutral in the conflict. When the Tutsis had been killed or driven away, the militia — still hungry for loot, and by then very much under the influence of banana beer and marijuana — began killing rank-and-file Hutus, particularly those who were well-dressed, educated, or drove cars. They were assumed to be moderates,[114] or at least had something worth stealing. As one Tutsi survivor put it, "The people whose children had to walk barefoot to school killed the people who could buy shoes for theirs."[115] It was this sort of killing by intoxicated youths that demoralized the Hutus and paved the way for the victory of the RPF.

At the same time, a number of the leading extremists had Tutsi wives or mothers, and sent them to the Hotel Milles Collines, where the manager, Paul Rusesabagina, made a heroic effort to save the lives of those who took refuge there. The presence in his hotel of Tutsi relatives of key figures in the extremist regime was one of the reasons he was successful,[116] a point overlooked in the film "Hotel Rwanda." Generally, Tutsi wives of Hutus were spared if their husbands were wealthy, and were willing to participate openly in the genocide.[117]

Who were the killers? The first violence was the work of elite military units — the Presidential Guard, the French-trained Recon Unit, and the paratroopers — who were generally recruited in the north, where Habyarimana had his strongest support. The Gendarmerie — a national police force — was also involved from the beginning, while the regular units of the army began participating a bit later,[118] as they had been preoccupied with fighting the invading RPA. The two militia groups — the *Interahamwe* and the *Impuzamugambe*— soon joined in, and appear to have done the bulk of the killing; but there were also cases of Tutsis being killed by ad hoc groups of civilians recruited on the spot. Soldiers who had been wounded at the front, fighting against the RPA, were particularly active in the genocide,[119] and Burundian refugees — Hutus who had been victims of Tutsi persecution — were also heavily involved.[120] Local political leaders — and religious leaders as well — played the part of enablers, along with opinion-makers in the radio and print media. There were accounts of teachers killing their students, doctors killing their colleagues and patients, and even a human rights activist implicated in the deaths of over 12,000 innocent victims.[121]

Often recruited from local soccer clubs,[122] the militia were nearly all unemployed young men, resentful of others' success; they could be easily turned against the Tutsis, because the latter were able to use their educational advantages to prosper in business even while excluded from political power. Ironically, some of the Hutu extremists had some Tutsi ancestry, among them Robert Kajuga, the *Interahamwe* leader,[123] and Froduald Karamira.[124] The *Interahamwe* marching song gives some idea of their ideological confusion:

> We are the MRND *Interahamwe.*
> We love peace, unity and development.
> We don't attack, we come to the rescue.
> We are not frightened, we frighten others.
> We don't let ourselves get downtrodden.
> On the contrary, we trample on others.
> We will silence wrongdoers.
> He [Habyarimana] has brought peace and we sleep safely.
> We are independent and imbued with democratic principles.[125]

Notice the emphasis on frightening others so as not to feel their own fear, and on trampling on others — so much for "democratic principles" — to avoid letting themselves get downtrodden. One key fear many Hutus felt was that of being reduced to a subordinate position once again if the Tutsis came back to power. Significantly, many of the militia wore banana leaves as they participated in the killings, reminiscent of what Hutus were expected to wear at ceremonies held by Tutsi monarchs in the past. Of course, the events in Burundi also raised the possibility that the Tutsis would kill the Hutus in revenge.

The fear that ordinary Hutus had of the Tutsis is indicated by the depiction of the RPF in the media "as creatures from another world, with tails, horns, hooves, pointed ears and red eyes that shone in the dark."[126] There was also an element of sexual jealousy of Tutsi women, who were portrayed in Hutu propaganda as beautiful, but scornful of Hutu men.[127] When French troops entered the Gisenyi region to protect the collapsing Hutu regime, RTLM called on "you Hutu girls to wash yourselves and put on a good dress to welcome our French allies. The Tutsi girls are all dead, so you have your chance."[128] The low self-image of the Hutus apparently survived nearly two generations of "Hutu power."

This low self-esteem may have been another factor in the swift collapse of the post–Habyarimana regime at the hands of the RPF. With 20,000 fighters, the rebel forces were outnumbered by the Rwandan Army by more than two to one,[129] and the latter had help from France. In fact, several prefectures in the southwest were occupied by French forces who tried to protect the collapsing extremist regime. As the French withdrew, the Rwandan government fled into neighboring Congo, accompanied by over one million Hutu refugees, while hundreds of thousands more fled to Tanzania or Burundi.[130] The RPF took over Rwanda, while the resulting influx of armed refugees — and their clashes with Congolese Tutsis — ultimately led to the collapse of Mobutu Sese Seko's decrepit dictatorship after four decades in power. Tiny Rwanda became a regional power, intervening in the Congolese civil war on behalf of the local Tutsis. Meanwhile, the RPF had to begin the slow and painful process of national reconstruction, punishing those guilty of instigating genocide, while seeking to rehabilitate many rank-and-file Hutus who simply went along with it, often in fear for their own lives.

Economic vs. Psychological Factors

The causes of the Hutu genocide against the Tutsis in Rwanda were numerous. The high population density of the country may have contributed to the problem, but cannot be defined as the chief factor; there is no correlation between population density and ethnic violence in Africa. Poverty was a contributing factor as well, since poor militia members hoped to benefit from looting their victims, but there are also poor countries in Africa, such as neighboring Tanzania, which have remained stable. Then there is the nature of the Habyarimana regime, which resembled the totalitarian systems responsible for genocide elsewhere in the world; yet Rwanda was in the process of transition to democracy by 1994, and members and leaders of moderate opposition parties were also caught up in the madness.

There were also psychological causes of the tragedy. Given events in Burundi, where Tutsis had been slaughtering Hutus, it was understandable that the Hutus in Rwanda, concerned about their own fate, might have turned on their Tutsi neighbors in a pre-emptive strike. There were still strong memories of the humiliation Hutus had experienced under the monarchy, and the Hutu extremists were quick to link the old monarchy with the radicalized but Tutsi-dominated RPF. In Rwanda, as in the urban ghettoes of the United States, the refugee camps of Palestine, and the "locations" in apartheid South Africa, the low status of oppressed groups contributes to their violence because of the lack of serotonin in the brain, which is produced by positive social interactions. Constant humiliation, or the fear of it, was a key factor in the genocide.

In addition, there was the weakness of the family in Rwanda *as a source of identity*, which differs from the situation elsewhere in the world. The killers even turned on members of their own families. Tom Odom mentions a Tutsi man's Hutu wife who joined the CDR, and tried to get Rwandan soldiers to kill her husband and two older sons, while protecting her baby.[131] Jean Hatzfeld describes a farmer telling a band of machete-armed youths to stop their mayhem, only to be killed on the spot by the gang, which included his own son. The killers then went on their way, cheerfully singing.[132]

Speaking in prison after the RPF victory, one Hutu told Hatzfeld that he and his friends knew that their Tutsi neighbors were innocent, "but we thought all Tutsis at fault for our constant troubles,"[133] in a mental leap reminiscent of Germany in the Nazi era. Trance logic prevailed, even as the killers themselves realized the insanity of it all. Stated another killer, "[I]t is as if I had let another individual take on my own living appearance, and the habits of my heart, without a single pang in my soul...."[134]

"Many of my friends turned into *genocidaires*," noted Paul Rusesabagina. "I was disappointed by them. I used to think of them as gentlemen — correct and reasonable — and yet when it came to a mass massacre, they followed the mob. This I will never understand."[135]

6

Sri Lanka

Emotional Repression, Social Stratification, and Ethnic Violence

There was a time, for nearly a decade following its independence in 1947, when the island nation of Sri Lanka (then called Ceylon) had the reputation of being a tropical paradise where its diverse ethnic groups lived in peace and harmony. As late as 1957, an article in *Readers Digest* described it as the "Isle of Delight," with a stable and democratic government, and a prosperous and literate population. About two-thirds of the Sri Lankans are Sinhalese, mostly Buddhist; Tamils, largely Hindu, make up about a quarter, and were originally about evenly divided between "Ceylon Tamils," long resident in the country, and "Indian Tamils," who arrived during British rule. Catholic and Protestant Christians are found among both Sinhalese and Tamils, making up about a tenth of the population. Muslims ("Moors") make up seven percent, and are typically bilingual. While Christians are counted as either Sinhalese or Tamil, Muslims are regarded as a distinct ethnic group.

Even when it was published, the *Readers Digest* account was already obsolete. Beginning in 1956, the Sinhalese and the Tamils were engaging in violent conflict, which continued on and off for more than fifty years, taking the lives of an estimated 60,000 victims, until it ended in the spring of 2009. Elections have been rigged, and political leaders assassinated, turning the country's once-vaunted democracy into a farce. The standard of living has been on a downward slide since independence, and began to recover only because increasing numbers of Sri Lankans have been finding well-paying jobs in the Persian Gulf nations, sending their wages home. Meanwhile, large sections of the capital, Colombo, have been burned down, with numerous enterprises reduced to ruins. The once-prosperous tourist industry has been hit hard, although it survives somehow, while most of the Indian immigrant workers, who kept the tea plantations running, have been repatriated as a result of the ethnic strife.

Economic factors alone cannot explain the ethnic conflict, since the worst of the violence took place in 1983 and after, following a brief period of economic recovery. The pat explanation that Sinhalese and Tamils were merely competing for jobs overlooks the fact that all the violence has cost the country so many jobs that neither group could possibly come out ahead.

From a psychohistorical perspective, there are three factors which are particularly important in terms of comprehending Sri Lanka's violence: (1) the psychological defense mechanisms of the Sinhalese, based on the Buddhist religion which trains them to deny their anger, but also teaches that they are a special people with a messianic mission; (2) the psychological dynamics of the Sinhalese caste system; and (3) the dual role of the Tamils as an Origin Folk and Catalytic Community. In addition, the widespread use of *ganja*, an illegal narcotic similar to marijuana, should not be overlooked.

The Sinhalese Origin Myth

The Sinhalese trace their origins to 543 B.C.E., when the legendary prince Vijaya landed on the island's shores with an army of 700 loyal followers. According to the Sinhalese national epic, the *Mahavamsa*, the island was then inhabited only by snakes and demons. Reading between the lines, scholars noted that these snakes and demons seem to have constructed a flourishing civilization, and concluded that the epic was referring to an indigenous people who *worshipped* snakes and demons — in other words, Tamils, who adhered to local religious sects.[1]

While the Tamil language belongs to the Dravidian family — found largely in the southern part of the Indian subcontinent — the Sinhalese language has North Indian affinities, leading some to assume that Vijaya was a genuine historical figure who led a mass migration to Sri Lanka from somewhere in Gujarat or Bengal. The prince might have been an actual historical figure, with his feats exaggerated beyond recognition by oral tradition, but there is no corroboration of the Vijaya legend from other sources. The figure of 700 soldiers sounds as if it might be mythical, as mythmakers are partial to multiples of seven. An army smaller than that could hardly have conquered a distant land, but the massive seaborne migration postulated by some scholars would have left evidence in terms of the physical appearance of the Sinhalese people, who are all but indistinguishable from their Tamil compatriots. And one scholar notes the lack of archeological evidence for any North Indian migration into Sri Lanka.[2]

Although the *Mahavamsa* describes events taking place during the life of Buddha, five to six centuries before the birth of Jesus, it may have been written more than a thousand years later.[3] The story describes Vijaya as the grandson of a lion — meaning, most likely, a courageous man with a beard — who abducts a princess in Bengal. The "lion" and his bride produce a set of fraternal twins, brother and sister. The brother slays his own father, and then founds a small kingdom, marries his sister, and produces sixteen more sets of twins, each one male, from this incestuous union. Vijaya is the eldest of these 32 offspring, presumably beating his twin brother out of the womb by a minute or two. Like his 31 brothers, Vijaya would have inherited leonine blood from both parents, making him half-human and half-beast. The tale describes Vijaya as being so evil that his father — himself an incestuous parricide — exiles him from the kingdom along with 700 followers.[4]

The Chinese traveler Hsuan Tsang, visiting the region in the 7th century C.E.— presumably after the *Mahavamsa* was written, and twelve centuries after the events in it supposedly took place — gives an account of a legendary Prince Vijaya which differs in important details. Hsuan Tsang's version takes place in South India, not in Bengal, indicating a possible Dravidian origin for the story. In this version, the lion is Vijaya's father, rather than his grandfather. The lion is slain by Vijaya on orders from Vijaya's father-in-law; and it is the father-in-law who then exiles Vijaya, accusing him of being a parricide while conveniently overlooking his own role in the matter.[5] The current Sinhalese tale thus seems to be an "Aryanized" version of a Dravidian legend, with his land of origin relocated a thousand miles northward in order to correlate Vijaya's place of birth with the Indo-European language spoken by his putative descendants.

Another heroic figure from the *Mahavamsa* is King Dutugamunu, a Sinhalese ruler who supposedly lived about three or four centuries after Vijaya. Like Jesus, he is miraculously conceived — as the reincarnation of a Buddhist monk. But if Dutugamunu's birth parallels that of Jesus, his life more closely resembles that of King Arthur. In his childhood, he learns of his destiny to fight the Tamil invaders of Sri Lanka, and curls up in a fetal position when his abilities are doubted. When his father urges caution, Dutugamunu becomes enraged — hence the *dutu* prefix of his name, which means "angry."[6] His foe, the Tamil king Elara, is presented in the *Mahavamsa* as a wise and just ruler, but is ultimately defeated by the Sinhalese under Dutugamunu.

Dutugamunu became a cult figure in post-independence Sri Lanka, more than two millennia later, as politicians competed with one another to identify themselves with legendary Sinhalese heroes. The king's supposed ashes were disinterred from their resting place in the old royal capital of Anuradhapura and placed on display for pilgrims; ironically, this grave was originally supposed to be that of his sworn enemy, King Elara.[7] Once again, a Dravidian myth was "Aryanized" for the benefit of Sinhalese nationalism.

A close look shows that Sinhalese and Tamils have many common characteristics. The Sinhalese language, for example, although classified as Indo-European, contains a great many Dravidian words.[8] Sinhalese Buddhists, in the past, attended Hindu temples and joined Hindu cults.[9] The ruler and his court in the quintessentially Sinhalese Kandyan kingdom in central Sri Lanka were mostly Tamil in origin.[10] In recent centuries, waves of Tamil immigrants have established themselves on the island, converting to Buddhism and incorporating themselves into the Sinhalese community, without necessarily abandoning all of their Tamil roots. The Sinhalese Karava caste is the same as the Tamil Karaiyars,[11] and some coastal Karava, officially counted as Sinhalese, speak both languages, adhere to Tamil religious practices, and have Tamil clan names.[12] The important Sinhalese Salagama and Duruva castes are also of Tamil origin.[13] Finally, the Colombo Chetties are descended from Tamil-speaking Chettiars from India who settled in the Sri Lankan capital during the 17th century, and also count themselves as Sinhalese.[14]

It is generally accepted that the Sinhalese language derives from Pali, the sacred tongue of Theravada Buddhism. One scholar — a sympathizer of the Tamil separatists — argues that it evolved from the body of religious literature produced by Buddhist monks during the 10th through 13th centuries C.E.[15] While this may explain the similarity with North Indian languages — since Pali is a dialect of Sanskrit, from which modern North Indian languages derive — it may, significantly, be the only case in history of a vernacular developing from a sacred tongue. Burma, Thailand and Cambodia all practice the same Theravada Buddhism as the Sinhalese, but have kept their original languages. That history proceeded otherwise in Sri Lanka may indicate a more intense conflict between the new Buddhist religion and its Hindu predecessor, a conflict which was isomorphic with the neurotic struggle between the real and unreal selves.

For centuries, the Sinhalese fought for their independence against repeated waves of

Tamil invaders from the Indian mainland, who sought to restore Hinduism; Sinhalese school textbooks refer repeatedly to these wars, seeking to "project an image of a Sinhala Buddhist identity which is defined fundamentally through opposition to and struggle against Tamil invaders in past history."[16] With some justification, the Sinhalese regard the Sri Lankan Tamils, now numbering about 12 percent of the country's population, as a legacy of these bygone invasions. During their colonial rule, the British imported many more Indian Tamils to work on the tea plantations. After independence, their descendants were stripped of their Sri Lankan citizenship, denied the right to vote, and repatriated in large numbers to India. The two Tamil communities generally did not live in the same areas, and supported different Tamil political parties. The Sri Lankan Tamils, heavily concentrated in the Northern and Eastern Provinces, favored territorial autonomy until, as a result of the continued ethnic conflict, they switched to a demand for total independence. This solution would have hardly benefited the Indian Tamils, who lived mostly in the Sinhalese-speaking part of the country.

A curious aspect of Sinhalese psychology is the common identification of Tamils with demons, which manifests itself not only in the Vijaya myth, but in exorcisms as well. Symptoms that would be identified as specific diseases in Western psychoanalysis — but as diverse expressions of the single phenomenon of neurosis in primal therapy — are objectified as demons by traditional Sinhalese healers. One of these demons is the *Demala Sanniya*, which — among other things — causes its victims to jabber in mock Tamil.[17] These exorcisms have parallels among Sinhalese Catholics, in which the demons "are frequently the gods of the Sinhala...,"[18] which would make them Hindu deities of Tamil origin.

In rejecting their own Tamil origins as demonic, the Sinhalese have projected all of their unacceptable characteristics onto the Tamils, who now constitute a classic Origin Folk in relation to them. In the Sinhalese mind, the Tamils represent the "Bad Child," who refuses to accept the moral order set down by the Buddhist religion and the parents within the Sinhalese family. Hating and rejecting Tamils makes Sinhalese feel that they are "good," because they are rejecting the rebellious and unacceptable aspects of themselves, thus becoming entitled to their parents' love. Yet, as we shall see, this psychological dynamic is sometimes inverted.

Although Buddhism repudiates caste, there is nonetheless a caste system among the Sinhalese. It differs, however, in a number of ways from its Hindu counterpart. First, there are no priestly (Brahmin), warrior, or merchant castes. Second, a Sinhalese caste's rank is closely correlated with its size; the larger castes hold higher status, while the untouchable Rodiyas number only a few thousand. Third, Sinhalese castes are not self-governing, and lack *panchayats* (councils) to run their internal affairs. Finally, customs and religious practices differ little from one Sinhalese caste to another.

Ironically, this more subtle caste system has proven to be even more rigid than India's. Among the Indian Hindus, some low-ranking castes have rewritten their genealogies, changed their customs, and altered their social status, through a process known as Sanskritization. But in the absence of caste *panchayats*, as well as distinctive customs, a low-status Sinhalese caste would not be able to take collective action to reinvent its identity; nor would any upward mobility result from a change in its customs, since all castes share the same practices to begin with.

As with the Hindus, Sinhalese Buddhist castes are named and socially ranked in relation to one another. They are hereditary, and generally endogamous. They are associated with specific occupations, and their members are reluctant to socialize or dine with other castes. They are also usually found living apart from one another, either in separate villages, or in different parts of the same village.[19] The largest Sinhalese caste are the Goyigama, or cultivators. Just below them in rank are the three castes of recent Tamil origin: the Karava, Duruva, and Salagama, who are found mostly in the coastal areas. Below these are service castes from the inland districts, traditionally clients of Goyigama patrons: the Vahumpera, Batgam, Achari, and Hena. The Rodiya and a few other small groups are outcastes, frequently living as beggars.[20] The Goyigama are themselves divided into nine ranked subcastes, which constitute a caste system within a caste system.

The introduction of universal suffrage in the early 1930s, under the British, gave the lower castes an opportunity to make their voices heard. Marxist parties such as the socialist Lanka Sama Samaja Party (LSSP) and the Communists drew most of their support from non–Goyigama, who had resented Goyigama domination for decades.[21] After 1970, some of these same lower-caste leftists abandoned the parliamentary-oriented LSSP and Communists for the more radical JVP (People's Liberation Front).[22]

Sinhalese Psychodynamics

Sri Lanka, along with the Philippines, had the longest experience of colonial rule of any country in Asia. The Portuguese first invaded in 1505, and ruled for about 150 years. They were followed by the Dutch, who stayed for another 150 years. The British supplanted the Dutch during the Napoleonic Wars, conquered the holdout Sinhalese kingdom of Kandy in the interior, and ruled for yet another one-and-a-third centuries.

Domination by the British, with their Victorian mores, encouraged the rise of puritanical morality among the Sri Lankan elite. In this regard, the contrast with Thailand, which escaped European rule, is particularly sharp. Among the Sinhalese, men and women live in separate worlds, husbands and wives having "little to do with each other. They sleep separately; they eat separately; they work separately; and when they have time to spare, they associate with persons of their own sex."[23] One scholar noted that it was possible to find mature Sinhalese men, with children and grandchildren, who had never seen a naked woman.[24] Nature did manage to take its course, however; for decades following independence, Sri Lanka had — along with Colombia — the highest rate of population growth in the world.

Men from the higher castes were allowed to have relations with women from lower castes, but not the reverse.[25] Similarly, members of high Sinhalese castes were not permitted to take food from low-caste people.[26] "There seems to be a deep psychological identity between eating and sexual intercourse," writes one anthropologist,[27] who notes the similarity between the Sinhalese words for milk (*kiri*) and semen (*kere*).[28] Both fluids are regarded with reverence, and may only be passed from higher to lower castes. The connection between food and sex stems from the common root of repressed need. Deprivation of any basic need in infancy can lead to either eating or sexual disorders in adult life, as postulated by Freud, and confirmed repeatedly in primal therapy. In the underdeveloped nations, where families are large and people are generally poor, infants may go hungry when there isn't enough food to go around; those who can contribute to the family's livelihood usually get fed first. The children who survive learn at an early age to repress their feelings of need.

Another emotion the Sinhalese have difficulty with is anger, which they either repress to displace onto the Tamils. Notwithstanding its peaceful reputation, "Sri Lanka is reputed to have the highest murder rate per capita in the world,"[29] and the rate is highest in the Southern Province, where the population is most heavily Sinhalese.[30] Violent crimes often stem from trivial breaches of status etiquette, and feasts and wedding ceremonies sometimes end in brawls.[31] Even overtaking the wrong person while riding your bicycle can turn out to be fatal.[32]

Devout Buddhists in Sri Lanka often display signs of severe depression and self-hatred — expressed, as in Northern Ireland, as extreme religiosity. The masochistic ceremonies at the Kalutera shrine, where pilgrims swing from metal hooks jabbed into in their bodies, are one example. Writes Gananath Obeyesekere, a Sinhalese psychoanalytic anthropologist, "Meditation on revulsion is a long and ancient tradition in Buddhism."[33] Pilgrims meditating in a Buddhist temple were overheard making the following comments: "My body is revulsive like a corpse." "[M]y body ... is like a clay pot full of feces." "The whole body is a heap of dirt." "My body is revulsive." "The body is a hell. A heap of dirt.... It is filth, filth." "When I think of my body it is thus: I think it is a heap of dirt. It is surely like a heap of feces."[34] One might compare this with Ian Paisley's sermons in Northern Ireland.

Most likely exacerbated by the widespread use of *ganja*, Sri Lankan violence — individual in the past, political in the present — originates in the caste system, which ascribes low social status to individuals solely on the basis of their birth. The correlation between low social status and crime is well-known, although the biological nature of this connection is not.

One would expect that low-status groups, who can hardly anticipate lenient treatment from the police or the courts, would take extra care not to run afoul of the law. This assumption does not take brain chemistry into account. Positive social interaction — being honored, applauded, treated with respect — causes the neurotransmitter serotonin to be manufactured by the brain cells. Social dominance correlates with high levels of serotonin.[35] In contrast, "Chronic stress lowers brain serotonin, particularly in the areas where painful memories are stored — the cortex and hippocampus."[36] A study of suicide victims showed that serotonin receptors were "unusually sparse" in their brains,[37] indicating a lifetime of unsatisfactory social relationships. "Goodbye, cruel world," may not be an entirely unwarranted response when one considers the deceased's life history. Whether the violence takes the form of self-annihilation, criminality, or politically-motivated attacks on other ethnic groups, low levels of serotonin are likely to be involved. In Sri Lanka, as in Soweto, the West Bank, and the South Bronx, status deprivation is directly responsible at the biochemical level for the high level of violence, which appears so counterproductive even to sympathetic observers.

Decline of the Westernized Elite

Beginning in the late nineteenth century, Sri Lanka underwent a rapid process of modernization, fueled by the swift growth of the cash economy, the high birth rate, and the rapid spread of education. Today, most rural Sri Lankans are members of the wage-earning agricultural proletariat, as opposed to the traditional peasantry which engaged in subsistence agriculture or exchanged its labor for payment in kind.[38] Landlessness is widespread, particularly among the lower castes.[39] At the other extreme, the wealthy British colonialists who owned the tea plantations in the highlands have now been largely replaced by Sinhalese.

For a quarter of a century, from the beginning of limited self-government in 1931 until the 1956 elections, Sri Lankan politics was dominated by a small Westernized elite who were "at the most about 7 per cent of the total population."[40] This group, drawn primarily from the Goyigamas and their Tamil equivalent, the Vellalas,[41] was mostly Christian. They often had English given and family names, wore Western clothes, entertained themselves with the pastimes of the British upper class, and sent their children either to schools in England or to English-medium schools at home. "Those not educated in English were condemned to subordinate roles in society."[42]

The Westernized elite faced opposition from both Marxists, who organized the trade union movement, and had a base among non–Goyigama Sinhalese, and from Sinhalese traditionalists — particularly the Sinhalese-medium schoolteachers, who strongly resented the higher pay received by their colleagues who taught in English.[43] Along with groups of village headmen, Buddhist monks, and traditional Ayurvedic doctors, the teachers were a primary force behind the formation of the Sri Lanka Freedom Party (SLFP), which was formed in 1951 to challenge the ruling United National Party (UNP). The first leader of the SLFP was S.W.R.D. Bandaranaike. He was born into a highly Westernized family, and was named after Solomon West Ridgeway, a colonial governor. Raised as an Anglican,[44] he converted to Buddhism and adopted traditional Sinhalese dress only when he entered politics.[45] Some of his countrymen believed that he even had to learn Sinhalese at that point in his life.

The UNP was able to survive one election after independence, but increasing labor unrest backed by the two Marxist parties set the stage for its downfall in 1956. A dissident faction of the socialist LSSP joined with the SLFP and some extreme Sinhalese nationalists to form the United People's Front (*Mahajana Eksath Peramuna*, MEP). This became known as the Buddhist political party, and drew strong support from monks belonging to the Amarapura and Ramanya sects, most of whose followers came from the lower castes.[46] On the other hand, the Siam sect, which is restricted to Goyigama, was divided over the election. The higher clergy, privately sympathetic to the conservative UNP, tried to rein in the lower clergy, which was pro-MEP, by insisting that all monks remain scrupulously neutral. But this backfired when Catholic, Protestant and Muslim clergy began ordering their own congregants to vote for the UNP.[47] In addition, the 2,500th anniversary of Buddha's death took place in 1956, just in time for the elections, and the Sinhalese were swept by a wave of Buddhist revivalism.

The MEP's victory constituted a revolution in style, if not in substance. The old elite, with their colonial ways, were gone from office; but there soon was a falling-out between the socialists and clericalists in Bandaranaike's coalition, particularly over the issue of land reform. The strongest opponent of land reform within the MEP was a charismatic monk, Tibbotuvave Budhharakkhita, whose synthesis of religion and political demagoguery, coupled with his corrupt life-style, made him the Sri Lankan equivalent of Rasputin and earned him the nickname "Buddy Racketeer."[48] He engineered the breakup of the MEP, a process which culminated in the assassination of Bandaranaike by one of Budhharakkhita's supporters in September 1959.

The Sri Lankan Tamils gave no support to the MEP, largely because of the latter's promotion of Sinhalese as the only official language, a policy which put Tamils seeking government jobs at a disadvantage. In the early years of independence, the Tamils generally voted for their own parties, the conservative Tamil Congress and the larger and slightly more militant Federal Party. Both of these parties were elite-led, and found it easy to make common cause with the UNP against the rising tide of Sinhalese communalism and its Marxist allies. The LSSP and the Communists were unable to win significant Sri Lankan Tamil support once they started aligning themselves with the SLFP, a process which began in 1964. As for the Indian Tamils, their leading party (Ceylon Workers Congress) backed the UNP, while the smaller Democratic Workers Congress ultimately aligned itself with the left and the SLFP; most of the Indian Tamils were unable to vote in any case.

This meant that the upland election districts containing the tea plantations, and their disenfranchised Indian Tamil workers, became "rotten boroughs," where a small number of Sinhalese voters could determine the election outcomes. The UNP and SLFP competed for these voters, using chauvinistic appeals. As political scientist Donald Horowitz notes, "There is no escaping the fact that two-party competition for the Sinhalese vote has made Sri Lanka's moderately serious ethnic conflict far more serious than it would otherwise have been."[49]

Concentrated on the crowded Jaffna peninsula, where shortage of land and inadequate rainfall make farming difficult, the Sri Lankan Tamils have learned to be hard workers. Many have sought their fortunes in Colombo as civil servants, businessmen or professionals. While Tamils living in the overwhelmingly Tamil Northern Province are often poor and uneducated, they are not the ones whom Sinhalese are likely to encounter. S.J. Tambiah observes that "there are no Sri Lankan Tamil slums in Colombo,"[50] a fact that may mislead some Sinhalese to think that all Tamils belong to the elite.

Generally preferring to send their children to English-medium schools during the colonial period, the Tamils gradually gained a significant edge over the Sinhalese. By 1956, they were strongly overrepresented in government service, particularly at the professional level, where they constituted 60 percent of the total.[51] The Bandaranaike government's "Sinhala Only" policy caused a drastic drop in the percentage of Tamils in government jobs.[52] As the Tamils tried to enter the universities, they found their way blocked by quotas.[53] Gradually, the Tamils — particularly the younger generation — were driven into the separatist camp.

Anti-Tamilism as a Defense Mechanism

Despite their majority status — about three-quarters of the population, now that most of the Indian Tamils have been sent back to India — the Sinhalese do not perceive themselves as a majority group. In their own eyes, they are a beleaguered minority in a predominantly Dravidian-speaking and Hindu region, perpetually on the brink of being overwhelmed by the Tamils. Alluding to the shape of the country, one prominent Sinhalese Buddhist monk said: "[S]ee how tiny, how fragile Sinhalese Buddhist society is. We are only a teardrop, a grain of sand, in an enormous sea. And it is in danger of being forever washed away."[54] A Sinhalese politician concurred: "In this country the problem of the Tamils is not a minority problem. The Sinhalese are the minority in Dravidastan. We are carrying on a struggle for our national existence against the Dravidian majority."[55]

This "Dravidian majority," needless to say, is a fiction. "Dravidistan" does not exist. Dravidian-speaking ethnic groups are themselves only a minority in India, where some have their own grievances against the Hindi-speaking plurality in the north. But some Sinhalese argue as if India is inhabited entirely by Tamils.[56] This distortion represents fear of annihilation, which has its roots in birth trauma, but also indicates a good deal of repressed childhood anger.

The most virulent of the Sinhalese Tamil-haters was Cyril Mathew, Minister of Industry under the UNP's President Junius Richard Jayawardena; their English names indicate their affiliation with the old elite. Mathew was the leader of the *Jatika Sevaka Sangamaya* (JSS), or National Workers Organization, the trade union affiliate of the UNP. He "effectively molded the JSS into an organization which controlled government offices and intimidated high officials."[57] It was less a union than a goon squad, used for breaking strikes led by Marxist unions and bullying voters at election time.[58] A sampling of quotations from Mathew's speeches and writings gives an idea of the man's views:

- "[T]he foreign Indians will, in the future, become the majority race and subdue the up-country Sinhalese."[59]
- "[A]ll the Tamil-speaking people living in Sri Lanka will unite with the Tamil-speaking people of Madras [now Tamilnad] and subjugate the Sinhalese people."[60]
- "[T]here is a systematic growth of Tamil forces in this country, in opposition to the Sinhala Buddhist culture...."[61]
- "[S]ubjecting the innocent and defenseless Sinhala people to extremely cruel torture and harassments such as beheading, bloodbaths, killing on the spike and setting whole villages on fire, the foreign invaders mercilessly suppressed the Sinhala people and forced Hindu, Catholic and Christian doctrines ... into their minds...."
- "[A] majority of the Sinhala people were undefiled and ... treated the honours, citations, wealth, prosperity, etc., obtainable from the foreign rulers as stinking infective dysentric excrement."[62]

Hardly an accurate account of Sri Lankan history, this last passage is more likely a symbolic expression of Mathew's own childhood. One can only wonder how such a man, seemingly a candidate for a padded cell, could end up in a position of power and responsibility in a country which once prided itself on its democracy and ethnic harmony.

The road to the eruption of full-scale inter-ethnic warfare in 1983 was not a straight one. For a quarter century after the 1956 elections, the government changed hands each time the voters were allowed to choose — even in 1960, when two elections were held in a single year. Key turning points were in 1965, when a UNP–led coalition including the Tamil parties came to power under Dudley Senanayake; and in 1970, when the United Front — a coalition including the SLFP, the socialist LSSP, and the Communists, and led by S.W.R.D. Banaranaike's widow Siramavo — won a huge majority in parliament, and then stayed in office for seven years by postponing the next election. The frequent changes of government at the top can be explained by the high rate of population growth and the five-year (or longer) time spans between parliamentary elections; this added up to huge contingents of first-time voters in every election, who voted against the ruling party because they were frustrated in their search for jobs. In Sri Lanka, politicians double as employment agents, trying to win voters' favor by finding them work. But this often backfires because for each voter who get a job, there are several more who are disappointed. Even the lucky few who get the jobs, Sri Lankans say, turn against their benefactors because they think they deserved better ones.

By 1970, when the leftist United Front took office, there had been a realignment in Sri Lankan politics. Most of the extreme Sinhalese nationalists had by then joined up with the conservative UNP, while the SLFP, shorn of its clericalist wing, was firmly aligned with the Marxist left. The LSSP and the Communists took posts in the cabinet, although the ultra-radical JVP, which had backed the United Front in the election, remained outside. This movement quickly became the voice of those — nearly all young, educated, and frustrated — who came to feel that the United Front was betraying its promises of social reform.

In 1971, Sri Lanka experienced a political explosion which may represent another example of an Adowa cycle. It had been fifteen years since 1956, when the Buddhist-nationalist coalition replaced the Anglophile elite in the government, amidst the celebration of Buddha's 2,500-year jubilee. Now, suddenly, the JVP launched an armed uprising against the very government that they had helped bring to power only months earlier. For a short time, the popularly-elected United Front government teetered on the brink of collapse, as the JVP's guerrillas seized poorly defended police stations and distributed the captured weapons to its followers. There was widespread backing for the uprising among the youth, and some members of the LSSP and the Communist Party youth groups joined it.[63] But a diverse group of nations gave military assistance to the beleaguered government, and not even Maoist China gave any backing to the rebels.[64]

The JVP was eventually crushed with brutality, and thousands of young people were killed, particularly among the lower caste groups, where the rebels had found the most support.[65] Neither the Tamils nor the Muslims were involved with the rebels to any significant degree. The timing of the rebellion has always mystified observers, who believed that "had the rebels waited one more year, they would surely have succeeded,"[66] due to the continued deterioration of the economy. It may have been due to competition within the movement's leadership, always a radicalizing factor in student movements; and government *agents provocateurs* may have been involved.

In the delayed election of 1977, the UNP made a spectacular comeback, reducing the SLFP to a powerless minority in parliament, and shutting out its two Marxist allies altogether. The UNP's strongest support came from the same lower castes which had followed the JVP in 1971. The UNP's leader was Ranasinghe Premadasa, later slain by an assassin. Cyril Mathew also served in the Cabinet. Mathew, despite his name, is a Vahumpera, the largest of the service castes in the up-country areas that once formed the Kingdom of Kandy. "Mathew is undoubtedly caste conscious," writes one participating observer of the Sri Lankan political scene. "But the alleged grievances the Vahumpera community had suffered were not from the Tamils but from the Goyigama community, who are Sinhalese. There is no particular reason for hatred against the Tamils."[67]

The reason for the anti–Tamil hatred, of course, is psychological rather than social.

Turning against the Tamils was a way for the once-rebellious Sinhalese lower castes to ingratiate themselves with the ruling elite. Parallels abound: German and Austrian workers became vulnerable to anti–Semitic appeals after their Marxist-led insurrections and strikes had been crushed; and white populists in the American South in the late 19th century became more racist after their struggle for economic justice failed.

As the UNP began recruiting more lower-caste Sinhalese, the JVP itself was reorganizing. But it had added Sinhalese chauvinism to its radical ideology. When new riots broke out in 1983, the JVP was in the forefront of attacks on the Tamils, in an attempt to upstage the UNP. The JVP was following a familiar pattern among Sri Lankan leftist parties: beginning as class-conscious Marxists, they increasingly adopt the rhetoric of Sinhalese chauvinism to win votes, until their anti-capitalist stance has become transformed into anti–Tamilism. This happened first with the long-defunct Labour Party of the 1930s and 1940s. History repeated itself when a dissident faction of the LSSP, which had been part of S.W.R.D. Bandaranaike's coalition in 1956, assumed an anti–Tamil stance and later merged with the UNP. Still later, the mainstream of the LSSP and the Communists also began taking an anti–Tamil stance. The JVP has been the latest addition to this list.

Tamil Separatism

Sinhalese extremism furthered the rise of separatist groups among the Tamils. Foremost among these has been the 20,000-strong Liberation Tigers of Tamil Eelam (LTTE), founded in 1976[68] by Velupillai Prabhakaran, a secretive but highly effective guerrilla leader. His Tigers have fought wars with the Sri Lankan government, rival separatist groups, moderate Tamils, Muslims, local criminals, and even the Indian army, which the UNP called in to maintain order. The war between the Indians and the LTTE began after a 1987 "peace agreement" was signed between India and Sri Lanka, with no involvement of the LTTE, allowing for Indian troops to occupy the Tamil-populated north of Sri Lanka. Despite thirty-to-one odds, the LTTE actually defeated the Indian army, forcing it to ultimately withdraw in disgrace.[69] Oddly, the Indians had originally been providing assistance to the LTTE,[70] out of sympathy for a largely–Hindu community being oppressed by non–Hindus, as in Bangladesh. But by 1990, the LTTE were actually receiving arms and ammunition from the Sinhalese government in their fight against the Indian "peacekeepers," whom the Sinhalese themselves had invited into the country.[71]

From the beginning of the armed conflict until the spring of 2009, when the Tigers were finally annihilated by the Sri Lankan army and their leader slain, no military force was able to inflict a lasting defeat on the LTTE. But they undermined their own popularity through massacres of non–Tamils: in May 1985, 148 Buddhist pilgrims were slaughtered by LTTE guerrillas in Anuradhapura[72]; and a few years later, 166 Muslims were killed in a village along the eastern coast while they were at Friday prayers.[73] Clashes within the Tamil community between the Tigers and their rivals often had caste-based overtones, and also involved competition over the *ganja* trade.

Repeated attempts at resolving the ethnic conflict in Sri Lanka resulted in failure, as hard-liners — particularly among the Sinhalese — sabotaged every peace settlement in turn. One consequence of the peace efforts was the eruption of clashes within the Sinhalese majority, between the conservative UNP and the once-radical JVP, with the Marxist-led unions caught in the middle. Ironically, it is this very conflict, with the rival camps appealing to different caste groups, which might lead to the end of the Sinhalese-Tamil ethnic violence. As the lower Sinhalese castes raise their status in the course of their conflict with the Goyigamas, their need to scapegoat the Tamils might be reduced. The very process which led, for so many years, to prolonged ethnic strife might thus contain the seeds of its own negation.

7

Cambodia

Displaced Anger and Auto-Genocide

The world has never seen a revolution like the one that ravaged the Southeast Asian nation of Cambodia during the late 1970s. It would be no exaggeration to say that "Democratic Kampuchea," as the followers of Pol Pot called their nation, proved to be the deathbed of Communism. In the course of less than a decade — from the onset of civil war in 1970, following Gen. Lon Nol's coup d'état, to the ouster of the Pol Pot regime by the Vietnamese in 1979 — at least a quarter of Cambodia's population of eight million was lost through massacre, disease, combat, or starvation.[1] This was an even higher percentage than were lost in Poland during the five years of the Nazi occupation.

Although American air raids, combat deaths, and killings by Lon Nol's troops accounted for many of the losses, most of the victims died one way or another at the hands of Pol Pot's fanatical followers, known to the outside world as the Khmer Rouge ("Red Cambodians"), to themselves as the Communist Party of Kampuchea, and to the Cambodian public as *Angkar*. This last word means "the Organization," but the similarity to the name of the vast Cambodian empire that ruled roughly half of mainland Southeast Asia from the ninth to the fourteenth centuries[2] — Angkor — is probably not accidental. This empire's temple, the celebrated Angkor Wat, even appeared on the Khmer Rouge national flag, although "[m]ost Khmers had not even heard of Angkor before French colonial archeologists began publicizing and interpreting their findings."[3]

During its reign of barely four years, Angkar selected entire categories of Cambodian citizens for extermination, in particular the intelligentsia (loosely defined), former members of the defeated Lon Nol army, and a number of ethnic minority groups, along with anyone who didn't appear to be working hard enough or who complained about the harsh conditions. When these groups were extirpated, the regime turned, like a paranoid cult, on real and alleged dissidents within its own ranks, purging tens of thousands of Angkar cadres. Simultaneously, it launched a suicidal war of aggression against neighboring Vietnam, whose defeat of the United States had enabled it to come to power to begin with. Only the Pol Pot regime's subsequent ouster by the Vietnamese prevented it from slaughtering even more victims.

Even after their defeat, Angkar continued to fight on from sanctuaries in Thailand, posing as an anti–Vietnamese nationalist movement, while continuing to kill innocent Cambodians as well as repeatedly purging their own leaders. Shrinking steadily in size, its rank-

and-file members falling in combat, and its leaders either defecting to the pro–Vietnam government in Phnom Penh or falling victim to internal purges, the movement finally disintegrated in 1999 with the capture of its last prominent figure, the bloodthirsty warlord of the Southwest Region, Ta Mok.[4] The horrors of the Angkar regime happened in a country long known for its gentle, pacific ways, a country which had, before 1970, escaped most of the violence that devastated Vietnam and Laos.

The Angkar holocaust against its own people, along with its war of aggression against Vietnam, seem to defy comprehension and explanation. Some attempts to understand Angkar's behavior lean on political analysis, others rely on anthropological understanding, and still others focus on psychological variables, particularly "the darker side of the Cambodian character...."[5] In fact, all three levels of variables are essential for a thorough understanding of the causes of the Pol Pot regime's horrific outrages.

Roots of Fanaticism

No commonality of language, religion or history unites Southeast Asia's various nations, and most of them are ethnically diverse to begin with. But throughout the region, there is a widespread tendency for people to present a public image of gentleness and charm, while reserving a far more violent code of behavior for times of stress, either personal or social. This pattern is the reverse of what prevails in the Middle East, where the public self is more belligerent than the private one.

The Cambodians, or Khmer, are distantly related to the Thai and Lao, with closer connections to various small tribal groups scattered from Vietnam to Myanmar and India. They are Theravada Buddhists, as they have been since the collapse of the Angkor Empire in the 14th century. At the same time, their religious practice remains mixed with Hinduism and ancient folk beliefs. Unlike Vietnam, Cambodia's culture has been heavily influenced by India.

> Before the Khmer Rouge took power, Cambodia was considered to be the most Buddhist country in Southeast Asia. To be Khmer meant being Buddhist. The countryside was dotted with more than 2,500 temples, and most men became monks at some point in life.... [M]ost males spent an average of two years as monks.[6]

Religion was linked to the state, and the king was the official head of the Buddhist clergy.[7]

While Cambodia was relatively homogeneous by the standards of the region, minorities still represented about 15–20 percent of the population, including Vietnamese, Chinese, Chams, Malays, tribal peoples, Thais, Lao, and a few others. Among the Khmer, there were important distinctions between lowlanders and hill-dwellers that took on an almost ethnic quality: "[N]o assumptions about Cambodian life, attitudes, mores, and beliefs based on observations of the central rice-growing and gardening zones," writes Michael Vickery, "are likely to be accurate for other regions."[8] Hill-dwelling Khmer tended to be suspicious of all outsiders, particularly those from the towns; they were self-governing and self-reliant, engaging in little trade outside their own villages.[9] Their typically sullen demeanor contrasted sharply with the amiability of Khmer from the towns and the rice-producing areas.

In 1980, after the ouster of Angkar, Prince Norodom Sihanouk — who ruled the country from 1953 to 1970 — observed that "the most fanatic Khmer Rouge soldiers were from the mountain and forest regions."[10] This would have included tribal peoples as well as ethnic Khmer from the hill country; Sihanouk's government, along with most lowland Khmer, made little distinction. It would be tempting to regard the horrors of "Democratic Kampuchea" (DK) as entirely the work of primitive illiterates, but it would be wrong for several reasons.

- First, the ruling clique in the DK (perhaps twenty people, often related by blood or marriage) were not only lowlanders, but also well-educated. Pol Pot (born Saloth Sar), his foreign minister Ieng Sary, and his defense minister Son Sen, as well as their wives, who also held important positions, had studied at French universities, where they were all acquainted[11] (Pol and Ieng were married to sisters). Khieu Samphan, the DK's leading ideologist, was a renowned French-educated intellectual. Ta Mok, the most brutal of the DK's regional commanders, had a Buddhist education.[12] While many low-level Angkar cadres were indeed illiterate peasants,[13] it was the Paris-educated clique that established DK policy.
- Second, had the horrors of Angkar's rule been the result of hill-peasant or tribal domination, we should expect to find even worse atrocities in Laos, where most of the Pathet Lao's membership was made up of mountain-dwelling tribals. Yet the Pathet Lao have been relatively restrained. No theory of why the DK degenerated into a charnel house is complete unless it also accounts for Laos' quite different development.
- Third, notwithstanding their reputation as gentle, the Khmers have a record of violence which cannot be attributed entirely to the presence of backward hill farmers or tribal minorities. Cambodia is almost the only nation in the world from which one still hears reliable reports of cannibalism, the custom being to eat your slain enemies' livers; this happened to two pro–Lon Nol politicians following the 1970 coup,[14] and there are reports of similar acts taking place under Angkar.[15] Atrocities were committed on all sides during the French-Indochina War, and the repression of the leftist opposition, beginning in 1963, was marked by considerable brutality.[16] Much of this can be laid at the door of Lon Nol, who served as Sihanouk's defense minister before he turned on the prince, but Lon Nol's record of oppression and corruption did not prevent him from emerging as the dominant figure after the 1966 elections. Haing Ngor, the physician-turned-actor who survived the Angkar holocaust, comments on the concept of *kum*, "a long-standing grudge leading to revenge much more damaging than the original injury," which he describes as an "infection that grows on our national soul."[17]

Rather than blame hill people and tribal minorities for the horrors of the Angkar regime, it might be more fruitful to scrutinize certain factors that may have caused so many Khmer to participate in the bloodbath. In particular, we might focus on three things:

1. The influence of Buddhist education on Khmer boys;
2. The Khmer inferiority complex, based on pigmentation, toward both their own aristocracy and neighboring peoples; and

3. The traumatic effect of the U.S. air war against Cambodia, which covered
the entire country, lasting from 1970 to 1973.

Khmer Child-Rearing

The Khmer family tends to be relatively unstructured by Western standards. In the
past, it was common for parents to give children to grandparents, aunts or even neighbors,
who raised them as their own. All the adults in the village participated in the socialization
of children, "parents hardly intervening more than others in the education of their own offspring."[18] The children were generally treated with affection, "but not fussed over and are
encouraged to take care of themselves from an early age.... Once the child begins to assert
his own personality, however, parental attentiveness diminishes."[19] Little attempt was made
to inform young children about sex,[20] perhaps because, in the close quarters of the family
home, they would have learned about it on their own.

At the same time, Philip Short says, in his biography of Pol Pot, that punishment of
children could be severe in Cambodia, at least during the colonial era. Children were beaten,
and sometimes forced to lie on nests of red ants.[21] However, this type of abuse may not
have been typical.

When boys reached early adolescence, the monks in the village pagoda took over
their socialization.[22] There is little reason to assume that the celibate monks exercised
superhuman control over their biological urges, and the probability is that sexual abuse of
the defenseless boys occurred; just how widespread this was requires further investigation.

One observer remarked that the monks "teach a tranquility that seriously inhibits even
fighting for one's rights."[23] This teaching was so effective that the Khmer expression for
"getting angry" acquired the slang connotation of "getting an erection"[24]—a private event
that one would not normally display in public. Cambodians, writes Ngor, "try to stay polite
even when we do not feel like being polite, because it is easier that way. To be in conflict
forces us to treat one another as enemies, and then we lose control."[25]

Anger, like hunger, is a biological reality in the human psychophysical system. It doesn't
disappear merely because it happens to be inconvenient to acknowledge it. Strongly repressed
anger can turn into paranoia, in which it takes on *the appearance of fear*. In Theravada Buddhist societies, such as Cambodia or Sri Lanka, the result is the emergence of a paranoid
political culture, in which clinical symptoms are replicated on the national level. Delusions
of reference are transformed into messianic national myths; delusions of imminent personal
annihilation become public concerns that the nation itself might disappear; and the individual paranoid's fondness for imagining himself in conflicts with powerful forces (the
Mafia, the CIA, space aliens) is paralleled by the pattern of paranoid nations seeking conflicts
with more powerful countries: Argentina attacks the British in the Falklands, Hitler invades
the USSR before subduing England, Japan attacks the United States while its army is bogged
down in China, Pakistan provokes repeated wars with India, and Angkar starts a conflict
with far more powerful Vietnam.

The Khmer have a strong sense of inferiority based on race. The earliest inhabitants
of Southeast Asia were dark-skinned and curly-haired, resembling Africans; such people,
who are still found in Melanesia, Australia and parts of the Philippines, were absorbed by

later migrants who came from China. Typically, Khmers are darker than their Vietnamese and Thai neighbors, who arrived in the region centuries later. Writes Ngor:

> To most Asians, including our neighbors, the lighter the skin color, the higher the status. They look down on Cambodians for having darker skins than themselves. Cambodians, who are shy by nature, sometimes outwardly appear to accept a lower status while inwardly resenting it.[26]

During the time of the Angkor Empire, the peasants were referred to as "black," while the ruling elite were termed "white as jade."[27] This was a class rather than a racial distinction — the peasants were darker because they worked outdoors in the sun — but the effect on the Khmer self-image was the same. When they were colonized by the French, the identification of dark complexion with subordinate status became even more intense. In addition, lighter-skinned Chinese immigrants came to dominate trade and commerce,[28] while Vietnamese — slightly less dark than the Khmer — staffed the lower levels of the French colonial administration.[29] Intermarriage between Chinese men and Cambodian women was common, since the Chinese usually immigrated without their own women, and the offspring of such unions, typically lighter-complexioned than the unmixed Khmer, became prominent in the civil service and the professions after independence.

From 1954 to 1970, when Prince Norodom Sihanouk dominated the political life of the newly-independent country, the economic gap between the mostly Khmer rural and urban poor and the heavily non–Khmer (or part–Khmer) urban middle class widened. The percentage of landless peasants increased from 4 percent in 1950 to 20 percent in 1970,[30] and this impoverished section of the peasantry made up most of the Angkar rank and file.[31] At the same time, American intervention in neighboring Vietnam and threats to China helped to push Cambodia's Vietnamese and Chinese communities into the arms of the Communists.

By 1968, "Economic hardships to the point of starvation were evident among the poorest people of both city and countryside...."[32] This was coupled with the rapid spread of education; Sihanouk opened nine universities and increased the number of secondary schools from 8 in 1953 to 200 in 1967.[33] As elsewhere in the underdeveloped world, the combination of increased poverty and rising levels of education proved to be explosive.

Sihanouk's Cambodia

French rule in Indochina ended as a result of a prolonged armed struggle, but the Vietnamese and Laotians did nearly all of the fighting; the Cambodian contribution was minor.[34] There were roughly 5,000 guerrillas operating in Cambodia during the French-Indochina War,[35] which lasted from 1945 until 1953. Known as *Issaraks*, they were not a united group. Some followed the extreme nationalist Son Ngoc Thanh, who supported a republican form of government, but was paradoxically backed by monarchist Thailand, which itself had territorial claims on Cambodia. The United Issarak Front was a rival group which was affiliated with the Vietnamese Communist movement, the Viet Minh. This movement was led by a Buddhist monk who used the nom de guerre Son Ngoc Minh (combining Son Ngoc Thanh and Ho Chi Minh), and attracted the support of many devout Buddhists,[36] despite its Communist connections. Other Issaraks, like guerrilla leader Dap Chhoun, were pro–Sihanouk monarchists.

Sihanouk himself remained in Phnom Penh, where he took advantage of the extensive fighting in Vietnam and Laos—and its echoes in Cambodia—to compel the French to grant him increasing power, his ultimate goal being full independence. To undermine Sihanouk's growing support, the French made secret arrangements with an Issarak leader, Prince Chantaraingsey, who shared their opposition to the Viet Minh.[37] This is an example of the uniquely surreal quality of Cambodian politics, in which movements take on opposite qualities simultaneously; there are collaborationist resistance groups, monarchist republicans, royal socialists, and, ultimately, fascist Communists.

The French were defeated in 1953 at Dien Bien Phu, and were forced to concede independence to the three Indochinese nations. In 1954, Vietnam was partitioned into a Communist North and a U.S.–controlled South. Laos remained a single country, but with rightist and leftist armies in charge of different zones. Cambodia's future looked more promising, with its territory intact and only a single army. The Issaraks disbanded, some ultimately rallying to Sihanouk, many emigrating to Hanoi with Son Ngoc Minh, and a portion following Son Ngoc Thanh into exile in Thailand and later South Vietnam.[38] Cambodia's new army was composed of troops who had fought on the side of the French.[39] Its leader was General Lon Nol, at the time a prominent figure in the small, strongly monarchist Khmer Renovation Party.[40] A larger group of secular republicans, the Democratic Party, failed to establish itself firmly in the post-independence era. Deference to the monarchy, loyalty to Buddhism, and admiration for Sihanouk's skill as champion of independence combined to undermine support for the Democrats. The elite supported them, but the peasant masses remained loyal to Sihanouk.

Sihanouk, like many "third world" leaders, preferred a single-party state. He created the *Sangkum Reastr Niyam* (Royal Socialist Community), which absorbed most of the other political forces. The small *Pracheachon* (People's Party), representing the radical left, was the only legitimate opposition. Despite widespread corruption and a degree of political repression, Cambodia was, even by 1966, "the most open and politically tolerant society in Southeast Asia."[41]

This was ended by America's anti–Communist crusade in Vietnam. As the war in South Vietnam heated up, both Communist guerrillas and Saigon army forces repeatedly crossed the border into Cambodia, followed by American troops and air attacks. Thousands of ethnic Khmer refugees from Vietnam's Mekong Delta—known as Khmer Krom, or Southern Khmer—fled into Cambodia to escape the intense fighting. Other Khmer Krom were recruited by the CIA into Son Ngoc Thanh's exile army, and were used to launch military attacks against Cambodia from Thai and South Vietnamese bases.[42] The U.S. government thought that this pressure would force neutral Cambodia to join SEATO; it had the opposite effect of promoting Sihanouk's closer alliance with China and North Vietnam.

In early 1967, a peasant uprising occurred in the Samlaut district, near the Thai border, provoked by Lon Nol's policy of forcing peasants to sell rice to the government at low prices.[43] This event seems to have convinced Cambodia's Communist leaders that peasant revolution was a possibility in the increasingly unstable country. At that time, the Communist Party of Cambodia was a tiny group that operated through the Pracheachon as its public front. Its first leader, Sieu Heng, defected to Sihanouk in the late 1950s and became an informer[44]; his successor, Tou Samouth, a former monk, was assassinated in 1962 by persons unknown,[45] most likely as a consequence of Sieu Heng's betrayal. Pol Pot and his close associates then took over the underground leadership of the party. They were contemptuous of the Issarak veterans in the party, whom they regarded as "'country bumpkins' with little theoretical knowledge,"[46] a glaring contrast with their own later animosity toward all intellectuals. The Pol Pot faction was more ambivalent toward three prominent left-wing political leaders — Khieu Samphan, Hou Yuon and Hu Nim — who also favored peasant revolution in Cambodia, but were more flexible in regard to alliances with pro–Sihanouk elements; the first of these three remained a loyal leader within the Khmer Rouge, but the other two were killed by Pol Pot during his years in power. Both Communist factions were impatient with the Vietnamese policy of supporting Sihanouk against American pressure; for strategic reasons, the Vietnamese were firmly opposed to any uprisings against the Cambodian government even as the Cambodian Communists were starting to look favorably on the idea. The later antagonism between the Cambodian and Vietnamese Communists can be traced in part to this disagreement.[47]

In 1966, open but non-partisan elections led to the victory of conservative, pro–American candidates. They formed a new government headed by Lon Nol, which began repressing the radical left. Not long after, Khieu Samphan, Hou Yuon and Hu Nim left Phnom Penh to join Marxist insurgents in the countryside, and were soon joined by many other urban leftists. It is still a matter of dispute how much Communist rebel activity there was in rural Cambodia during the 1967–1970 period. One source states that left-wing rebels were active in 13 out of 18 provinces.[48] But another writer dismissed them at the time as a minor problem, even less of a factor than Son Ngoc Thanh's CIA-financed exiles.[49] Ben Kiernan says that the estimated 2,400 Angkar-led rebels in 1969 were "hardly a major military threat to Sihanouk's army."[50] David Chandler, however, indicates that the guerrilla movement was growing, making inroads among tribal minorities in the northeast.[51] Given the poorly-equipped and ramshackle Cambodian army, with the ignorant and superstitious Lon Nol at its head, it would not have taken a particularly powerful guerrilla force to defeat it.

"Democratic Kampuchea"

Pol Pot, the fanatical Marxist intellectual, and Lon Nol, the superstitious and corrupt military chieftain, represented opposite poles of Cambodian politics. Yet they also shared certain characteristics:

- First was their lack of principle, a consequence of a society which de-emphasizes the role of the individual, and which relies more on external than internal restraints on human behavior.
- Second was their intense xenophobia. Lon Nol founded a "Khmer-Mon Institute" following his 1970 coup, which "tried to prove that the dark-skinned Khmer race was superior to the light-skinned people like the Chinese and Vietnamese."[52] Similarly, Pol Pot was in the habit of stressing his unmixed Khmer ancestry; as a student in Paris, he signed his articles "Original Khmer."[53] Lon Nol organized brutal pogroms against the Vietnamese minority after taking power; Pol Pot did likewise, also persecuting the Cham minority. Lon Nol, wrote American journalist Elizabeth Becker, "made no secret

of his dream of purifying the Khmer race, the Khmer culture, and Khmer Buddhism of the foreign pollutants he thought had sapped the country and eaten away its identity and territory."[54] Pol Pot's Angkar also often spoke of the need for "purification." "[W]e were to hear this word many times in the sermons of the Khmer Rouge officers," writes survivor Pin Yathay.[55]

- Third was territorial expansion. Lon Nol spoke of reconquering the Mekong Delta from Vietnam, and of uniting the Khmer minority in eastern Thailand—and even the related Mon people who lived in southern Myanmar— under his rule.[56] Pol Pot also laid claim to much of southern Vietnam,[57] which led to his self-destructive war against the larger neighboring country; and he also organized a branch of his party among the Khmers in Thailand.[58]

- Fourth was the notion of sacrifice. François Bizot, a French scholar of Cambodian Buddhism who was held captive by Angkar before they took Phnom Penh, noted the similarities between Pol Pot's version of Communism and the Buddhism in whose name Lon Nol attempted to rally his troops. They included renouncing family ties and material possessions, submitting to rigid discipline and publicly confessing one's shortcomings.[59]

The notion of "purification" appears in many countries during times of national weakness. It symbolizes the stage of the birth struggle when the infant is not yet out of the birth canal, and is receiving pollutants into its blood through the umbilical cord. Likewise, territorial expansionism is a projected memory of the infant's life-and-death struggle to get out of the womb as the mother goes into contractions. Unlike in Italy, where only the Fascists manifested it, birth symbolism was appearing at both ends of the Cambodian political spectrum; the psychological context, however, was different. Cambodians may have less birth trauma than some other peoples, but the tendency to repress anger was greater because of their Buddhist upbringing. This caused them to shift rapidly into birth-related feelings instead of merely symbolizing their childhood pain as in other countries. One specific example of this was Pol Pot's wife, Khieu Ponnary, who became psychotic in 1970, while in Beijing. She imagined that the Vietnamese were out to kill her by poisoning her water.[60]

Lon Nol's U.S.–backed coup in March, 1970, his ouster of Sihanouk, and his unsuccessful attempt to drive the Vietnamese Communists from their positions along Cambodia's eastern border, brought Cambodia into the Vietnam War. Throughout the rural areas of the country, peasants, students from the cities, and members of the Vietnamese and Chinese minorities rallied to Sihanouk, who promptly formed an alliance—the National United Front of Kampuchea (FUNK)—with Angkar, which had previously been in rebellion against him. Lon Nol's ineffective 35,000-man army busied itself along the Vietnamese border, attacking the South Vietnamese National Liberation Front, which swiftly defeated it. With extensive Vietnamese help, the Royalist-Communist alliance was able to establish itself in about half of the country in a matter of a few months. Only American air power, which was used extensively throughout Cambodia, kept the FUNK from capturing Phnom Penh. Writes Ervin Staub, "Between 1970 and 1973, the United States dropped three times the tonnage of bombs on Cambodia that it had dropped on Japan during all of World War II."[61] One effect of this was that a large part of the population joined the Angkar-led resistance; another was that millions of peasants fled the countryside for the relative safety of the cities.

The U.S. bombing campaign ended in the summer of 1973,[62] but the final Angkar offensive against Lon Nol only began in the spring of 1975. It appears that Angkar was less than eager to bring the war to a swift conclusion, even though the Lon Nol regime — limited by then to the major towns and the province of Battambang — was tottering, its inept leader partially incapacitated by a stroke. Pol Pot may have seen the isolation of his territory from Cambodia's cities as helpful for the establishment of his ideal society; this is consistent with his policy toward the urban areas once the war was over.

The Angkar's "Democratic Kampuchea" was one of the strangest societies the world has seen. The entire country was organized like a cult commune. All cities were evacuated, and the inhabitants were dispersed, the luckier ones ending up in the Eastern Zone, where the local Angkar cadres tended to be a bit more humane. Although this action was rationalized on the grounds that the Americans were planning to bomb Phnom Penh, the real reason appears to be Angkar's desire to control the population by putting them in isolated villages. Religion was outlawed; money was abolished; there were no newspapers or postal service; universities and secondary schools were closed, and primary education reduced almost to the vanishing point, at least temporarily. Diplomatic relations existed with only about a dozen foreign countries. The National Library was pillaged, and the regime even neglected the famous ruins of Angkor Wat. The calendar was reset at Year Zero, and the entire population was ordered to forget everything that had happened in the past — perhaps a reflection of Pol Pot's own feelings about his personal past.

The outside world regarded the little-known Angkar as Communist, and Marxism was soon to take the blame for its atrocities, but Pol Pot's regime rarely if ever made references to Marx and Lenin. The Cambodian people did not learn of Angkar's ideology until several years after its victory.[63] Angkar used the term *pativattana* to describe its revolution, a term which means "return to the past."[64] Years after the Vietnamese invasion, Khieu Samphan "emphasized that nationalist rather than Communist ideology had always been the driving force of the movement."[65]

Like most cults, Angkar saw enemies everywhere, and these enemies were perceived as acting in concert even when they were bitterly opposed to one another. "Enemies attack and torment us," declared Pol Pot. "From the east and from the west, they persist in pounding us and worrying us. If we are slow and weak, they will mistreat us."[66] It sounded like the Angkar leader was projecting his own early memories onto his country's situation.

Angkar imposed a manic-depressive state of mind on the entire population. All expressions of emotion other than officially-approved rage were prohibited. Crying was forbidden.[67] There was no flirting, gambling, bright clothing or jewelry permitted[68]; even soccer was outlawed.[69] An act of generosity toward a stranger could get one arrested.[70] A survivor recalls that one man was executed for sighing.[71] Even a young child was punished "for laughing and joking while at work."[72] A French-educated Cambodian who returned to Phnom Penh to work in a factory noted: "Everything was interpreted: words, gestures, attitudes. Sadness was a sign of spiritual confusion, joy a sign of individualism, [while] an indecisive point of view indicated a petty bourgeois individualism."[73]

In April, 1973, the final victory of Angkar over Lon Nol's army and its American backers gave its leaders a sense of invincibility. It was enhanced by the *Mayaguez* incident, when Angkar's soldiers fought to a draw with the U.S Marines. A few months after the fall of Phnom Penh, Pol Pot declared — uncharacteristically for a convinced Communist — that this achievement "is believed to be the work of God, for it is too imposing for mere humans."[74] Haing Ngor elaborates:

> The myth of defeating the Americans was something that the Khmer Rouge repeated over and over again until they believed it. They needed to believe in it, because it was the basis of their programs to develop the country. To them, defeating a superpower proved that they, the Khmer Rouge, were superior beings, like supermen. If they had defeated the largest superpower in the world, they were capable of anything. Nothing could stop them. Nothing could stand in their way. Not logic. Not common sense. Not even the laws of physics.[75]

This analysis of the state of mind of the Angkar leaders is valid, even though their military triumph over the U.S. was nonetheless real.

Angkar demanded absolute, mindless obedience from the people. At long indoctrination meetings held after work, cadres emphasized that people were not supposed to think.[76] Pin Yathay quotes one of their cadres:

> "You see the ox, comrades. Admire him! He eats where we command him to eat. If we let him graze on this field, he eats. If we take him to another field where there is not enough grass, he grazes all the same. He cannot move about, he is supervised. When we tell him to pull the plough, he pulls it. He never thinks of his wife or his children."[77]

While Angkar did not totally abolish the family, its role was diminished. In some areas, beginning in 1977, children were taken away from their parents and put to work.[78] They were not only used for farm labor — common enough in underdeveloped nations — but also, as young as age seven, for work on the railroad.[79] Many Angkar soldiers were pre-adolescents.[80] A Yugoslav television team, the only foreigners able to film what they saw in Democratic Kampuchea, showed a youngster of perhaps ten working as first mate on a coastal fishing vessel.

Even as the people were told that "hate was evil and had no place in the new society,"[81] the speeches of the Angkar leaders were filled with references to vengeance and blood.[82] Not many Cambodians actually heard these speeches, but the crude "cultural" performances put on by traveling troupes, the only entertainment permitted, had the same theme.

> At the end of the last dance all the costumed cadre, male and female, formed a single line and shouted "blood avenges blood!" at the top of their lungs. Both times when they said the word "blood" they pounded their chests with their clenched fists, and when they shouted "avenges" they brought their arms out straight like a Nazi salute, except with a clenched fist instead of an open hand.[83]

The Democratic Kampuchea national anthem, frequently heard throughout the country under Angkar, had a similar motif:

> The red, red blood splatters the cities and plains of the Cambodian fatherland,
> The sublime blood of the workers and peasants,
> The blood of revolutionary combatants of both sexes.
> The blood spills out into great indignation and a resolute urge to fight.
> April 17, that day under the revolutionary flag,
> The blood certainly liberates us from slavery.[84]

The identification of "blood" with "indignation" and the "urge to fight" points to the repressed anger that was the cause of Angkar's paranoia, and which is often symbolized by imagery of blood.

Angkar's rule was harsher on the non–Khmer minorities than on the Khmers. The Chams — a largely Muslim Malayo-Polynesian people, who made up perhaps three percent of Cambodia's population — were categorized as unreliable solely by virtue of their ethnic origin, and officially lumped together with the mistrusted urban evacuees.[85] Their villages were all dispersed[86]; their language was forbidden, even in private; and they were compelled to eat pork and work in pigsties to prove that they had abandoned their religion.[87] Ben Kiernan estimated that the Chams lost over one third of their number during the Angkar years.[88]

In earlier times, the Chams had enjoyed the reputation of being specialists in black magic and love potions.[89] It would be tempting to equate the Khmer Rouge persecution of the Chams with Nazi persecution of the Gypsies, but this could be misleading. The Chams appear to have suffered more under Angkar for three reasons: first, they spoke a different language from the Khmers, which would have made it harder for them to be kept under surveillance (as with the local Chinese and Vietnamese); second, they remained loyal to their Muslim religion, one key to their distinctive identity; and third, Angkar's mnemonist "return to the past" evoked ancient memories of the wars between the Khmers and the Cham kingdom.[90]

Thais, Lao, and Shans, all closely related, made up about one percent of Cambodia's population. The Thais, about 40,000, lived in Koh Kong province along the coast; many of them backed a local leftist guerrilla movement that opposed both the Lon Nol regime and Angkar, and they were all deported once Angkar came to power. Their ultimate fate is unknown.[91] The 2,000 Shans, immigrants from Burma who worked as gem miners near the Thai border, nearly all vanished.[92] Lao, in the north, were also apparently singled out for particularly harsh treatment.[93]

Angkar's policy toward the tribal peoples was more ambivalent. A number of these groups lived in the sparsely-populated Northeast, which was one of the first areas where Communist guerrillas had become active during the 1960s. Others, such as the Kuoy and Pear, were scattered throughout the country, living in close proximity to Khmer villages; these two largely indistinguishable groups may have been the descendants of untouchable castes in Hindu times. Many of the Kuoy and Pear were recruited into the Khmer Rouge.[94] Pol Pot himself employed Jarai bodyguards from the northeast, and the Jarai language, although related to Cham, was never banned.[95]

Ethnic Vietnamese who remained in the country after Lon Nol's massacres and expulsions in the early 1970s were particularly hard hit by Angkar's purges, including the one that decimated the East Zone in 1978.[96] The Vietnamese in Cambodia had been active in the Communist cause since French colonial times, and Vietnamese immigrant workers on the rubber plantations had promoted Marxism and inter-ethnic solidarity among their Khmer fellow workers. All Cambodians with any links to Vietnam became suspect according to Angkar's tortured logic once Vietnam had been identified as Democratic Kampuchea's main enemy in 1977. Angkar turned on Khmers with Vietnamese wives, Khmers who were half–Vietnamese, Khmer Krom who had resettled in Cambodia, and even Khmers who merely knew how to speak Vietnamese. Eventually, this hysteria spread to the entire population of the Eastern Zone, where the Communist movement had the strongest links to Vietnam.

While the Chinese were spared similar annihilation, this was primarily because of

Angkar's reliance on Peking for military and diplomatic support; ethnic Chinese still had to put up with racist taunts by darker-complexioned Angkar cadres, in addition to all the other hardships of life in Democratic Kampuchea.[97] Meanwhile, the Indian community, totaling only about 2,000, was completely wiped out. The few Europeans remaining after 1975 were also killed. Angkar seemed to be focusing its rage on anyone who was different from the poor-peasant "Original Khmer" norm it was trying to impose on the entire country.

The fate of intellectuals under Angkar is well known; defined as anyone with even a high school education, they were regarded as contaminated by the West, and were killed off, although some survived by hiding their backgrounds. Ironically, leftist intellectuals were less likely to do so, and consequently had a lower survival rate.[98]

Angkar's Leadership

Pol Pot and his colleagues governed from a compound in Phnom Penh, whose population had been reduced to about 20,000. The remaining two million had been deported and scattered throughout the rural areas, some of which were ill-prepared to receive them. Perhaps three quarters of these two million were not long-term residents of Phnom Penh, but refugees who had only arrived there in the previous five years; of the city's pre-war population of 750,000, many — particularly Vietnamese, but also the educated Khmer elite — had already been expelled or had fled before Phnom Penh's fall. Even some of the other permanent residents were only a generation or less removed from the countryside. Yet all were considered enemies by Pol Pot, and were forced to live on the starvation rations which Angkar provided them.

Angkar's small group of top leaders, known as *Angkar Loeu* ("Higher Organization") remained relatively isolated from the horrors being committed in their name.

> [They] were a dour, puritanical group of people who were rarely seen drinking alcohol, although they offered it to guests; it is said they never drank in private. Very few smoked cigarettes. They adopted an eerie habit of speaking so softly in conversation that they could barely be heard. They seemed to pride themselves on maintaining an outward appearance of calm — walking, talking, gesturing slowly and deliberate. They smiled but rarely laughed.[99]

Pol Pot himself, whose parents were wealthy landowners,[100] came from a strongly traditionalist part of Kompong Thom province, north of the capital, and belonged to the Thommayut sect of Theravada Buddhism. Only about four percent of the Khmers belonged to this sect, although that included the royal court; nearly all of the other Khmers belonged to the less strict Mohanikay sect.[101] Pol Pot spent much of his youth in a Thommayut pagoda, and later attended a Catholic school. He even lived for a while at the court,[102] where he was sexually abused by the young concubines of the elderly king.[103] Incredibly, in light of his horrendous deeds, acquaintances described him as "soft-spoken, courteous, friendly, and kind."[104] Elizabeth Becker, who interviewed him in Phnom Penh shortly before the fall of his regime, wrote: "[N]ot once, during a violent attack on Vietnam and the Soviet Union, did Pol Pot raise his voice or slam his fist on the arm of his chair."[105] His official biography "closes with the singular statement that he likes to live in the 'calm,' a profoundly Buddhist notion."[106]

Angkar's brutalities against the people began even before the fall of Phnom Penh, and increased with time. At first, the victims were individuals connected in some way with the previous regime. Later, ethnic Vietnamese, as well as other minorities, were singled out for persecution, along with anyone suspected of being an intellectual—i.e., influenced by foreign ideas. People who violated the strict regulations of Angkar, or complained about the bad conditions, risked nearly certain death. By 1976, Angkar began to turn on its own cadres. There were massive bloodbaths, even by the brutal standards of Angkar, in two of the eight zones into which the country had been divided. Troops from the Southwest Zone were first brought into the Northwest, and then into the East, to slaughter the local leadership, along with anyone else who appeared remotely suspect.[107]

There was enough food during the first year of Democratic Kampuchea—hoarded rice confiscated from the wealthy helped—but this soon changed. Decreased rations caused the government to lose support among its "base people," the inhabitants of the rural areas captured at the onset of the civil war from Lon Nol, leaving it with little following outside its own armed forces. The cause of the food shortage, which eventually reached famine proportions, was twofold: first, Angkar was selling the country's rice to China and elsewhere, largely in exchange for arms and military equipment, with which to fight the Vietnamese[108]; and second, labor was taken out of the rice paddies to build massive irrigation works. These dams and canals were poorly constructed, and were ultimately largely useless. The food shortage led to increased dissent, which led to more widespread killings. Epidemics of cholera resulted because of Angkar's habit of dumping the bodies of its victims into ponds and streams. Medical care for the epidemic victims was almost non-existent.

By 1977, relations with Vietnam had deteriorated sharply, and surviving East Zone cadres were taking refuge in Vietnam. Pol Pot targeted Vietnam largely because of his fear of internal dissent, a pattern we can see with other tyrannies that start suicidal wars, such as Idi Amin's Uganda, militarist Argentina, and Yahya Khan's Pakistan. The conflict began because Pol Pot claimed large amounts of Vietnamese territory, and Cambodia initiated nearly all of the armed clashes. "Far from just wanting to be left alone," write two Australian scholars, Pol Pot's regime "was spoiling for a fight with Vietnam."[109] Indicative of his intentions was a 1978 speech on Radio Phnom Penh, in which he called on each Cambodian to kill 30 Vietnamese. "We need only two million troops to crush the 50 million Vietnamese and we will still have six million Cambodians left."[110] Children, including girls, were drafted as soldiers.[111]

The 1979 war between Vietnam and Democratic Kampuchea was not caused by any centuries-old enmity, despite Angkar's repeated depiction of Vietnam as the "historical enemy," and its frequent use of the derogatory epithet *yuon* in referring to Vietnamese.[112] In its fight with Vietnam, Pol Pot's Cambodia ended up aligning itself with its other "historical enemy" Thailand—not to mention Thailand's ally, the United States, which had bombed Cambodia's countryside for years. Meanwhile, Cambodians who fled to Vietnam and rallied behind the National Salvation Front of Heng Samrin and Hun Sen were welcomed as liberators when they returned alongside the Vietnamese troops.[113] By 1980, Vietnamese troops could be seen "wandering around unarmed" in small groups throughout Cambodia,[114] indicating that they did not feel particularly threatened by their supposed enemies.

Driven from Cambodia, Angkar took refuge in Thailand and attempted to reinvent itself as a nationalist resistance movement against the Vietnamese and the new pro–Vietnamese government. They allied with exiled Royalists led by Sihanouk, and a small party of ex–Lon Nol supporters. This improbable alliance eventually fell apart, and most of its leaders — including some top Angkar figures — returned to Cambodia to enter politics, or live as private citizens. Only the Royalists and the Cambodian People's Party — representing the pro–Vietnamese former Communists — had any popular support. An Angkar remnant held out for another decade, protected by Thailand. Ta Mok, the Southwest Zone's commander and easily the most brutal of Pol Pot's satraps, played a major role in this rump movement. Ta Mok and Pol Pot eventually had a falling out, leading to the latter's arrest and show trial. Pol Pot died in 1998 of natural causes, while under arrest.[115]

Victory and Self-Destruction

From a psychohistorical perspective, the unprecedented self-destructiveness of the Angkar regime stemmed from identification with the aggressor — the United States — a process which is common among those who were traumatized as children by physical or sexual abuse. There is little evidence of such abuse in rural Khmer families, but the fact that boys are sent to the local Buddhist temples to be raised by supposedly celibate monks gives us a clue as to the origin of the nation's collective pathology. In a Khmer adage, the parent says to the monk: "I give you my whole child. Teach him everything you know. You set the rules. Whatever you do is up to you. I need only the skin and bones."[116]

Angkar's brutality was not generally accompanied by the kind of psychosexual sadism associated with the Nazis. There seemed to be little tendency to humiliate the victims. The difference between the two tyrannies probably resulted from the fact that Cambodia's small and incompetent army never exercised any influence over the country's civic culture, in sharp contrast to Germany. Few Khmer fathers were ever traumatized by having served in their country's military.

After 1975, Angkar saw itself, not without justification, as having scored an unprecedented historical victory over the United States. This experience proved to be as difficult for the Khmers to assimilate as the unexpected defeat in 1918 was for the Germans. Megalomania was one result. An Angkar document declares: "The standard of the revolution of April 17, 1975, raised by Comrade Pol Pot, is brilliant red, full of determination, wonderfully firm and wonderfully clear-sighted. The whole world admires us, sings our praises and learns from us."[117] Suddenly, a nation which had long feared annihilation at the hands of its two larger neighbors, Vietnam and Thailand, found itself in the role of victor over the most powerful country in the world.

This unanticipated success seems to have evoked feelings of anxiety among the Khmer, causing them to identify unconsciously with the United States, even as their leaders reviled it openly for its past and present actions toward Cambodia. Increasingly, Vietnam — not anti–Communist Thailand or the United States — was portrayed as Democratic Kampuchea's main enemy. The Khmer Rouge bloodbath resembled the Stalinist terror in the USSR, as revolutionaries were exterminated in the name of the revolution.

Pol Pot's expansionist ambitions were the opposite of Sihanouk's concerns that Cambodia's territory would be whittled away by its more powerful neighbors. His xenophobic persecution of ethnic minorities paralleled that of his enemy, Lon Nol, although it went much further. Vietnamese were singled out because of their long involvement with the revolutionary movement throughout Indochina. Local Chinese were hated for much the same reason, as many had been active supporters of Mao during Sihanouk's time.

The fact that groups such as the Kuoy and Pear were not persecuted, and even appear to have been favored by Angkar, gives us a possible insight into the mentality of the Angkar leadership. It is likely that the Kuoy and Pear were perceived as "pure" Khmer, untouched by either Buddhist or Western civilization. Democratic Kampuchea's tolerance of these two groups — in contrast to their persecution of so many others — illustrates the atavistic nature of its "return to the past."

Cambodia's self-destruction was undoubtedly a major factor in the downfall of Communism, which began in the 1980s, as the realization of what a "classless society" might mean spread throughout the USSR and Eastern Europe. Ironically, Cambodia's torment probably stemmed less from the shortcomings of Marxist ideology than from the repression of anger taught by the Buddhist religion. As elsewhere, catastrophes that appear to be political in nature actually have their origins in the psychological realm.

8

China

Mao's Cultural Revolution
as Reaction Formation

What happened in China during Mao Zedong's "Great Proletarian Cultural Revolution," from the opening shots in late 1965 until the fall of the Gang of Four in 1976, defies conventional description. Beginning ostensibly as a literary debate,[1] the Cultural Revolution soon turned into a mass movement that paralyzed the country with near-anarchy for two years, and stunted its economic and intellectual development for several years after that. Anywhere from 400,000 to 1,000,000 people may have been killed,[2] and from 1966 to 1969 there was "a major decline in clear evidence on virtually every economic 'front.'"[3] Universities were closed for more than five years,[4] and in the secondary schools, genuine education was replaced by mindless sloganeering.[5]

In 1958, Mao issued a famous quote:

> China's 600 million people have two remarkable peculiarities; they are, first of all, poor, and secondly, blank.... A clean sheet of paper has no blotches, and so the newest and most beautiful pictures can be painted on it.[6]

Danish journalist Hans Grandqvist echoes this sentiment when he argues, along with other leftists, that the Chinese Cultural Revolution was "the most extreme experiment in utopianism ever attempted, one based on the assumption that man can be re-educated to learn both self-discipline and unselfishness."[7] On the other hand, the Cultural Revolution has also been presented — by, among others, Mao's private physician, Li Zhisui, who observed the events from the inside — as nothing more than a cynical power struggle between Mao and his rivals, or his wife Jiang Qing and hers, with the millions of Red Guards and "Revolutionary Rebel Workers" playing the part of ignorant pawns.

Neither viewpoint does justice to the complex events that convulsed the world's most populous nation for a decade. While China's President Liu Shaoqi became the chief target of the Maoist radicals, ultimately dying of cruel neglect in his hospital bed, he had long been an ally of Mao, siding with him in disputes with the Party leadership during the 1920s,[8] and even taking the lead in the earliest days of the Cultural Revolution. Until early 1967, in fact, Mao protected Liu from Red Guard attacks.[9] The leftist radicals who toppled him ultimately fell out among themselves, with Jiang Qing and Mao's security chief Kang Sheng lining up against Party ideologue Chen Boda and Mao's designated successor,

Marshal Lin Biao. The Cultural Revolution was not a single struggle, but a host of conflicts, with different battles being fought in the schools, in the factories, and at the provincial and national level. And at least some of Mao's supposedly mindless followers had agendas of their own; hence their suppression by the army after 1969.

If the Cultural Revolution was an experiment in utopianism, it would have to be regarded as one of history's most monumental failures. "We were the most miserable, most unfortunate generation in China's history," stated one former Red Guard after it was all over. "Our ideals had been destroyed."[10] Presented as a rebellion against the restoration of capitalism, the Cultural Revolution virtually restored feudalism, as servile adulation of "the Great Helmsman" called to mind the Emperor-worship of past dynasties. Mao's death in 1976 was followed by the rise to power of Deng Xiaoping, purged twice before as a "capitalist-roader." Under Deng, agriculture was decollectivized, private capital and foreign investment — even from Taiwan — was introduced, and the goal of world revolution was totally abandoned, as symbolized by the 1979 attack on Vietnam. Mao himself set the stage for this "Great Leap Backward," repudiating the Red Guards, turning on once-trusted radical allies, and welcoming President Richard Nixon to Beijing even as the United States continued its war against Vietnam.

Losing the Faith

For the first part of the fifteen-year period between the final Communist victory over the Kuomintang (KMT) in 1950 and the outbreak of the Cultural Revolution, China was allied to the USSR, particularly during the conflict with the United States in Korea. The Hungarian uprising in 1956 seems to have created doubts in Mao's mind about the future of socialism. While Mao regarded events in Eastern Europe as evidence that socialism could be reversed, his Soviet counterparts simply blamed the unrest on the sinister machinations of the CIA. Russian tanks in Budapest and Prague, and Red Guard rampages in the streets of Beijing and Shanghai, represented alternate responses of the two Communist powers to the same ideological threat.

By the early 1960s, Mao "became increasingly obsessed with the possibility of historical regression."[11] The Sino-Soviet ideological dispute was underway by then, focusing on the question of whether there could be peaceful coexistence with the West and peaceful transition from capitalism to socialism, as the Soviets maintained, or whether armed struggle against imperialism was the only effective strategy, as Mao held. Most Communist parties sided with the Soviets, but China picked up support from Albania, North Korea, the massive Indonesian Communist Party, and some smaller parties and dissident factions elsewhere. Both Cuba and North Vietnam tried to remain neutral at the beginning.

The Chinese Communists believed that China's own peasant-based revolution could be duplicated throughout the less-developed regions of the world. Indeed, by the early 1960s, armed insurrections were already underway in a number of countries in Asia, Africa and Latin America. But by mid-decade, the tide had begun to turn. Left-wing governments were toppled in Syria, Iraq, Algeria, Indonesia, Ghana and Sri Lanka; the Indonesian Communist Party was destroyed in a massive bloodbath; radical insurgencies were smashed in Peru, the Dominican Republic, and the Congo. An Afro-Asian conference scheduled for Algiers was cancelled, to China's chagrin, and several African states broke relations with

Beijing. Worst of all, the United States was intervening massively in South Vietnam, while continuing to base troops in South Korea, Taiwan, the Philippines, and Thailand, posing a serious threat to China.

Few, if any, scholars have paid attention to the connection between these foreign setbacks and the outbreak of the Cultural Revolution — in fact, some have denied it explicitly[12] — but that may be because social scientists do not generally look at political events in a psychological context. The external setbacks caused the Chinese Communists to experience what is known as *cognitive dissonance*, a major discrepancy between what their ideology taught them to expect, and what they actually saw happening. The paranoid episodes that followed were similar in origin, if not expression, to the United States' experience a decade earlier with McCarthyism in the wake of Communist victories in the Far East and Eastern Europe. Rather than re-examine their expectations, people took the route of accusing their leaders of being in league with the enemy.

The American involvement in Vietnam posed a threat to China, as well as to the Communist movement in general. The logical move for China was to end its ideological dispute with the USSR for the sake of Communist unity, but that would have clearly meant the end of Mao's leadership of the Chinese Communist Party (CCP), since he had been so strongly identified with the critique of Soviet ideology. From 1964 on, Mao was concerned that his colleagues would toss him aside as Khrushchev had been in the Soviet Union.[13]

Mao's response to this dilemma was to extend his campaign against Soviet "revisionism" to his opponents in the CCP leadership. He termed them "capitalist roaders," defined as those who relied on expertise to develop China, rather than ideological commitment.[14] Mao wanted the Chinese to be "red" rather than "expert," and there was to be no middle ground. The problem, of course, was that it was impossible to pilot a jet, perform surgery, or run a factory with ideology alone; yet along with expertise comes the class division between those who hold it and those who don't.

In the spring of 1966, Mao and his allies made the curious claim that "since the founding of our People's Republic ... we have been under the dictatorship of a sinister anti-party and anti-socialist line which is diametrically opposed to Chairman Mao's Thought."[15] Echoing the belief of some Americans that their own government was controlled by "the Communist conspiracy" throughout the Cold War, this broadside set the stage for attacks on everyone in authority from high school teachers and low-level CCP cadres to the head of state. America was no longer the chief enemy, but rather "the persons in authority taking the capitalist road." A Chinese film about Vietnam from that period demonstrated the transition from one target to the other. "Now the imperialists are invading Vietnam," the film's narration began. "At the same time they are cooperating with the class enemies in our country. The class enemies who daydream of taking advantage of the Cultural Revolution to overthrow our government. We must watch out."[16]

Although triggered by events in Vietnam and elsewhere, the Cultural Revolution was, psychohistorically, an expression of the buried feeling of "I am angry at someone powerful," displaced from the authoritarian father of the Chinese family to a somewhat ill-defined group of "capitalist-roaders." Liu and Mao were not on the same wavelength when it came to their attitudes toward authority. Not the most filial of sons in his own youth, Mao blamed Confucianism — with some justification — for China's "slave mentality,"[17] whereas Liu, in his book *How to Be a Good Communist*, made favorable references to the ancient sage's teachings.[18]

At the beginning, teachers and school administrators came under attack, primarily at the hands of the children of CCP cadres,[19] a privileged group. The educational system had improved since the revolution, with corporal punishment formally abolished,[20] but it was still heavily dependent on rote learning. In the elementary and middle schools, children were identified by the class of their parents. At the top were the cadres' children, with the military cadres forming a distinct sub-group. Next came the children of workers, peasants, rank-and-file soldiers, and revolutionary martyrs. Below them were the intermediate classes — the intelligentsia, plus groups like street peddlers and self-employed artisans. At the bottom were the children of the "bad classes" — landlords, rich peasants, capitalists and former KMT officials. While the cadres' children monopolized the first Red Guard units,[21] students from intellectual families were also eager to join. "[M]any people could feel their initiative was stifled," said one such student about the school system before the Cultural Revolution. "I believe this was the thing people were most angry about."[22]

Anita Chan's research indicates that the cadres' children were generally involved in the "conservative" Red Guard units, which focused on attacking the "bad classes," along with their own teachers and school administrators, and generally defended the Communist Party. The worker and peasant children also tended to join the conservatives, while the intelligentsia, and to a lesser degree the other intermediate groups, were more often found among the "revolutionary rebels." The children from "bad classes" generally stayed out of the conflict, although some joined the rebels.[23] In the colleges, on the other hand, there were very few "bad classes," who were rarely admitted to begin with. Here, the "conservative" cadres' children fought against the "rebel" children of the intelligentsia, while the workers and peasants — brought into higher education through a form of affirmative action — simply went home when the fighting broke out.

Teachers were the first to be attacked by the Red Guard students, followed by CCP cadres, who had been brought in as "work teams" in an attempt to calm things down. This shift brought in the students from the pre-revolution elite families as a new wave of Red Guards. These new "revolutionary rebel" Red Guards clashed with the older Red Guard groups, and fighting broke out on secondary school and university campuses all over the country. This was followed by the spread of the violence to the cities, leading to civil war situations in many areas. The army was then brought in to arbitrate, but this inevitably led to political divisions within the army, as different units found themselves allied with different Red Guard factions. In addition, some Red Guard units accused army leaders of "following the capitalist road." At each stage, leaders at the center served as enablers, only to be denounced as enemies once they had achieved power. Beijing Mayor Peng Zhen, President Liu Shaoqi, regional CCP boss Dao Zhu, Defense Minister Lin Biao, and Mao's wife Jiang Qing all led the Cultural Revolution at some point, only to be overthrown shortly afterwards — in the last case, just after Mao's death.

It is not surprising that large numbers of ordinary Chinese students and workers should have taken the initiative during the turmoil. This had happened during collectivization, when the peasants — encouraged by Mao — raced ahead of the Party planners[24]; and during the Great Leap Forward, the peasants spontaneously attempted to turn their backward villages into centers of industry.

Overall, the results of the Great Leap were disastrous. This was officially blamed on widespread droughts and floods, and to some degree on the sudden withdrawal of Soviet aid as a result of the Moscow-Beijing rift, which brought a halt to a number of key projects. But the famine that killed millions of Chinese and created what Western China-watchers termed a "Downward Spiral" was primarily due to the reassignment of over 38 million peasants from farming to steel production.[25] This grandiose attempt to build "backyard furnaces" in every Chinese village bore all the earmarks of a primitive potlatch, as houses and trees were burned to provide fuel for furnaces that produced only useless, low-grade steel.[26] Ludicrously, household implements, bed-frames and doorknobs were used as raw material to make the worthless ingots.[27] Finished goods were being transformed back into the raw steel from which they were originally made, so that the total amount of steel produced looked good on paper. The wastage of manpower and electric power undermined agriculture and light industry, causing a three-year economic slump and a 40–45 percent drop in industrial production between 1960 and 1962.[28] Some peasants were heard rationalizing this, saying "It is better to waste the Communist fields than to plow a capitalist land."[29]

This economic collapse was an example of *growth panic*, resulting from the intensive development of previous years. Before 1957, Chinese industry had been growing at the phenomenal rate of nearly 20 percent a year.[30] As in oil-rich Iran under the Shah, rapid economic growth created feelings of unease — related to fear of surpassing the achievements of one's parents — which were resolved by the mass destruction of wealth. In China, this took the form of the excesses of the Great Leap, and the Cultural Revolution; in Iran, the country's wealth was sacrificed in the eight-year war with Iraq.

In addition to the fear of surpassing one's parents, increased wealth also created greater social inequality, as some Chinese became better educated and were able to command higher salaries. Maoism unsuccessfully attempted to retain social equality in the context of economic development and urbanization. "Mao's program," according to Maurice Meisner, "...envisioned the development and application of modern science and technology without professional scientists and technocrats,"[31] an impossible task. At the ideological level, the Cultural Revolution was a struggle between those who were willing to abandon equality for the sake of development, and those who — like Mao — preferred to forego development for the sake of equality.

The Beginnings of the Cultural Revolution

The Cultural Revolution was clearly not a conflict between Communism and capitalism. Both Mao Zedong and Liu Shaoqi were ardent Communists, notwithstanding Lin Biao's insistence that Liu was actually a "hidden traitor and scab" as far back as the early 1920s,[32] something that appears to have escaped Mao's notice for decades. While Mao's supporters were ardent devotees of the cult of personality, they were paradoxically the more democratic of the two camps in some important respects. Countless uncensored Red Guard newspapers appeared during the Cultural Revolution,[33] eagerly read by many until they were suppressed a year and a half later.[34] Hong Yung Lee indicates that, at least in Guangdong province, the large majority of these publications were issued by the radicals.[35] The Red Guards "freely elected their leaders, who were constantly subject to recall by those who had elected them,"[36] although in practice, dissidents were far more likely to defect to rival factions than to seek to replace their own leaders. Significantly, the first big-character poster, at Beijing University, demanded nothing more than the freedom to discuss a controversial play, *Hai Jui Dismissed from Office*, which appeared to some to be an allegorical attack on Mao.[37] This is not to deny that the Red Guards quickly descended to thuggery, but the "conservative" faction, backed by Liu and the CCP bureaucracy, were at least as bad as their opponents in this regard.[38]

Mao's greatest illusion was his belief that the "masses" were socially homogenous in China's socialist society. In fact, significant demographic cleavages existed among both the students and workers, accounting for much of the factionalism. Psychologically, everyone was expressing the same feelings of anger against someone they felt inferior to, but while some were directing it against the old upper classes dispossessed by the Communist victory, others were directing it against the Communist cadres, the so-called "power holders."

Ross Terrill's 1984 biography of Jiang Qing raises the question of to what degree she was responsible for the turmoil. Born in a small city in Shandong province, Jiang Qing became an actress on stage and screen in Shanghai. Her background was humble; her parents were divorced, and her mother worked as a servant, offering a close parallel to two other well-known first ladies of the twentieth century, Eva Perón and Imelda Marcos. She left Shanghai for Mao's base in Yenan in 1937, and attracted the Chairman's notice, becoming his fourth wife in 1939. Her marriage to Mao was approved by three other senior CCP leaders — army chief Zhu Deh, Zhou Enlai, and Liu Shaoqi — but only on condition that the former actress not engage in political activity for 30 years.[39]

Jiang Qing's adult life can be seen as an unsuccessful struggle to fit in with her surroundings. In the Shanghai theater world, she was regarded as an unsophisticated provincial, whereas in Yenan, her "bourgeois" Shanghai background made her equally suspect. Beyond that, she was a woman in a world where women were generally discounted. Jiang Qing never accepted such limitations for herself. A determined revolutionary, she tried to bend the world to her will, but ultimately failed.

During 1965, Jiang Qing — still officially prohibited from taking part in politics — involved herself in the revision of a theatrical piece being performed in Shanghai, *Taking Tiger Mountain by Strategy*. The story hinged on a heroic Communist officer who infiltrates a bandit gang in northeast China in 1946. Jiang Qing's revisions made the villains more villainous, the hero more heroic, and the entire story more melodramatic, if perhaps less realistic.[40] But her hopes of reforming traditional Chinese opera brought her into conflict with Beijing Mayor Peng Zhen, patron of playwright Wu Han who had authored the controversial *Hai Jui* play.[41] Peng, regarded as being on the far left of the CCP, had — along with Deng Xiaoping — played a major role in the Chinese denunciation of "Soviet revisionism."[42] At the onset of the Cultural Revolution, Peng headed a "Group of Five" which was supposed to direct it.[43] He had no sympathy with Jiang Qing's plans to tinker with traditional Chinese works for the sake of political correctness.

Another member of the Group of Five was Kang Sheng, Mao's security chief at the time. Kang was also a longtime associate of Jiang Qing, and coincidentally a native of her home town.[44] Educated in the USSR and trained by the NKVD,[45] Kang "enthusiastically cooperated with the NKVD in the hunt for mostly imaginary traitors among Chinese émigrés."[46] He directed the 1942 "rectification movement" against intellectuals who had gone to the Yenan guerrilla base to resist the Japanese.[47] He may have also assisted Mao against the "Returned Students Clique," made up of other Soviet-trained Chinese Communists.[48] He vouched for Jiang Qing's loyalty to the Communist cause during her Shanghai period.[49]

Kang Sheng disappeared from public life for many years after the Communist victory, and was reportedly suffering from mental illness.[50]

Mayor Peng's downfall was one of the many odd turns taken by the Cultural Revolution. In 1964, Peng permitted young people from "bourgeois" families to enter the Young Communist League.[51] His emphasis on performance, rather than proletarian background, made it possible for these youngsters to aspire to good careers.[52] It also echoed later demands by Maoists to include children from suspect backgrounds in the Red Guards. But children from cadre and poor families resented Peng's move, since they had difficulty competing for the rare college admission slots with peers whose parents were better educated.[53] It should be kept in mind that one likely consequence of Peng's approach would be that the future leadership of People's China would come largely from families that had run things before the revolution. The Red Guard slogan of the early phase of the Cultural Revolution, "From a revolutionary father, a worthy son; from a reactionary father, a vile son!"[54] was originally directed against Peng Zhen's policies.[55] One wonders, incidentally, whether Mao himself would have passed such a test.

Liu might never have become the chief target of the Cultural Revolution had it not been for the presence of his daughter at Tsinghua University in Beijing, an elite technical school, and a hotbed of Red Guard activity. Not especially political herself, she became a leader of the "conservative" faction of the Red Guards, with the support of her mother, Wang Guangmei, a sophisticated woman who was herself the object of intense jealousy on the part of Jiang Qing. Using a pseudonym and operating in a virtual cloak-and-dagger milieu, Wang Guangmei struggled against the charismatic student leader Kuai Dafu, head of a far-left Red Guard group known as the Regiment.[56] Kuai was the best-known of the Cultural Revolution's student leaders, and became an ally of Jiang Qing and the Gang of Four.

At the beginning, the Red Guards were mostly children of CCP cadres. Officially the only youths permitted to join were the "five kinds of Red": children of workers, peasants, soldiers, cadres, and revolutionary martyrs.[57] To the CCP, political outlook was inherited on the male line,[58] like the Y chromosome. In practice, this meant that the early Red Guard recruits were primarily the offspring of government officials. During the first stage of the Cultural Revolution, Red Guard rage was directed against "bourgeois" teachers and administrators, some of whom did in fact have ties to the old ruling elite. In the name of destroying the "four olds"— old ideas, culture, customs, and habits[59] — religious edifices and monuments left over from bygone dynasties were singled out for destruction.[60]

These early Red Guard groups were known as the *baoshu pai*, or "Proletarian Revolutionaries." Permanently employed, unionized workers, particularly from the larger enterprises, also backed them, as did a number of leaders of the minority nationalities in the border regions. All of these groups felt that they had gained something from the Communist revolution — positions of power, better wages, access to higher education, or regional self-government. The *baoshu pai* were regarded as "conservative," although this term must be used, obviously, in a very relative sense.

Opposed to them were the "revolutionary rebels," or *zaofan pai*, who included youths from bourgeois backgrounds who had been excluded from the earlier Red Guard units.[61] Dating from late 1966,[62] the *zaofan pai* had Mao's support.[63] In the factories, many temporary, part-time and contract workers joined them.[64] They were endorsed by the Central

Cultural Revolution Group, a small clique of leaders close to Mao: Jiang Qing, his private secretary Chen Boda (editor of the Party organ *Red Flag*), Lin Biao (Defense Minister, Mao's appointed successor, and editor of *Quotations from Mao Zedong*), and the secretive Kang Sheng.[65] Kang and Chen disliked each other intensely, and fought at each meeting.[66]

Once the rebels had taken the initiative away from their rivals, the cult of personality around Mao soared to unheard-of heights. The CCP had previously been the sole arbiter of right and wrong, and with the Party now discredited as "bourgeois" and "revisionist," Mao was the only unimpeachable authority left. As a Red Guard anthem put it, "Sailing the Seas Depends on the Helmsman." The "seas," in this case, were the uncharted waters to the left of Communism.

In another popular song of the period, "A Lamp in Front of Chairman Mao's Window," god-like powers are attributed to the CCP leader: "Chairman Mao's magic brush waves the east wind / The wind blows and the sky turns red throughout."[67] A sympathetic Italian Communist visitor, speaking with two Red Guards, was told: "Our most memorable experience [was] when Mao met with the Red Guards on Tien An Men square. Mao's warm greetings filled us with tremendous pride and showed us the way to further struggle."

"What did Mao say to you?" asked their interviewer.

"He said 'Good day to you comrades,' and waved to us," came the reply.[68]

There was much imagery of rising, red suns in Red Guard sloganeering. "Chairman Mao is the red, red sun in our hearts," they were fond of chanting. Curiously, the image of the rising sun was closely associated in the Far East with the Japanese Army, which had devastated China for years during the 1930s and 1940s.

Along with the deification of Mao came the kind of paranoia familiar to Americans who remember the 1950s. China perceived itself as surrounded by menacing enemies, all working together, with only "the heroic people of Albania," a small and distant nation, standing by China's side. To the east were the "Kuomintang reactionaries" on Taiwan; to the south, the "American imperialists" occupying South Vietnam and threatening to march north; to the southwest, the "Indian expansionists"; and to the west and north, the "Soviet revisionists" and their Mongolian allies. It was true that these forces did more or less encircle China. But China had already given India a severe drubbing in 1961; the Soviets had no diplomatic relations with Taiwan; and the Americans favored Pakistan in its interminable quarrels with India, and additionally had their hands full in Vietnam even without China's involvement. Most bizarre of all was Kang Sheng's concern about "treasonous activity" in China's northeast by secret agents of hard-line Communist North Korea,[69] the one country on earth with the least reason to want to see the People's Republic of China destabilized.

Paranoia was by no means limited to the leadership. Students, apparently projecting their own repressed doubts about their country's direction, discovered "hidden messages" in periodicals — shadows which appeared to spell out praise of Chiang Kai-shek, red flags which fluttered in imperialist *west* winds instead of socialist *east* winds, a "missing" ear on a portrait of Mao which showed him with his head slightly turned.[70] Maoists in Shanghai found fault with the size of one newspaper headline, the color of the ink in which Mao's calligraphy was printed, and the omission of a few words from a quote by Lin Biao.[71] It was all, they suspected, part of a capitalist plot.

Much Red Guard activity was purely symbolic. Street names were changed. Red traffic lights meant "go," and green meant "stop." Long hair was prohibited, and pointed shoes and tight trousers were prohibited as "bourgeois"; ironically, right-wing dictatorships in Greece and Argentina attempted to stamp out the same things. Many Red Guards chose new names for themselves, such as "Revere Mao," "Toward the East," "Anti-Revisionist," and so on. This was no radical departure, since Chinese often picked new names for themselves at key points in their lives. But no one could keep track of all their friends' new names when so many adopted them at once, so things soon reverted to the status quo ante.[72] Oddly, for a mass movement that proposed to change the world, the Red Guards seem to have spent a good deal of time playing cards and mah-jongg, flying kites, sightseeing, and just plain loafing.

Red Guards by the millions went on *chuan-lien*, or "link-up," traveling to distant cities at government expense, where they attempted to provoke revolts against local CCP authorities, with varying degrees of success. If the residents supported the Red Guards, the local authorities were in trouble. But if the latter enjoyed the support of their constituents, they were still in trouble. The visiting Red Guards then swiftly concluded that they had discovered an "independent kingdom" where the sacred writ of Chairman Mao, as interpreted by themselves, did not run. The only safe course for the local cadres was to run the Red Guards out of town as quickly as possible. There were also cases where the local inhabitants had no idea what the youthful tourists were talking about. In the Turkic-speaking Muslim region of Xinjiang, Red Guards from Beijing stenciled Maoist slogans on the sides of buses, to spread the word among the masses. But since they were unfamiliar with the Arabic script of the local Uighur language, the slogans appeared in mirror writing.[73]

"Not once during the Cultural Revolution," notes journalist Stanley Karnow, "did Mao outline a clear-cut, practical program aimed at precise objectives. Instead, he exhorted his followers to destroy his opponents so that an undefined utopia might emerge at some unspecified point in the faraway future."[74]

Civil Wars

At the end of 1966, as he celebrated his 73rd birthday, Mao toasted "the unfolding of nationwide all-round civil war" with his closest friends and allies.[75] In fact, there were many civil wars raging in China over the next year or more, as rival factions fought bloody battles with manufactured or stolen weapons.

Aside from the Red Flag Army, composed of ex-soldiers, none of these factions operated nationwide.[76] Each college and high school had its own set of rival activists, some of them nothing but small cliques of mutual friends. From time to time, various groups achieved a semblance of unity, but it was generally short-lived. When the workers began getting involved, coalitions were formed that spanned whole cities and provinces. Beijing had its "Heaven" and "Earth" factions,[77] named, respectively, after the Aeronautical and Geological Institutes, whose students were drawn from different social strata. Each citywide faction contained Red Guard movements that were ideologically opposed to their faction's leadership; "revolutionary" groups found themselves allied with "conservative" coalitions, and vice-versa.

Canton saw the radical Red Flags (mostly from bourgeois or intermediate families) make war against the conservative East Winds (mostly from families of workers, soldiers and cadres).[78] In Wuhan, in central China, the conservative Million Heroes fought against the radical Workers General Headquarters.[79] In Shanghai, the short-lived Scarlet Guards, nearly a million strong,[80] clashed with another Workers General Headquarters, headed by Zhang Chunqiao, one of the "Gang of Four," and the head of the Shanghai propaganda department.[81] The Shanghai Workers General Headquarters, which actually ran the city for a number of years, was started by Beijing Red Guards, and attracted temporary and contract workers.[82]

There was evidently a sub-ethnic component to the conflict in Shanghai. China's largest city lies just to the south of the densely-populated province of Jiangsu, which is bisected by the lower Yangtze River. Inhabitants of northern Jiangsu are looked down upon as bumpkins by southern Jiangsu residents; the northerners made up a large portion of the recently arrived temporary and contract workers, while the southerners, whose villages were closer to Shanghai, were more established in the city, more likely to be employed on a permanent basis, and ultimately more willing to back the conservative forces.[83] Not surprisingly, once the Workers General Headquarters had taken over Shanghai, it came under attack from the *Lian Si*, a group supposedly even further to the left. Strong among workers at the Shanghai Diesel Engine Plant — who were likely to be long-established in the metropolis — it also included former KMT members.[84]

In the Fujian seaport of Amoy, the radical *Tsu Lien* fought against the more moderate *Ke Lien*.[85] In Guangxi, where the fighting left an estimated 50,000 dead, the conflict between the Grand Army and the Alliance Command had ethnic overtones, with the ultimately victorious latter group being led by a member of the local Zhuang minority.[86]

Some of the most "radical" activists appear to have had ulterior motives when they accused Communist cadres of being "capitalist roaders." The head of Shanghai's ultra-leftist Workers Third Headquarters was the son of a Guomindang policeman.[87] And Ken Ling, a key figure in Amoy's *Tsu Lien*, was a particularly strange candidate for a revolutionary leader. From his own account, he was contemptuous of his fellow Red Guards, even those in his own faction. His family background was upper class, his mother was a practicing Christian, and his older brother had been arrested prior to the Cultural Revolution as a counter-revolutionary. When Ling denounced Communists as "capitalist roaders," he admitted that he "did so to avenge my family — grandfather, father and uncles — who had lost their considerable property and jobs because of such scoundrels."[88] Eventually, he and his brother fled to Taiwan.

Another group of allies of the radical Red Guards were the cadres who had been purged from the CCP in previous campaigns against "rightists"; they were now able to turn the tables against their accusers. Some Tsinghua students concluded: "To find honest revolutionary cadre one had to seek out those who had been isolated, oppressed, and attacked in the years prior to 1966. In other words, only those known as rightists and counter-revolutionaries in the past had some reason to rate as revolutionaries today."[89]

Inner Mongolia — A Case Study

Some of the most intense conflict during the Cultural Revolution occurred in the Inner Mongolian Autonomous Region (IMAR),[90] a vast area south of the Mongolian People's

Republic, and containing a population, at the time, of about 13 million, barely 2 percent of China's total. Current figures indicate that nearly 80 percent of the IMAR's inhabitants are Han (as China's majority ethnic group are called) and perhaps 16 percent Mongol, with other groups making up the remainder.

Following the Communist revolution, Beijing — faced with the problem of feeding the country's immense population — settled Han farmers in Mongol-populated areas, provoking Mongol resistance.[91] The conflicts between the two ethnic groups was less over language or politics than between settled agriculturalists and nomadic pastoralists, not unlike Rwanda or Sudan's Darfur region. The local political boss in the IMAR was a Sinicized Mongol named Ulanfu, who only learned the Mongol language after obtaining his position. While Ulanfu was no Mongol nationalist, he opposed Han chauvinism, saying in 1951: "We must educate the Han Chinese ... to respect the equal right and opinion of national minorities and to eliminate the tendency toward the superior outlook of a big nationality."[92] Statements like these, which echo earlier remarks by V.I. Lenin, caused Red Guards to attack him as a pan–Mongol separatist.[93]

In 1966, in response to the Cultural Revolution, Ulanfu began purging radical leftists, nearly all of whom were Han.[94] As in Shanghai, those groups who felt they had gained from the Communist takeover supported the status quo, even as they waved red flags and echoed Maoist rhetoric, while those who felt they had lost supported the more radical factions. In the IMAR, despite some Han support for Mongol factions, the political division tended to reflect ethnicity.

In 1967, Ulanfu came under attack by the left, who accused him of "being the agent of China's Khrushchev [Liu Shaoqi] in Inner Mongolia." At the same time, he was also accused to "trying to establish an independent kingdom,"[95] indicating that he may have had some degree of popular support; the incompatibility of these two claims was overlooked. He was purged in mid–1966 after coming under attack at a meeting in Beijing of the North China CCP leadership.[96] His critics included Liu Shaoqi and Deng Xiaoping, who were themselves purged as counter-revolutionaries not long after. "In presenting nationality considerations as equal to or more important than class ones Ulanfu had betrayed the Centre's ideology."[97] One wonders why the same criterion was not applied to Lin Biao's widely-read tract, *Long Live the Victory of People War,* where the world's "countryside" was seen as defeating the "city," hardly a Marxist class analysis. Ulanfu remained a threat to the Cultural Revolution's leadership, with some of his followers, by early 1968, fighting with the Maoists under the name "Genghis Khan Combat Squads,"[98] an appellation not likely to endear them to either the Chinese or the Russians.

Ulanfu was ultimately replaced by Teng Haiping, an army officer who became the head of the IMAR Revolutionary Committee, formed in late 1967. Run by the military, it had only one Mongol on it.[99] Teng's political outlook may be seen from his declaration:

> Let us reverently send greetings together, greet the reddest, reddest sun in our hearts, the contemporary Lenin, the greatest, most glorious leader of the proletariat of the whole world, Chairman Mao, a long and prosperous life [*sic*].[100]

Under Teng's Revolutionary Committee, Han chauvinism — warned against by Ulanfu — became official policy. Maoist activists described Ulanfu as "Mongolian trash,"[101] and insisted that "there are no good Mongolians."[102] In 1968, the leading IMAR newspaper eliminated the few words in Mongol which had appeared on its front page.[103] The following year, the IMAR's territory was reduced substantially, although this decision was reversed a decade later.[104]

Under the direction of the Gang of Four, whose chief figure Jiang Qing had a low opinion of non–Han cultures, the Mongolian CCP cadres were nearly all charged with being members of the Inner Mongolian People's Party, supposedly a secret irredentist group; although there was such a group in existence before the Japanese invasion, there is no evidence that it survived in the People's Republic.[105] Persecution of alleged Mongol separatists during 1968 may have taken as many as 24,000 lives.[106] By 1969, Teng Haiqing was himself purged, charged with the same offenses as Ulanfu.[107] Ulanfu survived the Cultural Revolution, and was ultimately rehabilitated.

As elsewhere in China during the Cultural Revolution, the violence was motivated by feelings of inferiority, in this case directed against an ethnic group that had once — during Europe's early Middle Ages — dominated the whole of China, along with Russia and Iran. Another ethnic minority, the Manchus, had also ruled over the Chinese, and their domination did not end until the overthrow of their dynasty by Sun Yat-sen in 1911. But unlike the Mongols, with their kin in the pro–Soviet Mongolian People's Republic and Siberia, the Manchus had no compatriots living across China's frontiers; they had nearly all forgotten their original language; and they were too scattered and urbanized to be regarded as potential separatists. Finally, the Han-Mongol conflict during the Cultural Revolution appears to have been, in part, an outgrowth of the farmer-herdsman conflict of the early days of the People's Republic.

The End of the Cultural Revolution

By the middle of 1967, most of the "capitalist roaders" had been purged — although, under Deng Xiaoping's leadership following Mao's death, China actually did restore capitalism and enter a period of unprecedented economic expansion. The leaders at the center suddenly began expressing concern about the "May 16th Regiment," a very small group in Beijing which had denounced Zhou Enlai. An estimated 10 million people were investigated in the witch-hunt against this group, and about a third of them were arrested.[108] Most of them were not even aware of the group's existence, which supposedly indicated its particularly sinister nature.[109] Almost a tenth of the alleged members lived in Jiangsu province; they were probably members of the Red Guard faction known as the Excellents, who were closely allied with Kuai Dafu's Regiment. Kuai had instigated the Excellents to attack Army headquarters at Nanjing and take over the city, and sent several hundred experienced Regiment fighters to assist them.[110]

By 1970, an ailing Mao could count only three top CCP leaders left by his side: Premier Zhou Enlai, Jiang Qing, and his anointed successor Marshal Lin Biao. It seems evident that the first two had both played important roles during the turmoil, Jiang Qing pulling Mao in a more radical direction, and Zhou Enlai dragging him back. Lin Biao, however, clearly saw himself as a loyal acolyte, the most likely reason he was chosen as Mao's official heir. A brilliant general in his time, Lin was not particularly concerned with ideology.

Although Lin and Jiang Qing were both regarded as radicals, they were leaders of rival cliques. As early as 1967, there was a split between them, when the ultra-radical student leader Kuai Dafu disrupted a cultural performance put on by the army. When Lin denounced the action, he was supported by most other radical leaders, even including Kang Sheng.[111] Three years later, when the CCP leaders met at the Lushan resort, Lin Biao made some indirect criticisms of the Shanghai leader Zhang Chunqiao, who opposed making references to "Mao Zedong Thought" in the new party constitution. Jiang Qing and her allies were clearly in the minority on this matter.[112] But when she managed to speak to Mao alone, Jiang Qing convinced him that the criticisms of Zhang had really been directed against Mao and his Cultural Revolution.[113] Jiang Qing had previously used her influence to bring about the downfall of Liu Shaoqi and Dao Zhu,[114] and Lin Biao had apparently become her next target. One should keep in mind that if Mao had died at that time, Lin would have automatically become the new leader of China, while Jiang Qing would have lost all her power.

The official story of Lin Biao's death is that he attempted to stage a coup against Mao, but that it failed, and that he died — with his family — in an airplane crash while trying to flee to the USSR. There are a number of reasons to doubt this:

1. Lin showed no signs of power hunger, and was totally loyal to Mao;
2. It is improbable that Lin expected that his soldiers could be turned against Mao, when they all carried his Little Red Books in their pockets — with introductions by Lin Biao himself;
3. Lin would have undermined his own legitimacy, both at home and abroad, had he overthrown Mao in a coup;
4. A few years earlier, Lin had commanded the troops that defeated the Soviet Army in the clash on Chenpao (Damansky) island, and he could hardly have expected a warm welcome in the USSR if he had fled there;
5. Lin was a highly competent military leader, and is not likely to have bungled a coup so badly, when lesser military leaders throughout the world have been able to succeed;
6. The Chinese government made no mention of any alleged coup until two months after Lin's death,[115] indicating that the story of his coup had been fabricated;
7. In 1980–81, when the Gang of Four were on trial, no mention was made of any alleged coup by Lin, although the prosecution often lumped the two rival leftist factions together[116];
8. Unit 8341, responsible for protecting the top CCP leaders, "dispatched troops to the airport before Lin's car left his residence, but when Lin's car passed, nobody intercepted it"[117];
9. Finally, the Central Investigation Group, which drew up the documents claiming that Lin had headed a widespread conspiracy against Mao, was strongly influenced by his rival Jiang Qing.[118]

The indications are that the "coup" was actually staged by forces loyal to Jiang Qing, who had Lin and his family killed, planted the bodies on an airplane, and told the pilot to head in the direction of the USSR and then bail out. Photographs of the airplane wreckage seem inconsistent with the official story that the plane crashed when it ran out of fuel;

a trained pilot could have set the plane down without too much damage on Mongolia's flat and treeless terrain, but it was totally destroyed.[119]

By April 1976, the Gang of Four still appeared to be riding high. By then, the Red Guards had been shipped out of the cities, eliminating any threat from the left; Zhou Enlai, the Gang's most powerful opponent after Lin Biao's demise, had just died; Wang Hongwen, a youthful Shanghai radical and Gang of Four member, was in a position to replace the ailing Mao. When Zhou's death was mourned by crowds, Jiang Qing and her associates were able to mobilize two million followers to march through Beijing over three days, denouncing the mourners as counter-revolutionaries.[120] This was to be her swan song.

A few months later, Mao died. One month afterwards, moderate forces led by Hua Guofeng moved against his widow. With the arrest of a mere 30 people, the Gang of Four's faction disintegrated.[121] None of the millions of people who had supported it in Shanghai and Beijing made a move to defend it.

Serving the People?

The essence of the Cultural Revolution might be summed up in a tale told by an old woman to a sympathetic European visitor:

> I was supposed to participate in a revolutionary criticism group, but my husband was very ill. He cried, he didn't want me to leave him. I finally persuaded him to let me go, telling him that in the old society we could certainly not have lived to be seventy, we owed that to Mao.... When I got back to the house my husband could no longer speak. The next day he was dead.[122]

For all the rhetoric about "serving the people," ardent Maoists were oddly unenthusiastic about doing it in practice. The indifference of the old woman to her dying husband parallels China's stand on Vietnam during the 1960s — loud support in words for the lofty principle of unity, but in practice, only disruption of what might have been a very effective Communist-bloc solidarity against the United States.

Critiques of the Cultural Revolution have overlooked the psychohistorical dimension. It was a movement rooted in childhood anger against the father, whose authority was sanctioned by Confucianism. It was triggered by the military threat from the United States, and motivated by growing doubts about Communism in some segments of the population, not least Mao himself.[123] It was as much psychological in nature as political — a reaction formation which undermined Chinese Communism while using ultra-revolutionary rhetoric. Those who attempt to explain the Cultural Revolution exclusively in political terms are making much the same mistake as the Red Guards themselves, who reduced everything in their world to politics.

9

Sudan

Entitlement Fantasies and Occidentophobia

For more than fifty years, since it gained its independence from Great Britain in 1956, the African nation of Sudan has been the scene of racial oppression and genocide on a nearly unimaginable scale. As many as 2.5 million Sudanese have been slaughtered, about 7 percent of the population, and the killing is still going on in the western region of Darfur and elsewhere. The victims have included Muslims and non–Muslims, primarily the latter. The Dinka of the Bahr al-Ghazal region in the South have been the main victims, but they have not been alone. Incredibly, slavery continues to exist, even into the twenty-first century. And Sudan's rulers have allied themselves with the international terrorist network of Osama bin Laden, even after the attacks of September 11, 2001, forced them to feign cooperation with the United States.[1] Years before that, Sudanese diplomats in New York were actually involved in the first World Trade Center attack of February, 1993.[2]

Sudan is the largest nation in Africa in terms of territory, although only the sixth in population, with about 34 million inhabitants. It is extremely backward, even by African standards, notwithstanding its advantages of adequate land and water, a seacoast, and deposits of oil and gold. Until the oilfields went into production, the country's chief export was gum arabic, extracted from the acacia tree, which is an essential ingredient in our popular colas and other soft drinks. Sudan has a literacy rate of roughly 20 percent; life expectancy is just 46, and there is only one doctor for every 35,000 people.[3] Parts of the country have no roads, and railroads barely exist in the Southern region.

Like many other African nations, Sudan is ethnically diverse, with hundreds of languages belonging to three major families, and several religions. The Northerners, mostly Muslim, and the largely pagan Southerners have little knowledge of each other, and there is a long history of antagonism between them caused largely by the slave trade. At the same time, different groups *within* each region are often hostile to one another as well. The Dinka and Nuer, both Southern pastoralists, who speak related languages, are frequently at odds, and both groups are feared by the ethnically unrelated agricultural tribes who live even further south, such as the Azande and the Ankole. And the Arabs who live along the Nile River regard the nomadic Baggara Arabs with disdain, and vice versa.

Arabs, taken together, are the largest group in Sudan, but are often found living intermingled with other peoples. The Nubians, descendants of the ancient inhabitants, are found in the North, along the Nile; although not regarded as Arabs, they often speak Arabic. In some Nubian villages, the name "Arab" is given to anyone who owns camels.[4] The Beja, also known in antiquity, are nomads who live in the northeast, spilling over the border into Eritrea; their language is distantly related to Somali and several others spoken in the Horn of Africa. The Fur, Zaghawa, and Masalit — all Nilotic-speakers — live in Darfur, in the west. The Nuba — a diverse group, quite distinct from the Nubians — live in the center of the country, primarily in the mountains of southern Kordofan; they include pagans, Christians, and Muslims, although the last are recent converts, and their Islam does not run deep. And Nigerian immigrants, from several tribes, are scattered throughout the North, where they are known as "Fellata."

A great many tribes live in the Southern region, which is overwhelmingly non–Muslim, but there are also many non–Muslims living in the North, some of them Southern migrants seeking jobs and refuge in Khartoum. Also living in Khartoum and other northern towns are non–Muslim immigrant communities — Egyptian Copts, Lebanese-Syrian Christians, Greeks, and Hindus — who settled there as diasporas in recent decades. Despite their religion, they live in Sudan unmolested. The key characteristic that marks any Sudanese group out for persecution is not race or religion, but low economic status; yet the rationalizations for oppression are invariably religious or ethnic.

African Nation, Arab Domination

Since independence, the country has been dominated by the Arabs, who strictly speaking constitute only about 40 percent of the population. "In Sudan," notes a Sudanese scholar, "'Arab' refers less to the appearance to which we usually affix stereotypical Arab physical identity, and more to a state of mind...."[5] Political power is monopolized by three Nile Valley Arab tribes — the Shayqiyya, Ja'aliyin, and Danaqla — who constitute barely more than five percent of the population.[6] They also dominate the higher ranks of the Sudan military, although the rank-and-file soldiers are frequently non–Arab Muslims.

The largest non–Arab group are the Dinka, in the South. Like their Nuer neighbors, the Dinka never had any chiefs, which made it all the harder for the British to control them.[7] This profound suspicion of authority carried over into independence, feeding the Southern separatist movement. "The pride of the Dinka was legendary, even among the Europeans," writes escaped slave Francis Bok, himself a Dinka. "My people believed that they already lived in heaven and that Dinka who went to live in the north or any place else were crazy."[8] Some Dinka did move north, however, settling among the Arab tribes and assisting them in raids against their fellow Dinka.[9]

Khartoum, the capital, with an estimated 6 million people, is now one of the most modern cities of Africa, with a downtown area filled with Western-style high-rises; meanwhile, photos of Darfur show the inhabitants living in thatch-roofed huts. Some of the Nuba can even be found in caves.[10] But Khartoum was not always such a showplace of modernity. "A more miserable, filthy, and unhealthy place can hardly be imagined," commented one English explorer during the mid–nineteenth century,[11] as he viewed the city founded only a few decades earlier as an Egyptian military outpost. The capital region contains three major towns: Khartoum itself, the commercial center of Omdurman, and the smaller industrial suburb of North Khartoum. The "Three Towns" are located at the Y-shaped juncture where the White Nile and Blue Nile combine. Its modern center is surrounded by a ring of refugee shanty-towns, where life is precarious, especially for non–Muslims. Writes historian Robert Collins:

> The gleaming towers soaring skyward and the luxury hotels of the new Khartoum were more an ominous symbol of the deep division between the "haves" at the center and the "have nots" on the margins than the rising phoenix of a new nation.[12]

Engaging in manual labor, which Muslims try to avoid,[13] Khartoum's non–Muslims face all sorts of social restrictions. Their children could not be enrolled in the capital's schools unless they adopted Muslim names.[14] They were denied assistance from government agencies, and turned away from hospitals.[15] Massive expulsions of Southerners from Khartoum took place under the military, reminiscent of South Africa's apartheid.[16]

The Slave Trade and Messianism

An understanding of the role of slavery is essential to any explanation of the ethnic conflicts in Sudan during recent years. Egypt expanded into the country in 1821, and began raiding the Southern region for slaves and ivory.[17] The slaves were sold off to the Middle East, and their descendants can be found there today. When the British arrived decades later, nominally serving the Egyptian monarch, they took a stand against slavery, but they were unable to abolish it without alienating slave-holding sheikhs whom they relied on for support. In the 1870s, some local Europeans owned slaves themselves.[18] Resistance to the Egyptian-British colonizers was strongest in the South, and it took almost 20 years to pacify the region.[19]

In 1885, conflict broke out between the British and their Egyptian clients, and the Sudanese Arabs took the opportunity to revolt against Anglo-Egyptian sovereignty. This took the form of a messianic movement headed by Mohammed Ahmad ibn Abdallah, who came from Dongola in northern Sudan.[20] Like many Sudanese, he was a Sufi, an Islamic mystic. Declaring himself the Mahdi (Messiah), he wiped out an Egyptian army under British command,[21] seized Khartoum, and established a theocratic regime. Although the Southerners supported him at the beginning, hoping to see an end to the slave trade, ibn Abdallah actually extended it.[22]

The Mahdist theocracy foreshadowed the Islamic regimes of a century later. Shoes and jewelry were outlawed, along with singing, dancing, hand-clapping, and flirting. Punishment was by flogging, stoning, and amputation.[23] Cursing, drinking, and smoking were considered capital offenses. The Mahdi intended to conquer Egypt, and then march on Mecca and Jerusalem and take over the world in the name of his version of Islam.[24] The jihadists of the twenty-first century call for the same thing.

Ibn Abdallah only survived his victory over the Anglo-Egyptian forces by a few months, dying from disease. He was succeeded by a Baggara Arab named Abdullah, who called himself the Khalifa (Caliph), in imitation of Mohammed's successors. Under the Mahdist Khalifate, the Baggara monopolized "almost every post of importance" in the regime.[25] This explains the current loyalty of the Baggara to the Mahdist Umma Party, which has widespread support in Sudan's rural areas. Multi-ethnic Darfur was annexed to the Khalifate, but remained restive. In the late 1880s, there was a famine in Sudan, which killed as many as 75 percent of the country's 9 million people.[26] In the 1890s, the British retook Khartoum, destroying the already weakened Mahdist regime; as a result, Darfur regained its independence.[27]

Heritage of Colonialism

Darfur did not become part of the Sudan again until the British annexed it in 1916. The South was ruled as a colony within a colony. Northerners were excluded from the three Southern provinces.[28] This permitted Catholic and Protestant missionaries to seek converts there without Muslim competition. But at the same time, Southerners were paid at a lower scale than Northerners.[29] There was serious neglect of education under the British. By the mid–1930s, only 9,000 boys were enrolled in the four-year elementary schools, and a mere 1,000 in the intermediate schools; there was only one secondary school in the country. Only 4 percent of the boys in the North were getting even a primary education, and the figures were even lower for girls and Southerners.[30] There were only a handful of Southern secondary school graduates by the mid–twentieth century, and they were mostly educated in Uganda, and knew little Arabic.[31] On the eve of independence, fewer than one percent of the senior posts in Sudan's civil service were held by Southerners.[32] Many of these posts had to be filled with Egyptians, but the British were wary of them because of the strength of nationalist sentiment in Egypt.[33]

From the British point of view, this was understandable. Egypt and Nubia had close links in ancient times, and had recently both been ruled by the Ottoman Turks. There were hundreds of thousands of Egyptians living in the Sudan; and Egyptian nationalists often thought in terms of uniting the Nile Valley — not to mention the entire Arab World — into a single state. The Sudanese Arabs were of two minds about this. Union with Egypt would vastly increase the Arab majority in the expanded state, reducing the danger of a possible takeover by a coalition of non–Arabs, perhaps backed by the Communists. On the other hand, the Sudanese Arabs would themselves be reduced to political insignificance by such a development, which would turn their country into a province of Egypt. Generally, the Mahdists opposed unification with Egypt during the period of British rule, while the rival Sufi order, the Khatmiya — strongest among the Nile Valley Arabs — supported it. This changed after independence, when the Khatmiya tribes found that they could rule Sudan themselves. There are other Sufi orders in Sudan, but they are apolitical.[34]

Along with the Mahdist Umma Party and the Khatmiya-backed National Union (later supplanted by the Democratic Union Party), there were a number of regional parties in the country at independence. Foremost among these was the Southern-backed Federal Bloc, which was an ally of the Communists.[35] The latter were strongest in Khartoum, and won about a sixth of the vote in the 1965 election,[36] although their support has declined sharply since. Pan-Islamists are another important group, deriving originally from the Egyptian Muslim Brotherhood. This movement, concentrated in Khartoum, recruited recent Arab migrants to the capital from the rural North.[37]

Urbanization and Pan-Islamism

Psychology students at the University of Khartoum see Sudanese society "increasingly experiencing pervasive depression and anxiety...."[38] These symptoms stem in part from the rapid social change occurring in the capital, fostered in part by massive migration, which is in turn caused by both drought and war. Throughout greater Khartoum, parental authority is beginning to break down, as young people take advantage of the frequent power cuts at night to engage in romantic liaisons, rejecting their fathers' politics along with their traditional morality.[39]

While highly mnemonist in character, pan–Islamism — or "Islamo-fascism," as American neo-conservatives term it — is a product of modern society. Its ideological roots stem as much from the secular Young Turks who took over the crumbling Ottoman Empire in 1908, as from long-established Islamic academies like Egypt's al-Azhar, until recently a hotbed of pan–Islamist ideology. Motivated by fear of change, pan–Islamism fights secularist tendencies of all kinds — Marxist, nationalist, consumerist, feminist — as well as demands by non–Arab and non–Muslim minorities. Sunni Pan-Islamists are also strongly opposed to the doctrines of Ayatollah Khomeini, whom they regard as a Shi'ite heretic, and whom they wrongly suspect of social radicalism. At the same time, Iran has generally had good relations with the current dictatorship in Sudan.

In Sudan in recent years, pan–Islamism has been associated with military dictatorship, first of Gen. Ibrahim Abboud, who held power from 1958 to 1964 and tried to Islamize the South[40]; next of Gen. Ja'afer Numeiri, who ruled from 1969 to 1985, originally preaching a variety of Nasserism, only to have a sudden conversion to pan–Islamism when he discovered, ten years after his coup, that he had serious heart problems[41]; and finally of Gen. Omar al-Bashir, who took over in 1989, proclaiming: "Anyone who betrays the nation does not deserve the honor of living."[42] He was still in power twenty years later, ruling over a totally impoverished and war-devastated nation. Al-Bashir was a protégé of Hassan al-Turabi, his former teacher. Al-Turabi's National Islamic Front (NIF) was founded in 1965. No mindless fanatic, al-Turabi has degrees from London University and the Sorbonne.[43] His wife is a feminist.[44] On the other hand, his niece is married to Osama bin Laden,[45] who once lived in the Sudan.

Al-Turabi, who served under Numeiri as attorney-general,[46] was in the beginning the *eminence grise* behind the al-Bashir regime. In the wake of the latter's coup, NIF militants attacked non–Muslims in Khartoum and closed churches, conducting a widespread purge of secularists among the civil servants and military officers.[47] The NIF was even permitted its own security force, the *Amm ath Thwara*, who had "their own arms networks and command operations," and ran private prisons where they held their political enemies. They also spied on the military.[48] Ultimately, al-Turabi and al-Bashir had a falling out when the former tried to concentrate too much power in his own hands. Al-Turabi soon joined with the opposition, even signing his own peace agreement with the Southern separtists.[49]

Al-Bashir, like Numeiri, shifted his ideological ground after coming to power. Originally a pan–Islamist who conducted genocide against non–Muslims, he has become an Arab racist, influenced by Libya's Muammar Qaddafi. His wars of extermination are now waged against non–Arab Muslims in Darfur and elsewhere. The consequence is further division within the country, as groups such as the Nuba, Beja, and Fur are driven into the arms of separatist guerrillas, further undermining the country.

Not all Muslim leaders in Sudan have been extremists. Mahmud Muhammad Taha was a religious reformer who favored equal rights for women, peace with Israel, and tolerance of non-believers, including the Communists. Strongly opposed to the Numeiri dictatorship, Taha was hanged in 1985.[50] His body was dangled from a helicopter, flown around Khartoum, and then dumped in the desert.

The Baggara Entitlement Fantasy

Key to the policies of the al-Bashir regime are the cattle-herding Baggara Arabs, who live in Darfur and Kordofan. Although they are Arabs, extensive intermarriage with the descendants of their female slaves has made them virtually indistinguishable from their African neighbors. The Baggara make up the bulk of the notorious *janjaweed* militia. Numeiri feared them, but his civilian successor, Sadiq al-Mahdi, descendent and political heir of ibn Abdallah, actively cultivated their support.[51] The Baggara were deeply involved in the genocide against the Southerners, and now against the Nilotic-speakers of Darfur. "No amount of things, hard work, courtesy or generosity of heart could one ever give the Baggara that can please them," noted a Dinka leader. "You can offer your wife to a Baggara in exchange for peace, and he will turn around before reaching home to come and demand your mother."[52] Although they are relatively isolated from the world, the Baggara share an entitlement fantasy with bin-Laden's terrorists: "We have been deprived, so therefore we are entitled to take anything we want." One Darfur African was told by a *janjaweed* leader: "We are the lords of this land. You blacks don't have any rights here.... We are the original people of this area."[53] In 1987, the Libyan-sponsored Arab Gathering promised "to kill all *zurqa* [dark-skinned people]. Darfur is now Dar al-Arab."[54]

Entitlement fantasies originate with the low status of women and children in the family. In the Sudan in particular, female circumcision (cliterodectomy) is widely practiced among most ethnic groups; this is extremely painful for the young girls, and is rarely done under sanitary conditions. Although the stated purpose is to protect the young women's virginity so that men will want to marry them, it makes it agonizing for them to have sex, particularly for the first time. Mende Nazer gives a chilling account of the operation as she experienced it in her Mountain Nuba village:

> I could feel [the female circumciser] take hold of me. I let out a bloodcurdling scream; with a swift downward cut of the blade she had sliced into my flesh. I was crying and kicking and trying to fight free. The pain was worse than anything I could ever have imagined.
> "No! No! Umi! Umi! [Mother!] Make her stop!" I screamed. But my sisters and my mother held me down and forced my legs apart, so the woman could continue cutting away. "I'm sorry, I'm sorry, I'm sorry," my mother mouthed at me silently, with tears in her eyes.[55]

Female circumcision reinforces the common belief that women exist only to serve the needs of men. When women are treated as chattels, they lose the sense of being in control of their lives, and their children are likely to suffer neglect and abuse as a result. The ultimate consequences are visible throughout the Muslim World. In Saudi Arabia, playground sets never caught on because the children only wanted to spend their time with their mothers; this is excessive closeness, hinting strongly of incest. And with the women kept in seclusion, the men begin developing sexual interests in young boys, a pattern similar to ancient Greece. Sexual abuse often causes children to regard themselves as "special," entitled to "anything I want," and in addition trains them to disregard the rights of others. One consequence is the continued existence of slavery.

Twenty-first Century Slavery

Officially, there is no slavery in the Sudan, although it is fairly common in practice, and even Sudanese military officers are involved in the trade.[56] It should be kept in mind, of course, that slavery survived much longer in Africa and the nearby Arabian peninsula than elsewhere. It was only abolished in British-ruled Sierra Leone in 1931, in Saudi Arabia in 1960, and in Oman in 1970, and there have been reports of it in Mauritania following independence in 1960. There is no reliable estimate of how many slaves there are in Sudan, and the figure sometimes given of 10–12,000 seems very low. Unlike in the nineteenth-century West Indies, Brazil, or the American South, the entire economy does not rest on the practice. Furthermore, many slaves have been able to escape, although they were still left with serious emotional trauma, especially if they were kidnapped as children, the typical practice. Sometimes it is hard to distinguish exactly who is a slave. During the 1990s, for example, many non–Muslim children were held against their will in Sudan's Islamic schools.[57]

Young boys are kidnapped by the Baggara to tend their cattle. Women and girls are used sexually, but their children are regarded as Arabs. Many women are used for housework, even in Khartoum, and the escaped Nuba slave Mende Nazer reports that she was even sent to London to work for a Sudanese diplomat, a relative of the family that had originally purchased her. Overall, the contribution of slave labor to the Sudan economy is so meager that it would be hard to deny that the motivations for the slave trade are actually political and psychological. On one hand, the slave owners are able to turn their entitlement fantasies into reality by dominating and exploiting others; on the other, in the past, the slave trade contributed to the destruction of the Dinka community, which was regarded by the rulers in Khartoum as a potential threat to Arab domination.

Anti-slavery movements in the West have made an issue of the Sudan, even raising funds to buy captives out of slavery. The famous abolitionist John Brown might have cautioned them against this. It only encourages the Baggara to continue raiding their neighbors, so they can capture even more slaves to sell to the foreigners, and then use the money to purchase guns and ammunition.

Southern Separatism

Northern policy toward the South after independence promoted the rise of the *Anyanya*, an openly separatist Southern guerrilla movement based largely among the Bantu-speakers in Equatoria province. Later, it was supplanted by the Sudan People's Liberation Movement/Army (SPLM/A), headed by the late John Garang, a Dinka politician and an effective guerrilla leader. Garang advocated a democratic and unified Sudan with autonomy for the South,[58] but many of his followers were probably more sympathetic to separatism. Spreading throughout the South during the late 1980s, and even into parts of the North, the SPLM/A was able to force the Khartoum government—then headed by the Umma Party—to the negotiating table. The NIF-backed coup of 1989, which put

Gen. al-Bashir in power, was intended to prevent a peace settlement between the two regions.[59]

Although the SPLM/A could never have survived without support from the population of the South, its soldiers have still been known to loot from the peasants[60] and use refugee children as unpaid labor in their camps.[61] Furthermore, it is often regarded by Southerners as a strictly Dinka movement. In 1991, a Nuer faction headed by Riek Machar broke away from Garang. Riek Machar proclaimed himself a Messiah and made war on the Dinkas.[62] Unlike Garang, he openly declared himself in favor of a separate state for the South; yet he made arrangements to obtain weapons from Khartoum, ultimately undermining his credibility.[63] The Garang–Riek Machar rift had been caused in part by the revolution in nearby Ethiopia, when the new government expelled thousands of Southern Sudanese refugees[64]; Deprived of their sanctuary, Nuer fighters believed that they had no choice but to make a separate peace with al-Bashir.[65] Ultimately, Riek Machar rejoined Garang.[66]

International mediation led to a peace agreement between the al-Bashir regime and the SPLM/A, signed in 2002 in Kenya, which permitted the South to secede if it wished after a nine-year interval, in the year 2011.[67] Garang might have persuaded his fellow Southerners to forego independence, but he died in an airplane crash only weeks after the signing; no foul play appears to have been involved. As a result, Sudan is the one country in the world least likely to remain intact over the next few years, although it would be unwise to make predictions.

One result of the peace agreement, unfortunately, was the extension of Khartoum's genocidal policies toward the Muslim Nilotics of Darfur. This policy was not altogether new. As early as 1992, al-Bashir had declared a jihad against the Mountain Nuba, some of whom are at least nominally Muslim. The Sudanese army "bombed and deported thousands of civilians, penning them up in concentration camps and selling them as slave labor to the large Arab-owned farms in Kordofan."[68] Arab settlers then took over abandoned Nuba land.[69] Once the conflict in the South had been settled, and the Nuba temporarily pacified, Khartoum began to turn its attention toward Darfur. In 2002, the governor of Southern Darfur vowed to exterminate the Fur people.[70]

Several factors were responsible for this tragic development. First, the Baggara were by then accustomed to raiding the Dinka for slaves and cattle, and with the Dinka and Nuba suddenly off-limits, the Fur were the next best available victims. A second major cause of the Darfur conflict was the extended drought, which began in the 1980s, and caused inevitable friction between settled peasants (Fur and Masalit) and nomads (Arab and Zaghawa, although the latter are Nilotic-speakers and support the local guerrillas).[71] Another factor was the influx of Arab refugees from neighboring Chad, another war-torn country, who were recruited into the *janjaweed.* Libyan dictator Muammar Qaddafi's egotism was yet another factor; he was the prime inspiration for the Arab Gathering, whose members were recruited into Sudan's regular and irregular militia movements.[72]

But the most important factor in causing the Darfur tragedy may have been al-Bashir's concern that the Baggara, deprived of their "right" to raid the Dinka, might become a threat to his own rather isolated and shaky regime. Al-Bashir was still identified with the Nile Valley Arabs, the "people of the river." The Mahdist Baggara had opposed regimes in Khartoum in the past, and could do so again in the future; and they were already well-armed. Setting them against the Nilotics was a way of keeping them busy.

Occidentophobia

The al-Bashir regime responds to outside criticism of its genocidal policies with the rhetoric of anti-imperialism. "The times of colonialism are over," declared Sudan's foreign minister in 1993, when his government was charged with human rights violations.[73] Insurgent leaders "were depicted as stooges in the pay of foreign enemies of Sudan and Islam, such as Israel and the U.S...."[74] Even the 1988 floods in Khartoum were claimed by one ex-cabinet minister to be part of a Christian conspiracy.[75] As long as it operates by such logic, the Khartoum regime is likely to remain invulnerable to foreign pressure. What it fears from the West, of course, is not some revival of colonial rule, but cultural influence which might lead to social change.

T. Abdou Maliqalim Simone suggests that "Perhaps ... the North displaces its frustration with its historical marginalization from the Arab world onto the South."[76] But "marginalization" has always been a vague concept, and many other Arab countries might also be regarded as "marginalized": Egypt with its long pre–Islamic history; Tunisia with its secular political culture; Morocco and Algeria with their large Berber minorities; Iraq with its Kurdish population; Christian-ruled Lebanon; Alawite-ruled Syria; Zaidi-dominated Yemen; and even Saudi Arabia itself, whose Wahhabi fanaticism sets it off from the rest of the Muslim world. One clue to the pathology of Sudanese pan–Islam is offered by Simone himself: "...Muslims will often not let blacks into their toilets because they are non–Muslim, but will let their white employers use them even though they are also non–Muslim."[77] Sudan's ruling Arab minority suffers from feelings of inferiority toward the West. These feelings are projected onto indigenous African groups who constitute their Origin Folk, and who are thereby targeted for either forcible assimilation or extermination.

10

The Muslim World
The Psycho-Geography of Hate

This chapter focuses on three case studies in the Muslim world: the Turkish genocide against the Armenians before and during World War I; the Pakistani persecution of the Ahmadiya sect from the early 1950s until the present; and the civil war in Algeria which lasted from 1992 to 1997, taking an estimated 100,000 lives. All of these cases illustrate the theories put forth in this book's first chapter, "A Psychohistorical Perspective on a Violent Century." The first two are examples of Shrinking Boundary Syndrome. The Algerian civil war, by contrast, is a unique case of a prolonged Adowa Cycle, and also an example of Occi-dentophobia.

Turkey and the Armenians

During World War I, the Ottoman Turkish government exterminated roughly one million Armenians living in their historical homeland, which straddled the border with Russia, in a genocidal act foreshadowing the events of World War II. Among the explanations put forth for this crime are traditional Muslim hatred of Christians, the desire by the Turks to eliminate a minority community that was increasingly successful in business, and the fear that the Armenians would assist the Russians by engaging in armed uprisings against the Turkish state.

Although all of these factors were involved to some degree, they fall short of a complete explanation. While the Turks bore considerable ill will toward Christians, who had already conquered much of their once-vast empire in both the Balkans and North Africa, Turkey was nonetheless allied to three Christian states — Germany, Austria-Hungary, and Bulgaria — during the very time that the genocide against the Armenians was taking place. There were, in addition, Christians living in the Ottoman Empire — particularly in Syria and Lebanon — who were not subjected to persecution. And the Jews, left unmolested during the period, were also prominent in commerce. Finally, while the danger of an Armenian revolt against Turkey may have been real, no such uprising actually took place. The Arabs, on the other hand, did rise up against the Turks, with help from the British; although the Turks hanged a number of their leaders, they never engaged in the kind of extermination they inflicted on the Armenians.

During the early nineteenth century, the Armenians in Turkey were known as "the loyal community," and were trusted by the Turks. This began to change as the Russians seized the Transcaucasus and created "a Russian Armenia ... where the Armenian Church was established and recognized and where Armenian governors and generals ruled provinces and commanded armies."[1] Subsequently, the Greeks and Serbs won their fight for independence, while the Habsburg and Czarist empires grabbed more Turkish territory, the British, French and Italians drove the Turks out of North Africa and Cyprus, and the Balkan states threw the Turks almost entirely out of Europe in the First Balkan War of 1912. As the Turkish empire continued to shrink, the Turks began to fear the total obliteration of their ethnic group. In addition, Turkish refugees from the Crimea began pouring into Rumelia, as the remaining Turkish territories in Europe were known; when Rumelia was lost, these refugees, along with others, moved to Anatolia (Asiatic Turkey), where an estimated 850,000 settled in Armenian-populated areas.[2]

One major factor in the decline of the once-dynamic Ottoman Empire was the method of recruitment of the Sultans. In the early days, the Ottomans chose their new Sultan from among the deceased ruler's numerous sons by his vast harem of concubines (the Sultans rarely married). But after 1566, the sultan's likely successors were held in a windowless prison called "The Cage," and were typically psychotic by the time they inherited the throne.[3]

Traditionally, Armenians had played a major role in Ottoman Turkey as merchants, craftsmen and architects.[4] "Muslim Turks lacked the most basic technical skills," notes Kemal Atatürk's biographer, Andrew Mango. "Famous as cavalrymen, they had to rely on Armenian farmers to shoe their horses."[5] Persecution of the Armenians began in the late nineteenth century, initiated by Sultan Abdul Hamid II, who was believed to have had an Armenian mother — a dancing girl in the royal palace who died when her son was seven.[6] This detail exemplifies another psychohistorical factor in the anti–Armenian campaign: the biological connection between the Turks and the Armenians.

In ancient times, Anatolia was populated by various Indo-European nations whose identities were submerged during Roman and Byzantine rule. They were later converted to Islam after being conquered by invading tribes from Central Asia, adopting the language of their conquerors. The Armenians, who clung to their ancient language and religion, were the main holdouts. The cultural affinity of the Turks with the Central Asians, along with their connection to the pre–Islamic Indo-European inhabitants of the peninsula, has created an identity crisis. "To this day," writes journalist Stephen Kinzer, "Turks are not sure who they are. It takes no deep psychological insight to see that beneath their veneer of racial and ethnic pride, which some of them take to absurd lengths, lies a strong sense of uncertainty and even inferiority."[7]

Under Kemal Atatürk, the official history claimed that eastern Turkey, the home of the Armenians, was "originally Turkish and Turanian, before the arrival of the Persians, of Alexander's Greeks, and of subsequent invaders. Later they reverted to their original Turkish owners: Armenians and others had no rights to these lands."[8] This denial of Anatolia's Indo-European past is connected to Turkey's pattern of persecution of ethnic minorities. The Indo-European Armenians were massacred beginning in the 1890s, with the slaughter culminating in 1915. In 1922, the Anatolian Greeks were expelled, in the wake of the Greek invasion, with hundreds of thousands killed. And the Kurds in Turkey have faced oppression and forced assimilation since 1924, when Atatürk abolished the Caliphate and simultaneously outlawed "all Kurdish schools, associations and publications."[9] Even Turkey's

Jews, occasionally the victims of official policy and popular bigotry, have fared better. What the Armenians, Greeks and Kurds share is that they all speak Indo-European languages, as did the original inhabitants of Anatolia. Significantly, in the course of its propaganda war against Kurdish separatists, the Turkish government has accused the Kurds of not only cooperating with Turkey's Greek and Armenian enemies, but of even *being* Armenians.[10]

This Turkish "anti–Aryanism" parallels the neurotic's rejection of his own original self. At the same time, Kemalist scholars claimed "Aryan" status for the Turks during the 1930s, postulating a fictitious Turkish identity for the ancient Hittites,[11] whose ancient state long predated the Turkish arrival. Turkish ultra-nationalists used the groups which had an ancient connection with Anatolia as poison containers. In the Turkish view, Armenians, Greeks and Kurds constitute Origin Folk — groups from which the dominant nation is derived. Yet, almost by definition, the dominant ethnic group is invariably in denial about this.

The Armenians were also victimized because of their role as a Catalytic Community. The Armenian Dashnag party, a radical nationalist group, held a congress in Paris in 1907 to which various forces opposed to the Ottoman Sultan were invited.[12] The Young Turk revolution took place the following year — less a revolution than a reformist military coup which put nationalist modernizers at the helm of what was still a traditional, multi-ethnic society. In 1909, killings of Armenians in and around the city of Adana took place, as part of a royalist uprising against the Young Turk government.[13] Ethnic violence was a defense against the anxiety caused by the threat of social change. The Armenian dead numbered 15,000 or more.[14]

Some of this anxiety clearly stemmed from birth trauma. The words of Sultan Abdul Hamid II, who initiated the persecution of the Armenians, reflect the neonate's fear of dismemberment as he struggles to escape from the birth canal:

> By taking away Greece and Rumania, Europe has cut off the feet of the Turkish state. The loss of Bulgaria, Serbia and Egypt has deprived us of our hands, and now by means of this Armenian agitation, they want to get at our most vital places and tear out our very guts.[15]

In little more than a decade, Turkey was obliged to fight no fewer than seven wars, beginning with the Arab uprising in Tripoli (now Libya) against Ottoman rule. Italy took advantage of the trouble to seize Turkey's remaining North African colony, and also seized the island of Rhodes. Before the Turkish-Italian War had ended, four Balkan states began the First Balkan War against the crumbling Ottoman empire and took nearly all that was left of European Turkey. But Turkey recovered part of this territory during the Second Balkan War, when the victors fell out with one another and Bulgaria was forced to surrender some of its gains. In 1914, the Young Turk government dragged Turkey into World War I on Germany's side, leading to the loss of its remaining Arab provinces. Then came the war with Greece, and another war with the short-lived First Armenian Republic, which was backed by France.

In 1911, a Young Turk leader, Enver Pasha, created a "Special Organization" to fight a guerrilla war against Italian forces in Libya. Other organizations with the same name were formed during World War I to organize the deportations of the Armenians.[16] In 1915, during the war, Turkish leaders blamed the Armenians for the disastrous defeat that January in the east, when tens of thousands of Ottoman soldiers died, primarily from the cold. The anti–Armenian agitation was coordinated by Turkish military intelligence.[17]

The primary excuse used to slaughter the Armenians was that they might rebel behind Turkish lines during the struggle with Russia. Another Christian minority, the Assyrians, who speak a language related to Arabic, actually did rebel against the Ottomans during the war[18]; but the Young Turk leader Talat Pasha, as late as July, 1915, ordered that "other Christians" not be included in measures taken against the Armenians.[19] Of course, the Turks' own fears of annihilation during the War should not be disregarded, and had the Czar's armies prevailed, the Turks might well have suffered the same fate they inflicted on the Armenians. Yet it was less fear of annihilation per se that motivated the Turkish genocide, so much as the Turks' *repression* of this fear. This, in turn, stemmed from the militarization of Turkish society, itself a product of the Ottoman Empire, where one ethnic group ruled by force over so many others.

Pakistan and the Ahmadiyas

The Muslim Ahmadiya sect was founded in 1899 in the Punjab, a religiously hetero-geneous province of British India, by Mirza Ghulam Ahmad, in response to the activities of Christian missionaries and the Arya Samaj, a Hindu militant movement. Ahmad pro-claimed himself a prophet, and defined jihad as merely an intellectual struggle against non–Muslims, as opposed to a violent holy war. After 1914, his followers split into two groups; a dissident faction in Lahore considered Ahmad to be merely a reformer of the Muslim religion, while the far larger group, known as Qadianis (after the town in which the sect originated), continued to regard him as a prophet. This put the Qadianis at odds with other Muslims, whom they dismissed as *kafirs* (pagans). The Ahmadiyas number per-haps 250,000 altogether, concentrated in Pakistan and Bangladesh, with smaller groups in England, Africa and Israel. They tend to be well-educated, and in the past have occupied important posts in the Pakistani government and army.[20]

In 1931, another group appeared among the Muslims of the Punjab which developed a long and bitter history of antagonism toward the Ahmadiyas. These were the Ahrars, formed to defend Muslims against the perceived threat from Hindu militants. Originally supporting Islamic socialism, they were also allied with the Congress Party of Mahatma Gandhi and Jawaharlal Nehru, who had their own differences with the Hindu zealots.[21] Unlike the Ahmadiyas, the Ahrars came from the lower social strata. The antagonism between the two groups was exacerbated by Hindu-Muslim clashes in nearby Kashmir, as the Ahrars and Ahmadiyas took different stands on the issue, with the former siding with the Hindus.[22]

The partition of India in 1947 provoked a mutual slaughter in the Punjab, coupled with a massive exchange of population. The Punjab was divided more or less evenly between India and Pakistan. As Pakistan's Hindus and Sikhs all fled to India, the Muslims in the Indian half of the Punjab fled to Pakistan. The well-educated Ahmadiyas, heretics by ortho-dox Muslim standards — because most of them believed that their founder was a prophet who came after Mohammad — nonetheless emerged as leaders in the new Pakistani state, which did not originally pursue sectarian policies against dissident Muslim groups. Pak-istan's original leaders, in fact, were a highly secularized group; Mohammad Ali Jinnah, the governor general and founder of the Muslim League, wore European dress, drank whiskey, and was married to a Zoroastrian, while the first prime minister, Liaquat Ali Khan, had a Christian wife.[23] The Ahrars, in contrast to the Ahmadiyas, tended to end up as penniless refugees in the new state. They did not even endorse the existence of Pakistan until 1949.[24]

In the wake of partition, the Ahrars initiated the campaign against the Ahmadiyas. In part, this appears to have been an attempt to establish their credentials as loyal Pakistanis, which may have been in doubt. There was also the matter of Mohammad Zafrullah Khan, Pakistan's foreign minister, and an Ahmadiya. He was blamed for Pakistan's failure to obtain Kashmir and other territories that went to India at partition, and at least part of the anti–Ahmadiya agitation was directed against him personally.[25] At the same time, the trauma of partition was also a factor in the anti–Ahmadiya agitation. The political space of undivided India's Muslims in general, and of the Punjabi Muslims in particular, had contracted, and — as in Ottoman Turkey — a sense of pollution, stemming from birth trauma, translated into a desire to persecute "impure" minorities. With the Hindus and Sikhs already gone, and the Christians able to count on Pakistan's Western allies for protection, the Ahmadiyas remained as an easy target.

There was also the obvious desire on the part of some Pakistanis to obtain the Ahmadiyas' property and jobs; however, other Muslim communities — such as the Memons, Chiniotis, Bohras and Khojas — were also wealthy,[26] but never suffered persecution. Nor was there any mistreatment of Pakistan's Zoroastrians, a highly-educated and prosperous group numbering only about 50,000, who are not even Muslims.

The issue between the orthodox Muslims and the Ahmadiyas stems primarily from the former's *fear of impurity*, with economic rivalry playing at best a secondary role; the Ahmadiyas, after all, are only 0.1 percent of Pakistan's population. Once the Ahrars had begun the campaign against the Ahmadiyas, they were joined by Pakistan's Islamist parties and many of the *ulama* (religious scholars). Notes Nasim Ahmed Jawed:

> The declared objective of the *ulama* was to preserve the purity of the Islamic faith by indicating that the Ahmadi belief against the finality of Muhammad's prophethood was an innovation and not a part of the true Islam. Another demand was to deprive the Ahmadis of the full rights of full Muslim citizenship, and particularly of their high governmental positions.[27]

The attacks on the Ahmadiyas occurred in two separate waves: the first was in response to partition and the refugee crisis; it began in 1948 and peaked five years later. The second climaxed in the mid–1980s, and appears to have been a delayed reaction to India's defeat of Pakistan in the 1970–71 war over Bangladesh (the former East Pakistan). While the second wave is a good example of the 15-year Adowa Cycle, described in Chapter 1 above, the first wave was far too soon after the initial trauma to qualify. This foreshortened Adowa Cycle is probably due to the rapid turnover in Pakistan's leadership after partition; the leadership of the Muslim League, which campaigned for the creation of Pakistan, had its base in the Hindu-majority provinces of India, not in the Muslim-majority areas such as Punjab, East Bengal and the Northwest Frontier which became part of Pakistan; Muslims in the first two areas generally voted for regional parties, while the Pushtoons in the Northwest Frontier tended to vote for Congress. When the Muslim League leaders relocated to the new state, they left most of their political following behind in India. The army, which was rooted in the Punjab and the Pushtoon-speaking Northwest Frontier Province, soon forced the civilian politicians aside and took over the country.

In early 1953, anti–Ahmadiya riots broke out in towns throughout Pakistani Punjab when Islamist parties demanded that the Ahmadiyas be declared non–Muslims, a serious disadvantage in Pakistan.[28] Large crowds attacked the police, burned public property, and then took refuge in mosques. Provincial Chief Minister Mian Daultana backed the anti–Ahmadiya movement, but quickly reversed his stand after the army declared martial law.[29] The national Prime Minister — Khwaja Nazimuddin, a Bengali — was ousted as a consequence of the riots, marking "the beginning of the political instability that lasted for the next five years...."[30]

The Islamists eventually scored a success in 1974, three years after India's victory in the Bangladesh War, when Prime Minister Zulfikar Ali Bhutto gave in to their demands and formally declared the Ahmadiyas to be non–Muslims. "[A]lthough they were free to practice their religion," comments Christophe Jaffrelot, "they could not proselytize...."[31] They were also forbidden from holding high office. The leader of the Ahmadiya sect fled to London.[32]

In 1977, Bhutto was overthrown and subsequently tried and executed by General Zia ul-Haq. Zia was politically close to the Islamists, who began to campaign anew against the Ahmadiyas. The Ahmadiyas were forbidden to call themselves Muslims, preach their faith to others, use Islamic terminology, or practice Muslim rites.[33] They could not refer to their leader as a "prophet," call their places of worship "mosques," or use the Muslim term *azan* to refer to their call to prayer. Many Ahmadiyas went into hiding, while others emigrated.[34]

While the anti–Ahmadiya campaign of the 1950s was promoted by various militant groups and opposed by some elements of the government, the events of the 1980s had the full blessing of the regime. The Pakistani government published a booklet in 1984 entitled *Qadianism—Threat to Islamic Solidarity*, which charged the Ahmadiyas with having "originated under the instigation of a colonial power."[35] This may have been true, but the same could also be said of the Muslim League, the party that founded Pakistan. The anti–Ahmadiya movement of the 1980s and beyond wraps itself in the banner of anti-imperialism, as if Pakistan had not accepted massive U.S. military and economic aid, joined the SEATO and CENTO pacts, and allowed American bases on its soil. According to General Zia, the Ahmadiyas offended true Muslims because they passed themselves off falsely as Muslims.[36]

Between 1984 and 1988, according to pro-government sources in Pakistan, nearly 2,700 Ahmadiya "miscreants" were arrested. Among the charges against them were displaying badges, calling themselves Muslims, spreading rumors, distributing anti-government literature, and using Islamic terms to describe their prayer meetings or places of worship. Such "provocations" had led to the deaths of 19 Ahmadiyas. More than 100 Ahmadiya mosques were damaged or destroyed by mobs, or closed by the police. Even the dead were given no rest, as a number of Ahmadiya corpses were disinterred from Muslim cemeteries.[37]

Unlike the Armenians in Turkey, the Ahmadiyas had no putative link with any hostile neighboring powers. They became a poison container because they practiced an "impure" version of Islam, rejecting eternal warfare against non–Muslims. This made them the target of pollution fantasies, which in the 1980s stemmed from the traumatic loss of East Pakistan nearly 15 years before.

In a bizarre twist to the anti–Ahmadiya persecution, Mirza Tahir Ahmed, the sect's exiled leader, claimed in June 1988 that within one year's time, the enemies of the Ahmadiyas would be punished by God. Sure enough, two months later, Pakistan's military dictator Zia ul-Haq, chief supporter of the anti–Ahmadiya campaign, died in an unexplained helicopter crash, along with his aides and several U.S. advisors.[38] What might one make of the continued activities of the anti–Ahmadiya movement, which was not even fazed by this sign of divine disfavor? The most likely explanation is Muslim fatalism, which rejects the notion of the effect of human wishes on God's actions; to a Muslim, prayers merely acknowledge the supremacy of God, and requesting divine intervention on one's behalf would be considered both presumptuous and futile.

The Algerian Civil War

From early 1992 to 1997, a civil war raged in Algeria that may have taken as many as 100,000 lives. Like the war of independence against France, which lasted from 1954 to 1961, the Algerian civil war was a guerrilla conflict, featuring small-scale skirmishes rather than major battles. Most of the victims were unarmed civilians, killed because of their opinions, dress, or the place where they happened to live. Although the worst atrocities were committed by the Armed Islamic Group (GIA), the most extreme of the insurgent armies, there were also atrocities committed by other forces, not least the government itself. Although the army finally succeeded in stamping out the insurgency, terrorist attacks continued on a small scale even a decade later, as remnants of the GIA affiliated with al-Qaeda.

To understand the Algerian civil war, one must appreciate the nature of the country's colonial experience at the hands of the French; it was unique in the Muslim world. Once an Ottoman province, Algeria was seized by the French in 1830, long before the rest of the Middle East, or even most of Africa. The French conquest, justified in the name of France's "civilizing mission," was accompanied by wholesale atrocities against the local population. Whole villages were wiped out on suspicion of being sympathetic to the local resistance. Commented one French parliamentarian, "[W]e have outdone in barbarity the barbarians we have come to civilize...."[39]

Algeria, with its subtropical climate and pleasant beaches, attracted European settlers, and they ultimately reached 10 percent of Algeria's population — a higher ratio than anywhere on the continent except South Africa. Although the country was ruled by a Governor-General appointed by France, it was officially not a colony but part of the metropolis, the main reason why France was willing to expend lives and treasure to retain it, even as its other African colonies — from Morocco to Malagasy — were granted independence.

The European colonists, who were drawn from Spain and Italy as well as France, monopolized the best farmland and the better urban neighborhoods, and many of them grew wealthy exploiting cheap native labor; on the other hand, by no means all of them were affluent, but — as in South Africa — even the poorest Europeans were privileged relative to the native inhabitants. The Europeans were granted representation in the national parliament, where they formed a vocal bloc in opposition to decolonization; Algeria's Muslim majority had a separate bloc of representatives, the same size as that of the European minority, and chosen through largely fraudulent elections. Of the indigenous peoples of Algeria, only the Jews were granted full legal equality with the Europeans, a cynical divide-

and-rule maneuver passed off as an example of French enlightenment. Under a law passed in 1865, Muslims were denied equal rights as French citizens unless they renounced their Muslim civil status; only a handful of Muslims ever did so.[40] Throughout the colonial period, there were frequent uprisings by the Muslims, which were put down with extreme brutality.

European settlement was concentrated in the more fertile lowland areas, while the Muslims living in the less accessible and more arid mountain areas were less directly affected by colonization. Many of the mountain dwellers were not Arabs but Berbers, who spoke several distinct languages and even used a unique alphabet related to ancient Phoenician. Most of Algeria's "Arab" population actually consists of Arabized Berbers; despite this — or more likely because of it — there were clashes between Arabs and Berbers during the Revolution, which the French were quick to take advantage of.[41]

Algeria's religious leadership played an ambiguous role during the colonial period. "Throughout the 130 years of colonial rule," writes Milton Viorst, "the *ulama* [religious establishment] and its Islamic allies had been at the forefront of resistance to the French."[42] On the other hand, Reinhard Schulze points out that "[S]ome important leaders of the powerful mystical order of the Tijaniya ... were prepared to cooperate with the French."[43] By the twentieth century, "the colony depended for much of its religious support upon the movement that had been the principal mobilizer of resistance to its implantation in the nineteenth."[44]

Algeria's war of independence cost hundreds of thousands of lives, and attracted notice all over the world. After 130 years of colonial rule, the Algerians were left with a weak sense of national identity. In 1936, Ferhat Abbas, a moderate who later became the leader of the National Liberation Front (FLN), denied that an Algerian nation even existed.[45] Even decades after independence, French remained the language of the educated minority, and the political parties which called for an Islamic state had French names.

Unlike in Vietnam, the liberation struggle was led by a movement which spanned the ideological spectrum. It included secular nationalists, Marxists, and Islamists — although pan–Arabists of the Nasserist or Ba'athist variety were not particularly evident. On the eve of independence, there was a brief but bloody civil war between the followers of Ahmed Ben Bella, based in Morocco, and the official government-in-exile, based in Tunisia. The division was at least partly along Arab-Berber lines.[46]

Three years after independence, President Ben Bella was overthrown by his former ally, Col. Houari Boumedienne, who ruled from 1965 to 1978 until he died from natural causes. Boumedienne pursued a policy of Arabization of the education system, importing teachers from Egypt — including members of the extremist Muslim Brotherhood — and fostering classical Arabic at the expense of both French and Berber.[47] This policy alienated the Berbers, particularly the Kabyles — the largest Berber group — who feared the loss of their distinctive culture. Second, it introduced Egyptian pan–Islamist ideas to Algerian youths. And finally, it created a distinction between French-educated Algerians, who continued to have access to the better jobs, and younger Arabic-educated graduates, who were finding it increasingly difficult to get work. Boumedienne's education policy was a major reason the discontent among the unemployed youth took the form of Islamic extremism. There was little piety among Algerians in the early days of independence. During the 1960s, notes Michael Willis, Algerians — especially the young — were largely indifferent to religion. He estimated that, at least in the capital, less than 1 percent of the population were particularly devout.[48]

To some degree, the secularist–Islamist conflict masked the struggle over the country's economic direction. In 1971, the Boumedienne regime turned sharply to the left, seizing large estates and promoting collective farming, while aligning itself with the Communist Party.[49] This was opposed by the landowners, who made common cause with the ulama (religious teachers); when the ulama denounced the regime's land reform, the landlords reciprocated by subsidizing their mosques.[50] There was also opposition to the leftward turn by elements in the ruling FLN, as well as in the army.

Boumedienne's successor, Chadli Benjadid, reversed his socialist policies. Regarded in the West as a democrat, he favored increased political liberalization, but primarily for the purpose of benefiting the growing Islamist movement, to offset the left. At the time, there was considerable agitation by Berber cultural revivalists, as well as feminists and Marxists. Complicating the matter was the fact that the Kabyles, under the secular political system, had become more upwardly mobile than the Arab majority thanks to their better knowledge of French,[51] replicating the Sinhalese-Tamil disparity in Sri Lanka. "By 1980 it was evident that the Islamists had friends in high places and were benefiting from considerable if tacit indulgence on the part of the authorities, despite their increasing resort to violence in the prosecution of their mission."[52]

Chadli's economic policies led to massive unemployment and increasing inequality, exacerbating the tensions between the French-educated and Arabic-educated sections of the population. The worldwide decline at the time in oil and gas prices virtually bankrupted the state, and the high birthrate and massive urbanization created a vast population of young Algerians with nothing to do but hang around in the streets; they came to be known as *hittistes*, meaning those who hold up the walls. The first sign of serious trouble came in 1982, when an ex–FLN guerrilla, Moustafa Boyali, launched an uprising in the mountains near the capital in the name of Islam. He held out for five years before he was killed in combat; some of his surviving followers later joined the Islamic guerrillas during the civil war.[53] The FLN didn't take the hint. In October 1988, the entire country exploded in riots, leaving hundreds of dead and wounded, as angry youth attacked all symbols of the state.[54]

The political liberalization of the Chadli era gave the Islamists the space to organize, just as the reversal of the socialist course provided them with masses of young, unemployed recruits. The question is why it was the Islamists who benefited from the situation, rather than the radical left. There are two answers to this. First, the events in Cambodia during the previous decade had discredited the left everywhere — although, ironically, the events in Algeria during the 1990s, in which the left played no significant role, bore no small resemblance to the auto-genocide of the Khmer Rouge. The second reason is the fear of change, in part a reaction to birth trauma, which informs politics throughout the Muslim world. While birth trauma can be found in every society to one degree or another, Islamic theology *politicizes* its symptoms, causing the radicalized masses to turn against such catalytic communities as the Jews, the Armenians, or the United States, which now — thanks to the revolution in communications — plays that same role on a global scale. In consequence, revolutionary movements are typically sidetracked into ethno-religious chauvinism, as in Ba'athist Syria or Iraq, Khomeini's Iran, or even Kemalist Turkey. Algeria's particular tragedy is that its catalytic community consisted not of some small minority group or a foreign country, but of roughly half the population — the half that was educated in French, wore Western dress, and had only a nominal identification with Islam.

One curious aspect of the Algerian civil war was that the two warring sides were in basic agreement about the rightward economic direction they wanted the country to take. The main Islamist party, the Islamic Salvation Front (FIS), favored economic privatization, even though "it imposed enormous burdens on the poor, and the urban poor above all,"[55] the core of the FIS's own support.[56] This, comments Hugh Roberts, was "abnormal to the point of being bizarre in the extreme,"[57] although one might compare the appeal of the Religious Right in the United States to working-class families whose economic interests might lead them to support liberal Democrats. At the same time, the Algerian army, which had essentially run the country since independence, had been undergoing an important change; the guerrilla fighters against France, typically trained in the Arab countries, were gradually being replaced by former rank-and-file soldiers from the French colonial army who had defected to the nationalist side only after independence looked inevitable.[58] This latter group was fiercely anti–Islamist, and also less committed than the ex-nationalist combatants to social equality.

In 1990, Algeria held municipal elections, and the FIS won everywhere except in Kabylia, where the Berbers had their own parties, and the Sahara region, where the Tuaregs remained loyal to the FLN. The FIS generally did best in the larger urban areas, and in one extremely poor rural district.[59] It received more support from men than from women, and among the less educated and unemployed, and had about twice as much following among the 18-to-19-year-olds than from the 50–59 age bracket.[60] These figures must be regarded with some caution, since the FLN may have stuffed the ballot boxes in the more remote rural areas; but, at the same time, the FIS was seen intimidating voters inside urban voting stations, with no interference from the police.[61] Fouad Ajami believes that the fall of the FLN was due to its corruption, its "cynical *nomenklatura* that talks left and lives right."[62] But as in Palestine, where Fateh was defeated by the pan–Islamist Hamas for ostensibly the same reason, there were a number of other parties competing against the incumbents, so that the choice was never just between corrupt secularists and Islamic militants; Islamist ideology was simply more appealing to the voters than secular nationalism or Marxism.

While benefiting from Algeria's hesitant steps toward democracy, the FIS was undemocratic in its ideology. It favored the suppression of Berber culture, opposed women's rights, and featured banners in its demonstrations reading "Death to Democracy." Its firebrand deputy leader declared: "In Islam sovereignty belongs to the divine law; in democracy, sovereignty belongs to the people, to the mob and to charlatans."[63] Islamic activists targeted women who wore Western clothes, provoking reprisals by secularist youth against women in Islamic dress.[64] In the towns it briefly controlled, the FIS closed liquor stores, banned concerts during Ramadan, and ordered women to sit in the back on public buses. At the same time, it also set up literacy classes in mosques, and provided food and other services to the poor.[65]

Late in 1991, the FIS won the first round in the parliamentary elections, taking 188 seats out of 430, and trouncing the FLN, which won only 18. The army cancelled the second round and seized power in a coup, ousting Chadli and declaring a state of siege.[66] This paved the way for the five years of armed conflict which followed. The Armed Islamic Movement (MIA) was the first guerrilla group to fight against the military regime. It included

FIS activists, veterans of Bouyali's unsuccessful uprising, and returned pan–Islamist volunteers who had served with Ayman al-Zawahiri and Osama bin Laden in Afghanistan, where Algerians were among the largest national contingents. Another guerrilla group, the Islamic Salvation Army (AIS), declared itself the official military wing of the banned FIS.[67]

"Beginning in March 1993," writes Giles Kepel, "a steady succession of university academics, intellectuals, writers, journalists, and medical doctors were assassinated."[68] The Islamists were targeting not the government which had been repressing them, but all representatives of secularism and modernity.

The MIA and AIS soon found themselves competing with the Armed Islamic Group (GIA), which was even more fanatical. It was the GIA, which incorporated common criminals within its ranks,[69] that was responsible for most of the worst atrocities against civilians; this alienated it from the other Islamist tendencies, while strengthening the hand of the most hard-line elements in the army. The GIA targeted economic enterprises, rationalizing its destruction of the economy on the grounds that it reduced the influence of Jews, Christians and secularist Muslims. Stated one of its top leaders, "Our jihad consists of killing and dispersing all those who fight against God and his Prophet." His number two man described the FIS's aims as "throat-slitting and murder until the power is God's."[70] Algeria was no stranger to such violence, which was more common during the war of independence than its Western sympathizers might care to admit. The FIS's pronouncements echoed those of Saadi Yacef, leader of the FLN forces in the Casbah during the Battle of Algiers, who declared: "[W]e are assassins.... It's the only way in which we can express ourselves."[71] There is an echo here of Palestinian extremists, who justify terrorist attacks on Israeli civilians on the grounds that they are calling attention to their grievances. In both cases, terrorism appears to be the result of childhood neglect.

Late in 1994, the GIA turned on the AIS, which coincided with the army's declaration that it planned the "total eradication" of the Islamist guerrillas.[72] The next year, following the election of a new secularist president of Algeria, the GIA executed nearly two dozen of its own leaders who had condemned the indiscriminate killings of civilians.[73] One consequence of this was a split in its ranks, as the Groupe Salafiste pour la Prédication et le Combat was formed by disaffected GIA militants who sought to avoid attacks on civilians.[74]

The Algerian civil war is a unique example of a *delayed Adowa Cycle*, taking thirty years for completion — from independence to the outbreak of civil war — instead of the usual fifteen. This may be due to the slower turnover among the country's leadership, drawn from the military. The Algerian army began as a guerrilla force, and was led by younger men, although it soon became an exile army based in Tunisia and Morocco. Once the army seized power in 1964, the same people remained in control for decades. The turnover in the population, on the other hand, was particularly rapid due to the high birth rate — as well as the large rate of emigration to France. But the Islamist uprising could not have taken place without the encouragement of a segment of the national leadership, who served the role of enablers.

More than thirty years after independence, in a country where most of the population was too young to remember colonial rule, the Algerian rage against the West was more psychological than political in origin. The West represents modernity to Algerian Islamists, and what they fear about modernity is that it gives people endless opportunities to make choices, from deciding which candidate to vote for in a democratic election, to choosing where to go on vacation, to picking one brand of product over another. Birth trauma often leaves its victims in a feeling of "I don't know what to do," and for such people, living in a consumerist democracy, with its constant choices, can be agonizing. They often end up joining cults, or letting others run their lives. In the Muslim world, where such feelings are expressed in the political sphere, they become followers of Ayman al-Zawahiri, Osama bin Laden, or Ayatollah Khomeini.

11

Iran

Khomeini's Islamic Revolution: Shadow and Substance

Two group fantasies play important roles in Iran's long history. The first is that some day a "just king" will arrive, bringing about an era of social justice without the Iranian people having to struggle for it. Following the Arab conquest of Iran during the mid–seventh century and Iran's subsequent conversion to Islam, the "just king" was transformed into the Hidden Imam, whose role in Shia Islam is to return and usher in the millennium. The Shias are a large majority of Iran's Muslims, but only about a sixth of the world's total; until recently, when it was joined by Azerbaijan and later Iraq, Iran was virtually the only Shia-ruled country in the Muslim world.

The second major Iranian fantasy is that all the evil in their country is the work of outsiders, and that Iranian political leaders are their hapless pawns.

Satarreh Farma Farmaian, the American-educated daughter of an Iranian aristocrat, founded the first school of social work in Iran. Although she was no supporter of the fallen Shah, she was forced to emigrate from her country shortly after the Islamic Revolution of 1979. In exile in Los Angeles, she wrote her autobiography, *Daughter of Persia*. Throughout her book, she refers to the self-image of common Iranians as "nobodies," incapable of making any difference in their own personal lives, much less in the life of their nation. She gives the example of Mashti, a male servant in her childhood home, whom she was close to. A dishonest grocer sold him an unripe watermelon, which got him into trouble with his employer. Although Mashti was a physically strong fellow, it never occurred to him to return to the market and confront the grocer. Either the latter had cheated him, so he maintained, or some evil spirits had ruined the melon. Whatever the case, there was nothing he could do about it.[1]

Scholars such as Daniel Pipes and Ervand Abrahamian have observed that Iranians are paranoid even by Middle Eastern standards. They seem incapable of seeing their political leaders as actors in their own right. All of their leaders, in their opinion, must be mindless puppets of some foreign power — typically England, but also the United States, the USSR, or Israel. Writes Hooman Majd:

> Iranians have traditionally, at least in the last few centuries, despised their leaders no matter their character or their deeds, been quick to turn on and mock them, but at the same time yearned for strong leadership and someone to look up to.[2]

Not even Ayatollah Khomeini escapes suspicion. According to *New York Times* journalist Elaine Sciolino, Iranians have been known to ask, "Why did the United States put Khomeini in power?"[3] as if the Iranians themselves had nothing to do with it. She attributed this mindset to Iran's history of domination by foreign powers.[4] But Iran was one of a handful of Muslim countries which escaped Western colonization, while European interference in China never produced the same attitude of helplessness — if anything, judging from recent Chinese movies, quite the opposite. Iranians not only see themselves as nobodies, they also see other Iranians, even the most powerful, in the same way.

The Psycho-Geography of Passivism

The central part of Iran is an arid plateau, surrounded by mountains and, beyond them, largely fertile lowland provinces. Ethnic Persians, about half the population, inhabit the plateau, while the surrounding areas contain a variety of other groups. About a quarter of Iran's people are Turkic, primarily Azerbaijanis. Kurds and their Baluchi relatives number another 8 percent, while Arabs, who live in the southeast, are 3 percent. There are smaller communities of Christians, Jews, and Zoroastrians. Some groups are very closely related to the Persians, such as the Luris, Bakhtiaris, and Shomalis ("Northerners"). The last are actually two groups speaking distinct dialects — Gilani and Mazenderani — who inhabit a narrow, densely-populated stretch of well-watered land along the southern Caspian coast.

In sharp contrast to China, Vietnam, Indonesia, or even India, there has been relatively little peasant unrest in Iran,[5] even though land ownership had been highly unequal prior to the Shah's limited reform, with half of the cultivated land belonging to absentee landlords, and 40 percent of rural households holding none at all.[6] In the first serious political conflict in twentieth-century Iran, the civil war of 1908–09 the peasantry backed the moribund Qajar dynasty, while the constitutionalist reformers were supported by the urban middle class. Outside the cities, the reformers were supported only by the nomadic Bakhtiari.[7] During the 1950s, Mohammad Mossadegh's nationalist followers were also primarily middle-class, and the peasants failed to fight for his regime against the CIA–backed group. The 1979 Islamic Revolution was entirely an urban affair, with the peasantry playing no significant role.[8]

The Caspian region, on the other hand, is an exception to the rule of Iranian peasant passivity. This narrow crescent is a region of "thatch-roofed wooden houses with verandas, dense green forests, rice paddies, [and] water buffalo,"[9] more reminiscent of Southeast Asia than the Middle East. Gilan province, the western end of the crescent, has long been the most radical area in Iran. Between 1917 and 1921, a guerrilla insurgency raged there, heavily influenced by the Bolsheviks in nearby Russia.[10] Later, the Communist Tudeh party had its only peasant following in this same area[11]; and Gilan was the locale of the first guerrilla uprising against the Shah, as early as 1971.[12] In 1981, two years after the Islamic Revolution, a leftist group also launched a brief uprising in the Caspian religion.[13]

In the central plateau, landlords traditionally dominated their tenants through the ownership of water rights, as well as land. Water "becomes a factor of life and death," writes Reza Baraheni, "and whoever has this natural resource will use it as an instrument of economic and political power."[14] This is even reflected in the blue domes featured in Iranian architecture, "conveying a life-enhancing reference to water."[15] The ability to provide life-giving water is also an instrument of psychological power, promoting identification with the oppressor. Not surprisingly, when the Shah's reforms distributed land to the peasants, the landlords were allowed to keep their rights to the water, leaving the peasants almost as dependent on their masters as before.

Family life in Iran is different from elsewhere in the Middle East; fathers socialize more with their families, rather than spend all their free time with their male friends, as in Pakistan or the Arab countries.[16] But, at least among the elite, the family structure is strongly authoritarian. "For Moslems," says Farmaian, "disagreeing with a parent or indeed any family elder, is among the worst of all sins, and its punishment is everlasting hellfire."[17] Her own father had four wives, each with her own household; they took turns spending the night with their husband. The father was proud of his children — all thirty-six of them — but needless to say, his relationship with them was not quite as close as one finds in monogamous families. He met with them weekly, for which they dressed up and prepared recitals, as if he were the principal of their school. They addressed him as *Ghorban*, "a word suggesting an almost untranslatable reverence on the part of the speaker. Although it is sometimes rendered in English as 'Excellency,' its truer meaning is 'You for whom I sacrifice myself.'"[18]

While this may reflect the lives of the elite, conditions were different among the less affluent, where men could rarely afford more than one wife. Farmaian herself envied the less formal relationship between Mashti and his own daughter. But the poor regarded themselves as dependents of their wealthy landlords or employers, and it was the heads of the wealthy families who were regarded as the authority figures on the rural estates, or within the walls of the urban compounds. This pattern of dependency was developed even further when the military officer Reza Khan seized power in 1921 at the head of a Czarist Russian–trained division, with British support; he founded the Pahlavi dynasty four years later. His appetite for other people's property[19] made him the personal owner of much of the country, a situation which interfered with his sincere desire to modernize Iran. Landlord and ruler became one and the same for many Iranians. But Muslim religious institutions continued to own much land as well.[20] The income from this property was important for the survival of the Shia hierarchy, since while the Sunni clergy is supported by the state, the Shia are dependent on voluntary contributions,[21] not easily forthcoming in times of economic uncertainty.

The Iranians — unlike the Arabs — are Indo-Europeans (called "Indo-Aryans" before World War II), and "Iran," adopted by Reza Shah in place of "Persia," is cognate to "Aryan." Even today, thousands of years after their ancestors migrated to the region, Iranians still feel a sense of not belonging there. Their non–Middle Eastern origins are attested to by the tomb of the first Persian Emperor, Cyrus the Great — a relatively modest structure compared to the Egyptian pyramids — which still stands in southern Iran. It has a gabled roof, similar to houses designed for northern climates with heavy snowfalls, where the Indo-Europeans originated.[22] Like their relatives in Europe, the Iranians received their religion from Semites, and Iranian resentment of Arabs — even Ayatollah Khomeini referred to them contemptuously as "camel grazers" and "barbarians"[23] — forms a curious parallel to Europe's anti–Semitism. But whereas Europe was pagan before it adopted Christianity, Iran followed the ancient monotheistic faith of Zoroastrianism.

Essential to Zoroastrianism is the concept of eternal struggle between externalized good and evil — in contrast to Christianity and Judaism, which see it taking place within each individual, as did Mohammad. This pre–Islamic doctrine was incorporated into Shia Islam, along with Islamic fatalism. But at the same time, Iran's national epic, the *Shahnameh* ("Book of Kings"), is replete with tales of mighty heroes, each as tall as a cypress tree, slaying villains and dragons, winning battles, and falling in love with beautiful heroines who smell, invariably, of musk. Like the costumed super-heroes of American comic books, the *Shahnameh*'s heroes are bigger than life and always win in the end. Divine intervention seldom figures in the lengthy epic, and Islam is never mentioned, although the poem was written after the Muslim conquest. An account of the battle of Qadisiya, where Muslim Arabs defeated the Persians, takes place before the time of Alexander, and results in a Persian victory.[24] Foreshadowing Khomeini, the *Shahnameh* derides Arabs as cowardly primitives.[25] Inspired by Iran's pre–Islamic history, the *Shahnameh*, like our own comic books, teaches that the individual can make a difference, and is not prevented by Fate from achieving his own ends; it is the anti–Koran.

Sunnis vs. Shias

The Sunni-Shia division goes back to the political conflict that emerged just after Mohammad's death between his son-in-law Ali and his young widow Aisha. The latter was backed by wealthy Arab merchant clans which had adopted Islam only after the Prophet's triumphant return to Mecca. These clans wanted an elected Caliph to rule the growing Muslim community, while Ali's supporters wanted leadership to remain in Mohammad's lineage. Elected leaders often turn out to be strong, having been chosen for their abilities; hereditary leaders are often weak. Ali's supporters, the Shias, have traditionally perceived themselves as being in opposition to all existing governments. Following a series of inconclusive battles between the early Sunnis and Shias, Ali briefly became Caliph, but he faced a Sunni revolt, and was then assassinated by a member of yet another faction opposed to any Sunni-Shia reconciliation. Ali was ultimately succeeded as Caliph by Yazid, a Sunni.[26]

Yazid's army clashed with a small band of Shias, led by Ali's son Hussein, near Karbala in 680 c.e. The heavily outnumbered Shias were slaughtered, and only a few of their women survived. "[T]he Battle of Karbala changed Shi'ism from a loosely knit group of Ali's devotees into a separate sect inspired by the potent themes of sacrifice, guilt, and death."[27] It is interesting that following the Islamic Revolution, a portrait of Khomeini showed him standing in his black and white robes against a backdrop of orange sky, his hands clasped in prayer, surrounded by adoring cherubs; the painting was copied from a 17th-century portrayal of the Virgin Mary by the Spanish artist Murillo.[28] The similarities between Shi'ism and Christianity are the result of both diffusion and convergence.

A legend associated with the Battle of Karbala is that Hussein brought his infant son with him to the front. As his thirsty followers approached the Euphrates River, facing thousands of Yazid's heavily armed troops, Hussein held the baby up, "to show the enemy how urgently water was needed." Perhaps misunderstanding the gesture — or, more likely, unconcerned with the enemy's suffering — the Sunnis let loose a barrage of arrows, one of which killed the baby.[29] As the story is presented to Iranians today, it appears to justify the sacrifice of children for political ends. And it epitomizes the psychohistorical role played by Shi'ism in Iran: It is an expression of the feeling, "I am a helpless victim."

The Karbala legend parallels the death of Jesus, and is recounted in passion plays throughout Iran — again, a parallel with Europe. "Go to any village or remote tribal area," says Baqer Moin, "and you will find people replaying the martyrdom of Hussein."[30] Sometimes the legend coalesces with Iranian nationalist sentiment. A modern Iranian historian writes: "It is perfectly evident that not a single person among the evil-doers in Karbala was either Iranian or of Iranian extraction."[31] True enough; they were Arabs. But the revered martyrs were also Arabs, since the vast majority of the recently conquered Iranians still adhered to Zoroastrianism and played no role in the Sunni-Shia conflict.

The Shia emphasis on Islam's rulers being from the bloodline of the Prophet "coincided with [Iran's] pre–Islamic traditions of legitimacy."[32] Yet the Shias did not become the dominant sect among Iranian Muslims until the rise of the Savafid dynasty, around 1500 C.E.,[33] which promoted a particularly fanatical strain as part of its struggle with the expansionist Sunni Ottoman Empire.[34] The triumph of Shi'ism in Iran was preceded by seven centuries of Shia opposition to Sunni domination, followed by another four hundred years of Shia dynastic rule — first under the Savafids, when Iran experienced a Golden Age, and then under the Turkic Qajars, who allowed the country to stagnate. Reza Shah took power from the last Qajar king, ironically — considering the events of 1979 — with the support of the Shia clergy.[35] His regime was far more nationalistic than Islamic, fostering a cult of Cyrus the Great.[36] The Shia clergy — who generally preferred the Pahlavis to chaos, Communism, or democracy — nursed their grievances until they were able to establish their theocratic rule on the ruins of his son's regime.

According to Sandra Mackey, Iranians have an "ancient idea that true kings are born into difficult circumstances, hidden away until the moment they are needed, and then emerge to save the nation."[37] In Shia Islam, this is transformed into the belief, similar to Christianity's Second Coming, that Imam Hasan Al-Askar (died 873 C.E.) left an infant son who was supposed to be the Mahdi, "the savior that Shia eschatology said would return at the end of time to deliver the suffering faithful from injustice."[38] For the next 11 centuries, the Hidden Imam was believed to be in "occultation." This messianic expectation not only divided the bulk of the Shias from Sunnis, but also from rival Shia groups such as Yemen's Zaidis and the Ismaili sect. It also explains how Khomeini was able to gain such widespread support from exile; he reminded his followers of the Hidden Imam.[39]

Fear of Change

Muslim societies frequently display evidence of birth trauma, but the symptoms differ between the Sunnis and Shias. Many Sunni nations are expansionist — such as Iraq, Morocco and Indonesia — whereas Iran's extremists have been less concerned with expanding their country's borders than with "purifying" it of alien influence. This began under Reza Shah, who campaigned against words in the Persian language of non–Persian origin.[40] Both territorial expansionism and obsession with purity are birth-related, but reflect different phases of the birth process: the expansionist is reenacting his (rarely her) memories of not having enough room in the womb, while the obsessive purifier is reliving his passage down the birth canal, when toxins are reaching his bloodstream through the umbilical cord.

This significant difference between Iran and other Muslim states indicates that birth may be somewhat less traumatic for Iranians. This is likely a reflection of the higher status of women in Iran, inherited from pre–Islamic days. Arabs (other than Egyptians) and Pakistanis have less conscious awareness of their pre–Islamic civilizations — officially, it is described as the "Age of Darkness." With their higher status and greater emotional freedom, Iranian women produced less birth trauma in their offspring. This raises the question of why birth trauma suddenly started to be reflected in Iran's politics in the 1970s.

Part of the answer may lie in the paradox that while the Pahlavi dynasty imposed a tyrannical rule on Iran for more than half a century, it was only when the standards of living and education began to rise precipitously, as a result of the boom in oil prices, that massive popular resistance to the monarchist regime spread throughout the country. Prior to that, the Shia clergy had supported the Pahlavis, even encouraging Reza Shah to declare himself king out of fear of democracy and social change.[41] At least part of the clergy supported the 1953 royalist coup against nationalist Prime Minister Mohammad Mossadegh, whom Ayatollah Khomeini denounced as pro–Communist.[42]

Reza Shah's ambition was to modernize Iran, along the lines of Kemal Ataturk's Turkey. As a result, the Iranians today are more Westernized than any other Muslims except the Turks, even though both nations escaped colonial rule. But the mass support that Ataturk enjoyed in the wake of the Ottoman Empire's collapse following World War I did not exist in Iran. After the feeble Qajar ruler declared Iran neutral in the "Great War," the country was invaded from all directions: the warring Turks and Russians marched into Iranian Azerbaijan to outflank each other; the British seized the oil fields in the south, while the Germans sent an agent to stir up the local tribes against them; and the Afghans invaded from the east to steal whatever they could lay their hands on. Epidemics followed, and total collapse of society — what Iranians called the *harj-o-marj* — loomed as a possibility. Reza Shah's coup, following his defeat of the Marxist rebels in Gilan, came as a relief to many.

But Reza Shah's later affinity for Nazism persuaded the British and Soviets to depose him in favor of his young son, Mohammad Reza Shah, in 1941. Mohammad Reza had grown up in the shadow of his father. A diminutive and indecisive man, he was dominated by others, including even his twin sister Ashraf.[43] Threatened by the widespread support for Prime Minister Mossadegh in 1953, he fled the country, leaving it to an army coup to restore him to power. The army was assisted by mobs rented by the CIA. After the Communists began toppling the Shah's statues, the royalists filled the city with their own demonstrations, and sent Mossadegh fleeing.[44] However unpopular the Shah may have been, many Iranians were terrified at the thought of life without him; some of this may have resulted from smash-and-grab looting in the streets of Tehran directed by royalist *agents provocateurs*. The Shia clergy, later his fierce opponents, were happy to direct public rage against the Baha'is, a small religious group who split off from Islam in the 19th century.[45]

During the early 1960s, the Shah launched a modest reform program, absurdly ballyhooed in Iran and America as "the Shah-People Revolution." The United States, then under President John Kennedy, favored reforms in the underdeveloped nations as a way of preventing radical revolution, while the Shah's young wife, Queen Farah, also pressed him to improve the living standards of the people.[46] The massive increase in oil prices only began about ten years later. Many, both in Iran and the United States, concluded that the country was on its way toward an era of stability, modernization, and prosperity. There was talk of Iran becoming a great power like Japan by the year 2000.[47] Iran had the advantage of its vast oil wealth, but the Japanese did not adhere to Muslim fatalism. As a result, fifty years after its opening to the west, Japan was able to defeat large nations like China and Russia and emerge as a world power. But almost fifty years after the Shah's coup in 1953, theocratic Iran had a declining standard of living, and was unable to impose its will even on Afghanistan.

In his opulent palaces, ignorant of the lives of most of his subjects, Mohammad Reza Shah was hardly the revolutionary his American publicists made him out to be. His limited land reform allowed landlords to keep one village each, distributing the remainder to the sharecroppers. Some of the landlords were able to put their villages in the names of family members or retainers, evading the reform. And when the remaining land was distributed, hired laborers, on the bottom of the social scale, were excluded altogether. It was this underclass of propertyless, uneducated ex–farm laborers who began migrating to the cities, causing the urban population to double between 1966 and 1980.[48] Tehran alone, by then, contained 5 million people.

> The abrupt, unplanned, and uncontrolled influx of young migrants into the cities had created sprawling shanty towns. These, in turn, had produced a vast social problem with its typical symptoms — prostitution, alcoholism, drug addiction, delinquency, suicides, and, of course, a crime wave.[49]

Another consequence of urbanization was a shift in the ethnic composition of Tehran. Prior to the oil boom, most of the city's workers were Azerbaijani or Shomali,[50] but the later migrants came primarily from the Persian region south of the capital. It was these uprooted and uneducated laborers who became the strongest supporters of the various forms of politicized Islam during the late 1970s,[51] while the long-established workers, hailing from the northern provinces, tended to be more sympathetic to Marxism.[52]

The Shah was himself a factor in the rise of oil prices during the early 1970s, although Americans tended to blame it all on the Arabs. His head filled with visions of grandeur, the Shah spent much of the country's newfound wealth on armaments purchased from the United States; he entertained prominent guests from abroad in a 1971 celebration of Iranian history at the ancient city of Persepolis which cost up to $200,000,000.[53] Oil, while it produced few jobs itself, financed the growth of other sectors, particularly construction and service. The Iranian GNP grew at a rate of 30 percent in 1973–1974, compared to only 8 percent in 1962–1970.[54] Oil revenues, a mere $593 million in 1966, rose sharply and steadily each year until 1972, and then skyrocketed. Revenues for 1974 were $22 billion — thirty-seven times those for 1966, and about four times those for 1973. There was a drop of 10 percent after 1974,[55] causing a sharp rise in unemployment.[56] This economic retrenchment has been regarded as a major cause of the Islamic Revolution, but psychohistorians might argue that the previous rise in the country's economic wealth was a more important factor than the relatively small subsequent decline. At the same time, while Iran may have been flush with petrodollars, much of it was wasted on grandiose projects or deposited in the Pahlavi family's foreign bank accounts. The gap between rich and poor widened enormously, and even the government-sponsored recession of 1975–77 failed to halt the 30 percent inflation rate.[57]

Oil wealth also led to the expansion of higher education, although about half the population remained illiterate.[58] Iran's first university had been founded only in 1935.[59] During the 1950s, "the number of university students per one thousand population was far below that of Egypt, Turkey, and other Asian countries."[60] But by 1970, there were eight Iranian universities, mostly state-run.[61] University students increased from 29,000 in 1963 to 135,000 in 1974,[62] and 154,000 by 1977,[63] a more than five-fold increase in 14 years. In addition, there were an estimated 60,000 Iranians studying in American universities,[64] plus thousands more in Europe and India. Many young Iranians were radicalized by their overseas education, and the existence of a large contingent of youth who were better educated than their parents paved the way for a fierce clash of values between the two generations, as it did elsewhere.

Iran's Drug Problem

Because Iran started modernizing so late, nearly all aspects of mid–twentieth century life reached the country at about the same time, under a widely unpopular government. And this social change was occurring in a society in which the use of opium had become common. "What alcohol is to Americans, opium is to Iranians,"[65] writes William Forbis. The most hard-core addicts numbered in the hundreds of thousands, and opium was regarded as "almost a part of Iran's heritage...."[66] In 2005, *Iran News* reported that Iran had the highest drug consumption in the world, with perhaps more than 15 percent of its population using it."[67]

While the drug had long been known in Iran, it only became a major cash crop in the nineteenth century.[68] Iranian opium was regarded as the world's best,[69] and found a market in China through British middlemen. By 1869, cultivation of opium poppies was so common that it interfered with food production, resulting in a series of famines.[70] In 1924, the export of opium provided the Iranian government with a tenth of its revenue.[71] One of the most popular forms in which it is used is *shir'e*, made from the ashes of previously smoked opium.[72]

The Shah outlawed opium cultivation in 1955, but smugglers were able to bring it in by the truckload from Afghanistan and Pakistan to satisfy the cravings of Iran's addicts; the ban was finally recognized as ineffective, and was lifted. Following that, opium became universally available.[73] Even under the puritanical Islamic Republic, 60 percent of the large prison population had been convicted of drug addiction, and Afghanistan remained the chief supplier of "plentiful and cheap" heroin.[74] It was especially popular in Qom, Iran's main center of religious learning, where it was a "major form of male entertainment" in the absence of alcohol and cinemas.[75] The Shah's own family was involved in the trade, even while it was supposedly illegal. Princess Ashraf was arrested in Geneva in 1960 when she was found to be carrying suitcases containing $2 million worth of heroin.[76] At the time of the Islamic Revolution, she was still regarded as the country's main drug dealer.[77]

The widespread use of opium, which kills pain, appears to have been a factor behind the unexpected spread of religious fanaticism in Iran. Consider the spread of the "Jesus Freak" movement in the United States after drugs became widespread during the 1960s. As with alcohol, emotionally defended people become less repressed when their pain is dulled by drugs.[78] As long as they remain unconscious of the source of the pain, people tend to *act their feelings out symbolically*, without feeling them. Even allowing for Iranians' legitimate grievances against American policy toward their country, the sheer intensity of the anti–Americanism following the Islamic Revolution indicates its largely symbolic nature. During the 1979–80 seizure of the U.S. Embassy, for example, Elaine Sciolino noted that "the same Iranian demonstrators who chanted angry slogans about the 'den of spies' in the mornings followed me down Ferdowsi Avenue in the afternoons asking me to help them get visas or contact their relatives in Los Angeles or Dallas."[79] On one level, America, which for many years dictated the Shah's policies, represents the harsh and distant father — or the powerful landlord who was the authority figure for many rural Iranians. On another level, America was the source of Westernization — "Westoxication," as it was called by Shia fundamentalists and militant nationalists alike — which symbolized the confusion triggered by consumer freedom, and typically associated with birth trauma. For many Iranians, the need to blindly follow some charismatic leader is an acting out of the feeling of "I don't know what to do," a birth feeling which was evoked by the country's sudden rise in prosperity.

Perinatal Origins of Totalitarianism

From 1957 to 1975, Iran had a two-party system in which both parties, Melliyun and Mardom, were indistinguishable instruments of the Shah,[80] each headed by his own personal friends.[81] Their candidates for the powerless Majlis (parliament) had to be approved by SAVAK, the secret police.[82] To outsiders, the system appeared to be democratic, since the two parties alternated in office, but in fact all political power — and much of the country's growing wealth — was concentrated in the hands of the ruler. In 1963, the Shah's proposed reforms evoked violent opposition from the Shia clergy, led by Ayatollah Khomeini, in a revolt which was finally crushed in 1964 — fifteen years before the Islamic Revolution of 1978–79. Khomeini's opposition focused on the extension of largely meaningless voting rights to women and non–Muslims minorities.[83] The Shah's land reform was also a threat to religious institutions, although the clergy were careful not to make this the main issue. Khomeini was supported by nationalists whose slogan was "Yes to reforms, no to dictatorship," but they were outflanked by the better-organized clergy, whose goals were precisely the reverse. The Shah was furious with the Shia clergy, calling them "a stupid and reactionary bunch whose brains have not moved for a thousand years."[84] This, of course, came from a man eager to revive glories from more than *two* thousand years ago. Khomeini's enforced exile extinguished the revolt, and Iran once again appeared to be a pillar of stability in a volatile region.

Then, in March 1975, the Shah's two tame parties were suddenly dissolved.

> In an unanticipated initiative [the Shah] announced the establishment of a new single party, called the Rastakhiz or National Resurgence Party. All Iranians were pressured to join it, and whereas the two earlier entities had had little real organization outside the Majlis this was to become a mass party. By 1977 it was claimed that five million Iranians had joined and local cells were established throughout the country.[85]

Iranians opposed to the new state of affairs were invited by the Shah to go to prison or into exile.[86] The opposition was weak and disorganized at that time, and the Nixon administration had no objection. Almost overnight, the nature of Iranian politics changed.

> [D]issenters who for years had been left alone so long as they did not air their opposition now suddenly found themselves with no choice but to enroll in the party, sign peti-

tions in favor of the regime, and even march in the streets singing praises for the 2,500-year-old monarchy.[87]

Newspapers featured photographs of the Shah and his family almost daily, and newsreels in movie theaters invariably portrayed the activities of the monarch, at which point the audience was expected to jump up and shout, "Long live the Shah!" This proved to be an effective way of convincing the regime's opponents that they were an isolated minority; no one in the darkened theater was likely to catch on to the fact that everyone else was pretending.

In 1976, servile academics at Tehran University drew up the document *The Philosophy of Iran's Revolution*, which spelled out the new political style:

> The Shahanshah ["King of Kings"] ... stands above class or the interests of special groups in society. He is king of all the people. He is also in a father-son relationship to the nation.... The Shahanshah is not just the political leader of the country. He is also in the first instance teacher and spiritual leader, an individual who not only builds his nation roads, dams and qanats [aqueducts] but also guides the spirit, thought and hearts of the people.[88]

A first-grade textbook reflected the same outlook: "At home we love and respect our father.... The Shah is like the father of this large family and we are like his children. The Shah loves all of us. We love our kind Shah like our own father."[89] Of course, the identification of the Shah with "father" also made him the target for a good deal of repressed childhood rage.

That Iran's sudden leap from authoritarianism to totalitarianism was motivated by perinatal factors is indicated by the Shah's own comment in 1975 that "Iranian culture should be cleansed of all pollution which might have crept into it through foreign elements."[90] This pollution fantasy, which played a major role in Khomeini's rhetoric as well, stems from the stage of the birth process when the newborn's placental link with the mother's bloodstream is cut off. Traumatic events at the social level, such as war, can evoke such feelings. For example, during the peak of the Vietnam War, Americans suddenly became extremely aware of air and water pollution, a concern which faded as the war wound down, and "Earth Day" was largely forgotten. Iran had not been involved in any wars during the 1970s, but it would seem that the widespread use of opium had a similar result; its ability to numb pain allowed buried memories to surface, even from birth.

Khomeini's Reactionary Revolution

The first major outburst of anti-regime sentiment following the establishment of royalist totalitarianism took place in Washington, D.C., in November 1977, during the Shah's visit to President Jimmy Carter. At least 4,000 Iranian exchange students showed up to demonstrate against him,[91] and there were clashes with the police and with a smaller number of pro–Shah demonstrators. There were many injuries, and both Carter and the Shah got a whiff of the tear gas used by the police. News of this show of opposition shattered the myth that the Shah was beloved by his "children," and energized the long-smoldering resistance back in Iran. If privileged university students were so vehemently opposed to the regime, other social classes had even less reason to regard the Shah with affection.

Early in 1978, an article attacking Khomeini was printed in a government-controlled newspaper, causing an intense reaction among religious scholars in Qom. By the next day, perhaps 20 demonstrators had been slain by the police.[92] Over the next few months, there were more uprisings throughout Iran, and by the middle of the year, the oil workers also got involved. They struck in October, demanding higher wages, an end to political oppression, and equality for women.[93] The pro–human rights policy of the Carter administration made Washington reluctant to come to the aid of the beleaguered (and ailing) monarch. And, although this was rarely mentioned in the press, the Shah's role in raising oil prices also may have worked against him with the United States. For these reasons — and because Khomeini's ultimate intentions were sadly misconstrued by American policy-makers — the U.S. was not entirely unwilling to let the "King of Kings" depart.

His leading opponent, Ayatollah Ruhollah Khomeini, was a very different kind of man from the Shah. Born in relative poverty in 190s, he lost his father only a few months later, and was raised by his mother and aunt; the latter was a respected figure in her community despite living in a male-dominated society. Both of them died when Ruhollah was sixteen.[94] This was at the end of World War I, when Iran was reeling from the effects of foreign invasion, domestic unrest, weak Qajar government, and the flu epidemic. Khomeini's older brother, who also became an Ayatollah, took responsibility for the younger man's further education.[95] Only in 1962, when his mentor Ayatollah Boroujerdi died, did Khomeini get involved in politics.[96] But during the following two years, he quickly became the spokesman for the most anti-government elements of the Shia clergy. The collapse of the 1963–64 revolt forced him into exile, first in Turkey, then in Iraq, and finally in Paris.[97]

Like the Christian fundamentalists in the United States, Khomeini argued that his religion's sacred book contains everything that is needed to run society, and that the only function of government is to interpret its texts: "[S]overeignty belongs to God alone and law His decree and command," he has written. "The law of Islam, divine command, has absolute authority over all individuals and the Islamic government."[98] Any government which does not derive its authority from the Koran is, by his definition, unjust and illegitimate[99]; but all Islamic governments are just, regardless of what they might do. Khomeini elaborated: "If a just ruler orders the arrest of any person or burning down the house of another, or the extermination of a community which is detrimental to Islam and Muslims, his order is just and must be obeyed."[100]

Corruption was another one of his major themes. Leaders are installed by God, Khomeini argued, so that men will not "fall prey to corruption."[101] Western culture was identified as "Satan" because of its freedom. Khomeini recognized that his "Satan" imagery was a projection of repressed inner urges:

> It is Satan that is ruling us too; we follow him, and our vain desires are a manifestation of him. As long as that great Satan that is our unredeemed soul exists within us, whatever we do will be done in egoism. We must destroy the government of Satan within us.[102]

Khomeini's writings abound in condemnations of "passion" and feelings, indicating a thoroughly repressed mental state. "In his unredeemed state," Khomeini writes, "man is like an animal, even worse than other animals. Left to his own devices, he will always be inferior to the animals, for he surpasses them in passion, evil, and rapacity."[103] Music is condemned "became it involves pleasure and ecstasy,"[104] and sexual activity is likewise considered sinful because of the feelings it might arouse.[105] Revealingly, when he was asked by an American reporter upon his return to Tehran after sixteen years of exile, "Ayatollah, would you be so kind as to tell us how you feel about being back in Iran?" he chillingly replied, "Nothing."[106]

In 1977, Khomeini's son Mostafa, also his aide, died mysteriously in Baghdad, causing some to suspect the Shah's SAVAK, as the last two people to see him were Iranians. With its close ties to the CIA, however, SAVAK would have been unlikely to assassinate an oppositionist outside its own borders, since the U.S. government doesn't tolerate such actions. Washington allows a dictator to kill as many opponents as he wants inside his own country, but killing even one opponent in another land qualifies him as a rogue. And Khomeini hired SAVAK's chief, Hossain Fardost, to head his own secret police after he took over, indicating that he must have known SAVAK was not involved in his son's death. Mostafa's apparent murder played into Khomeini's hands, since the Shia clergy in Iran were at the time trying to settle their differences with the Shah, and the son's martyrdom allowed the father to grab the spotlight once again. The Ayatollah's only response to his son's death was to repeat a Koranic verse: "We belong to God and to Him we shall return."[107] But two years later, when radicals assassinated Revolutionary Council Chairman Morteza Motahhari, Khomeini was devastated. "[H]e sat clutching his handkerchief, sobbing and sometimes crying out loudly for his friend."[108]

Under the guise of religion, Ayatollah Khomeini established a new totalitarian regime on the ruins of the Shah's, hijacking the revolution from the youthful Marxists and Islamic socialists who initiated it. The central theme of the Islamic Republic has been sacrifice of the young. The red tulip, Iran's national flower,[109] symbolizes martyrdom. As with the cherry blossom in Japan, the tulip falls from the stem before it wilts, representing the sacrifice of men in wartime before they grow old.

More than twenty years after the Islamic Revolution, an American reporter still noted graffiti in Isfahan reading "Martyrdom is prosperity for us."[110] In 1979, Khomeini wrote to Pope John Paul II: "[A]s Shiites we welcome any opportunity for sacrificing our blood. Our nation looks forward to an opportunity for self-sacrifice and martyrdom."[111] That opportunity was not long in coming. In 1980, Iraq's dictator Saddam Hussein invaded Iran, hoping to seize the oil-rich province of Khuzistan, where the population was largely Arab, and which he apparently thought could be held against an Iranian counter-attack. The result was one of the longest wars of the twentieth century, costing perhaps a million dead, the large majority of them Iranian.

Iran has three times Iraq's population, and Iraq was already facing unrest among its Kurds and Shias, while the Iranians swiftly united against the attack. With Basra, its second largest city and only seaport, just a few miles from the Iranian border, Iraq was quite vulnerable. Yet the war finally ended in a draw, eight years later. This took place immediately after Iran Air flight 655 was shot down by an American warship which mistook it for a combat plane, there having been minor clashes in the Gulf at that time. In a country which had stoically accepted as many as 800,000 dead in the war, there was an outpouring of grief for the 290 passengers.[112] These deaths were *unexpected*, unlike the war losses, and after Iranians began feeling their pain from the tragedy, it was no longer possible for them to deny their grief for a while generation which had been sacrificed. Khomeini was forced to accept a cease-fire, an act he termed "more deadly than drinking hemlock."[113] His murder contract on the Indian Muslim novelist Salman Rushdie, issued shortly afterward, may have been in part his response to the humiliation of having to agree to a cease-fire; the controversial novel, clearly offensive to most Muslims, had actually been published months earlier with little reaction from Khomeini or any other Islamic militant. One way or another, Khomeini had to be involved in a struggle he could not win.

The war had unanticipated consequences for Iran. The enormous demand for manpower forced the government to tolerate women working outside the home.[114] At the same time, many young men were able to evade military service by enrolling in Qom's seminaries.[115] From the Islamic Revolution to the end of the century, Iran's clergy increased from 80,000 to at least 600,000.[116] The war's economic cost was astronomical, and was a major factor, along with the huge birth rate, in the decline of the standard of living. Hashemi Rafsanjani, the army's commander-in-chief, estimated it at about 1 trillion dollars.[117]

During the war, Iran developed the Basij militia, which began as a civil defense force which also spied on the population. It recruited young boys, old men, and even women. Sent off to the front, the Basij were trained to walk across minefields to clear the way for the regular army.[118] The sacrifice of children, reminiscent of the death of Hussein's infant son at Karbala, became the primary goal of Iran's war effort—not the defeat of the Iraqi enemy, which Tehran repeatedly identified with Caliph Yazid, the victor at Karbala. During the war, a seven-year-old girl wrote to Khomeini:

> [W]e children used to play with our dolls.... When you came we had no desire to play with dolls any more. They became old and after a while they broke. Then we began to make wooden guns.... Childish games had no meaning for us any more. We felt grown up, very proud of the wooden guns we carried on our shoulders.[119]

The psychological purpose of child sacrifice, of course, is not to make children feel "grown up," but rather to reverse the normal state of affairs in which children live to bury their parents. In conditions of extreme birth anxiety, people become willing to bury their own children, thus making themselves, in their own unconscious minds, immortal.

The More Things Change...

Khomeini's death in 1989 led to a temporary softening of his harsh theocracy, but the hard-line fanatics organized in the Society of Militant Clergy still held a great deal of power. "Virtually every branch of government has a shadow position or institution with equal power—at *least* equal—usually led by, loyal to or largely made up of clerics."[120] The hardliners also run huge foundations which confiscated the property left behind by the Shah and the millions of others who fled Iran after 1979. Since the revolution, Iran has actually had two governments: a secular one in Tehran, chosen by relatively free, if imperfect, elections; and a theocratic one in Qom, led since Khomeini's death by Ali Khamenei, originally a relatively low-ranking cleric.[121] Dyarchy has never survived for this long a period anywhere, but it has a precedent in Iran, during World War I, when a weak Qajar government competed with the nationalists.[122]

The system is inherently unstable, but with the election in 2005 of the hard-line Mahmoud Ahmedinejad, the secular and theocratic governments were for once on the same wavelength.[123] For eight years, when the reform-minded cleric Mohammad Khatami was president, it appeared that the Islamic Republic was evolving into a democracy, but Khatami was unable to cope with the hard-liners, who still controlled the judiciary, the para-military forces, most of the media, and much of the economy. And even Khatami's reformism had its limits; in July 1999, he ordered the crackdown on a widespread student uprising.[124] By 2005, when Ahmedinejad — the populist mayor of Tehran — replaced him, it was clear that the reformist forces had been defeated. This could be blamed in part on George W. Bush's invasion of neighboring Iraq two years before. By 2005, the United States had troops or bases in nearly every country surrounding Iran, and Bush was linking Iran to Iraq and North Korea, the "Axis of Evil," making it clear that Iran risked a U.S. invasion; this played into the hands of the hard-liners.

But Ahmadinejad's popular support among the Iranians has had its ups and downs. As mayor of Tehran, he was considered remarkably effective, and his baiting of the United States — through his holocaust denial, and his identification with Latin American Marxists like Hugo Chavez — appeals to Iranian nationalist sentiment. Yet his links to neo–Nazi elements alienated potential friends among the governments of Europe. In 2006, for example, he wrote to German Chancellor Angela Merkel, "proposing, in all seriousness, an alliance of the two countries against 'the victors of the Second World War.'"[127] He seemed oblivious to how hard Germany has worked to put the Nazi past behind it. It also appeared that he was unconsciously walking in the footsteps of the pro–Nazi Reza Shah, daring the United States, out of masochism and the desire for martyrdom, to invade Iran and depose him.

Ahmedinejad's blatant anti–Semitism has both religious and political roots, and is closely linked to his belief in the imminent coming of the Mahdi, or messiah.[128] Both of these have roots in birth trauma. Expectation that a messiah is coming to "deliver" us stems from first-line memories of needing to be delivered during a difficult birth process; and the anti–Semitism comes from fear of a group which is typically seen as promoting change.

The 2009 election was also regarded by many, in Iran and abroad, as fraudulent, and the mass demonstrations against it that spring resembled the uprising that had toppled the Shah thirty years earlier, even to the point of prominent clerics being arrested by the government. In the forefront of the demonstrations were the young, the educated, and women. The rural and urban poor, who had suffered the most under the Ayatollah's as their standard of living fell, either stood aside or supported Ahmedinejad. If there was ever a case of psychoclass initiating a revolution, vindicating deMause's psychogenic theory of history, this was it.

A wide spectrum of Iranians had been involved in the original revolt against the Shah, and most of the armed struggle was the work of groups which later found themselves in opposition to the Khomeini regime. Khomeini hijacked the revolution in part because he was able to organize through the mosques, but also because he outcompeted the other groups in terms of martyrs. On "Black Friday," September 8, 1978, 1,600 people were killed by the Shah's forces when half a million marched on the Majlis to support Khomeini.[129] His left-wing rivals were equally militant, but a bit more careful with the lives of their followers. None of them — the Communist Tudeh, the Marxist Fedayin al-Khalq, the Islamic socialist Mujahhedin, and the Islamic Marxist Peykar — are likely to return to center stage. The Tudeh compromised itself by its support for Khomeini, who subsequently destroyed them, while the Mujahhedin did the same when it backed Saddam Hussein during the war. The

Fedayin fought on in Kurdistan for a while, but were defeated; and Peykar, for its part, had only limited support.

There have been very few gains for the Iranian people as a result of Khomeini's revolution. The continued survival of the Islamic Republic might best be attributed to the Iranian fear of chaos — another *harj-o-marj* — which is a reflection of birth trauma. Iran's standard of living has now declined to perhaps a quarter of what it was before the revolution,[130] when most of the population was already poor. Women lost some of the rights they had under the Shah, particularly the right to sue for divorce — although men could still divorce their wives by simple declaration.[131] The age of consent for women was briefly lowered to nine, although this was later changed. The Islamic militants saw the role of women as "Religious piety, revolutionary chastity, and breeding soldiers for the revolution...."[132] This was scarcely distinguishable from Nazism.

The Shah's limited land reform was never extended, despite the rhetoric about supporting the "oppressed." Religious institutions even managed to recover some of their land the Shah had distributed to the peasants. In the urban slums, the Islamic Republic has failed to provide basic services for the rural migrants who continue to flock to the cities,[133] just as under the Shah. Political dissidents are assaulted at their lectures and assassinated by Islamic death squads. The *komitehs* (committees), which originally mobilized the population against the monarchy, degenerated into gangs of racketeers that shook down people for bribes if they allowed Western music or alcohol at their private parties.[134] The Kurds, who rose against the Shah in 1978, helping to topple his regime, found themselves at war with Khomeini from the beginning.[135] Their leading political party estimated that 50,000 Iranian Kurds were killed in the struggle against the Islamic Republic. The Baluchis, who had remained more or less loyal to the Shah, managed to fare better; their own uprising resulted in fewer than a hundred dead.

Along with workers and women, intellectuals were subjected to repression. Academic organizations were abolished, university faculties were purged, and student leaders were killed. Books were banned,[137] with even the revered *Shahnameh* coming under suspicion by the clergy.[138] Elections continued to be rigged,[139] and members of the Shah's elite Imperial Guard swiftly became loyal soldiers of Khomeini.[140]

One odd aspect of Khomeinism has been its efforts to transform Shi'ism. The Ayatollah claimed to speak for all Muslims — indeed, to some degree, all non–Western peoples — but in practice, his support outside Iran was limited to Shias, who were often, as in Saudi Arabia, Ba'athist Iraq, or Bahrein, the victim of neglect and discrimination on the part of Sunni governments. But even the Shias of Iraq failed to rally to Iran's cause, which would have brought about a swift end to Saddam Hussein's war effort. In January 1988, Khomeini issued a *fatwa* declaring that the Islamic state had power over all religious matters, "even over prayer, fasting, and the pilgrimage to Mecca."[141] Having failed to spread its Islamic Revolution, Iran was creating a state religion, not entirely unlike what the Shah had hoped to do with his mnemonist revival of Iran's Zoroastrian past. In fact, the Shi'ism of the Iranian Revolution might be interpreted as a disguised form of nationalism; the Iranians are asserting their identity, against the Arabs and the West alike.

Like the Shah, Khomeini had no interest in Shia martyrology. "There were no grand observances of Ashoura [the anniversary of Hussein's martyrdom] presided over by Khomeini.... Khomeini and his coterie discouraged popular Shia piety, and even more, Shia traditions."[142] Vali Nasr regards this "excessive legal-mindedness" as something of a "Sunni-fication" of Shi'ism — a reflection of the influence exerted in recent decades by Sunni fundamentalism, with its Puritanism and intense political activism.[143] Of course, the Islamic Revolution in Iran also inspired Sunni fanatics in the Arab countries, and the jihadists of 9/11 might never have launched their war of terror against the United States if Iran hadn't paved the way with the seizure of the U.S. Embassy in Tehran.

After nearly three decades of Islamic Revolution, Iran found itself alienated not only from the "Satanic" West, but also from many of its Muslim neighbors, including devout Saudi Arabia. Its only friendly neighbor is Christian Armenia, supported by Iran during its conflict with Shia Azerbaijan.[144] By 2008, however, Ahmedinejad's fiercely anti–American regime was cozying up to Iraq, whose Shia-dominated government had been installed under the aegis of U.S. troops. It was ironic that four thousand Americans had to die in order to further the ends of a hostile regime in Tehran.

Iran's Islamic Revolution has accomplished less for its people than most of the other revolutions of the twentieth century. One of its hard-line supporters, a student named Abdullah, was drawn into a conversation about the revolution's achievements. Before, he insisted, his female relatives were exposed to liquor stores and billboards featuring women in scanty bathing suits. "Now there are no more billboards and no more stores selling alcohol. That is the victory of our revolution." That was it? he was asked. "That's enough," he replied confidently.[145] Little wonder that by the 1990s, Iran had the world's highest suicide rate. It increased by 14 times between 1990 and 1995.[146]

Demographic factors put the survival of the Islamic regime at risk. The population has nearly doubled between 1979 and 2009; meanwhile, illiteracy has been largely wiped out, while university graduates have increased nearly tenfold.[147] These graduates — and recently, a majority of them have been women — are too young to remember the struggle against the Shah, and are unable to find suitable work in Iran's economy, which has been damaged by the effects of the war with Iraq, international sanctions, and a massive brain drain. Moreover, they are far better educated than their parents. By 1999, notes Robin Wright, "Iran's mosques were virtually empty."[148] Clerics were receiving angry gestures in the street, and taxi drivers were refusing to pick them up. These were strong indications of a political explosion in the making.

In 1982, Khomeini addressed the youthful followers of his opponents, the Mojaheddin, asking them rhetorically: "What have you seen from your corrupt leaders other than [empty] claims and misguidedness? ... Why have you surrendered your mind to others? Why do you lack independence of judgment?"[149] His successors had better hope that Iran's young people weren't listening.

12

Italy

Birth Trauma, Expansionism, and Fascism

Along with Hitler's Germany and Franco's Spain, Mussolini's Italy was one of the three major regimes classified by historians as "fascist dictatorships." The term "fascist"—derived from an Italian word meaning "bundle"—was almost accidental. Had Franco been the first to seize power, rather than Mussolini, the Soviets could just as easily have termed World War II the "Great Anti-Falangist Struggle," and U.S. anti-war demonstrators might have been shouting "falangist pigs" at the police during the 1960s.

The three regimes shared much in common. They were all one-party systems, headed by a glorified leader; they repressed the organized working class, women, and ethnic minority groups; they abolished rule by law; they gave their loyal followers arms and military-style uniforms and used them to intimidate dissenters; they opposed land reform; and they promoted extensive state intervention in the economy, while permitting continued private ownership of most industry, and denying the existence of class struggle. Yet there were differences: Franco's Spain, unlike the other two, was never territorially expansionist, while Nazi Germany was uniquely committed to biological reductionism. Mussolini was the only one of the three dictators who sought to change the character of his people, something he had in common with the Communists rather than his fellow fascists.

Unlike Nazi Germany, where biology became ideology, or Falangist Spain, where Catholic ultra-conservatism was the official ideology, Fascist Italy had no real ideology at all. Listen to their Minister of Education, Balbino Giuliano, blathering amphigory as he attempts to explain his party's doctrine in 1932:

> We are unable to determine ... the Fascist content of any particular idea, because this "Fascist content" partakes of the nature of any great religious idea. Like the sun, such ideas are ever-present, always themselves, and never anything else, but are not contained in any particular concept; from within themselves, they produce theories of concepts because ... these ideas are religious and not theological.[1]

In 1919, Mussolini himself admitted: "It is a little difficult to define the fascists. They are not republicans, socialists, democrats, conservatives, or nationalists. They represent a synthesis of all negations and all affirmations."[2] That sounds much like they added up to nothing.

Italian Fascism—the capital "F" indicates Italy's ruling party, as opposed to the style of government—is a paradox. It produced a totalitarian regime in a country where the people were known for their emotional expression, hardly the sort of thing one might expect if one followed Theodor Adorno or Wilhelm Reich. For a generation, the regime tried to inculcate its subjects with militarism, but its soldiers accomplished nothing when put to the test, being beaten by the British, Russians, Americans, Germans, Greeks, Yugoslav and Albanian Partisans, the International Brigades in Spain, and the Afar tribesmen in Ethiopia. They achieved even less during World War II than they had during World War I.[3] Italian Fascism had the appearance of a fanatical ideology, but Mussolini never expressed "a single belief or idea in all his voluminous writings that he did not directly contradict somewhere else."[4] At various times, Mussolini had been a socialist and a defender of private property; a monarchist and a republican; a fervent opponent of war and an equally avid warmonger; an enemy of religion and an ally of the Vatican; pro– and anti–Jewish; pro– and anti–German; pro– and anti–British; a revolutionary and a reactionary. In a typically self-contradictory pronouncement in 1919, he declared: "We are strongly against all forms of dictatorship, whether they be of the sword or the cocked hat, of money or numbers. We will accept only one dictatorship, that of will and intelligence."[5] In the final analysis, he believed in nothing except himself, and given his bouts of depression, may not even have been sure of that.

Joseph La Palombara comments: "There is much in the Italian personality that Fascism managed to reach and touch deeply, and there is much about the Italian family concerning which Fascism was in part a macrocosmic manifestation."[6] Describing the Italian family as "fundamentally authoritarian in character," La Palombara notes that parents "are capable of administering severe physical punishment," and that the children are quick to learn obedience.[7]

But La Palombara's description could apply equally to families in most Western countries, or in the Far East. Italy's distinction is that it was the only nation, other than Germany, where a reactionary totalitarian movement came to power with some degree of mass support (the Falange in Spain, never a mass movement, triumphed largely as a result of foreign intervention). But unlike in Germany, Italian Fascism's support was so shallow that when Mussolini was ousted during July 1943, "the Fascist party simply dissolved without offering the slightest resistance."[8]

Luigi Barzini observes one significant difference between his countrymen and other Europeans:

> *"Mamma mia!"* is the most common exclamation. What other people call for their mother
> in time of stress or danger? Do the Germans say *"Mutter,"* the French *"Maman,"* the
> English *"Mother of mine,"* when faced by a disappointment or an emergency?[9]

This curious habit points to a high degree of birth-related first-line pain. Italian culture—and, under sufficient stress, its political life as well—is suffused with symbolic representation of very early trauma. In what other nation did artists portray so many nurturing mothers in the form of Madonnas? What other nation produced so many intrepid explorers eager to break out of Mediterranean confinement? Where else were demagogues like Savonarola and Mussolini hanged by their heels in imitation of the birth process?

The Italian Fascists, like other ruling parties, attracted opportunists, who joined only to further their personal interests. But every political party must also contain a hard core of true believers, or the opportunists will have nothing to attract them in the first place. Typically, a party's hard core consists of devoted converts to its ideology. But if an ideology is defined as a) an accepted body of facts; b) a set of shared values; and c) a theory of cause and effect, then Italian Fascism had no ideology. What it had was a leader, Mussolini; that was all.

Mussolini — The Myth and the Man

Benito Mussolini was born in 1883 in Predappio, a small town in the relatively urbanized region of Romagna, which had been part of the Papal States, but had rebelled against the rule of the Pope in 1860 and had joined the new Italian kingdom. In the post-fascist era, Romagna became the heart of the "Red belt," where the Communists were stronger than elsewhere in the country. Mussolini's own father, a blacksmith and later an innkeeper, was an active leader in the local Socialist Party, and had spent time in prison for his convictions; Mussolini's schoolteacher mother, on the other hand, was a devout Catholic. The second of three children, Benito — named after Mexican revolutionary Benito Juarez — acquired a childhood reputation as a bully and thief, stabbed three of his classmates, got himself expelled from school, liked to rip chickens' feathers out for fun, once threw rocks at churchgoers, and boasted of raping one of his girlfriends. His nickname was "the Mad One."[10] His father beat him with a strap when he was little — common enough in the late 19th century — but was unable to make him behave.[11] Despite the prevalence of what we would now term physical abuse, though, children were very much valued in Italy. They were allowed to get away with actions that would have been forbidden in Germany, for example, where children were regarded as "useless eaters." It may have been the distinctive combination of lenient codes of conduct and physical punishment when these codes were broken that produced the mindset — common to both the Fascist squads and organized crime families — that welcomed violence if an authority figure served as an enabler.

In his early days, Mussolini described himself as a "Socialist of the anarchist kind,"[12] according to sympathetic biographer Nicholas Farrell; he sported a cravat in anarchist black rather than Socialist red.[13] The anarchist philosopher Max Stirner, who believed that nothing mattered outside the Ego, and advocated "total revolt against the state," was a major influence on Mussolini.[14] Even in 1920, only two years before he took power, he could declare: "Down with the state of all types and incarnations. Down with the state, yesterday, today and tomorrow. Down with the bourgeois state and the socialist one."[15] His affiliation with the Socialist Party before World War I may have been a product of pure expediency; foreign anarchists would not have been permitted to live in Switzerland, where he spent several years,[16] and it was easier to sponge off Socialists than anarchists, since a few of the former were wealthy. In 1913, he had a relationship with Leda Rafanelli, an anarchist, mystic, and — unusually for the time — convert to Islam. "She soon discovered that he had no firm opinions but embraced those he had taken from the last book he had read...."[17] This pattern continued throughout his life.

Mussolini's appeal to his followers never depended on his ideas, but on his ability to resonate with his listeners' buried feelings. "I did not create Fascism," he confessed at the end of his career. "I extracted it from the subconscious of the Italians."[18] In his 1925 autobiography, he repeatedly indicated that his decisions were made on sudden impulse: "...as if a revelation had come to me..."; "I suddenly understood..."; "Up leaped the idea...."[19] Even Fascist slogans were singularly devoid of meaning. The famous motto of the Fascist Youth, "Believe! Obey! Fight!" gives no indication of what the uniformed youngster is supposed to believe. Among their other favorites were such intellectually provocative catchphrases as: "Eeya, eeya, alala!" "To us!" "We go straight ahead!" and the always endearing, "Let's arm ourselves and you go and fight!"[20]

Notice the Pope addressing his faithful in St. Peter's Square. Standing on a balcony, he slowly moves his outstretched hand up and down, and from side to side. This is actually a form of hypnotic induction. Mussolini, likewise, "conveyed as much through gesture and tone as through his formal argument," according to R.J.B. Bosworth.[21] His body language was typified by his "jutting fleshy chin, rolling eyes, [and] florid gestures...."[22] With his "chest and jaw thrust out, hands on hips, or ... dancing up and down like an orchestra conductor, the theatrical rolling of his eyes," his words were "delivered in a high-pitched falsetto tone,"[23] making him appear something of a buffoon to non–Italians. "It is bewildering," writes Laura Fermi, "to read the words that aroused such boundless enthusiasm and find that without Mussolini's presence, deprived of his voice, they are banal and hollow."[24] But demagogy rarely appeals across cultural barriers, and Mussolini's adept use of body language retained a grip on the unconscious minds of his fellow Italians even as they consciously began to have grave doubts about his regime.

The Duce's gestures brought to mind the little boy he once was, standing up to his punitive but ineffective father, along with the infant trying to break out of a confining womb. Symbols of birth trauma appear constantly in Italian Fascism, from the expansionist foreign policy to the promotion of large families, the ubiquitous obsession with fast vehicles, Party songs, paintings and exhibitions, and even Mussolini's own claustrophobia.[25] The origin of this first-line pain can be traced back to the Roman Empire, where the sexual use of children was common. Women who are shut down sexually as a result of early rape may find giving birth particularly difficult. Christianity's anti-sensual bias undoubtedly has its roots in Roman degeneracy, to which it is a reaction formation; passed on from generation to generation, it laid the groundwork for the birth trauma — stronger in Italy than in Rome's more distant provinces such as Spain or France — that fed into Fascism.

Psychology of Colonialism

Italy, finally unified only with the capture of Rome in 1870, was late in joining the European quest for overseas colonies. Aside from whatever dubious economic gains were to be had from the annexation of such unproductive lands as Eritrea and Somalia, the underlying drive for overseas expansion was the feeling, stemming from birth trauma, that Italy had too many people, and that colonies were needed as an outlet for the nation's surplus population. Even under the best of circumstances, however, Italy's colonial empire could never have absorbed more than a million European immigrants, fewer by far than had emigrated to the United States or Latin America. But this fact had no effect on the unconscious feeling of "I need to break out of the womb."

For most colonial powers, Italy included, empires satisfy the desire to rule over others, as others have ruled over oneself, both in childhood and in the socially stratified societies that built the empires. The false sense of superiority which colonial conquest engenders allows the colonizers to project onto the colonized the unacceptable aspects of their own character. Italy's first king hinted at the psychological roots of Italian foreign policy when he said, in his last public speech in 1897, that it was not enough for the outside world to respect Italy; Italians, rather, must be feared.[26]

Having established itself in northeast Africa following reunification, Italy turned its attention to the ramshackle Ethiopian empire in 1895, hoping to make it an Italian colony, which would place Italy among the major colonial powers. But Ethiopia's Emperor Menelik inflicted a series of defeats on the invaders, notably at the Battle of Adowa in 1896. This marked the first time that a European power had lost a war to an African nation. The humiliating setback sparked massive social unrest in Italy over the next few years,[27] but it also proved to be "the critical event which set the founders of the Nationalist movement on their path."[28]

Birth Symbolism

The unexpected defeat triggered a collective birth feeling in Italy, which began in 1910–1911, fifteen years after the catastrophe in Ethiopia, the delayed reaction being a result of the inevitable turnover in the population and the leadership of the nation. We see this feeling manifesting itself first in the futurist school of art; then it entered the political arena, sparking the Turkish-Italian War, which led to the Italian capture of Libya and Rhodes. The expansionist mood and the desire for a liberating "bath of blood"[29] dragged Italy into World War I — on the Allied side, as it happened, although it might have been otherwise. The veterans of this war were the main recruits to the *squadristi*, the shock troops of the new Fascist movement.

Understanding the psychodynamics of Italy's prototypical Adowa Cycle requires recognizing the distinction between first-line and second-line pain. First-line pain, buried in the deepest regions of the brain, stems from birth and other very early traumas; second-line pain, located in the limbic system, reflects the traumas of later childhood. Most people symbolize predominantly on the second-line level. Social expressions of second-line pain include chauvinism, idealization of the past, paranoid delusions, and blind obedience to authority. First-line pain is more likely to lead to delusions that "the world is coming to an end," anarchic opposition to all authority, anomic violence, and territorial expansionism. Xenophobia and fear of change tend to be both first- and second-line.

Entire cultures may be first- or second-line, depending on their obstetrical and childrearing practices. England, Germany and Japan are examples of predominantly second-line cultures; while birth may be traumatic, childhood is even worse. On the other hand, Italy, India and possibly Iran are predominantly first-line cultures, with most pain stemming from birth rather than childhood. Because Italian children are often indulged, much of the pain they repress will connect directly to birth memories. Sexual repression among Italian women has been in steep decline since 1945, but things were different for women during the late nineteenth century whose sons became adults between 1914 and 1922. In that era, birth was more traumatic; the result was a permanent sense among their offspring of being too crowded, of not having enough room, of needing to "get out."

Italian psychoanalyst Alessandra Piontelli, who works with young children, observed the results of birth trauma in one three-year-old girl:

I show her the drawer with the toys.... She takes the ambulance and says, "It is closed ... one cannot open it...." In fact the ambulance has a very large and evident opening at the back. As she looks at it, two small figures that were inside it fall on the floor. She says, "They can't come out ... they can't get out...."[30]

Fascist loyalists often expressed birth memories in the course of their adulation of Mussolini. Wrote one informant in Naples in 1931, reporting on Mussolini's speech in that city: "[S]omething great and tremendous was about to take place for Italy and the world, and ... Benito Mussolini was the invincible and undefeated man who would bring that something about."[31] This ineffable anticipation stems from the birth experience. Images of beating hearts were common in the Duce's fan mail from adoring women. A Sicilian widow wrote him in 1937: "I am poor and ill, and I place great hopes in Your magnificent heart, the greatest heart we Italians have known from the Roman Empire to the present day."[32] A 14-year-old girl declared: "Duce ... my life is for you.... [I want to] rest my head on Your broad chest so as to hear still alive the beating of Your great heart." This last breathless accolade came from Claretta Petacci, who later became Mussolini's mistress, and died by his side in 1945.[33] And not to be outdone, the regime's leading philosopher, Giovanni Gentile, exclaimed in 1936 after the victory in Ethiopia, "When Mussolini again raises his great voice and calls us to the harvest, he must find tomorrow as today and yesterday, ready hearts, just one heart, with the same thought, the same political line."[34]

A 1921 poster advertising a Fascist Party congress shows a grim man strutting toward a mound of dirt topped with a skull. The man is holding the fasces in one hand and a sinister-looking dagger in the other. Aside from a cap with a long tassel — probably symbolizing the placenta and umbilical cord — he is stark naked.[35] Would any other party advertise its gatherings that way?

Birth symbolism appeared in song lyrics as well, as with this unduly optimistic Fascist victory song released in time for the 1941 invasion of Greece: "Forward youth, together we shall break every bond and overcome every obstacle. We shall smash the slavery that is *suffocating us as prisoners in our own sea!*"[36] (Emphasis added.) This echoed the speech of the Duce the previous year declaring Italy's entry into the war.[37] In the event, the Greeks pushed the Italian army back into Albania.

Back to the Past and the Future

Italian Fascism was preceded by two movements, one political and one artistic, that contributed to its pageantry: the Nationalists and the Futurists. The Nationalists were founded in 1910 by Enrico Corradini, who argued that "nationalism was the antithesis of democracy; liberty and equality should be replaced by obedience and discipline."[38] He was an admirer of Japanese nationalism, noting that "Japan is the God of Japan."[39] The Nationalists were opposed to the 1912 reforms that granted universal male suffrage, and called for the annexation of Malta, Corsica, and Dalmatia.[40] They were monarchists, but were not necessarily averse to replacing the king if he proved uncooperative. Corradini was the first to argue that Italy's expansionism should be perceived as a "proletarian" revolt against "bourgeois" nations such as France and England, adopting the rhetoric of the left to support the policies of the right.[41] Interestingly, the Nationalist paper, *L'Idea Nazionale*, issued its first edition on March 1, 1911, the fifteenth anniversary of the Italian defeat at Adowa.[42]

A prominent figure loosely affiliated with the Nationalists was the poet and novelist Gabriele D'Annunzio, who might have emerged as Italy's dictator instead of Mussolini had he not been quite so eccentric. A prominent interventionist during World War I who later led the freebooting Italian nationalists' seizure of the city of Fiume (now Rijeka), it was D'Annunzio who gave Fascism the Roman salute, its war cries, and the anthem *Giovinezza*.[43] In a curious anticipation of Mussolini, his novel *The Flame* included a character fond of haranguing crowds from a balcony.[44]

If D'Annunzio and the Nationalists represented the second-line element in Fascism, the first-line element was represented by artist and writer Filippo Tomasso Marinetti, founder in 1909 of the Futurist movement. Futurism, according to Gaetano Salvemini, "advocated an explosive art and life, the carrying of Italian pride to the point of apoplexy; the abolition of culture and logic, of museums and universities, of the monarchy and the papacy ... 'heroism and buffoonery in art and in life'; and other humbug of the same kind."[45]

Marinetti and D'Annunzio had much in common, although they disliked each other,[46] perhaps because they were competitors. In Marinetti's novel, *Mafarka le futuriste*, he told a fantastical tale of an African king "who manages to give birth, without female help, to a winged and mechanical son."[47] This flying Pinocchio was intended as a substitute for Mafarka's deceased brother, who died from rabies after cannibalizing his new wife,[48] a likely reference to traumatic birth, often symbolized by images of dismemberment. In addition to being an allegory about Italy's response to the Ethiopian victory at Adowa, this fable was also subtly autobiographical. Marinetti was himself born in Africa — in Alexandria, Egypt.[49] A 1914 "self-portrait" shows him, revealingly, as a mechanical stick-figure[50]; he later became a proponent of the "aeropittura" school of art, which was obsessed with airplanes and flight.

Involved in politics, the theater, and art, the Futurists were similar to the cubists who appeared at the time in France, but they made the cubists seem like "squares" by comparison. Futurism "gloried in the cult of speed and progress, sport, heroism, danger, courage and violence,"[51] all of which was adopted by Fascism. Marinetti described his followers as "the mystics of action,"[52] presaging Mussolini's own glorification of action for its own sake, which he regarded as more important than thinking.[53] The Futurists opposed the conservative Nationalists on social questions, and sought to separate the nationalist ideal from the church and aristocracy[54]; but they shared the Nationalists' antagonism toward the large and growing Socialist Party, as well as the pro-clerical *Populari*, who later became the Christian Democrats.[55] The Socialists and *Populari*, motivated by humanitarian idealism, were to lead the opposition to Italian intervention in World War I.

Futurist productions from the immediate pre-war period display extensive birth symbolism. Even Marinetti's automobile accident in 1909 became a birth metaphor in his eyes: "Oh! Maternal ditch, almost full of muddy water! Fair factory drain! I gulped down your nourishing sludge; and I remembered the blessed black breast of my Sudanese nurse...."[56] There are repeated representations of birth contractions in paintings produced by different artists. By 1910, with images of birth starting to show up in its artists' creations, Italy was once again ready for war, this time against the increasingly weak Turkish Empire, which was already facing rebellion by the Arabs in Libya, its last North African possession. The Italian people were informed by their leaders that Libya was a "garden of Eden," overflowing with fresh water and abundant mineral wealth.[57] In reality, it was a vast desert, featuring some of the hottest areas on earth, with European settlement possible only in a narrow

belt along the coast. Its mineral wealth consisted entirely of oil, which the Italians never bothered to exploit.[58] Ironically, Mussolini went to prison for opposing the invasion of Libya.[59]

The Turkish-Italian War was merely a rehearsal for the long-awaited bloodbath that
followed. Although an ally of Germany and Austria-Hungary prior to 1914, Italy had territorial claims on both rival camps. From Austria, Italy sought Trentino, the Italian-speak-
ing part of Tyrol; Istria, a small province east of Venice with a mixed Italian-Slav population;
and Slavic Dalmatia, which had once belonged to Venice. But the Nationalists also wanted
Corsica, Savoy, and Nice from France, as well as Tunisia and Malta. The growing list of
territorial demands became an oft-repeated slogan in the Fascist era.

As a result of World War I, Italy could have acquired some of these territories with
minimal risk by waiting until the war had been decided, and then pouncing on the losing
party — France or Austria — as it collapsed. But the real motive for entering the war went
beyond the understandable desire to liberate "Italia irridenta." There was still the unsatisfied
need for a wholesale bloodletting — this time, of the younger generation of Italians themselves.

June 1914, the same month Archduke Franz Ferdinand was assassinated in Sarajevo,
witnessed a near-revolution in Italy, "Red week," as entire towns were taken over by Socialist revolutionaries. Red flags were raised over public buildings, rail lines were sabotaged,
the property of the rich was distributed to the poor, and rumors spread that the royal family had gone into hiding.[60] The outbreak of the war, which doomed the three major dynasties of continental Europe, also saved the House of Savoy in Italy, as rebellious young men
were sent off to the front lines, and the population's anger was redirected against the foreign enemy. As his country hesitated on the brink of war, philosopher Giovanni Gentile
said that it didn't matter which side Italy fought on, as long as it entered the war, because
war would "cement the unity of the country in blood."[61] If this is what their philosophers
were saying, one can only imagine what was going through the minds of their generals.

Why did Italy join England and France, rather than its original allies, Germany and
Austria-Hungary? Unlike in the United States, the cultural ties were no stronger with one
camp than with the other. The territorial claims could have been used to argue for joining
either side — Corsica was as worthwhile a prize as Trentino, Nice even more appealing than
Trieste. And the argument, so compelling to Americans, that England and France were
fighting for democracy carried little weight in Italy, where the strongest interventionists
were the least enthusiastic democrats.

There appear to be two related factors influencing Italy's decision to join the Allies
during World War I: first, Italy had a long history of defining itself in opposition to the
Germans, dating back to ancient struggles with Teutonic barbarians, and extending through
the Dark Ages to the anti–Habsburg struggles of Reunification. Second, there was an expectation that the Central Powers would win the war, given the fierce reputation of the Prussian army. Italy, it seems, was unconsciously hoping to get in on the losing side; masochism
is yet another symptom which is partly birth-related. This goal would be achieved during
World War II.

But even during World War I, Italy lost over half a million soldiers in battle, plus
another million lives in war-related epidemics.[62] After two years of indecisive trench warfare in the Alps, fighting an Austro-Hungarian army that was suffering massive losses on
two other fronts, the Italian army was badly beaten at Caporetto, only a few miles inside

Austria. In the wake of that battle, 350,000 soldiers deserted the Italian army; only the hasty dispatch of 11 British and French divisions held the Austrians at the Piave River.[63] A dubious last-minute victory over the collapsing Austrians in late 1918 — little more than a skirmish — gave Italy the opportunity to claim, with no justification, that it had won the war for the Allies single-handedly. This may have convinced more people in Italy than elsewhere, but it raised expectations of major territorial gains at the peace settlement.[64] When the gains proved modest, the Italian Nationalists argued that they had been betrayed by the British and French. The notion of *betrayal* is a common group fantasy, and has no factual basis in this case. At the peace settlement, Italy got virtually all the Italian-populated parts of the Habsburg Empire, and more as well; and its failure to obtain Albania and part of Turkey was due to the resistance of the local population. But the Italian *perception* of having been short-changed — D'Annunzio described it as a "mutilated victory,"[65] once again echoing traumatic birth imagery — was a major factor in pushing the country toward extremism. This perception stemmed in large part from the unconscious feeling that there "wasn't enough room" in Italy for its growing population.

Fear of Chaos

The question of intervention vs. neutrality had bitterly divided the Italian public during World War I, but the conflict between the camps had grown even sharper following the war's end. The anti-war camp included the Marxists, by then divided into four parties, and the Catholic *Populari*. The pro-war camp included the Nationalist movement, the avant-garde Futurists, and a number of political leaders known as liberals (actually conservatives by contemporary standards). These last had dominated pre-war Italian politics, when only a small minority of the adult population was enfranchised. The liberals, like the Fascists later on, favored colonial expansion, fraudulent elections, and the violent suppression of the working class. They were not, however, an organized political party, which put them at a disadvantage after 1912, when all men got the vote — a concession granted as a way of winning popular support for the war in Libya.[66] Perhaps not surprisingly, the sons of these elitists flocked to the Fascists from the beginning, with the blessings of their fathers.[67]

Mussolini formed the first Fascist group in March 1919, in Milan.[68] The Fascists originally put forth a leftist program, and presented themselves as revolutionary.[69] This claim merits examination. The Italian state enjoyed only limited legitimacy in the post-war period: the Nationalists rejected its universal franchise, the Republicans its monarchy, the *Populari* its secularism, the Marxists its bourgeois character, and the Anarchists were opposed to it by definition. There were German and Yugoslav minorities in the north who didn't want to be in Italy in the first place, and even the Sardinians had some doubts about their national identity.[70] The loosely-organized liberals and conservatives, the small Radical Party, and the Agrarians were the only political forces that accepted the state in its existing form, until the appearance of the Fascists. Far from being revolutionary, the Fascists were merely the most violent champions of the status quo.

The earliest Fascists were largely veterans of the *Arditi*, the shock troops of the Italian army, who were sent into the most dangerous situations at the front, and suffered the heaviest casualties. Mussolini spoke glowingly of how they "threw themselves into the battle with bombs in hands, with daggers in the teeth ... singing their magnificent war hymns."[71]

Many of the *Arditi* were recruited directly from the prisons; the ruling elite regarded criminals as expendable at the front, but failed to consider the possibility that some of them might survive. They brought their uniforms and songs into the Fascist movement, along with the violence they had learned during their outlaw days.

The Fiume incident of 1919, in which many *Arditi* participated under D'Annunzio's leadership, taught Italians what might be accomplished through bold and violent initiative. Although the port city remained with Italy until World War II, D'Annunzio's thuggish regime there was short-lived. Facing opposition from both the Yugoslavs and the Italian government, D'Annunzio delivered an hysterical oration:

> We are standing alone against a threatening and insatiable monster. We are standing alone "against the foolish and vile world".... We are standing alone against the immense power established and supported by thieves, by usurers, and by forgers....[72]

The vaunted Fascist "revolution" of October 1922, culminating in the March on Rome — a re-enactment of Julius Caesar's crossing of the Rubicon — was little more than a disguised coup d'état. Trounced in the 1919 elections, Mussolini had moved toward the right, picking up support from social classes fearful of Marxism.[73] He was backed by demobilized army officers, who were paid four-fifths of their former salaries by the government for their services as leaders of the Fascist squads.[74] The King was already surrounded by Fascist sympathizers,[75] and readily capitulated. Thirty thousand Italian troops, backed up by 4,000 mounted Nationalist militiamen, caved in to about 5,000 undisciplined Fascist blackshirts, many of them armed with nothing more than cudgels and daggers.[76] Mussolini formed a broad-based government, as liberals, Nationalists, some *Populari*, and even a few moderate leftists flocked to his banner. The key to Mussolini's success at this juncture was fear: the ruling elite's fear of social reform, and the deeply held fear of chaos among all strata, stemming — as in Iran during Khomeini's revolution — from birth trauma.

At the outset, the Fascists still had limited support. In the 1921 elections, they took less than 7 percent of the seats in parliament, while the *Populari* took 20 percent and the divided Marxists 25.[77] But by the decade's end, all democratic rights had been swept away, the press was under Fascist control, and opposition parties and labor unions were dissolved. The National Fascist Party (PNF) had become the only party. The blackshirt squads were organized into a Volunteer Militia for National Security, sworn to obey Mussolini or their local bosses rather than the king,[78] Although it took far longer than in Germany, a democratic, if unstable, political system had been transformed into a totalitarian dictatorship.

Surviving a Crisis

Despite the widespread backing of the Fascist regime by parties of the right and center, there are indications that Mussolini was not particularly popular during his early years in power. Late in 1924, a rumor spread in the southern city of Reggio Calabria that Mussolini had resigned. A contemporary observer wrote: "[I]n an instant, the city burst into celebration. Work was suspended everywhere and the shops were closed in sign of jubilation. A vast popular throng hailed the representatives of the opposition and carried them aloft in triumph."[79] This occurred in the wake of the crisis caused by the murder of moderate Socialist leader Giacomo Matteotti, one of the fiercest enemies of Fascism in the Italian parliament. Matteotti was kidnapped by five members of a goon squad nicknamed the Cheka, which took orders from Mussolini himself. Indications are that the intention was merely to give him a beating in response to a speech in the parliament that was received by the Fascist deputies with "constant heckling, whistling, and banging of fists on tabletops...."[80] But Matteotti was a large and strong man, and apparently fought back against his assailants, who ended up killing him.

There have been times in the 20th century when bloody dictatorships have doomed themselves by killing just one prominent opponent: Javier Chamorro in Somoza's Nicaragua, Benigno Aquino in Marcos' Philippines, Steve Biko in apartheid South Africa, Gregory Lambrakis in the colonels' Greece. But Mussolini managed to survive the crisis caused by Matteotti's death, and even used the event to bury what was left of Italy's democracy. There were three reasons for this. First, the landlords, aristocracy, military, and business elite were more afraid of Marxist revolution than of Mussolini's thuggery. Second, there were the "intransigents" in the Fascist Party itself, led by Cremona boss Roberto Farinacci, who were threatening a second March on Rome to replace Mussolini and purge the government of its non–Fascist members.[81] This seems to have encouraged the elites to back Mussolini to avoid even worse terror at Farinacci's hands. (Ironically, the rebellious intransigent Farinacci became PNF secretary for more than a year after the crisis was resolved.[82]) Finally, when Mussolini addressed the parliament during the crisis, virtually admitted his culpability in the Matteotti murder, and dared Italy's establishment to remove him, he was addressing a body from which all the opposition parties had temporarily withdrawn, setting up their own rump body.[83] It proved to be a serious tactical error.

Remaking the Italian National Character

Some have considered Mussolini a consummate opportunist, "an actor pretending to be the person Italians wanted him to be,"[84] in the words of playwright Luigi Pirandello, himself a Fascist party member. There may be more to it than that. In his Socialist youth, Mussolini identified with his father; interestingly, in this respect, his wife Rachele was the daughter of his father's mistress,[85] and there is some evidence that she was actually his half-sister.[86] Partly as a result of his pre-war sojourn in Trentino, Mussolini began combining his socialism with Italian nationalism, and became a champion of intervention against Austria when the war broke out. He ultimately repudiated the values of both his Socialist father and Catholic mother: "Enough, red and black theologians, of all churches," declared Mussolini in his newspaper, *Il Popolo d'Italia*. "No more false and sly promises of a heaven which will never come! Enough, ridiculous saviors of the human race. The human race does not give a damn for your infallible prescriptions granting happiness. Leave the path open to the primal forces of the individual."[87]

Italian Fascism is replete with images of endless struggle, the need to break out, to expand into new territory, to break loose from confinement, to break new speed records (the last a preoccupation for Americans as well). There was a constant effort to increase the Italian birth rate, notwithstanding the country's inability to support its existing population, and, in what may be a defense against feelings of infantile helplessness, a demand to transform Italians into a tough, hard "master race" like the Prussians, culminating in the adaptation of the Nazi goose-step by the Italian blackshirts and the ill-fated alliance with the Third Reich.

The regime made use of the developing technology of the 1920s. "The dashing and irresistible Duce appeared in a succession of fast cars, airplanes, and motorcycles...."[88] Soccer stars and race car drivers "were endlessly exalted as the proper models for youth, bold, amoral and anti-intellectual."[89] The obsession with fast-moving machines came to dominate art, as Marinetti lauded "swift machines that deflower the earth, the sea, the clouds."[90] The "aeropittura" school was so obsessed with airplanes that even female nudes were typically entitled "Mistresses of Pilots." While the French might look at an airplane and think of a naked woman, the Italians under Fascism were doing the opposite.

The imagery of being trapped in an overcrowded place, of needing to break out — which may have had particular significance for the former convicts who joined the *Arditi* — manifested itself most obviously in the Fascist regime's foreign policy. For years, Mussolini aligned himself with Britain, the dominant power of the day; this can be attributed to the influence of his long-time mistress, the sophisticated Margherita Sarfatti. But he lost interest in her during the mid–1930s, taking up with the younger and less worldly Claretta Petacci. On the eve of World War II, Mussolini declared: "Italy ... is really a prisoner in the Mediterranean, and the more populous and powerful she becomes, the more she will suffer from her imprisonment. The bars of this prison are Corsica, Tunisia, Malta, and Cyprus; its sentinels are Gibraltar and Suez."[91] Early on, the Fascists had persuaded England and France to transfer modest portions of their African colonies to Italy. "These crumbs were accepted by the Fascist regime in anticipation of British support for an eventual banquet in Ethiopia."[92]

While insisting on the need for colonies to absorb Italy's expanding population, the Fascist regime simultaneously urged Italians to produce more children to populate the hoped-for colonies,[93] and incidentally to provide more soldiers for Mussolini's wars. Under the Fascists, "procreation and child rearing were set forth as the exclusive functions of all women. There was even a 'Day of the Mother and Child' proclaimed in 1933."[94] Every year, Mussolini "honored the ninety-five most prolific Italian mothers at an elaborate ceremony in the Palazzo Venezia,"[95] his official residence.

The regime's most ambitious project was the remolding of the Italian national character, reflected even in the party anthem, *Giovinezza*, which contained the line, "In the Italy with its natural borders, Italians are remade."[96] Italians would learn to be "more serious, more hard-working, less talkative, less rhetorical, less corrupt...." Under Fascism, the Italian "would sleep less and spend less time on pleasure and entertainment." He would "know the joy of obedience to a single will."[97] The 1941 film *Uomini sul fondo* ("Men on the Bottom"), a tale of sailors rescued from a damaged submarine — yet another birth/deliverance image — portrayed this ideal of the new Italian man. The imperiled sailors "do not gesticulate or emote, and their rarely used voices are always low and controlled; the news of their rescue elicits only a laconic 'finally.'"[98] But in 1940, Mussolini was forced to admit to Count Ciano, his Foreign Minister and son-in-law, that 18 years of Fascist rule had failed to turn the Italian people from a "race of sheep" into a nation of wolves.[99]

Nonetheless, the lengthy period of totalitarian rule was not entirely without effect. "Foreign visitors noted that people in fascist Italy smiled less readily than before, and even young children used to adopt 'a fierce and gladiatorial pose ... as though all their sense of humor had been lost.'"[100] There is a parallel here to what happened in Cambodia decades later under the Khmer Rouge.

Refounding the Roman Empire

While the Italian Nationalists looked back to a glorious and romantic past, to a time of Italy's preeminence in art, music, science and exploration, they had to face the uncomfortable fact that Italy had not been a nation prior to 1860, but a collection of petty kingdoms and republics. This had been the case since the Lombard invasion during the Dark Ages. In competing with the Nationalists, the Fascists carried mnemonism to even greater lengths; they restored the imagery of the Roman Empire.

The Romans regarded the state as a virtual deity. This concept was inherited by modern Europe, with its divine right of kings and — later still — its totalitarian dictators. England departed from this tradition with the Magna Carta, and the United States went even further by making the people sovereign in its Constitution.

There was no comparable concept of popular sovereignty in Fascist Italy. Mussolini defined Fascism as follows: "[A]ll is for the state, nothing is outside the state, nothing and no one are against the state."[101] In this, he echoed Gentile, who hoped for a "new state" which would reflect the national will.[102] The state would protect society against chaos, the *excessive* fear of which is a birth memory, although even normal concern about societal collapse might easily persuade some to turn to dictatorship as the lesser evil.

The key to mobilizing public opinion behind an oppressive state is war, and Mussolini's Italy spent most of its existence involved in one kind of war or another. "War," Mussolini was to declare in 1943, "is the most important thing in the life of a man, like maternity in a woman...."[103] First, there were the clashes between the Fascists and their opponents leading up to the March on Rome, in which an estimated 3,000 people, most of them anti–Fascists, were killed.[104] Next came the clash with Greece in 1923, and the brief occupation of Corfu.[105] From 1921 to 1933, the Fascists — along with their liberal predecessors — were involved in fastening their rule on the rebellious colony of Libya, which had nearly gained its independence when the Italian army was preoccupied with the Austrians. From the first year of Italian rule in 1912 to 1933, the Arab population of the colony dropped from 1.2 million to 825,000.[106]

In 1934, there was a war scare over Austria, where Hitler had assassinated Viennese dictator Engelbert Dollfuss. In 1935, Italy invaded Ethiopia. From 1936 to 1939, Italy sent troops to help Franco in the Spanish Civil War. As this war ended, Mussolini ordered the annexation of Albania, where there was only token resistance at first. In 1940, he declared war on France, and his army made a lamentable attempt to drive the French back from their common frontier. Then came the ill-fated invasion of Greece. The following year found Italian troops at war with the British in Egypt and East Africa, and on the Russian front against the Soviets; all these campaigns led to disaster. Finally, Italy was bombed and then invaded by the Allies, the Germans occupied the north, and civil war broke out in the German zone. During the few years of peace, Italians were constantly exposed to militarism through the party militia and youth groups, and even the regime's campaign to become self-sufficient in wheat was described as a "battle." This battle, too, was lost.[107]

Nostalgia for the Roman Empire, gone for fifteen centuries, permeated Mussolini's regime. From the beginning, the Fascist militia used Roman terms like "century" and "legion" to describe its units.[108] The Fascist salute and the eagle symbol, along with the fasces themselves, were borrowed directly from the Romans. The deification of the Roman emperors was echoed by the personality cult around Mussolini, who was described thus in a school textbook: "The Duce is semi-divine. His will is without limits, His courage annuls fear, His Heart is the synthesis of 40 million hearts.... He is universal."[109]

One important aspect of Mussolini's mnemonist revival of Roman antiquity was "God-stealing." The Romans were fond of borrowing deities from enemy nations as a form of psychological warfare. Defeated by Carthage in 217 B.C.E., they responded by building a shrine to Astarte, chief goddess of the Phoenician settlers in western Sicily, who were related to the Carthaginians, and whose loyalty had become suspect.[110] And when they sought to conquer Egypt, they adopted the Egyptian gods Isis and Serapis.[111] Similarly, the Fascists — bitter enemies of Marxist socialism — borrowed Stalin's plans for celebrating May Day and the anniversary of the October Revolution and used them for their own party's celebrations.[112] The glorification of work, the justification of Italy's colonial expansion as the legitimate demands of a "proletarian nation," and Mussolini's ceaseless belaboring of the comfort-loving "bourgeoisie," even as his own associates enriched themselves and settled into luxurious villas, were all examples of God-stealing from Marxism.

Just as the Roman Empire dominated the Mediterranean region, so did Fascist Italy aspire to make the sea an "Italian lake." Since that was impractical, Mussolini turned his attention to Ethiopia, virtually the only uncolonized part of Africa, and — more important — a nation that had inflicted a humiliating defeat on Italy decades earlier. Although Italy had an overwhelming advantage in terms of weaponry, and even used poison gas against the Ethiopians,[113] the conquest took longer than expected, and the original commander — General Emilio de Bono, one of the Duce's four top lieutenants in the March on Rome — had to be replaced with General Pietro Badoglio, who in 1943 was to rally Italy to the Allied side.[114] The annexation of Ethiopia in 1936 was hailed by crowds in Italy's piazzas,[115] and the conquered nation was merged with already-colonized Somalia and Eritrea to form the new empire of "Italian East Africa." One important consequence of this was to place a large number of Italian troops on the far side of the Suez Canal, allowing the British to cut them off from supplies and reinforcements after Italy entered World War II. It also provoked the British into invoking sanctions against Italy, which in turn aroused Italian ire against a country which would deny Italy its rights to an empire, while enjoying a far larger one of its own. As a result, Italy moved closer to Nazi Germany. Ironically, as it turned out, Italy's adherence to the Axis may well have doomed Hitler's plans.

The Rise of Anti-Semitism

Italian Fascist anti–Semitism had its roots in the conquest of Ethiopia, where Mussolini began imposing a strict policy of racial separation, beginning in 1938. Africans and Europeans were forbidden from working together or living in the same neighborhoods. Theaters and restaurants were segregated, and whites could not be employed by blacks.[116] The Italian residents in Ethiopia preferred to ignore these regulations. "Colonial government reports admitted that Italians and Ethiopians went together to a café or were seen walking on the street or sharing a taxi."[117]

The prohibition against interracial sex was also observed in the breach, as — with few white women available — many Italian men acquired Ethiopian girlfriends. This prompted the fear that Italian "blood" would be "polluted." Coupled with the xenophobia promoted by the international sanctions, it laid the groundwork for the anti–Semitic legislation which was passed, with little warning, in 1938.

Italy's anti–Semitic legislation never went as far as Nazi Germany's, but its sudden enactment evoked surprise. The Italian Jewish community was small — perhaps 0.1 percent of the population — and thoroughly assimilated, except in Trieste, where Jews were originally German by culture, and proportionately more numerous than elsewhere in the country.[118] Severe discrimination against Jews had existed in the Papal States prior to Reunification, but the new Italian state prided itself on its religious tolerance and secularism. Italian Jews, as Mussolini himself noted, were prominent in many fields. There had been a Jewish mayor of Rome during the liberal era, along with two prime ministers and twenty-four members of the Senate; an impressive 8 percent of Italy's academics were of Jewish origin.[119] A number had even been Fascists. Among them was his long-time paramour, Margherita Sarfatti, who had converted to Catholicism, but was still forced to leave Italy after 1938. Nonetheless, Mussolini believed as early as the 1920s that Jewish bankers controlled world finance, and were also linked with Communism.[120]

Cremona's fanatical Party chief Roberto Farinacci was among the most prominent Fascists to become anti–Semitic after the conquest of Ethiopia. "The Ethiopian conflict," he declared in his newspaper, "had brought to the surface the requirement to think harder about a 'totalitarian vision of the complex Jewish problem.'"[121] And as anti–Semitism became law, Mussolini stated in Trieste:

> The racial problem has not erupted out of the blue.... It relates to the conquest of the Empire; since history teaches us that empires are conquered with arms, but maintained with prestige. And prestige requires a clear and severe racial conscience that establishes most clearly not just differences but superiorities. The Jewish problem is therefore but an aspect of this phenomenon.[122]

Mussolini is saying here that the conquest of people they regarded as inferior evoked feelings of inferiority among the Italians themselves in respect to the Jews. This was a pattern similar to the one seen in 19th-century Germany, where anti–Semitic parties flourished in the wake of the scramble for Africa. Imperial conquest is supported by people who think it will enable them to overcome feelings of inferiority, but since the roots of their inferiority complex lie in their personal history, rather in their nation's history, it never works.

Anti-Semitism also had roots in birth trauma, as indicated by the reference by Giuseppe Bottai, one-time Party secretary and editor of Party journal *Critica Fascista*, to the "pollutions" of Italian art by "certain artists ... infected by Jewish elements...."[123] With the conquest of Ethiopia, the need to break out of confinement had been largely satisfied; the next repressed feeling the Fascists experienced was the sense of being polluted, a memory of the toxins entering the infant's bloodstream through the umbilical cord during the birth process.

Unlike in Eastern Europe, where anti–Semitism was widespread, Italy's racist policies received no popular support. "The passage of the anti–Semitic laws," writes Tracy Koon, "was received by the populace at large with dismay, disgust, or contempt...."[124] By 1939, the regime had established an "Aryanization" program, through which "a special commission could simply declare arbitrarily that a Jew was not a Jew."[125] This gave some Italian Jews an opportunity to bribe their way out of oppression. Jews who were declared "Aryans" suffered no disabilities for the time being, although these exemptions were revoked when the Nazis occupied the country.

Coupled with the appearance of anti–Semitism was a virulent xenophobia, directed primarily against the British, the leading movers in the weak but irritating League of Nations sanctions against Italy. There was a campaign to "purify" the Italian language of English terms, as resorts were ordered to change their names from "Grand Hotel" to "Albergo Grande," and *zuppa inglese* became *zuppa Impero*.[126]

Fascism Goes to War

Mussolini was a master of sham, of striking postures that had little relation to reality. He and his local bosses appeared to enjoy popular support as they addressed enthusiastic rallies that filled vast piazzas, but the crowds were organized from above; registered Party members were ordered to turn out, with repeated absences resulting in possible loss of employment.[127] The public championing of the working class coexisted with policies that favored the rich,[128] and the glorification of modern technology and architecture hid a backward social system in which many southern peasants remained landless and illiterate, and beggars were still found in the cities.[129]

At times, the fakery showed, if one knew how to read between the lines. In 1932, there was a well-publicized exhibition celebrating the 10th anniversary of the March on Rome. Giant fasces decorating the display were stylized to "look like some futuristic industrial chimney or the funnels of a liner...."[130] Elongated, tilted, tapered toward the top, with the bindings and sticks merged into a single body and the axe-head distorted beyond recognition, these objects nonetheless displayed a curious familiarity. Turn the image upside-down, and one can see a rough representation of the Italian peninsula — the inversion being a symbol both of distress and birth. The exhibition as a whole also manifested a subtext that communicated the message of a deified ruler leading his country toward death. Little wonder Margherita Sarfatti was aghast.

The exhibition's subtext was prophetic. Italy entered World War II in a state of total unpreparedness. It had a mere 2 months' reserves of ammunition, and only 3 tons of oil per capita, compared to 3,810 in Germany, 6,300 in the USSR, and 17,000 in the United States.[131] Mussolini's obsession with speed caused him to neglect the armoring of his ships and planes, which proved disastrous. Half the Italian fleet was sunk in one British attack at Taranto in November 1940,[132] and by March 1941, it was largely finished as a military force.[133] The Italian air force entered the war with only a few hundred serviceable planes and six weeks' supply of fuel, and the country produced fewer aircraft in 1943 than the United States could turn out in one week.[134] The army failed to provide its conscripts with adequate boots, in a country renowned for its footwear; rifles dated from before World War I; and the troops sent to fight in the Russian winter were expected to use mules for transport.[135]

Italy's ill-fated invasion of Greece forced Germany to come to its rescue, postponing Hitler's invasion of Russia for a crucial five weeks, and tying down a number of German divisions for the remainder of the war. The Italian assault on British positions in Egypt was a similar fiasco, as Hitler once again was forced to divert some of his troops to an unwanted front. Mussolini's worst mistake was his failure to seize the British island of Malta when it was nearly undefended; Malta was reinforced and never fell, costing the Axis forces in Africa dearly.[136] By February 1941, 130,000 Italian troops had surrendered to the British in North Africa, with only 550 deaths on the Allied side.[137] The Italians in Ethiopia were captured by a British-Indian force.[138] There were also heavy casualties on the Russian front, where Italy lost 70,000 men during the 1943 Axis retreat along the Don.[139] Eleven thousand Italian troops surrendered without a fight on Pantelleria, an island south of Sicily, in 1943,[140] and Partisans in the Yugoslav and Albanian mountains discovered that Mussolini's warriors put up little resistance. A revealing photograph published in R.J.B. Bosworth's *Mussolini's Italy* shows half a dozen Italian soldiers who had just been taken prisoner in 1943; they appear to be enjoying the happiest day of their lives.

By the summer of 1943, Italy had suffered huge losses of men in East Africa, North Africa, the Russian front, the Balkans, and even Sicily, which had already fallen to Britain and America. Its cities had been bombed, the country was running out of food, and hunger strikes were breaking out. German troops were already in the country, doing most of the fighting against the Allied invaders. The navy and air force had proven useless. The fighting in Sicily, more than anything else, shattered the myth of Mussolini's infallibility, and led to his downfall; most of his own Grand Council, including his son-in-law Count Ciano, voted for his removal. The next day, their action was seconded by the King. Three million strong — not counting a far larger number in affiliated groups — Italy's Fascists folded their hands as their once-idolized Duce was ousted and placed under house arrest.

> [T]here was no revolt against the King in Italy, not a cry was raised for the Duce, not a single platoon of fascist militiamen decided to go out and die for Mussolini. The people of the country streamed into the streets, tore the fascist buttons from their lapels, and not seeing any fascist symbols on anybody felt that nobody was a fascist, that nobody had ever been a fascist, and the whole thing had been a long ghastly nightmare.[141]

An Ideology at Last

The Fascist regime had a sequel, the Italian Social Republic set up by the Germans, with Mussolini — rescued by Nazi commandos — as its puppet leader. The Duce still retained some of his legendary ability to persuade the masses, when he was able to address them in person. It should be noted though, that while a strong resistance movement arose in the German-occupied north, there was no comparable guerrilla activity by Mussolini's loyalists in the Allied-controlled south, even though that was the region where the post-war neo–Fascists of the Italian Social Movement were the strongest.

Reviving Fascism in the German zone was a task of Herculean proportions. The PNF had to be rebuilt almost from scratch, as the Republican Fascist Party (PFR). A purge took the lives of Count Ciano and four other Grand Council members who had voted against Mussolini in July 1943, and had been unlucky enough to get caught. A new army under General Graziani — who had lost North Africa — was recruited from German POW camps, although most captive Italian soldiers refused to join it. It was backed up by a Republican National Guard, and a "Black Brigade" militia. These units, along with others such as the Ettore Muti Brigade, which was under direct Wehrmacht control,[142] were used primarily against the local Partisans. Another outfit siding with the Germans, but not under Mussolini's control, was the *Decima Mas*, headed by the monarchist Prince Junio Valerio Borghese, whom Mussolini suspected — not without justification — of plotting to replace him.[143] Almost the only Italian unit fighting the Allies at this time, as opposed to the burgeoning Partisans, was the SS Italia brigade.

The puppet republic was estimated by the Germans to have had the backing of only two percent of the Italian people.[144] Laura Fermi notes that "All appointments in the new government had to be approved by the Germans,"[145] who kept close watch on their protégés. There wasn't even a genuine capital of the new state, and the various ministries were scattered around German-occupied Italy, with only tenuous communication between them and the Duce.

What it did have going for it, as the cult of an infallible Duce continued to collapse, was the beginning of an ideology. One of its prominent advocates was Nicola Bombacci, a former Communist, who believed that Mussolini — rather than the Russian followers of Lenin — would build socialism. Bombacci was personally close to the Duce, and died with him.[146] Another leftist who rallied to Mussolini at this late date was Carlo Silvestri, a Socialist journalist who became his confidante.[147] There was talk of the nationalization of industry, and even a brief experiment with freedom of the press.

Coupled with this sham leftism — reminiscent of Fascism's early days — was increased anti–Semitism, promoted by such racist thinkers as Julius Evola and Giovanni Preziosi. Evola argued that the Jews were "spiritual" opponents of Italian civilization, and that Jewish immorality, if not Jewish genes, was the source of all crime.[148] Preziosi was made the puppet regime's "Inspector General of Race" in March 1944, arguing for the "total elimination" of anyone with even a drop of Jewish blood.[149] It was under the Social Republic that thousands of Jews were deported to the gas chambers from Rome and other northern cities. Most Jews in Italy were able to escape this fate, however: some lived in already-liberated Naples; some escaped to nearby Switzerland; some were hidden by the Church or sympathetic individuals; and a large number were able to disappear into the crowds of refugees, claiming to have lost their identity papers.

At its demise, Italian Fascism had already gone far toward evolving into the local variety of National Socialism — although, even then, figures like Preziosi and Evola cringed at Nazi excesses, not least because Italians themselves were increasingly their victims. The post-war Italian Social Movement found its soul-mates among Europe's neo–Nazis, rather than on the left, although it did align itself with a small monarchist faction. National Socialism found it easy to replace Italian Fascism because the latter had no ideology to begin with. Evola himself, after the war, was to correctly dismiss Mussolini's entire enterprise as little more than a "hypnotic" side-show.[150]

This was a far more accurate description of Fascism's essence than, say, A. James Gregor's judgment that "Fascism as an ideology was a far more complex and systematic intellectual project than many ... have been prepared to admit."[151] In an age before television, in a country where few had radios, the key form of propaganda available to Mussolini's Fascists was the mass rallies in the piazzas of the towns and cities. The regime "wanted its citizenry to find its total self, public and private, in the piazza. Ideal fascist citizens would carry the piazza with them wherever they went."[152] And what was going on in the piazza — with its uniformed crowds giving their regulation salute, shouting their inane slogans, hanging on their leader's stultifying phrases[153] — was nothing other than a form of stage hypnosis. Mussolini's mentor Marinetti may have been thinking of this when he said that "Everything of any value is theatrical."[154]

13

Argentina

Fear of Abandonment,
Caudilloism, and the Dirty War

In 1978, the British magazine *New Statesman* noted, "The failure of Argentina as a nation is the biggest political mystery of this century."[1] Indeed, given the country's size, relatively well-educated population, absence of threatening neighbors, long coastline, oil resources, and fertility of its rich grasslands, it is hard to see how Argentina — one of the world's ten most prosperous countries in 1929[2] — could have collapsed into virtual bankruptcy and ungovernability by the turn of the millennium.

To understand Argentina in psychohistorical terms, one must first consider the various cleavages in its society. To begin with, as elsewhere in Latin America — and, for that matter, the world — there is the cleavage between rich and poor. This is more evident in the countryside than in Buenos Aires, but even in the capital there are massive disparities between the neighborhoods populated by the wealthy and those inhabited by workers, especially recent migrants from the rural areas. Second, there is a sharp cleavage between the littoral and the interior. The former consists of the city of Buenos Aires (the Federal District) and the surrounding province of the same name, Argentina's largest; the latter consists of the other 22 provinces. The littoral contains nearly two-thirds of the population.[3] In many ways, the littoral and the interior seem like two different countries, and at one point, early in Argentina's history, they actually were.

The third cleavage, which overlaps considerably with the second, is between the racially-mixed population, the Creoles, which originated during the Spanish empire, and the immigrant communities which began arriving in the late nineteenth century. These immigrants settled primarily in the littoral, although some reached major towns such as Cordoba in the interior, and many became farmers in northeastern provinces like Entre Rios and Misiones. At the same time, economic development brought hundreds of thousands of Creole migrants into the greater Buenos Aires area, even as developments in Europe reduced the flow of immigration from the Old World.

What distinguishes Argentina from the rest of Latin America is the division between the Creole and European political cultures, which transcends the class divide. Without massive European immigration, Argentina's history would resemble that of Paraguay, where democracy never took root until very recently. Without the Creole component, it would be more like Uruguay, where military interventions have been few, and political conflicts are over ideology rather than personalities. With both, Argentina's history is a unique example of a centuries-old tradition of Caudilloism — loyalty to a powerful military chief— being transformed into a modern political movement even without losing its traditional character.

Indian Denial

"In Argentina," writes Julia Rodriguez, "native peoples were, literally and figuratively, erased from the national memory."[4] Argentina prides itself on its supposedly European population, all but denying the presence of Native Americans. In fact, culturally Indian Argentines make up a substantial, if undetermined, part of the population, and together with Spanish-speaking mestizos may comprise as much as 25 percent of the total.[5] The northwestern part of the country had belonged to the Inca empire, and the local clothing still shows Inca influence.[6] Although some believe that the Diaguita people, the original inhabitants, were only loosely ruled by the Incas — from whom they derived their language, religion and music, as well as dress — the presence of stone fortifications indicates that the Inca state, as firmly governed as Pharaoh's Egypt, did indeed overlap with today's Argentina.[7]

In the central province of Santiago de Estero, the rural population still speaks Quechua, the language of the Inca empire.[8] Other Indian languages are spoken in Formosa province, adjacent to Paraguay, and in Patagonia in the south. Since many of Argentina's original inhabitants were nomadic, the Spanish conquerors "tended to see nothing but emptiness" in the land.[9] The denial continues today. Indians didn't count as people because they didn't believe in private property.

There is even Inca influence on current Argentine political culture. For example, the Argentine flag contains a sun symbol bearing a human face, much like the one which the Incas placed over the Temple of the Sun in Cuzco.[10] Argentines believe that the symbol represents the sun breaking through the clouds on May 25, 1810, at the moment independence was decided upon.[11] However, while there are a number of countries throughout the world that feature suns on their flags, the only other one that has a face on it is Uruguay's, and that is because Uruguay borrowed its flag motif from Argentina, of which it was originally a province.

There is a shrine to an Argentine saint, called La Difunta Correa (The Deceased Woman Correa), unrecognized by the Church, who died in the 1840s while following her soldier husband; her baby survived, sucking at her lifeless breast. Still drawing worshippers, the shrine is similar to the cult of Pachamama, the Indian mother goddess worshipped by the Incas.[12] Noting that "we never speak of Indians in Argentina," one Argentine writer suggests that the process of Indian denial might be analogous to the way in which political dissidents were "disappeared" during the 1970s.[13]

In his 1839 *Voyage of the Beagle*, Charles Darwin described how the Argentines massacred all Indian adults they caught, keeping the children as servants.[14] The subsequent conquest of Patagonia did not proceed smoothly. Civil wars among the Argentines diverted so many troops from the Indian wars during the 1850s "that by 1860 the frontier line in some places lay closer to Buenos Aires than it had forty years before."[15] Ultimately, the independent Indian tribes were subdued, converted, and absorbed into the dominant Spanish culture. But photographs from the interior in a recent tourist guide show many people who are obviously either pure Indians or mestizos.[16]

Creole Racism

Surviving Indians, mestizos, and Africans who arrived by way of Brazil[17] constituted a powerless underclass from the beginning of Argentine history. In colonial times, urban residents "were divided into two groups: the white *vecinos*, who enjoyed full civil rights, and the usually nonwhite *moradores* or simple 'dwellers,' who did not."[18] By the late eighteenth century, David Rock notes, whites and non-whites constituted virtual castes, with intermarriage forbidden.

> The [lower] castes were assigned distinctive modes of dress and, among other restraints, were prohibited from bearing arms and consuming alcohol. In some parts severe penalties were exacted against the castes if they ventured to acquire the blessings of literacy.[19]

During the nineteenth century, social prejudice prevented non-whites from renting land or running country stores.[20]

The subordinate groups were kept down through religion. Missions abounded, where converted Indians were treated like children and not permitted to make their own decisions.[21] In colonial times, only candidates of unmixed European ancestry were allowed into the priesthood.[22] "[R]eligious instruction prepared Indians and the poor to accept their permanently subordinate role in colonial society."[23] At the same time, the racial lines were never drawn as sharply as in South Africa or the United States. The populist president Hipólito Yrigoyen, elected twice between World War I and the Great Depression, had some Indian ancestry,[24] as did Juan Perón.[25] And Bernardino Rivadavia, president from 1826 to 1827, was part black.[26]

The notion that Argentina is engaged in a struggle between "Civilization and Barbarism," in the words of Domingo Sarmiento, one of its most illustrious literary figures, and its president from 1868 to 1874,[27] is a constant theme in the country's history. More often than not, "civilization" is identified with white Europeans, and "barbarism" with Creoles of mixed race. This is despite the fact that when Buenos Aires was permanently established in 1580, the majority of its founders were mestizos.[28] When large numbers of migrants from the interior began arriving in Buenos Aires during the 1930s, the local *porteños* described them contemptuously as *Negros*. And anti–Perónistas used the term *cabecitas negras* ("little darkies") to describe Perón's supporters.[29] In 1940, the prominent Argentine economist Alejandro Bunge published a book entitled *Splendor and Decadence of the White Race*, in which he called on the affluent to have more children,[30] echoing a theme common in Nazi Germany; and as late as 1975, journalist Roberto Aizcorbe — a fierce anti–Perónist — attributed his country's "cultural reversal" to "the integration of aboriginal elements into the Argentine population."[31]

Gauchos

The gauchos — the famous semi-nomadic cowboys of the Pampas — were originally regarded as a particularly barbaric part of the non-white underclass, and did not begin to be romanticized until after the turn of the twentieth century. By then, they had largely disappeared,[32] because the authorities forced them to become peons.[33] Gauchos were violent, fond of settling their disputes with knives, and then riding away to avoid retribution. Their lives were primitive, their diet consisted entirely of beef, and their houses were mud and thatch, containing only ox skulls for furniture. They would work for a few months, and then request their pay and move on, causing the elite to regard them as "uncivilized."[34] The gaucho "detested learning, weakness, restraint, rules, work, settled society, and order in general," and "His sense of honor consisted of loyalty to the chief who was strong enough to control him...."[35] Marriage was rare among them, "and it was the unmarried mother who formed the nucleus of the rural family for she was the only permanent parent."[36]

Like the American cowboy, however, the gaucho became an important cultural icon after he had vanished from the scene. "[T]he mythologizing of the gaucho ... heralded the birth of cultural nationalism," notes Judith L. Elkin. "The feeling of racial superiority, originally enlisted in the war against gauchismo, now adopted gauchesque virtues in the struggle to naturalize the immigrants."[37] At the same time, according to Robert Crassweller, the lifestyle of the now-vanished gauchos contributed to "the mental attitudes and psychological values of individualism, fragmentation, tenuous personal relationships beyond the family, and a lack of social cohesion."[38] He continues:

> [T]here would never be any close connection between people and land. Everything would be temporary, migratory, tentative, half-hearted. The consequences for social psychology were enormous and half a century later Perón would be the beneficiary.[39]

Immigration

Racism was one of the reasons the Argentine ruling elite sought to encourage immigration from Europe. The "Generation of 1880," which transformed Argentine politics, was on much the same wavelength as the Progressives in the United States, with their panacea of eugenics. It was led by President Julio Roca, a former general. Although some regarded him as "the originator of economic dependency and a murderer of innocent Amerindian women and children, he has also been seen as a champion of order and progress."[40] Argentina's new rulers identified their mestizos as an obstacle to modernization. In 1910, one deputy declared: "We do not need yellow immigration, but rather European fathers and mothers of the white race to improve the hybrid and miscegenated elements that constitute the base of our nation's population."[41]

There were also strong economic factors as well that promoted immigration, particularly the need for more labor to raise the alfalfa needed to feed the improved strain of cattle on which Argentina's economy depended.[42] Immigration took off during the late nineteenth century. "Between 1870 and 1914 almost 6 million immigrants, mostly Spanish and Italian, arrived in Argentina, although only a little over half of these settled permanently...."[43] Some of the immigration from Italy was seasonal; laborers called *golondrinas* (swallows) spent three months in Argentina working on the harvest, and then returned to Italy, where the seasons were reversed, to do the same.[44] There were also immigrants from other countries. Along with Italy and Spain, Argentina received people from the UK, Germany, France, Austria-Hungary, Russia and Ottoman Turkey. Significantly, just as many of the Spanish immigrants were Basques, Gallegos and Catalans, so were many of the British immigrants from Ireland, Scotland or Wales, while the immigrants from the Habsburg domains were mostly Slav, those from Russia typically Jewish or Polish, and those from the Ottoman Empire either Syrian/Lebanese or Greek. Like the Creole underclass they were expected to replace, these were people who had been kicked around a lot.

As Jonathan Brown points out, referring to the 1890s, "Creole workers lacked a cohesive family structure that could have provided security and advancement in society."[45] But the same thing held true for many of the immigrants, particularly the Italians and Spaniards, who frequently arrived without their women (the pattern among the Jews, who were fleeing persecution, was quite different). From these two developments — the unstable family life of the rural mestizo underclass, and the absence of a solid family structure among many immigrants — came the dominant repressed feeling of the Argentine political culture: *I am afraid of being abandoned.*

This feeling was not unique to Argentina. As psychohistorian David Beisel shows in his discussion of the origins of World War II, fear of abandonment was a major factor determining French responses to the Nazi threat. This fear derived from both the massive loss of male heads of households during World War I, and to the practice among the wealthy of farming their babies out to distant wet nurses during the nineteenth century.[46] The consequence was France's abandonment of collective security during the 1930s, its supine acceptance of England's appeasement policy, and — one might add — its cult-like adoration of the collaborationist Marshal Pétain.

The Dance of Love

One inevitable consequence of the influx of largely male immigrant workers into Buenos Aires was the rise of prostitution. Between 1875 and 1934, prostitution was legal in Argentina, coinciding with the period of massive immigration, allowing for a few years' time lag.[47] By 1901, registered prostitutes in Buenos Aires numbered over 6,400, with the unregistered ones estimated at 10,000.[48] A dozen years later, there were 300 registered brothels in the city.[49]

These brothels were the locale for the development of Argentina's national dance, the tango, still immensely popular after well over a century. Compare its longevity with our own once-popular Charleston, which livened our evenings for only about forty years — or the lambada, which lasted about two weeks! The tango emerged from the Buenos Aires slums, its steps and music a mixture of African, Spanish, Italian and German styles; the dance was originally done by two men, evidence of how serious the shortage of women must have been. "[B]y the 1880s it had become associated with prostitution.... Only after 1910, when tango became a fad in France, was it accepted by the upper classes of Argentina."[50]

Notes Crassweller: "Nostalgic and forlorn, viewing time present as a misfortune, the tango reflected a total style of life, a psychology, a creative sensibility that nevertheless expressed the viewpoint of the loser with a fatalism recalling the Moorish strain in the Creole heritage."[51] The writer Ezequiel Martínez Estrada referred to tango as "the dance of pessimism, of everyone's sorrow: a dance of the never-changing, enormous plains and of a subjugated race that crisscrosses them without end and without destiny, in the eternity of a forever-repeating present."[52] Tango lyrics speak of the "impossibility of a meaningful relationship between a man and a woman" in a corrupt world, symbolized by the fact that the dancers look away from each other. A common figure in many tangos is "the naïve little man," who thinks he can survive while remaining moral, or even change the world. Tango seeks to disillusion him.[53]

Caudilloism

Coupled with fear of abandonment, one often finds blind loyalty to a father-figure, a dynamic typical of cults. In Argentina, this is usually coupled with profound disillusion-ment at the end of his presidential term. The first dictator, Juan Manuel de Rosas, died in exile. Yrigoyen was toppled in a coup, having lost his popular support. Perón suffered a similar fate, and returned to power eighteen years later only to alienate his youthful sup-porters. Raul Alfonsín, who came to power on a wave of popular enthusiasm after the ouster of the military, was forced to resign before his term was over; and his successor Carlos Menem, who served out two full terms, ended up facing criminal charges.

During Argentina's early years, caudillos ruled in each province, fighting wars with one another. Rosas, the caudillo of Buenos Aires province, ultimately emerged as the supreme leader of the country from 1840 to 1852, until he was finally defeated by his rivals. His tyranny "was one of the bloodiest in the history of any American nation,"[54] and featured the severed heads of political opponents, captured by the dreaded Mazorca (secret police), put on display.[55] The postal service was eliminated,[56] and the government no longer sub-sidized education, which survived only through public contributions.[57] Yet Rosas was loved by the gauchos, as well as by the Afro-Argentine community, at the time a significant pres-ence in the capital. "With Rosas as leader, the common people took great delight in put-ting the city folk in their proper places."[58] Everyone had to wear the color red, to show loyalty. "Portraits of Rosas were carried in triumph through the streets and placed upon the altars of the principal churches. Sermons glorified the dictator...."[59] The Unitarists, oppo-nents of the Federalist Caudillos, were excoriated as "savages," and a theatrical performance featured one of them being murdered by a Rosas supporter.[60] Rosas hated them because they believed in progress,[61] which in Argentina has often been associated with contempt for the poor and oppressed; there is a parallel with Perón's excoriation of the oligarchy, and his opponents' suppression of the working class in the name of democracy. In another parallel with Perón, Rosas' wife Doña Encarnación was politically active, and helped him win sup-port from the underclass.[62]

Notwithstanding massive immigration, industrialization, urbanization, and the emer-gence of powerful unions and militant left-wing parties, the landed oligarchy continues to dominate the economic and political life of the interior, and to a great extent the entire country. No serious land reform has ever been carried out, as in neighboring Bolivia or Chile. As late as 1968, Indian peasants in sparsely-populated La Rioja province, in the Andes, lived "in a virtual master-slave relationship that harkened back to the days of the Spanish conquest."[63] The landowners, "who care little about the quality of national poli-cies," dominate the local parties, and the legislators are beholden to them.[64]

The oligarchy also dominates the military, which has ruled Argentina for much of its history. They do this by placing their sons in the military, particularly the Navy; by mar-rying off their daughters to up-and-coming officers; and through the influence of the Church, which is aligned with the oligarchy, and of which military officers are typically devout adherents. The Argentine Church hierarchy is "perhaps the most conservative in

South America,"[65] and has always been in the forefront of reaction. Unlike in Brazil, Chile or Venezuela, the Argentine Church does not exercise its political influence primarily through Christian Democratic parties; the Christian Democrats in Argentina, who frequently align themselves with the left, are a relatively small group. Instead, the leading pro-clerical movement in Argentina has always been the Nationalists.

The Argentine Nationalists

Nationalism in Latin America is generally regarded as a movement of the left, a less-sophisticated version of Marxism which targets the overbearing influence of the *Norteamericanos* on the economy, culture, and politics. This does not hold true for Argentina. There, Nationalism is usually — though not always — identified with the radical right, and characterized by hostility to modernism, women, democracy, Marxism, Jews, foreigners, Protestants, and a host of other bogeys. Nationalists even rejected the French Revolution because it undermined "natural hierarchies,"[66] which are of overriding importance to ultra-rightists. They have enjoyed considerable strength within the Army, which "was largely formed by German officers...."[67] According to David Rock, the Nationalists "were pure reactionaries who always looked to the past...."[68] Distrustful of cosmopolitan Buenos Aires, they believed — much like Europe's fascists — that democracy would ultimately lead to Communism; among their sources of inspiration were the Spanish clericalists and the French monarchist followers of Charles Maurras.[69]

The Nationalists never became a mass movement in Argentina, unable as they were to compete with the Perónists for the loyalty of the underclass, while the lower middle class which made up much of fascism's support in Europe was relatively weak, and its members not always assimilated into Argentine society. The Nationalists served instead as paladins of the oligarchy, defending its privileges from left-wing threats, while occasionally issuing calls for social reform as a smokescreen. They were devoutly Catholic, favoring clerical control of education, something the liberals opposed.[70] They enjoyed an ambivalent relationship with the Perónists, supporting them at the beginning, but turning against them when Perón began catering too much to his working-class base. Unlike the Perónists, the Nationalists drew much of their following from the European ethnic groups (other than Jews, needless to say), particularly the generation whose parents had never become citizens. This was a large group, since immigrants, early in the twentieth century, made up about 30 percent of the population, and according to Rock, "Between 1850 and 1930 fewer than 5 percent of immigrants took Argentine citizenship, partly because as noncitizens they remained legally exempt from military service."[71] The extreme nationalism of some of their sons was in part a reaction to their lack of it; this was the reverse of the pattern in the United States, where immigrants typically acquired citizenship with enthusiasm, while their children often became involved with radical *left* groups.

The alliance between the Nationalists and Perónists in Argentina resembles the association between the Nationalists of Luigi Federzoni and Mussolini's Fascists in Italy: an ultra-conservative movement latches on to another movement with a larger base but a less coherent ideology. Psychohistorically, though, Argentina is the opposite of Italy. In Italy (see Chapter 12, above), the dominant Fascist movement was characterized by birth (first-line) feelings, while the less numerous Nationalists reflected unfelt childhood (second-line) pain. In

Argentina, however, the Perónists were motivated by fear of abandonment, a second-line feeling; the Nationalists, on the other hand, appeared to be deeply into birth trauma.

This was indicated by their xenophobia. In early 1919, a general strike in Buenos Aires led to anti-police violence, and troops were called in. In response to the threat from the left, Nationalists formed the *Liga Patriotica Argentina*, a paramilitary group, which launched attacks on radical immigrants.[72] During the *Semana Tragica* that year, a right-wing pogrom directed primarily against Jews cost as many as 1,500 lives.[73] Interestingly, another group singled out were the Catalans,[74] possibly because of the anarchists among them. The *Liga* promoted what it regarded as the Argentine values of "piety, obedience, punctuality, [and] deference,"[75] as opposed to skepticism, tolerance, and relativism, which, along with Marxism, were seen as essentially Jewish.[76] By 1980, the Nationalists were able to add a few more demons to their list: Masons, Zionists, Mormons, Jehovah's Witnesses, homosexuals, hippies, and even the Rotary Club were all identified as subversive.[77] The Nationalists also flirted with territorial expansion during the early 1940s, suggesting the annexation of Uruguay, Paraguay, and Bolivia, and a possible war with pro–Allied Brazil.[78] Also indicative of birth trauma was the Nationalist call for "moral purification" of the national soul.[79]

Perón's Regime

In 1930, the demagogic Radical president, Hipólito Yrigoyen, clearly losing his faculties due to the ravages of advancing age, was overthrown in a military coup, and the oligarchy was restored to power. This initiated the so-called "Infamous decade"—actually thirteen years—which "witnessed the reimposition and maintenance of the conservative elite's political power through a system of institutionalized fraud and corruption."[80] The coup's leader was Gen. José Uriburu, a former leader of the *Liga*.[81] The brief manifesto issued on his behalf was filled with condemnatory references to the Yrigoyen regime's sins of "chaos," "collapse," "anarchy," and—significantly—"the exaltation of the subordinate."[82] The rigged 1932 elections were won by the *Concordancia*, a coalition of conservatives, anti–Yrigoyen Radicals, and defectors from the Socialist Party.[83]

In June 1943, this coalition, then headed by Ramón Castillo, was overthrown by the United Officers Group (GOU, also standing for "Government, Order, Unity"), who were disturbed by his incompetence,[84] and in addition "feared that the forthcoming elections would result in the victory of the popular front led by the Communists."[85] Perón was sympathetic to the GOU, but did not join the coup until it was clear that it would succeed.[86] Although the coup was interpreted in the United States as pro–Axis, its leaders were originally divided on the issue of World War II, as were those they had replaced. About six months after they took power, however, the GOU removed the pro–Allied moderates from the cabinet, outlawed all political parties, restricted the press, and re-established compulsory religious instruction in the schools,[87] after half a century of secularism. This was primarily the work of Gustavo Martínez Zuviría, Minister of Education, an anti–Semitic novelist who wrote under the name Hugo Wast.[88]

Even before he joined forces with Evita, Juan Perón saw the potential of recruiting organized labor into the camp of the GOU. Spanish dictator Primo de Rivera had also courted labor's support for his military regime, and there was Rosas' cultivation of the underclass in mid–nineteenth century Argentina. Perón was a strange candidate for friend of the working man, however, having machine-gunned demonstrating workers during the *Semana Tragica*.[89] Although he defined himself as the ideological successor to Yrigoyen,[90] he really had no ideology, but only sought "to assure the undisputed loyalty of different sectors of society to the Perónist regime and to Perón in particular."[91] His doctrine of "Justicialism" was poorly formulated, and his books on the subject were contradictory.[92] He favored an "organized community" under the guidance of the state, but overlooked the question of who would control the state. He excoriated the oligarchy while calling for conflicting interests to be harmonized.[93] "We want capital and labor, in a tight embrace," he explained, "to forge the greatness of the fatherland, while the state watches over the good of both, assuring justice for the rich and the poor."[94] Condemning both Communism and capitalism, Perón described his "Third Position" in 1940 as "not a middle-of-the-road position. It is an ideological position which is in the center, the left, or the right according to circumstances."[95] The best word in English would be "opportunism."

In one sense, Perón was an ideal figure to mobilize the Argentine poor, particularly the Creoles. Like so many of them, he came from an unstable family of racially-mixed background. His father deserted the family when he was a child, after bringing them to Patagonia, and Juan was subsequently raised by relatives in Buenos Aires.[96] Bright and energetic, Perón sought a career in the Army, but he never adopted the ultra-conservative ideology so popular among his colleagues. If my understanding is correct, Perón's longing for an "organized community" reflected his fear of abandonment, common among many of the poor at the time, while most of the military were still responding to birth-related feelings such as fear of chaos, change, and pollution. In key speeches, Perón would directly address his listeners' unconscious feelings, evoking his "poor old mother" in words that "echo[ed] exactly a dominant refrain of tango — the poor grief-laden mother whose pain symbolizes the pain of her children, of all the poor." And he would urge the men in the audience to protect the women, "also a constant theme of both tango and other forms of popular culture."[97]

The conflict between Perón and the other GOU leaders came to a head in 1945, when he was removed from his position as minister of labor and exiled to a small island in the Rio de la Plata. His courting of organized labor bothered the ultra-conservatives in the government,[98] while the regime's diverse opposition also regarded him as a threat. His military rivals opposed his common-law arrangement with the beautiful radio actress Evita Duarte, whose poor and illegitimate origins offended their devout Catholic sensibilities. As it happened, after strikes and demonstrations by the CGT (General Workers Confederation) forced the military to reinstate him, Evita became his most valuable asset.

Perón was elected president in 1946 in the cleanest elections up to then in Argentina's history. He was backed by the CGT, along with dissident factions of the Radicals, conservatives, and Socialists. Most of the latter groups opposed him, along with the Communists. U.S. Ambassador Spruille Braden's support for the opposition backfired, as the Perónists convincingly portrayed him as the hidden hand behind the anti–Perón coalition.[99] Braden was still able to persuade many in the U.S. that Perón was a South American version of Hitler, although his fervent opposition to right-wing totalitarianism didn't stop him from later becoming a leading figure in the John Birch Society, which had a few Nazi skeletons rattling in its own closets.

Perón defined his constituency as the *descamisados*, or "shirtless ones." This had originally been a term of contempt. Crassweller states: "[P]roper attire in public was one of the deep and hitherto unchallenged values of the Argentine civilization. Anyone appearing in public in less than tie and jacket, regardless of heat, was at the very least a boor and a clod."[100] The mass mobilizations of 1945 and 1946 brought the shirtless poor into the Plaza de Mayo, the capital's central square. Workers were not even allowed in the area previously if they weren't well-dressed. One observer recalls: "[W]hen the voices began to ring out and the columns of anonymous earth-colored faces began to pass by we felt something tremble which until that day had seemed unmoveable."[101]

The workers felt empowered by Perón, even though the inequitable social structure remained intact. One of their favorite songs claimed that Perón's sexual organ was "bigger than a ham."[102]

Saint Evita

Although Evita's role in restoring Perón to power after his ouster has been exaggerated, she did play a major role in winning the support of the poor. Appearing before them draped in expensive Parisian gowns, furs and diamonds, she would declare: "You, too, will have clothes like these some day."[103] It worked; many common people loved her. "To be in the Señora's thoughts," said one woman, "is like touching God with a person's own hands. What more does anyone need?"[104]

The Eva Perón Foundation, which she ran personally, managed to build 12 up-to-date hospitals, 1,000 schools, old age homes, holiday resorts, and thousands of residences; it even had its own Red Cross.[105] There were warehouses filled with bicycles, sewing machines, and other useful items which were distributed to the poor. Both businesses and unions were dunned to pay for them. Those who benefited from her largesse typically became enthusiastic Perónists; indeed, no other Latin American political movement until then ever gained so much popular support. After her death, there was a movement to pressure the Vatican to declare her a saint, but this only helped turn the Argentine Church against Perón.

There was a seamy side to Evita's political career, however. She liked to appoint relatives to high positions. Her brother Juan, with whom she was extremely close, became her husband's private secretary; one brother-in-law, an elevator operator, became Director of Federal Customs; another became a senator, and another first became governor of Buenos Aires province and then a member of the Supreme Court, while her mother's boyfriend was appointed Minister of Communications.[106]

Some of the Foundation's activities, moreover, appear to have been versions of the Potemkin villages of Czarist Russia. A "Children's City" was built in a wealthy suburb of Buenos Aires, supposedly a boarding school for up to 300 underprivileged youngsters. An unsympathetic visitor noted that the well-fed and well-dressed children, who greeted her with a cheerful song, had no pencils or notebooks in their classrooms, and there was nothing written on the blackboard, causing her to wonder what they had been doing before she arrived. There was no sign of wear and tear on the furniture or toys. The kitchen was immaculate, and when the cooks were asked how much milk the children drank each day, they could only reply, "Lots and lots." The director knew none of the children by name. It was the same at a home in the capital for poor girls who migrated from the interior: the furnishings were luxurious, but showed little sign of use. "These were designed not for the children or the women or the girls," observed the visitor, "but for the child and girl Eva never had a chance to be."[107]

One interesting clue to Evita's traumatic childhood came during a much-publicized official visit to Franco's Spain. Housed in the Prado palace, she asked her friend and advisor Liliane Guardo to stay overnight in the room with her. The two pushed heavy furniture against the bedroom door, as if for protection,[108] although nothing ill was likely to befall an official guest. Was this an indication of childhood rape, perhaps in her father's mansion? Could that have been the ultimate origin of her hatred of "the traitorous and perfidious oligarchy ... the cursed race of exploiters and the dealers in humanity"?[109]

Evita was the foremost promoter of Perón's cult of personality. "[Y]ou have purified me," she wrote to her husband as she left on her European trip, "your wife with all her faults, because I live in you, feel for you and think through you...."[110] In her book, *History of Perónism*, she elaborated:

> If a person believes himself to be somebody without our movement, if he makes the mistake of believing that he is a being with a personality of his own will in our movement, we stare at him astounded, for how far his ignorance can reach, how much can ambition bring man to a loss, making them think they are somebody, while in this very century and in this very country there already is a leader, a guide, a master.[111]

In 1950, she stated that "all Argentine children, I believe, even before they learn how to say 'Papa,' should say 'Perón.'"[112] And after 1952, children's textbooks replaced the phrase "Mommy loves me" with "Eva loves me."[113]

For all Evita's devotion to Perón, however, the two did not appear particularly close as a couple. Evita spent so much time making speeches and meeting with supplicants that there were times when she and her husband hardly saw each other,[114] leading Crassweller to suspect that neither of them had much of a sex drive.[115]

Evita's cancer, which killed her in 1952 at the age of 33, may have contributed to that situation. Without her, Perón lost his sense of direction, and "became in no time at all an old-fashioned run-of-the-mill Latin American military dictator, relying on the violence of his followers to curb his enemies...."[116] By 1955, he was beginning to sound paranoid, accusing an "International Synarchy," led by the U.S. and the USSR, of plotting disorder.[117] His xenophobia, coupled with his growing preoccupation with speedboats and motorcycles,[118] indicated that Evita's death may have plunged Perón into birth feelings.

Perónism in Practice

Perón's political base of urban workers and rural landlords was not unprecedented, if one recalls that Franklin D. Roosevelt also enjoyed the loyalty of the powerful labor movement as well as Southern Dixiecrats. Perón's appeal to the workers, according to James McGuire, resulted not from his charisma, "but rather because he was plainly responsible for a large and sudden increase in the wealth, power, and status of the urban working class."[119] And, as Daniel James observes: "Almost anyone enquiring of a Perónist worker why he supported Perón has been met by the significant gesture of tapping the back pocket where the money is kept, symbolizing a basic class pragmatism of monetary needs and their satisfaction."[120] Given their hero's use of tango lyrics in his speeches, however, and the absurd extremes of the Perón personality cult, the reality may be a bit more complex.

To start with, there were gains for workers in the form of medical compensation, maternity leave, and paid vacations, as well as the more intangible matter of dignity. Between 1945 and 1948, real wages rose 22 percent for skilled workers, and 30 percent for the unskilled.[121] Far more workers became unionized; the number grew from 529,000 in 1946 to 2,257,000 in 1954, shortly before Perón's overthrow. However, this still constituted only 43 percent of all wage earners,[122] while 20 percent had already been organized — mostly by Marxists — even before the 1943 coup.[123]

Perón opposed the independence of the unions, and used gangsters to oust the Communist leadership from the important meatpackers' union.[124] A wave of strikes in 1950 was broken by force.[125] Purges crippled the CGT until it had little to do except "issue interminable exhortations to 'loyalty,' while battening down the slightest signs of unrest."[126] Perón told the workers that they were to go "From home to work, and from work to home."[127] Ultimately, the 40 percent inflation wiped out virtually all the gains of the workers,[128] and at times real wages actually declined.[129]

There was no serious land reform,[130] hardly surprising given the fact that Perón's party was dominated in some areas by large landowners.[131] "By 1955," writes David Rock, "Perón's colonization and land redistribution measures had aided only 3,200 farming families."[132]

Although Perón's government was far from totalitarian, and could barely even be described as a dictatorship, it was no model democracy. Judges and civil servants were replaced with Perónists, and Congressmen could be ousted or imprisoned if they were too critical of the government. Anti-Perónists were unable to hold large meetings or have free access to the media. In the 1951 election, the Communist presidential candidate was assassinated by armed Perónists, as other opposition politicians were jailed or went into hiding.[133] As early as 1946, all six universities were purged, with 70 percent of the professors removed. Right-wing nationalists took over their administrations.[134]

Perón's Downfall

Just as war-time and post-war prosperity helped stabilize the Perón regime, so did recession in the early 1950s contribute to its collapse.[135] In addition, the Church — and the far right in general — was alienated by Perón's enfranchisement of women, the legalization of divorce and prostitution, and the ending of support for Catholic schools,[136] along with his further initiatives on behalf of labor.[137] There was also the issue of Catholic Action, which competed with the Perónists in the universities and working-class neighborhoods.[138] Finally, if Evita wasn't unacceptable enough, she had been replaced in Perón's bedroom by a 13-year-old nymphet.[139] As massive demonstrations and counter-demonstrations erupted in Buenos Aires, promoted by Perón's separation of church and state, the Air Force rebelled and bombed the city. After more than 150 civilians had been killed, a number of churches were destroyed by the Perónists in reprisal, and a priest was killed.[140]

It is significant that between 1946 and 1954, Perón's strength had continued to grow among the poorly-educated *descamisados*, even as it declined among the better-off workers, generally of immigrant background.[141] Notwithstanding the country's substantial economic progress, the old Creole-European cleavage still existed, and the military were able to make good use of it. Perhaps Perón should have listened when Evita suggested, in 1951, the creation of a workers militia.[142]

In 1955, Perón was overthrown by a military coup led by Gen. Pedro Aramburu, as the Air Force overflew the capital in a cross and "V" formation, meaning "Christ Conquers."[143] Hailed in the U.S. as a return to democracy, this "Liberating Revolution" ushered in a long period of instability, coups, economic deterioration, resistance by labor unions still loyal to Perón, and meaningless elections in which Perónists—still roughly a third of the population—were prevented from participating. The elections twice led to victories by Radical Party candidates—Arturo Frondizi and Arturo Illia—but they were both overthrown in coups. After eighteen years, Argentina's leaders finally decided that the aging ex-ruler, then living in Franco's Spain with a young and attractive new wife, Isabel, should be allowed to return. And that was when Argentina's troubles truly began.

The "Dirty War"

The stage was set for the bloody conflict by the 1969 uprising in Cordoba—the *Cordobazo*—in which students and workers fought together, and even took control of Argentina's second city for two days. There were other uprisings, both in Cordoba and elsewhere, and it became clear to the ruling military that their ability to govern the country had been lost. Argentine juntas differ from military dictatorships elsewhere in Latin America by their lack of permanent leaders; junta heads there tend to come and go, unlike in the Dominican Republic, Haiti, or Nicaragua, where tyrants rule their country for life and may even pass it on to their sons. Given Argentina's long-standing cultural divide, it was difficult for any military figure to relate to the unconscious feelings of the majority of the population. They governed, instead, by terror and violence.

By 1970, half a dozen armed movements were advocating revolution in the name of Marxism, Perónism, or a mixture of both. These included the short-lived Argentine Revolutionary Movement, the Perónist Armed Forces (FAP), the Liberation Armed Forces (FAL), the Revolutionary Armed Forces (FAR), the Montoneros, and the People's Revolutionary Army (ERP). The FAP, FAL, and FAR were all absorbed in 1973 by the Montoneros. The ERP, further to the left, remained apart.[144]

Interestingly, as early as 1964, Perón had encouraged the formation of a Perónist Revolutionary Movement, which called for an armed insurrection by the workers,[145] but it seems that his purpose was to undercut CGT head Augusto Vandor,[146] leader of the "Loyal to Perón" faction within the confederation's Perónist wing,[147] which was actually *opposed* to Perón, and wanted him only as a figurehead, whereas the rival "Standing Up Beside Perón" faction, whose followers ranged from fascists to radical leftists, sought to put him in complete control.[148] The exiled leader subsequently withdrew his support from the movement, and it collapsed.[149]

While the ERP's origins were Trotskyist, the Montoneros had different roots. One of their activists remarked: "Most of our leaders had studied at the military school in Argentina. They were from the ultra-right side of our society...."[150] Some had been involved with the neo–Nazi Tacuara.[151] Their leader, Mario Firmenich, was identified as an agent of Argentine military intelligence,[152] which casts the group's history of revolutionary activism in a quite different light. During the early 1970s, for example, "There were no assaults on military garrisons and no instances of Montonero *comandos* deliberately setting out to do battle with the army or police."[153] This contrasts sharply with the ERP, which attacked army bases with almost enough courage to make up for their lack of military professionalism. In 1970, Firmenich had been involved in the kidnapping and subsequent murder of former president Aramburu, who was at the time intriguing against the regime of Gen. Juan Onganía. The regime made few efforts to find Aramburu, leading some to suspect their complicity with the kidnappers.[154]

In 1973, the increasingly unpopular military regime caved in and permitted Perón to return, denying him only the right to run for president. The elections in March gave about half the vote to a Perónist-dominated coalition, while the Radicals received only 21 percent, the conservatives 20, and the anti–Perón leftists a mere 9.[155] Hector Campora, a relatively unknown left-wing Perónist, became president; later, Perón was elected in a landslide, with his wife Isabel — a folk-dancer with no political background — as his vice president. On June 20, huge crowds gathered at Ezeiza airport to welcome back the returning ex-president and his entourage. Many were members of the Montonero-oriented *Juventud Peronista*, or other pro–Perón leftist groups. They were ambushed by heavily armed rightists. The official death toll in the massacre was at least a dozen, but many believed that was far too low.[156] One eyewitness estimated hundreds killed.[157]

The ambush had been instigated by José Lopez Rega,[158] an extreme rightist and author of "incomprehensible books about astrology and the occult."[159] In 1964, he became Isabel's "spiritual master."[160] His influence grew as Perón's health declined.[161] Known as *El Brujo*, (the Witch Doctor), Lopez Rega was behind the Argentine Anti-Communist Alliance (AAA), which began the "Dirty War." Originally, it was directed by the Perónist right against the Perónist left, with Perón's full support. In 1975, Lopez Rega's opponents forced him into exile,[162] but the witch hunt continued, even without the Witch Doctor directing it. After 1976, when the Army overthrew the hopelessly incompetent Isabel, the military got involved in the repression, and dissidents of nearly all persuasions were targeted.

The justification for the Dirty War was the armed actions of the Montoneros and the ERP. From 1969 to 1979, there were 239 kidnappings and 1,020 murders by the guerrillas. During the same period, however, the military kidnapped 7,844 and murdered 7,850.[163] Not that other governments would have failed to respond to the death of over a thousand people, but the brutal killings and torture went on long after the guerrillas had been wiped out.[164] Furthermore, "the two top leaders of the purportedly powerful leftist Perónist Montoneros were actively — and secretly — collaborating with Argentine army intelligence...."[165] As for the ERP, its ambitious attempt to establish a liberated zone in impoverished Tucuman province — with fewer than 100 guerrillas[166] — was a complete failure, with no support forthcoming from the local population.[167] By the end of 1976, "the ERP had been eliminated as a guerrilla force."[168]

With the Perónists out of the government after Isabel's fall, Argentina was dominated by military men with Nationalist leanings. They saw themselves in a holy war against Marxism on behalf of the Catholic Church. Junta head Gen. Jorge Videla defined as enemies all those who "spread ideas contrary to western civilization,"[169] even as his subordinates inflicted tortures that rivaled anything seen under Genghis Khan or Idi Amin. "We are fighting against nihilists," said his fellow junta member, Admiral Emilio Massera, "against agents of destruction whose only objective is destruction itself, although they disguise this with social crusades."[170] It was a fair description of the junta itself. And the pro-junta National Patriotic Movement, composed largely of youth, stated that "[W]e are fighting against Marxism: so that we can continue to believe in God; so that the family can continue to be the center of Argentinian life; so that fathers can continue to be the main educators of their children."[171] Writers had to conform to the official line, as in any totalitarian state: they were ordered to put only happy endings in their scripts, and nothing was to be said about divorce, abortion, or domestic violence.[172]

When the junta's leaders were put on trial, they admitted to having killed 30,000 people[173]—although there could have been some duplication, and other estimates run a good deal lower. It was clear, though, that their intentions were close to genocidal. "First we will kill all the subversives," declared Gen. Ibérico Saint Jean, "then we will kill their collaborators; then their sympathizers, then ... those who remain indifferent; and finally we will kill the timid."[174] As it happened, "few of the victims were actually militants or had information to give their tormentors."[175] By the time a year had gone by, perhaps a million Argentines had gone into exile, in Europe, Mexico, Venezuela or elsewhere. They included nearly half of the country's scientists, researchers, and professionals.[176]

At the same time, partly due to the country's long-standing if weakly rooted democratic traditions, and partly to pressure from the human rights-conscious administration of President Jimmy Carter in the U.S., the junta's leaders sometimes posed as champions of freedom. They claimed to see themselves "as guardians of an emergency regime that would cleanse the body politic and eventually restore a liberal democracy."[177] In 1976, shortly after his coup, Videla said, "Liberty is the proud mother of the Republic and its children; to lose her, in any way, would be to lose that which we love most. Let's protect her and conserve her."[178] And Massera, later convicted of 90 murders, said in 1977: "We believe that the best proof that a country is civilized resides in its scrupulous protection of the right of its minorities to peacefully dissent."[179]

This was the same man who declared that all the ills of Western society could be traced to three men: Marx, Freud, and Einstein.[180] They were guilty of challenging established ideas—and, Massera hardly needed to emphasize, all three were Jews. The junta's terror was directed more against Jews than against other groups; although they made up only 1 or 2 percent of the population, they were about 10 percent of the disappeared.[181] During the late 1970s, an Argentine National Socialist Front, "made up of Federal Police and state intelligence agents," took credit for bombing synagogues and machine-gunning Jewish-owned stores.[182] Rumors abounded that Israel was plotting to seize Patagonia or northern Argentina.[183]

One odd consequence of U.S. pressure on Argentina was that the anti–Marxist dictatorship began aligning itself with the USSR, on the basis of their common opposition to Washington. The Soviet presence in Argentina grew significantly, while the USSR defended the junta against American criticism. As a result, the pro–Moscow Argentine Communist Party "declared that the Argentine generals were progressive and said it supported General Videla."[184] There were only a few cases of repression directed against its members.[185] Similarly, the military persecuted Freudian psychoanalysts, who tended to identify with the political left, but had no trouble with Lacanians, whose arcane doctrines presented no threat to their beloved social order.[186]

The Junta Self-Destructs

Some of the twentieth century's worst tyrannies have brought about their own destruction by starting unwinnable wars. Pol Pot's Cambodia attacked Vietnam; Idi Amin's Uganda invaded Tanzania; Japan's militarists attacked the United States; Hitler invaded the USSR while still fighting England; and Pakistan got itself into a hopeless conflict with India in 1970. The junta's Argentina fit this pattern when it invaded the Falkland Islands (Islas Malvinas to the Argentines) in 1982. Although Argentina had once owned this desolate and sparsely-populated archipelago, losing it to Britain in the early nineteenth century, the dispute "seemed buried and almost forgotten" as early as 1933, when it was revived by Nationalists in response to British economic penetration of Argentina.[187] In 1977, after Videla's coup, a quarrel with Chile over three tiny, remote islands in the Strait of Magellan was settled by British arbitration in favor of Chile. This prompted Massera to call for the forceful recovery of the Falklands.[188] When Gen. Leopoldo Galtieri took over the junta in December 1981, "The streets of Buenos Aires were flooded with thousands of citizens screaming for an end to military rule. These cries of hatred turned suddenly to cheers on April 2 when Galtieri announced that he had sent Argentine troops to invade and take over the Falkland Islands."[189] Argentina's troops performed poorly in battle, and were defeated in short order by the British and their Nepalese mercenaries. After that, the junta was finished.

The junta left behind not only a legacy of terror, but a bankrupt economy. Worried about the instability, "Argentina's rich sent an estimated US $82.5 billion to foreign banks during the 1974–82 period, while evading taxes in Argentina."[190] The cost of the repression itself was also huge.[191] Saddled with debt, neither the Radicals under Raúl Alfonsín nor the Perónists under Carlos Menem were able to tackle Argentina's serious economic problems; only after the political system collapsed and Nestor Kirchner defaulted on the country's loans did things begin to improve. Meanwhile, the militancy of the working class grew even stronger. The junta's worst torturers, put on trial, were often unrepentant. Said one: "What I did I did for my Fatherland, my faith, and my religion. Of course I would do it again."[192] They regarded their crimes as a preemptive strike against potential revolutionaries to save civilization; in fact, the Dirty War was a replay of dictator Rosas' campaign of terror against his educated opponents.

Hopefully, Argentina has passed the point where militarist thugs can hijack the nation's destiny — although there have been many times in the past when high expectations were cruelly dashed. Yet it is important to distinguish between the junta of 1976–1983 and previous caudillos, including Perón. The junta ruled entirely by terror; there was no charisma involved. The disappearance of the charismatic caudillo may be related to the gradual development of stable families in the urban areas, as the male-female ratio has become more balanced, and the rural migrants from the interior become second-generation *porteños*. Deference to powerful father-figures has been replaced by class consciousness as the old repressed feeling of fear of abandonment has receded. The Nationalists' birth-related fear of chaos and need to break out, on the other hand, has never resonated with the majority of the population. Ironically, the very family values which the military and Nationalists used to rationalize their horrendous repression may have undermined their always shaky grip on the Argentine people.

14

Haiti

A Nation of Origin-Folk

Even before the devastating earthquake of January 2010, Haiti was the poorest nation in the Western Hemisphere. Its problems have long seemed virtually insoluble. In 2005, the country's annual gross national product was a mere $3.88 billion. Eighty percent of its eight million people are illiterate. Most are still rural, despite the massive influx into the capital, Port-au-Prince, whose population now exceeds one million. Yet the size of the average farm is a mere three-quarters of an acre. The typical Haitian consumes just under the minimum daily calorie requirement.[1] Over one-third of Haitians now suffer from malnutrition.[2] The distribution of wealth is the most unequal in Latin America, with the top one percent controlling about half; most Haitians live on the equivalent of under one dollar per day.[3] Since the earthquake, which killed 100,000, much of the capital's population have been living in tents, and the slowness of the cash-strapped government to respond has caused increased political instability.

With 11,000 square miles, Haiti ranks with El Salvador as the most densely populated nation in the Americas. Its land is severely eroded, due to the massive deforestation caused by peasants who chop down trees to make charcoal for cooking; this began in 1954, when peasants burned the trees toppled by Hurricane Hazel.[4] With the erosion comes severe flooding every time a hurricane strikes the island; this is increasingly frequent due to global warming, itself due in large part to worldwide deforestation.

Haiti's soil is exhausted. It produces only about one-sixth as much rice per hectare, just over one-tenth as much corn, and little more than half as much sugar as the U.S., and only one-third as much coffee as Mexico.[5] There are few jobs available in the cities, and unemployment fluctuates at around 70 percent.[6] People survive on money sent home by relatives abroad.[7] Some are forced to turn to crime, which has destroyed the tourist industry; even guidebooks to the once-popular destination can no longer be found.

Haitian-American anthropologist Michel-Rolph Trouillot criticizes the "dangerous ... idea that the Haitian political quagmire is due to some congenital disease of the Haitian mind."[8] Yet if Haiti's current situation is to be attributed to slavery or colonialism, what is one to make of the relative success of other West Indian nations such as Barbados or St. Lucia, where slavery lasted two generations longer, and colonial rule for more than another 150 years? Even nearby Jamaica, which is also extremely poor, has managed to function for nearly half a century as a somewhat stable two-party democracy; but Haiti took almost two centuries before it held its first free election, and the winner — populist ex-priest Jean-

Bertrand Aristide — managed to become the first elected political leader in Latin America to be overthrown *twice*.

It is not a congenital disease, but a pattern of child sexual abuse which — along with overpopulation, soil erosion, foreign intervention, and domination by a socially irresponsible elite — has been the cause of Haiti's difficulties. As Lloyd de Mause notes, sexual abuse of children can be more destructive to a nation's life "than just the violent behavior instilled by beatings."[9] Certainly, those who would argue that fascism emerges solely as the result of corporate capital would be hard-pressed to explain the 14-year dictatorship of François Duvalier in a country where large industries are unheard of. When ordinary Haitians pick up guns or machetes and butcher their fellow citizens in order to protect the interests of a tiny clique of corrupt power-holders, something is going on with them that requires a psychological, rather than purely economic, explanation.

A Troubled Beginning

The island of Hispaniola, first colonized by Christopher Columbus, remained entirely under Spanish rule for two centuries, but French buccaneers established a base on the small neighboring island of Tortuga off its northwest coast, and eventually colonized the western third. France annexed this area in 1697,[10] and it became known as Saint Domingue, with Spain retaining the rest of the island. The first slaves brought to the colony were actually whites, recruited under false pretenses in France and then reduced to servitude[11]; women were also purchased to provide wives for the earliest settlers.[12] But during the 18th century, slaves were imported from Africa, and Saint Domingue ultimately accounted for about 10 percent of the entire African-Atlantic slave trade,[13] which peopled an area stretching from Brazil to Baltimore.

Slavery in Haiti was particularly brutal, even compared to the U.S. South.[14] In the early days of the colony, sugar was the main industry. The sugar mills had 18–20 hour shifts, and the field work — where the slaves risked cutting themselves on the sharp cane — wasn't much easier.[15] A slave could expect to survive for about 10 to 15 years.[16] Since the work was considered too hard for women, few were imported.[17] It was cheaper to purchase new slaves from Africa than to invest in children.

The slaves were originally brought from West Africa, with a large contingent of Fon from Dahomey (corresponding roughly to present-day Benin). Later, as the colonists expanded into the mountains to plant coffee, they imported Bakongo from Central Africa, and these eventually became the largest group of Africans in the colony.[18] Unlike in the U.S., where the masters took care to disperse the tribes, this was not done in Haiti, and more of the African culture survived than elsewhere in the Americas.

Colonial Haitian society was very hierarchical, ruled from the top by a small minority of *grand blancs*, or wealthy plantation owners. Just below them were the *petit blancs*, not poor whites in the U.S. sense, but typically overseers, artisans and professionals; they too owned slaves, although not as many. Beneath the whites were the *affranchis*, or "free persons of color." These were mostly mulattoes — children of white masters and black female slaves — although they included some people of pure African descent. While they were denied full social equality with the whites, many of them were well-off and owned slaves and plantations.[19] Unlike many of the whites, who spent much of their time in Europe dissipating their wealth, the mulattoes stayed in Haiti and worked to increase their fortunes. From 1758 on, however, there were increasing restrictions on their rights; they were forbidden to gather in groups for any reason,[20] and were subsequently excluded from the medical and legal professions.[21] At the same time, they made up most of the local armed forces,[22] and were relied on to fight bands of escaped slaves in the mountains, known as maroons.[23]

Below the *affranchis* were the slaves, although even among them, there were cultural distinctions, particularly between the Haitian-born Creoles and the African immigrants. There was a privileged caste of slaves, consisting of foremen, coachmen, cooks, butlers, maids, nurses and concubines. "Permeated with the views of their masters and mistresses, these upper servants gave themselves airs and despised the slaves in the fields."[24] Outside the system were the maroons, typically African-born, who had often escaped to the mountains as soon as they arrived in Haiti.[25] Their resistance laid the groundwork for the revolt that ultimately abolished slavery and achieved independence.

The mulattoes often maintained close ties to their white fathers, and their women were very much in demand by the white men, lawful wedlock being more the exception than the rule.[26] By 1789, 5,000 out of 7,000 mulatto women in Haiti were prostitutes or concubines.[27] Writes Doris Garraway: "[T]he free mulatto woman in the eighteenth-century French Caribbean ... was deemed superior in charms, intelligence, and sexual savoir faire to white women, thus leading white men to shun women of their own race in favor of colored lovers and concubines."[28]

The Haitian war of independence, triggered by the French Revolution, represented the first successful slave revolt in modern history. During its early stages, there were a number of conflicting factions: *grand blancs* who supported restoration of the monarchy; *petit blancs* who favored the Republic; mulattoes who demanded equality with the whites; and slaves who fought for their freedom. Britain and Spain, each with their own quarrel with revolutionary France, also got involved. At the end, former slaves fought together with the largely mulatto *affranchis* against Napoleon's armies, which intended to restore slavery. Little quarter was given by either side. By 1803, when the French withdrew in defeat, having lost 60,000 men to the rebels and yellow fever,[29] much of the country was in ashes. At least 100,000 Haitians were killed, out of fewer than 700,000.[30] "The transformation of slaves," writes C.L.R. James, "trembling in hundreds before a single white man, into a people able to organize themselves and defeat the most powerful European nations of their day, is one of the great epics of revolutionary struggle and achievement."[31] But the more difficult struggle of building a viable nation had only begun.

Elite Internalization of Racism

Independence ended the white presence in Haiti, but the mulattoes remained. They were a tenth of the population, concentrated in the towns of the south; many of them were former slaveholders themselves. "[R]ace prejudice against the Negroes permeated the minds of the Mulattoes who so bitterly resented the same thing from the whites," states James.[32] Looking down on the Creole language, spoken by most Haitians, and on the African religious practices known as Voudou, the mulattoes "learned to identify everything that was French, white European, light, with beauty, purity, intelligence, and correctness."[33] This continued into the twentieth century. "[T]he Haitian intellectual has taken pride in aligning himself with French culture, and, in racial terms, has been particularly self-conscious about his Negroid origin."[34] The black independence leaders, Toussaint L'Ouverture and Jean-Jacques Dessalines, never trusted the mulattoes. Toussaint once boasted that he could do away with the mulattoes by raising his left hand, a reference to the black magic he professed not to believe in.[35] And Dessalines was murdered by rebellious southern soldiers acting on orders from mulatto general Alexandre Pétion.[36]

By 1807, Haiti had split into two countries—a black kingdom in the north, and a mulatto-dominated republic in the south.[37] This situation prevailed for more than a decade before the country was reunited. "Many of the problems which confront modern Haiti," says James Ferguson, "can be traced to this initial period of divided independence."[38] The social structure in each state was different. While the south promoted land reform—even as some wealthy mulattoes were able to acquire formerly white-owned plantations[39]—the north kept all the plantations intact under black owners.[40] One consequence is that the Haitian elite has exercised its influence less through land ownership, as in the rest of Latin America, than through its greater education and control of business.[41] In the north, which has always been the more rebellious part of the country, much of the land is still owned by a small oligarchy, but cultivated by individual sharecroppers in small parcels.[42] There are only a few large plantations left, which grow sisal and sugar cane.[43]

Elite rejection of everything African was reflected in the use of Parisian French as the official language, even though eighty percent of Haitians speak only Creole,[44] which is derived from French, but barely mutually intelligible. Disapproval of Voudou was even more intense. Toussaint outlawed it a few years before independence.[45] The elite instigated campaigns to chop down silk-cotton trees, which are sacred in the Afro-Caribbean religions.[46] In the late 19th century, Haitian writers denied that Voudou existed, or claimed that it was practiced by only a few people.[47] Official tolerance of Voudou, however, varied from district to district, with Jeremie, in the south, being the most repressive. "[O]ne may spend months in the region without hearing a single drum beat," observed Maya Deren.[48] Not coincidentally, Jeremie was also known as the leading stronghold of mulatto anti-black prejudice.

Some have argued that "the line that divides Haitians most is *not* a color line,"[49] and that what appeared to be a racial conflict between blacks and mulattoes was really a clash "between two cliques within a single class."[50] The Haitian leftist leader Ben Dupuy says that the country's past intra-elite conflicts were actually between landlords and merchants,[51] which might have *appeared* to be racial in nature, given the fact that the landlords were usually black and the merchants mulatto. And Peter Hallward notes, "Whenever the elite finds itself threatened from 'below,' the routine tensions between mulattoes and blacks ... vanish immediately...."[52] "Mulâtre political factions," Trouillot reminds us, "almost always included black intellectuals and military men."[53]

It may be true that the class struggle between rich and poor often overshadowed the black-mulatto conflict within the elite, but the latter was real enough—"routine," as Hallward admits—and the poor, as elsewhere in the West Indies, were not always on the brink of overthrowing the rich. The struggle for Haiti's destiny went on at the psychological as well as economic level, and even the most elite blacks found it harder to reject their African identity, not necessarily for lack of trying, than any mulatto. That some Haitian parties could be defined as "mulatto factions" is telling, given that the mulattoes were only a tenth of the population. Furthermore, the mulatto elite liked to rule through cooperative black politicians for the sake of legitimacy, a practice known as *la politique de la doublure*.[54]

Even the most elitist blacks often found themselves fighting the mulattoes. The mulatto leaders Alexandre Pétion, Jean-Pierre Boyer and Andre Rigaud all opposed Toussaint during the Haitian Revolution, and were defeated in 1799 by Toussaint, Dessalines, and Henri Christophe, all of whom were black.[55] When Boyer reunited Haiti in 1818, he suggested turning the country back over to France because he was afraid that the blacks would overthrow the mulatto elite.[56] In 1848, the black president Faustin Soulouque ordered his armed thugs, the *zinglins*, similar to François Duvalier's *Tontons Macoutes* a century later, to massacre the mulattoes in preparation for his crowning himself emperor.[57]

The mulatto elite's internalized anti-black racism stems from fear of abandonment — a repressed feeling similar to what characterizes the *masses* in Argentina (see Chapter 13). This is evidently the result of the weak family structure in Haiti, which dates back even before the beginning of the slave trade, and then was exacerbated by the loose morality which prevailed among the slave-owners and their mulatto companions. It is fear of abandonment which led Haiti's mulatto elite to cooperate with foreign powers — England, France, and ultimately the United States — against the interests of their own fellow-citizens, whom they reject as "Africans." Haiti is a nation of Origin-Folk.

The Haitian Masses

Generally poor and illiterate, "[r]ural Haitians have always taken the state for granted and expect nothing from it but a hard time."[58] The 2010 earthquake is likely to have reinforced this belief. Even Toussaint reestablished the plantation system, and defined the owner as the "father" of his "family"; peasants were paid, but were not allowed to leave.[59] Their subordinate status "was rendered immutable and permanent."[60] Up until Aristide's election in 1990, peasants were officially defined as second-class citizens.[61] In the southern republic, they were denied the right to vote, along with "women, criminals [and] idiots...."[62] In the northern kingdom, of course, there were no elections to begin with.

Haitian governments have traditionally placed the burden of taxation on the peasants, who had to part with 40 percent of their miniscule incomes.[63] The government taxed coffee, raised by peasants, along with imported necessities such as kerosene and matches. But luxury imports remained untaxed, and the rich paid nothing on their incomes.[64]

Family life for Haitians today is unstable, due both to the country's poverty and its tragic history. Even at the beginning of the 19th century, as if anticipating psychohistory, Toussaint blamed the country's continuing disorders on the "negligence with which fathers and mothers raise their children...."[65] By the mid–19th century, reports Elizabeth Abbott, Haitian peasants were rarely married, but lived in "often polygamous unions...."[66] Even today, polygamy remains common in the rural areas.[67] Polygamy depends on a high birth rate, so that there are enough women to go around, as older men marry much younger women; and because the women marry young, they tend to produce more children.

As the country became increasingly urbanized, polygamy tended to mutate into promiscuity. Kathie Klarreich is a white American woman who married a Haitian musician and lived in Port-au-Prince. "Haitian men," she says, speaking from experience, "think it is their right to have as many mistresses as they want, but they will not tolerate such behavior from their women — wife, girlfriend, or mistress."[68]

Of course, with the few economically successful men monopolizing so many of the available women, both male homosexuality and child sexual abuse have become common. Prior to the AIDS crisis, Port-au-Prince had many bars and hotels that catered to gay tourists from the U.S.[69] Randall Robinson observed American tourists cruising for both men and boys along one of the capital's main streets.[70] Needless to say, these sex tourists would not have been flocking to Haiti unless such behavior was already acceptable there. Abbott notes that street urchins were frequently arrested by the police, and then pimped out by prison guards to the inmates.[71] Widespread sexual abuse of children — particularly male children, since women play a smaller role in political life — leads to the kind of rage that finds expression in violent political movements such as the *tontons macoutes* and its successors.

Haitian Voudou

African culture survived in the New World wherever black people lived in large numbers. Cuba's Santeria religion is originally Yoruba, and the popular Charleston dance in the United States came from Liberia by way of South Carolina's Sea Islands. But only in Haiti did African culture — Voudou and its accompanying dances — remain so widespread. This was because of (1) the small percentage of whites in the country, virtually zero after the war of independence; (2) the fact that so many slaves had been born in Africa at the time of the revolt; and (3) the fact that slavery, along with its process of cultural displacement, ended earlier than elsewhere in the Western Hemisphere.

Haitian Voudou is a complex religion, deriving its deities from different parts of Africa, and often merging them with Catholic saints. The famous Voudou dolls were invented elsewhere, most likely New Orleans, and are not found in Haiti. Zombies, on the other hand, are real. Unlike in Hollywood movies, Haitian zombies do not stagger about, grabbing and eating people. "A zombie is nothing more than a body deprived of its conscious powers of cerebration," writes Maya Deren. "[F]or the Haitian, there is no fate more terrible."[72] Zombies are created, as Wade Davis discovered, when a *bokor* (sorcerer) poisons someone who has behaved badly to his family or local community. The poison creates the *appearance* of death, and the target is buried while still alive. Subsequently, he is disinterred, beaten up by the *bokor* and his associates, and then sold as a slave to a plantation. The zombie may remain in his dissociated state for years, obeying his master's orders and subsisting on one meal a day — salt-free, since even a small amount of salt is supposed to bring the zombie back to his conscious state. One victim's life "had the quality of a strange dream ... and conscious action was an impossibility."[73] The poison itself could hardly be the cause of such a long-term effect; a Japanese poisoned by a similar substance from a *fugu* fish recovered from seeming death and walked out of the hospital within half a day.[74] The zombie's condition is a trance state, resulting from the experience of being abandoned by his family, who buried him, and then the beating from the *bokor*, a symbol of authority. Haitian zombies are similar to the "mussulmen" in the Nazi death camps, who gave up their will to live.

There is no moral code in Voudou, unlike in Judaism or Christianity. Everything is about power,[75] the creation of zombies being an example. There are over 400 Voudou gods, or *loa*,[76] and two distinct rites, Rada and Petro. Experts disagree on the details, but the general sense is that Rada derived from Benin and western Nigeria, while Petro originated among the Bakongo, but may have also been influenced by surviving Indians in the mountains. Petro *loa* "are more unpredictable, temperamental, and at times violent than the Rada,"[77] notes Laurent Dubois, and even the drumming that accompanies Petro ceremonies is more "frenzied"[78] and "off-beat."[79] Not surprisingly, the Petro cult was involved in the slave revolt.[80]

Some of the Voudou gods have counterparts in classical paganism, which raises questions about how far back in human prehistory they might actually go. There is Agwe, like Neptune the ruler of the sea; Ogoun, the god of fire and metal (Vulcan); Erzulie, the goddess of love (Venus); Guede, also known as Baron Samedi, the god of the underworld (Pluto, later reinvented as Satan); and Legba, the god of communication (Mercury).[81] Unknown to classical or Norse mythology is the serpent *loa* Damballah, who speaks only in a "barely intelligible hissing."[82] Identified with water, Damballah is probably a symbol of the umbilical cord; memories going that far back are non-verbal.

The same *loa* may appear in both Rada and Petro rites, but their behavior is dramatically different. "As Rada Goddess of Love," says Maya Deren, "Erzulie speaks in diminutive, soprano accents; in her Petro aspect her voice has a primordial, almost beast-like growl."[83]

The Voudou theory of personality is complex. An individual's soul includes a *gwo bon anj* (divine particle), *ti bon anj* (intellect), *namn* (energy), *zetwal* (guiding star), *loa met tet* (disposition), *loa rasin* (link to ancestors), and *wonsiyon* (guardian angels).[84] Both the concept of the *loa*, in their various aspects, and the theory of the personality indicate dissociation, which is typically a consequence of severely repressed anger. In Voudou ceremonies, the participants are possessed by the *loa*, who "ride" them like horses. What would pass for Dissociative Identity Disorder in the U.S. is normal behavior in Haitian Voudou, although the causes may well be the same.

Foreign Intervention and Racial Domination

From 1804 to 1988, there were 35 rulers in Haiti. Twelve of them served for one year or less.[85] Political instability increased as time went on. From 1843 to 1915, notes historian Max Boot, "there were at least 102 civil wars, coups d'état, revolts, and other political disorders. The period between 1908 and 1915 was particularly chaotic. Seven presidents were overthrown during those seven years."[86] To some degree, this near-anarchy was the result of foreign intervention, which had bankrupted the country and strengthened the rule of the least patriotic elite factions. However, during the late 19th century, the elites displayed "a readiness to compromise the autonomy of the country by inviting foreign intervention rather than allowing their political opponents to gain power."[87]

In 1825, France demanded "reparations" from Haiti for the loss of its slaves during the war of independence. Haiti had no choice except to agree, and allowed the French to control her finances, which "had a catastrophic effect on the new nation's delicate economy."[88] Haiti was forced to take out huge loans, which it was still paying off 100 years later.[89] Other European powers — notwithstanding the Monroe Doctrine — also intervened; the British sent gunboats to suppress a revolt against an unpopular government in 1865,[90] and Germany landed troops in Port-au-Prince in 1911 to protect its economic interests.[91] But the most frequent interventionist was the United States. Between 1849 and 1915, the U.S. intervened no fewer than 25 times.[92] It was then that a full-scale occupation began, provoked by the public lynching and dismemberment of President Vilbrun Guillaume Sam, in retaliation for his massacre of 167 political prisoners.[93] This 19-year-long occupation had profound consequences.

Although there were some positive aspects of the U.S. occupation in terms of political stability and improvement of the infrastructure, the Americans imposed their racial prejudices on the Caribbean country. U.S. advisors "openly showed their preference for light-skinned officials,"[94] while black peasants engaged in guerrilla resistance.[95] This was overcome after the insurgent leader, Charlemagne Péralte, was killed in 1919.[96] Tens of thousands of peasants were displaced as American corporations seized large tracts of land; it was supposed to be used for rubber plantations, but no rubber was actually produced.[97] The Americans created chain gangs of unpaid workers to build the roads.[98] There were also attempts to stamp out Voudou.[99]

The mulatto elite cooperated with the Trujillo dictatorship during the 1937 massacre of up to 35,000 Haitian farm-workers in the Dominican Republic.[100] Since 1920, Haitians had been emigrating to the Dominican Republic to cut sugar cane, but the Great Depression had made them redundant.[101] In addition, the Dominican elite was overtly racist toward the Haitians, notwithstanding its own frequently mulatto ancestry. Trujillo worried about "a weakening of the national blood" by "despised Negro aliens."[102] And as late as 1983, Dominican President Joaquín Balaguer wrote in his book, *The Island in Reverse*, that "the black, abandoned to his instincts ... multiplies with a rapidity which is almost comparable to that of vegetable species."[103]

In 1946, following the fall of fascism, demands for democracy and racial equality spread throughout the Caribbean, and the elitist regime of the mulatto President Elie Lescot was overthrown.[104] Haiti then entered a period which was dominated by *Noirisme*, which achieved its final expression under the regime of François (Papa Doc) Duvalier.

Noirisme and Papa Doc

Neither an ideology nor a program, *Noirisme*—called Pan-Africanism in Anglophone Africa, *Negritude* in Africa's former French colonies, and black nationalism in the U.S.—stands for the abolition of the low self-esteem of oppressed black people throughout the world through the conquest of political power and cultural revival. It has had both left-wing and right-wing adherents, Papa Doc being the foremost example of the latter. Originating in the West Indies, *Noirisme* first spread to French-ruled Senegal, where its chief advocate was Leopold Senghor, a poet and later the country's first president. Like the West Indies, Senegal, France's first African colony, was a black-populated land whose people were acculturated to the West.

The first *Noiriste* intellectual in Haiti was Jean Price-Mars, whose 1928 work, *Ainsi Parla l'Oncle*, defended Voudou as a legitimate religion.[105] François Duvalier, who studied under Price-Mars,[106] followed suit in 1938, when he founded the journal *Les Griots*, which emphasized Haiti's African roots.[107] One of his early poems was entitled *An Exile's Lament*:

> I then remembered the route crossed by my ancestors
>   of distant Africa —
> The sons of the jungle
> Whose bones during the centuries of starry silence
> Have helped to build the pyramids
> And I continued on my way, now with heavy heart,
> In the night.
> I walked on and on and on
> Straight ahead.
> And the black of my ebony skin was lost
>   in the shadows of the night.[108]

In 1946, after the fall of Lescot, the moderate *Noiriste* Dumarsais Estimé became president.[109] Chosen by the parliament, rather than the people, he enlarged the school system, promoted more blacks to government jobs, raised government workers' salaries, built hospitals, allowed workers to unionize, brought electric power to the capital, and encouraged the tourist industry.[110] Estimé's term was "the first time Africa, and not simply France, became an important part of the nationalist dialogue."[111] He lasted four years, and was then overthrown in a military coup by Col. Paul Magloire. Duvalier, who was Director of Public Health in the Estimé government,[112] never fully trusted the army as a result.[113] Magloire's corrupt regime, backed by the elite, ruled Haiti for another decade, following which elections — the first in which all Haitians were allowed to vote,[114] but rigged by the army[115] — put Duvalier in power.

Duvalier was a physician, hence the nickname Papa Doc. He had a good reputation in Haiti at the time, partly because of his work eradicating yaws, a widespread disease similar to leprosy, during the 1940s.[116] His father, Duval Duvalier, was originally from Martinique[117] and published a newspaper which opposed the U.S. occupation.[118] His mother had been mentally ill, and died in an insane asylum when he was fourteen.[119] In 1957, Duvalier appeared to be a democrat, calling for a free press, union rights, political freedom and economic justice.[120] Several of his close associates at the time were leftists, including Lucien Daumec, his brother-in-law.[121] But the Duvalierist "revolution" was soon to sour.

Despite the highly negative image Duvalier's regime had in the U.S., there were some positive achievements. He forced the Catholic Church to Haitianize its clergy,[122] and more blacks were able to find government jobs than under previous leaders.[123] Thanks to Duvalier's close associate Clovis Désinor, Port-au-Prince's International Airport was built without U.S. aid, and for less than half of its estimated cost.[124] And unlike in other dictatorships, the opposition continued to publish its newspapers — although they had limited effect in a country where most people were illiterate, and were occasionally banned.

Nevertheless, the bad heavily outweighed the good under Duvalier. While the elite prospered, conditions worsened for the rural poor, and 80 percent of Haiti's children were malnourished.[125] (This rate, far higher than that of the adults, indicates the degree to which the welfare of children is neglected, and not only by the government.) The *Noiriste* philosophy of government resembled European fascism. As its intellectual spokesman stated: "Authority is a sacred thing. Let us establish the mystique of authority. Force remains a beautiful thing, to be respected even when it crushes us."[126] Luckner Cambronne, a cabinet minister and close Papa Doc associate, insisted that "A good Duvalierist stands ready to kill his children, or children to kill their parents."[127] Ironically, Duvalier benefited from the fact that Haitians generally dislike violence, their arguments rarely escalating into fights, unlike elsewhere in Latin America. Haitians "could not believe such ruthlessness, such contempt of human life, as demonstrated by Duvalier were possible in another Haitian."[128]

Duvalier was opposed at the beginning by "the vast majority of the light skinned elite,"[129] along with many leftists. As early as July 1957, an armed band of Haitians and Americans invaded the country from Florida and seized an army barracks near the presidential palace, locking up the soldiers, and almost bringing about the downfall of the government as Duvalier packed his bags and prepared to flee. They were finally overcome by the *tontons macoutes*, Duvalier's loyal paramilitaries. The invaders numbered exactly *eight* men.[130] This gave Duvalier another reason to distrust his army. This invasion was the first of many — from Cuba, the Dominican Republic, and the Bahamas — none of which numbered more than thirty men, and which never came close to success. Their main effect was to stoke Duvalier's paranoia.

Another blow to the dictator's mental state came in 1959, when he sunk into a diabetic coma following a heart attack. Dr. Jacques Fourcand, his personal physician and a U.S.–trained neurosurgeon, administered insulin to him, which anyone with even a limited understanding of diabetes should have recognized as potentially fatal. But the Tonton Macoute leader Clement Barbot managed to get the glucose tablets that saved his life.[131] Of course, after nearly being killed by your doctor, and then rescued by your chief killer, who wouldn't be a bit paranoid?

By 1961, Duvalier had completely overwhelmed his political opposition, and was elected to an unconstitutional second term of six years; the vote was 1.3 million for his Party of National Unity, and none against.[132] In 1964, the constitution was changed to make him President for Life.[133] "I shall be lord and master," Duvalier ranted at the time. "I have always talked with the wild energy that characterizes me; with all the savagery which characterizes me.... The revolution is the revolution.... Why can't the Haitian people turn their ass the way they want? Why not? They are starting to recognize that Duvalier is not the Lucifer of the Caribbean...."[134] A government pamphlet, *The Catechism of the Revolution*, harnessed the Lord's Prayer on behalf of the dictatorship:

> Our Doc who art in the National Palace for life, hallowed be thy name by present and future generations. Thy will be done at Port-au-Prince and in the provinces. Give us this day our new Haiti and never forgive the trespasses of the anti-patriots who spit every day on our country; let them succumb to temptation, and under the weight of their venom, deliver them not from any evil....[135]

The Tontons Macoutes

Typically, Latin American dictatorships rely on the army, the Church, and the large landowners. Haiti's army was small, ineffective, and unreliable from Papa Doc's point of view; the Church was a potential enemy, and certainly no friend of Voudou-influenced black nationalism; and the landlords had relatively little influence over the behavior of their sharecroppers. It was the wealthier land-owning peasants, rather, who "formed the basis of Duvalier's national support, and among them he was genuinely popular."[136] The mulatto elite soon made peace with the regime, which never threatened their economic interests, and for a while, Papa Doc was also supported by some black intellectuals, who believed his promises of revolution.

Papa Doc ruled through the *tontons macoutes*, the term referring to bogeymen whom children are told might carry them off in their baskets if they misbehave. There were about 300,000 Macoutes altogether, of whom perhaps 40,000 were armed.[137] The latter were organized into the denim-clad National Security Volunteers (VSN), but *macoutes* from affluent backgrounds disdained this militia.[138] These more elite *macoutes* were often seen in the capital, driving expensive cars and wearing stylish clothes and sunglasses. "Except for the Port-au-Prince units, the militia was composed mostly of untrained youths who carried battered rifles, clubs, or machetes."[139]

Government employees were almost all *macoutes*,[140] particularly the Section Chiefs, who were like county Sheriffs in the U.S., but had "unfettered authority over the lives of the peasants...."[141] Papa Doc "was the first national president to take a direct personal interest in the appointment of each chief de section."[142] Also targeted for recruitment were the *houngans*, or Voudou priests[143]— supposedly distinct from the *bokors*, although many were both. Catholic and Protestant clergy were also recruited into the *macoutes*,[144] and in fact the 1966 concordat with the Vatican gave Papa Doc the right to appoint Haiti's bishops, making him the effective head of the country's Catholic Church.[145]

Political repression under Papa Doc was severe — worse than in previous regimes, few of which managed to last as long. The *macoutes* targeted whole groups of people — neighborhoods, clubs, or extended families — if they found a single one involved in opposition activity. "Infants were raped and killed for offenses against the state committed by cousins twice removed, or even by former neighbors...."[146] Peter Hallward estimates that 50,000 political murders were committed by the *macoutes* during the Duvaliers' rule, nearly all under Papa Doc, not counting thousands more under their military successors.[147] Such violence is not unknown in the Caribbean region; El Salvador, with about the same population, may have lost 75,000 during its civil war, and the Guatemalan death squads, from 1957 on, killed about 250,000, out of a population fifty percent larger. And tens of thousands died in Nicaragua in the struggle against the Somozas. But those countries, at the time, were engulfed by armed insurrections; in Haiti, there was no war going on.

When Papa Doc declared himself ruler for life, it was hardly a departure from Haitian tradition; seven previous rulers had done likewise.[148] And many, going back to Dessalines, came to be known as the "father" of the people.[149] But Papa Doc's followers actually considered him a deity. "Man talks without acting," went a Duvalierist slogan. "God acts without talking. Duvalier is a god."[150] Duvalier openly identified himself with the *loa* Baron Samedi, "a sinister figure who symbolizes death in Voudou."[151]

But if God acts without talking, Duvalier did plenty of the latter. His public speaking style was distinctive, as described by Bernard Diederich and Al Burt:

> Dressed in his favourite colour, black, his smooth, round face assumes a special sheen. He moves hyperslowly, speaks in a whisper. [This appears to be a form of hypnotic induction—R.M.] His eyelids droop. Wearing a slightly bemused, unshakeable half-smile, he does nothing for disconcertingly long periods of time, and Haitians, receptive to the unusual, are awed. The man appears to be as calm as death."[152]

During his 14 years in power, Duvalier brought about "the transformation of the authoritarian political model of the past into a totalitarian apparatus."[153] This was done not only through the *Noirisme* doctrine, but also through the co-optation of the *Bizango*, a secret society of *houngans* originally descended from the pre-revolutionary bands of maroons.[154] Duvalier based his *tontons macoutes* on the *Bizango*, which evidently accounts for the survival of Duvalierism for decades after the overthrow of his unpopular son. The mulatto elite retained their position in the economy, as any serious attempt at ousting them would probably have brought in the U.S. Marines. But the rural middle class — the wealthier section of the peasantry, along with the *houngans*, who were frequently the same people — gained a share of political power that they were unwilling to forfeit.

My Son, the Doc?

Despite widespread belief that personality traits are inherited along with physical traits, there are few cases in history of great leaders founding dynasties and then being succeeded by their equally great sons. Far more typical are instances where the dynasty's celebrated founder is followed by a son of far lesser ability. Iran under the two Shahs, Nicaragua under the Somozas, and North Korea under Kim Il-Sung and Kim Jong-Il are good examples, and one might even add the U.S. under "Poppy" and "Dubya" Bush.

Haiti may be yet another case. Ability and personality clearly did not pass from the crafty and sinister François to his amiable but oafish son Jean-Claude, popularly known as Baby Doc, as well as by the less flattering nickname of Melonhead. In fact, photographs of François together with Jean-Claude reveal virtually no physical similarity between the two. Besides their disparate height and girth, their facial features are completely different.

But one photograph of Duvalier with his cabinet shows Luckner Cambronne facing the camera, and the latter's resemblance to Jean-Claude is striking.[155] Cambronne was known to be the lover of Papa Doc's wife Simone,[156] and Papa Doc was impotent from diabetes, which he had developed as a young adult.[157] So the genetic theory of inheritance remains unchallenged, but it is curious that none of those who wrote about the Duvalier regime seem to have noticed Baby Doc's evident parentage.

When Papa Doc died in 1971, Cambronne proposed the constitutional amendment to allow Jean-Claude — still only 19 — to succeed him.[158] He was assisted in arranging the transition by U.S. Ambassador Clinton Knox, neither the first nor the last time the U.S. was to intervene directly in Haitian affairs.[159] Baby Doc had no interest in governing the country, and spent his time racing cars and motorcycles, holding parties, and seducing women and the occasional man. His older sister Marie-Denise, along with his mother and Luckner Cambronne, essentially ran the country.[160] The political terror was greatly reduced, but the corruption grew even worse. In the single month of December 1980, according to an IMF estimate, Baby Doc embezzled $20 million from his impoverished country.[161] Cambronne was a major player in the kleptocracy; he was involved in the drug trade,[162] tore up Haiti's railroads to sell them to Africa while pocketing the proceeds, snatched corpses from private funeral parlors to sell them to U.S. hospitals, and founded Hemocaribian, which sold Haitian blood — rich in antibodies — to American laboratories at a 600 percent profit.[163]

In 1979, Simone decided to make a pact with the devil to keep her son in power for another 22 years (22 was Papa Doc's magic number). The *loas* said, through the *houngans*, that only a wife could do that, not a mother. Undaunted, Simone went through a Voudou wedding rite with Jean-Claude.[164] Unfortunately for the couple, the devil failed to keep his end of the bargain; Baby Doc's regime fell only seven years later.

The following year, Baby Doc married again, to Michelle Bennett, daughter of a struggling businessman. This marriage didn't go over well with anyone. The Catholic Church was unhappy because Michelle was divorced; *Noiristes* objected because she was mulatto (of course, so was Baby Doc, since Simone was the illegitimate daughter of a wealthy mulatto); and Simone herself was furious because Michelle's family, totally corrupt themselves, soon became the dominant faction in the kleptocracy. Worse yet, Michelle's first husband was the son of the very man who had launched that ill-fated eight-man invasion back in 1957.[165] Freudians should have a field day with this one—after "marrying" his mother, Baby Doc ended up adopting the grandchildren of the man who had tried to kill his own father!

Although the mulattoes were back in power after Papa Doc's death, the Duvalier regime survived for another 15 years, at least in part through the continued legitimization of Voudou and the cooptation of the rural middle class. It also had the tacit support of the U.S., partly because the terror had clearly been reduced, and partly because Haiti welcomed American investment—the only criterion at that time for considering any country part of the "free world." From 1967 to 1986, the number of American firms doing business in Haiti increased from 7 to more than 300. But real wages dropped by 50 percent between 1980 and 1990.[166] The cocaine trade flourished in the later years of Baby Doc, and continued afterward.[167] Michelle's own brother was arrested in the U.S. on drug-related charges.[168]

Baby Doc's regime fell in 1986, having lasted one year longer than Papa Doc's—although, to be fair, Papa Doc would have remained in office longer had he lived. One serious problem that helped bring down the dictatorship was the 1981 outbreak of African swine fever, which caused the American Agency for International Development to order the eradication of Haiti's entire black pig population. Pink pigs were brought in from the U.S. to replace them, but they were unsuited to Haiti, since the food and shelter they required was so expensive that few Haitian peasants could afford them.[169]

Another serious miscalculation was the 1983 appointment of a bloodthirsty *macoute* leader, Roger Lafontant—like Papa Doc a physician—as Minister of the Interior. Lafontant didn't last long in that job, but it provoked massive opposition.[170] As demonstrations against the government spread over the next three years, and Baby Doc's supporters began defecting, he made preparations to leave for exile in France. But first, he and Michelle had two male infants sacrificed in the presidential palace in order to curse the next occupant.[171] This indicates, among other things, the strength of Voudouist beliefs even among the mulattoes.

The Rise of Lavalas

The Duvalier regime was followed by a series of military dictatorships and short-lived civilian governments. The chief strongman during this transition period was mulatto Gen. Henri Namphy, who had played a key role in forcing Baby Doc out. By 1987, Namphy "had openly gunned down more civilians that Jean-Claude Duvalier's government had done in fifteen years."[172] Small landholders in the fertile Artibonite valley were turned into sharecroppers as the rich seized their land with Namphy's help.[173] In September 1988, an attack on populist priest Jean-Bertrand Aristide's church in Port-au-Prince by hundreds of armed thugs resulted in the deaths of at least a dozen congregants.[174]

Aristide represented the worst nightmare for both the Haitian elite and their backers in the Republican administration in the U.S. Born in a small town on the south coast, he moved to Port-au-Prince when he was a child, following the death of his father.[175] He was educated, having done post-graduate work in psychology[176]; he had a massive base among the people, especially in the shantytowns of the capital, this movement calling itself *Lavalas* ("The Flood"); and he was an uncompromising adherent of Liberation Theology, which was gaining followers throughout Latin America. One of the military dictators of the post–Duvalier interregnum, Prosper Avril, formed a death squad to assassinate Aristide's supporters.[177] After the attack on his church, Aristide's *Lavalas* following became so widespread that he was chosen as presidential candidate by the National Front for Change and Democracy (FNCD), a reform-minded coalition whose leaders soon began to distrust him as too radical.[178] In 1990, in the first completely free and fair elections in Haiti's history, Aristide won two-thirds of the vote against 11 other candidates.[179] There was an 80 percent turnout,[180] impressive under the circumstances.

The Aristide government lasted a mere seven months before being overthrown by the army. But during this short period, there was a significant reduction in government waste and corruption, as well as drug trafficking and human rights abuses, even according to an official U.S. source.[181] Much was made of instances of mob violence under the *Lavalas* government, but the victims were typically *macoutes*, who were still engaging in political violence themselves; they even attempted a coup, led by Lafontant, just before Aristide's inauguration.[182] An estimated 25 people were killed by mob violence during Aristide's interrupted reign,[183] but stories of thousands murdered "were a fiction."[184] This number compares with 1,500 slain in a few days by the military after Aristide was overthrown.[185] Aristide was hated passionately by the elite,[186] but these were the same people who had backed the Duvaliers, Magloire, Namphy and other brutal tyrants. What they feared was the loss of their privileges.

The Cédras Regime

The three-year dictatorship of Gen. Raul Cédras was made in the U.S., and endorsed by the CIA's top Latin America analyst.[187] Cédras himself—a mulatto so light-complexioned he could easily have been taken for a Frenchman—was a member of the Haitian National Intelligence Service (SIN), subsidized by the CIA; the elected government was not even aware of SIN's existence.[188] In three years, an estimated 3,000 to 5,000 Haitians were slain,[189] many of them by the uniformed goon squad, similar to the *tontons macoutes*, named FRAPH (Front for the Advancement and Progress of Haiti).[190] Headed by Emmanuel "Toto" Constant, FRAPH was closely connected to the Haitian army. It used a salute similar to totalitarian parties, and flew the Haitian and U.S. flags.[191] It was subsidized both by the CIA[192] and the Defense Intelligence Agency.[193] The connection with the former may explain the polished image Cédras had in the U.S. media; TV news programs showed him, casually dressed, strolling down the street with his wife and dancing at a local block party. Meanwhile, his FRAPH supporters were running rampant, killing 70—including 30 children—in a 1993 post–Christmas attack on the Cité Soleil slum, an Aristide stronghold.[194] In the first three months after his coup, at least 200,000 Haitians fled the country.[195] Meanwhile, the CIA was peddling the tale that Aristide was mentally ill, "a psychotic manic depressive with proven homicidal tendencies."[196] This is now the standard line on any third world leader who opposes U.S. interests.

A year after the Cédras coup, Bill Clinton was elected U.S. president with a plurality of 43 percent of the vote, a substantial part of it coming from the African American community. The Congressional Black Caucus was no friend of the Cédras dictatorship, which had in fact been recognized only by the Vatican.[197] They were able to put pressure on the Clinton administration to undermine Cédras, and in September 1994, American troops began another occupation of Haiti, replacing Aristide in office, but at the same time protecting his military and paramilitary enemies. Aristide finished out his interrupted term, and abolished the Haitian army in 1995.[198] The same year, his ally René Préval was elected president, winning 88 percent of the vote, but in a very light turnout,[199] and served for five years. Aristide ran for a second term in 2000, and won. Despite Cédras' persecution, which killed or exiled most of its leaders,[200] electoral results continued to show massive support for *Lavalas*.

Aristide's Second Coming

In the 2000 presidential election, boycotted by some parties, the "psychotic" Aristide managed to win over 90 percent of the vote against six relative unknowns. The turnout was described by Aristide critic Michael Deibert as "very light,"[201] but the pro–Aristide writer Peter Hallward gives it as 60 percent,[202] marginally less than the 61 percent in the historic 2008 presidential election in the U.S. The Haitian turnout might have been higher had it not been for the elite's history of not accepting the results.

Aristide's inability to improve his people's condition was caused by the fact that the U.S. was once again under a right-wing Republican administration; by the absence of any rival superpower that might have come to Haiti's aid; and by the Haitian elite's refusal to abide by the will of the Haitian people. The CIA, through the mass media, manipulated American public opinion into thinking that Aristide, not his elitist opponents, was the one who was undermining the country's fragile democracy.

There were still some positive achievements under Aristide's second government. One anti–Aristide businessman described "a lot of social investment" in and around Haiti's second city, Cap-Haitien: "[N]ew schools were built, irrigation canals were dug, literacy centers opened, that kind of thing."[203] The number of high schools in the country was increased by 300 percent, a free medical school was established,[204] and an agrarian reform begun.[205] But oppressive social systems cannot be overthrown without force, and Aristide was unwilling to take that route. "Rather than seek to develop anything like an organized military wing of *Lavalas*, Aristide had done everything possible to discourage it."[206]

In December 2000, immediately after the election, the badly defeated opposition formed its own "provisional government," headed by lawyer Gérard Gourgue.[207] It included the Democratic Convergence (CD)—an alliance of old Duvalierists, other right-wingers, disappointed former allies of Aristide, and criminal gangs like the Cannibal Army (coyly renamed the Artibonite Resistance Front[208]) whose loyalty could be bought. Former members of the disbanded Haitian army were trained in the Dominican Republic by U.S. Special Forces.[209] The Dominican oligarchy feared Aristide's example.

Even in the capital, where much of the elite was concentrated, the CD had limited support. Its mass demonstration in December 2003 brought out only 20,000.[210] Strangely, the former dictator Prosper Avril returned to Haiti and endorsed the CD, allying himself with politicians he had arrested and tortured during his brief rule. When the police arrested him, the CD declared that it would never negotiate with the government as long as Avril remained in jail.[211]

The CD's strategy was to provoke violence, blame it on the government, and then use its claims of "violations of human rights" to advocate a U.S. embargo on aid to the impoverished nation. Ultimately, the U.S. embargoed $500 million in foreign aid to Haiti,[212] This explains Kathie Klarreich's unhappy observation "that for the vast majority of the poor — the very people Aristide had promised to help — things hadn't improved. There was still no reliable electricity, no decent health care, education, or government services."[213]

Among the alleged victims of the Aristide government were broadcasters Jean Dominique and Brignol Lindor, Cannibal Army leader Amiot Metayer, and Syrian-Haitian businessman Gerald Khawly. None of these killings could be definitively pinned on the *Lavalas* government. Significantly, in December 2003, the Haitian Press Agency reported that the CD was planning to murder some of its own supporters in order to discredit Aristide[214]; this would be hard to believe if it didn't match the CIA's advice to its beloved Contras during the undeclared war against the Nicaraguan Sandinistas.

Jean Dominique, who generally supported *Lavalas*, had made many enemies through his broadcasts, mostly on the right. Although his death was blamed on Aristide's supporters, after the 2004 overthrow of *Lavalas* the new government of Gerard Latortue never even bothered investigating his murder.[215] Death threats directed at him had come from a group of ex-soldiers loyal to former dictator Prosper Avril.[216] Brignol Lindor, unlike Dominique, was a strong supporter of the CD. He was killed by a pro–*Lavalas* gang known as the Forest Dwellers, but it was in reprisal for the severe beating of one of their own members by CD supporters.[217] There was no indication that anyone higher up in *Lavalas* had ordered it. Amiot Metayer, nothing but a thug, was probably killed by a rival gang leader. At his funeral, rumors were spread that the police were planning to seize his casket.[218] This soon became the CD's preferred way of stirring up violence; needless to say, Haiti is the last place on earth where one might want to leave a dead body unburied! Finally, Gerald Khawly was a known mobster, whose mansion in Jacmel "had been built amid rumors of involvement in drug trafficking...."[219] He was killed in a drive-by shooting — typical of gangland slayings, but rarely used by governments to liquidate their opponents.

Despite some degree of disenchantment and defection, Aristide retained the support of most Haitians, and by late 2002, the CD had nearly collapsed, despite financial support from the U.S. National Endowment for Democracy.[220] Opposition to Aristide was by then under the control of a group of ex-soldiers, led by Guy Philippe, once the police chief in Cap-Haitien,[221] who had been trained by the CIA in Ecuador.[222] Philippe led an armed attack in 2002 on the presidential palace, but faced stiff opposition from the population of Port-au-Prince.[223] The American media spoke of pro-government gangs called *Chimères* terrorizing the opposition, but these were unorganized and poorly-armed groups of street urchins.[224]

Early in 2004, the anti–Aristide forces launched their full-scale revolt against the freely-elected government. There were only a few dozen of them, led by Philippe and former FRAPH leader Louis Chamblain.[225] Crossing from the Dominican Republic, they soon captured Cap-Haitien and Gonaives. In the former city, with half a million inhabitants, "fewer than one hundred came out into the streets to welcome the rebels...."[226] In Gonaives, the Cannibal Army was an important ally.[227] But on March 1, when the rebels arrived in Port-au-Prince, their sympathizer Michael Deibert could only report that "[s]mall groups of residents clapped in their wake."[228]

The revolt's success was due less to popular support than to the absence of any armed force committed to defending the government. Since the army had been dissolved, there were only the lightly-armed police, who included some former *macoutes*. Thanks in part to Cédras, the popular movements had been seriously weakened, and the *Chimères* were in no position to replace them. The weakness of the rebels was illustrated by the fact that U.S. Marines had to be called in to help kill *Lavalas* supporters after their victory.[229]

Once Port-au-Prince had fallen and Aristide whisked away to exile in the Central African Republic by the Americans, Philippe and Chamblain were shoved aside, and Gerard Latortue was installed as the new president. He was a resident of Florida, and a retired official of the World Bank.[230] His short-lived regime killed an estimated 4,000 people,[231] and there were massive purges of *Lavalas* supporters from state institutions; in the telephone company alone, 3,000 people lost their jobs.[232] Aristide's literacy program and agrarian reform were ended, taxes were suspended for three years for the elite,[233] and the new medical school was closed.[234] Two American writers noted that "Washington set patently lower standards and expectations when it came to issues of social justice and quality of life in regard to the black republic than for any other Latin American country."[235]

None of this, however, went over particularly well with the people; in September 2004, a revolt in the capital by Aristide supporters resulted in nearly 700 deaths.[236] Two years later, elections were held once again, and Aristide ally René Préval won a bare majority, but in an extremely crowded race.[237] Two supporters of the "democratic" anti–*Lavalas* coalition received barely a tenth of the vote between them.[238] As Préval was inaugurated, angry crowds outside the presidential palace chanted "Tie up Latortue!"[239]

The Failure of Liberation Theology?

Even as Préval took over the reins of government once again, Aristide remained in exile. Although portrayed as a bloodthirsty tyrant in the U.S. media, it seems clear that he had been far too easy on his opponents, whose own record of violence and corruption ranked with the worst regimes in the Western Hemisphere. Spiritual leaders like Martin Luther King or Mahatma Gandhi may not make the most effective politicians, since politics may involve moral compromises. Nor are they necessarily the best leaders to deal with economic crises, and Haiti's — partially because of deforestation and erosion — has been prolonged and catastrophic. As a result, about 1.5 million Haitians now live abroad, in the U.S., Canada, the Dominican Republic, the Bahamas, Europe and Africa.[240] This is what Mao Zedong was referring to when he said that political power grows out of the barrel of a gun. Without an armed force of their own, the Haitian people were defenseless against the economic elite and the Duvalierist thugs who supported them.

Yet Haiti's problems are not entirely political and economic. The unexpressed rage of the masses, which takes the form of Duvalierism in Haiti's politics, stems not only from oppression at the hands of the elite, but also from abuse — sexual and otherwise — of children at the hands of adults. If even Jean-Claude Duvalier could be raped as a boy by an army officer,[241] one can imagine the likely fate of the thousands of *restavèks*, poor children who live as unpaid servants with wealthy families.[242]

If Haiti is ever going to cease to be "the orphan of the Americas,"[243] Haitians themselves are going to have to take the initiative in protecting their children from abuse. Otherwise, the victims of this abuse are going to become the brutal oppressors of their own people once they reach adulthood. And self-inflicted disasters will combine with natural ones to keep the nation in poverty and degradation.

15

South Africa

The Psychology of Apartheid

Understanding the political dynamics of South Africa, and its transition from apartheid to democracy at the end of the twentieth century, presents a challenge to any paradigm. The country — with ample land, adequate water, an extensive seacoast, and enormous mineral wealth — was unique in the world, except for parts of the United States before the Civil Rights movement, because racial discrimination was written into its laws. With more than 80 percent of its population treated as second-class citizens or worse, most outside observers anticipated that South Africa would end up experiencing a bloodbath of immense proportions, as White families were slaughtered in their beds by their own servants — or more likely, so the common joke went, by their neighbors' servants, as their own servants proceeded to slaughter the family next door. Despite considerable violence as the mass-based resistance brought down the pillars of White supremacy, the worst was avoided, and the liberation struggle cost far fewer lives than in Kenya or Angola.

South Africa also represents a challenge to psychohistory. If our purpose is to identify the dominant group fantasy of a nation, exactly how many nations exist within the South African state, and whose fantasies are we talking about? There were four official racial categories under apartheid — African, European, Colored, and Asian — but at least three of these were culturally diverse. Among the Europeans, the English and Afrikaners spoke different languages and went to different churches; the Zulu, Tswana and Venda spoke mutually unintelligible languages; the Asians were divided along both religious and linguistic lines; and even the relatively homogenous Coloreds contained several distinct subgroups. Even today, with racist laws abolished, it would be hard to say whether South Africa is one nation, or four, or eleven, or fifteen. The political struggle for equal rights, and the class struggle for decent wages and conditions, coexisted with equally intense struggles over the definition of each group's identity.

Almost three-quarters of South Africa's population of 44 million is African. Europeans are now about 15 percent; 10 percent are Coloreds, who are of mixed racial origin; and 3 percent are Asians, nearly all of them from the Indian subcontinent. Under apartheid, your race decided your destiny. It determined whether you could vote, which jobs you could hold, where you could own land, where you could live or worship, which schools you were permitted to attend, and which public and private facilities you were allowed to use. Even public beaches and taxicabs were reserved for either "Whites" or "non–Whites." The huge

economic and educational gaps between the various social strata might have been daunt-
ing to any government, even the most democratically inclined, but the assumption behind
apartheid was that *every* member of a racial group was to be treated as if he or she shared
the education level of the *average* member. A semi-literate European had more rights than
an African with a college degree. And after 1948, the disenfranchisement of the non–White
majority was perceived by the Whites as permanent.

All this was justified in the name of maintaining "white, Christian civilization." Africans
were regarded as insufficiently civilized to participate as equals in society. Yet they were typically hired to raise the children of the Whites.

South Africa Before Apartheid

Settled by Dutch colonists in the 17th century, who encountered and enslaved the
Khoisan-speaking peoples at what is now Cape Town, South Africa was annexed to the
British Empire as a result of the Napoleonic Wars. Further to the north, the land was occupied by Bantu-speaking African tribes, unrelated to the Khoisans; they were in the process
of migrating southward. When the British freed the slaves of the Dutch farmers, or Boers,
the latter objected and many of them migrated north in the Great Trek of 1840. Clashing
repeatedly with the Africans, the Boers prevailed and established their two independent
republics, Transvaal and the smaller Orange Free State. Both of these states had African
majorities who were allowed to own land only on reservations, and were used as cheap labor
on European-owned farms. As the Boers fought Africans in the north, the British subjugated other African peoples in the east, particularly the Zulu and the Xhosa.

The first Africans to become British subjects were the Mfengu, a Xhosa subgroup who
lived in the region known as the Ciskei. Originally Zulu refugees who had fled the tyranny
of King Shaka,[1] the Mfengu had low social status among the Xhosa, and became prime targets for missionaries.[2] Many other Xhosa distrusted the Mfengu as British collaborators.[3]

As both Franz Fanon and Albert Memmi have pointed out, colonial systems, analo-
gously to dysfunctional families, typically rely on *identification with the aggressor* in order
to retain power over the colonized. Once the latter begin to regard their conquerors as a
reference group, they supposedly lose interest in recovering their independence. But dysfunctional families may also produce a second defense mechanism, *dissociation*— generally
found in the most severely disturbed families — through which the victim denies reality and
withdraws into a fantasy world, sometimes expressed in religious terms. British rule in South
Africa, as elsewhere, sought to co-opt the elite among the colonized, while at the same time
relying heavily on divide and rule and, in South Africa's case, extensive European settlement. But the Boers — rough and unlettered pioneers who spoke a dialect of Dutch,
Afrikaans, rather than a world language — preferred to keep their distance from the conquered Africans. This continued after the two Boer republics fell to the British in the Boer
War.

Most elements of apartheid were in place even before 1910, when South Africa became
a White-ruled dominion within the British Commonwealth. Transvaal and the Orange Free
State were two of the country's four provinces, the others being Cape of Good Hope (or
Cape Province) and Natal. Cape Province was bilingual, while Natal's colonists were predominantly English-speaking. All non–Whites were kept off the voting rolls in the Afrikaans-

speaking provinces, and for all practical purposes in Natal. But Cape Province had some non–White voters, most of them Coloreds, who at the beginning made up 15 percent of the electorate.[4] They were disfranchised after 1948.

The Nationalists in Power

The 1948 victory of the Nationalist Party (NP; it was later renamed the National Party) over the United Party meant the imposition of the stricter form of White supremacy practiced in Transvaal and the Orange Free State over the less rigid policies of Cape Province. The ideological architect of apartheid was Dr. Hendrik F. Verwoerd, Prime Minister from 1958 to 1966, when he died at the hands of an assassin. The Dutch-born Verwoerd, who came to South Africa as a small child, held a degree in behavioral psychology, which he taught at Stellenbosch, the leading Afrikaans university.[5] His doctoral dissertation was on "The Blunting of the Emotions."[6] To the extent that White domination lasted as long as it did, even after neighboring countries had achieved majority rule, it was partly due to Verwoerd's sophisticated psychological strategy, a variation of the colonialist policy of divide and rule.

Although it defined itself as a single "White South African" nation, the European minority was divided between Afrikaners and English. The Afrikaners are descended from Dutch, German, and French Calvinist settlers, and are about 60 percent of the Europeans. They have always lagged behind the English in terms of wealth and education, although NP rule helped narrow the gap. An English South African psychologist notes that "Afrikaner affairs from 1830 onwards have been dominated by an obsessive hatred and antagonism toward the British,"[7] exacerbated by the Boer War, when thousands of Afrikaner civilians perished in British concentration camps. Prior to 1948, opposition to "British-Jewish capital" was a common theme in Afrikaner politics.[8]

The NP openly pursued policies that favored Afrikaners over the more advantaged English. State-owned corporations were established in various industries to provide them with guaranteed jobs, while English South Africans were gradually replaced in government service. Many Afrikaners came to depend for their livelihood on continued NP rule.[9] It was this dependence on political power, coupled with the modest majority held by the Afrikaners over the English, which made it impossible for the ruling group to follow the usual pattern among dominant elites of co-opting the upper strata of the oppressed communities. If educated non–Whites had been allowed to vote, they might have coalesced with the English and outvoted the NP. Some other method had to be found.

This method was apartheid, or "separate development," as it was termed in English. It involved the transformation of the scattered Native reservations — about 13 percent of the country — into tribally homogeneous "independent nations," or "Bantustans." All Africans were expected to become citizens of the Bantustans, even if had been living outside them for generations. If they continued to live in the "White" 87 percent of the country, they had to carry pass books. Millions of Africans were ultimately expelled from the urban areas and relocated in the Bantustans, where vast shantytowns grew up, populated almost entirely by migrant workers and their dependents. Starting with the largest, Transkei, some of the Bantustans were granted a sham independence, with the South African government holding the reins of power.

The purpose of this, in the words of the South African government, was "to provide areas in which each of the races will be able to develop on its own lines free from interracial frictions and animosities which (as experience has shown) would otherwise exist...."[10] M.D.C. de Wet Nel, Verwoerd's cabinet member in charge of implementing apartheid, elaborated:

> At least 80 to 90 percent of the Native population in the urban Bantu townships have one or other link with the ethnic group, and furthermore, a very strong link.
> That is why it has always been felt that an injustice is being done to the Bantu in the cities as a result of the fact that these Natives from the reserves simply lose all contact with the reserves when they come to the cities. This is an injustice to these Natives which we want to rectify.[11]

Apartheid also involved the tribalization of African education, as small universities were established, mostly in rural areas, for the major tribes. There were also separate universities for the Coloreds and Asians.

Radio and television played an important role in propagating the pro-apartheid message. A recurring theme was "that happy Blacks are those who confine themselves to consumerism, who stay away from trouble-making politics, and who strive hard to live in harmony with their circumstances."[12] And even after the fall of apartheid, the Nationalists issued an appeal in comic book form to the Coloreds in which a son asks a father what the NP has done for his people. Replies the father: "You are at university, we have a roof over our heads and I have a reasonable income. What more do you want?"[13]

Another role of television was to represent Europeans and Africans as if they were living in separate worlds. This was at least consistent with the traditional Zulu outlook. As the Zulu poet Mazisi Kunene said, "When the first white men came ... the elders went to those men and said: 'Tell us about your world.' There isn't one world, there are many worlds ... in the African system, there is diversity. The ideal is diversity, not symmetry."[14] On the government-owned Zulu-language TV station, "Zulu gangsters and Zulu detectives could fight it out in a Zulu city where Zulus owned bars and hotels and drove fancy cars and a white face was seldom seen...."[15] This was the apartheid ideal, but it had little relation to reality.

By the end of the 1980s, Verwoerd's program had already been partly implemented. Four of the ten projected "Bantu nations"—Transkei, Ciskei, Bophuthatswana, and Venda— were supposedly independent, although no nation aside from South Africa ever recognized them. Around three and a half million Africans had been deported to the homelands.[16] Bophuthatswana's Sun City casino resort was attracting big-name entertainers, while the Ciskei army fought alongside South African troops against nationalist guerrillas in Namibia. Yet, with the accession of Frederik W. de Klerk to the presidency in 1989, the NP began making concessions that eventually led to the total abolition of White supremacy, and the 1994 electoral victory of Nelson Mandela's African National Congress (ANC).

African Nationalism versus Zulu Tribalism

Founded in 1912,[17] the ANC was the oldest African nationalist movement on the continent. Its first president was John Dube, an educated member of the African elite, and a member of the Zulu ethnic group. He published a Zulu-language newspaper, and favored government recognition of the Zulu monarchy. In 1917, he was replaced by a more radical group of leaders, and left the ANC.[18] But even by 1949, the ANC had fewer than 3,000 members. "It continued to identify itself with the interests of the governing elites rather than with African workers and the unemployed."[19] In 1952, Chief Albert Luthuli, also a Zulu, became ANC president. The next year, the ANC launched its Defiance Campaign against pass books and other onerous apartheid regulations, raising its membership to 100,000.[20] It was at this time that many ANC youth leaders joined the Communist Party.[21] As it happened, a number of these younger and more radical leaders — such as Nelson Mandela, Oliver Tambo, Govan Mbeki and his son Thabo — were all Xhosa. Part of the reason for this was that educated youth were prone to develop radical ideas, and the only college that accepted non–Whites in South Africa was Fort Hare in the Transkei, where the Xhosa lived.

One might, of course, make too much of the ethnic differences among the Africans. For example, the Zulu, Xhosa, Swazi and Ndebele all speak varieties of the Nguni language, although the Xhosa dialect — Southern Nguni — has absorbed some Khoisan words and phonemes. The Tswana, Basuto and Pedi groups all speak Sotho. Most of South Africa's "Bantu nations" are rather arbitrary designations made up of diverse ethnic groups; the Venda, for example, are two separate tribes, one of which is descended from Yemeni Jews.[22] Some, like the Zulu, had established kingdoms before they were conquered, while others, like the Xhosa, were still at a tribal stage, not having merged into a single polity. Tembu tribesmen can be found among both the Xhosa and Zulu.[23]

The country's European rulers were clearly eager to foster tribalism among the Africans, but it is not self-evident why such a strategy was more successful among the Zulu in particular. As one Zulu noble explained to an American journalist in the wake of apartheid's collapse, "I support apartheid. It makes you have an identity. You know that you are an African, and an Indian is an Indian, and a white man is a white man. People have lost their identity now."[24] But did Zulus and only Zulus need pass books and discriminatory legislation to remind them that they were African?

Prior to the electoral victory of the ANC, the western press hailed Chief Mangosutho "Gatsha" Buthulezi as a "moderate nationalist" who was opposed to violence. In fact, he was a tribalist, rather than a nationalist, and he only opposed violence when it was directed against the Europeans' government. His organization, Inkatha — now called the Inkatha Freedom Party — was quick to direct violence against other Africans, as in 1976, when Zulu migrants attacked residents of Soweto,[25] or in 1980, when his armed followers clashed with striking students at the Zulu university at Nongoma.[26] In 1983, Buthelezi declared, in the wake of armed clashes between Ikhatha and the ANC: "We are sick and tired of people of Xhosa extraction here in our midst.... [They] cannot be allowed the freedom to wreak havoc among our people and our youth."[27] The Xhosa were about 5 percent of Natal's African population, but were solidly pro–ANC.

Like other forms of colonial rule, apartheid was able to create a stratum of privileged collaborators, but what needs to be explained is how such an atavistic movement as Inkatha could have gained any degree of mass support. Part of the explanation may stem from Anglo-Afrikaner rivalry. Having fought a series of wars against the English with some initial success, the Zulus — who lived mostly in Natal — may have been more prepared than other Africans to make common cause with the Afrikaners. Significantly, the Zulus who live in the eastern Transvaal (now Mpumalanga province) do not follow Inkatha.[28] At the same time, there may have been some resentment about the role played by Xhosa leaders in the ANC, as well as the presence of many Indians in the overall liberation movement; Indians are about a tenth of Natal's population, and there has been friction in the past between them and the Zulu majority.

Inkatha recruited many migrant workers because of its close association with the chiefs, who allocated land in the reserves and helped their subjects find jobs in the "White" areas. Inkatha also had connections with the police and military; many Zulu recruits in the South African police were Inkatha sympathizers.[29] Inkatha also sponsored a credit union, which won it support in some urban areas,[30] although its trade union affiliate, UWUSA, had only a negligible following, barely two percent of the ANC–leaning COSATU.[31] In addition, since the ANC was banned for three decades after the Sharpeville massacre of 1960, Inkatha was able to grow without competition. But in addition to these purely societal-level factors, there are also strong psychological factors behind Zulu tribalism. One of these is the sacred coil, made out of woven grass, which represents the unity of the people, and is also called *inkatha*.[32] Psychohistorians will recognize it as a symbolic placenta.

Prior to the English conquest, the Zulu emperor Shaka built a militaristic kingdom which overran most of what later became Natal. The last area he annexed was south of the Tugela River, where the local people are dismissed as "Lala" by the northerners because of their distinctive accent. These southerners were the first Zulus to be conquered by the British, like the Mfengu in the Eastern Cape, and were more exposed to Christian missionaries and Western education. "The north-south divide remains a combustible element in the region to this day, and even something of a line marking political affiliations."[33]

Traditional Zulu society was highly stratified: "[T]he chiefs and their women lived lives of conspicuous luxury and ease. This can be attributed to the greater control by the ... chiefs over the labour-power of their commoners."[34] The militarization of Zulu society was based on "[s]ubmission to authority, obedience to law, respect for superiors, order and self-restraint, fearlessness and self-sacrifice, constant work and civic duty...." These traits became "a second nature" to the Zulus,[35] and while useful in the struggle against the British, they also served to help them adjust to colonial rule once the conquest was complete. In fact, these values were virtually the same as what European institutions were teaching their own constituents.

The British, consequently, developed respect for Zulu traditions — the Zulus, after all, were among the few peoples who had ever beaten them in battle — and favored a policy of indirect rule, governing their new subjects through their own chiefs and laws.[36] Roughly a quarter or more of Natal remained in Zulu hands. This contrasted with Afrikaner policy of leaving the Africans with little of their own land and social order; the Basuto, who live in the Orange Free State, had only about 2 percent of its territory for themselves. Some of the Zulu chiefs prospered under colonial rule, and increasingly perceived their interests as being linked to the European rulers. The Zulu king opposed the Defiance Campaign, causing a small faction of the ANC to split off and side with the monarch.[37]

Chief Buthelezi was originally an ANC supporter, but remained out of jail when the ANC was banned after Sharpeville. He founded Inkatha as a "cultural" movement, taking care to use the ANC's colors of black, green, and gold.[38] Unlike the Transkei's Kaiser Matanzima, Buthelezi refused to accept "independence" for the Zulu Bantustan, and a glance at the map will show why: nearly all of the Transkei formed a single block of territory, while Zululand (or KwaZulu) was split into dozens of isolated sections. Buthelezi may also have thought that the Western powers would back him as South Africa's acceptable Black leader, rather than Nelson Mandela or Oliver Tambo, who leaned toward the Soviet camp in the Cold War.

In 1983, the United Democratic Front (UDF) was formed, composed of a large number of African, Asian, and Colored civic groups and unions, and calling for universal franchise and an end to apartheid and all forms of racial discrimination. Zulu chiefs opposed the UDF "because it threatened to undermine and delegitimate their personal power bases."[39] In 1995, one Inkatha member, an unlettered filling station attendant, explained to an American political scientist how his loyalties had shifted over the decades. During the 1950s, he had supported the ANC, and when Inkatha was formed as a Zulu traditionalist organization, he saw no problem with supporting both groups. But later, the violence between UDF and Inkatha forced him to take sides, and he chose Inkatha, regarding the UDF as too socially radical, and led by inexperienced youths. By the mid–1990s, however, with the ANC in power at the federal level, this Inkatha supporter was already considering defecting to the ANC.[40]

Buthelezi, however, became ever more hostile to the ANC as de Klerk's government began negotiations with it, in preparation for a negotiated end to White supremacy. He "entered an extraordinary alliance with the strongest defenders and beneficiaries of apartheid: right-wing Afrikaners who accused de Klerk of selling out the white man, and the leaders of the 'independent' Bantustans of Bophuthatswana and Ciskei."[41] Armed by South African army intelligence,[42] Inkatha engaged in a bloody conflict with its ANC/UDF opponents that took an estimated 20,000 lives over a period of 10 years.[43] This fighting was described by the *New York Times* as "a resurgence of earlier battles between rival ethnic groups," a judgment echoed by other U.S. media,[44] but in fact the violence was political, with Zulus on both sides. The same thing held true in other parts of South Africa, where groups ranging from soccer teams to ultra-militant parties claiming to be to the left of the ANC were armed by the apartheid regime to start fights with the ANC and prove to the world that Africans were incapable of governing themselves.

Buthelezi's opposition to sanctions and his support for foreign investment earned his Inkatha the reputation of a responsible alternative to the ANC in the West, but "Inkatha was less a 'party' or a 'movement' than a syndicate of rural Zulu chiefs and urban bosses backed up by the coercive power of the KwaZulu Police (KZP)."[45] A product of apartheid's divide and rule policy, it was also an example of dissociation, mnemonism, and Shrinking Boundary Syndrome.

Identification with the Aggressor: The South African Coloreds

The Coloreds in South Africa are less a community than a statistical category, although this may change as the memory of oppression recedes. For the most part, they are of mixed racial origin: former slaves of Khoisan, Malay, Indian, West African, and Malagasy origin, who interbred with both their Afrikaner owners and local Africans. Among the Coloreds, those who practice Islam are classified as "Cape Malays," although they appear to have as much African ancestry as their non–Muslim neighbors. Another subgroup are the Griquas, descendants of Coloreds who migrated north during the Great Trek, and subsequently intermarried with the Africans. Their darker complexion gave them lower status in South Africa's color-conscious society, and few identify themselves as such. A third distinct subgroup among the Coloreds are the descendants of English-Zulu intermarriages in Natal. And finally, a handful of European immigrants and their offspring were classified as Coloreds because they were too swarthy to be White; the existence of Coloreds whose native language is listed as Italian, Greek, or Yiddish testifies to this miscarriage of injustice.

Coloreds slightly outnumbered Whites in the old Cape Province, and constitute majorities in two of the three new provinces carved out of it. They are overwhelmingly Afrikaans-speaking, although half belong to mainstream English-speaking denominations, another 30 percent to the Dutch Reformed Church, 7 percent to the Catholic Church, and 6 percent are Muslims.[46] This last group, who are least likely to identify with the Europeans, tend to be prominent among the community's leadership.

Afrikaners were divided over how to deal with the Coloreds. Should they be regarded as allies of the Europeans on the basis of their language and culture? Or were they untrustworthy on grounds of their complexion? If Coloreds were acceptable as first-class citizens, would it be possible, given their ancestry, to draw a clear line between them and the African majority? Generally speaking, Afrikaners from Cape Province such as J.B.M. Herzog (Prime Minister during the interwar period) and Daniel Malan (the first NP Prime Minister, elected in 1948), favored extending voting rights to Coloreds and dropping restrictions against their employment.[47] But NP leaders from the north, such as Cornelius Mulder and Andries Treurnicht, were opposed to this; it might have increased the political weight of Cape Province. "The Coloreds are a nation on their own," argued Mulder, "and they must be led in that direction."[48] When Prime Minister P.W. Botha allowed the Coloreds and Indians to each have their separate houses of Parliament to manage their own affairs in 1982, Treurnicht seceded from the NP and formed the Conservative Party.[49]

The Coloreds themselves are unsure of their own identity. "One the one hand," observed a Colored Anglican bishop, "we're black and oppressed.... But socially and biologically and culturally, whites are our brothers and sisters...."[50] In 1995, a prominent Colored politician declared "We are Afrikaners," and "We are not Afrikaners," in the same speech.[51] Writes Pierre Van den Berghe:

> [T]he Coloreds have traditionally been caught between their feelings of racial superiority vis-à-vis the Africans and their constantly frustrated hope of acceptance by the Whites. This has led to ambivalent attitudes towards the Whites, to political passivity, and to a failure to identify with the Africans.[52]

The first Colored political movement was the African People's Organization (APO), founded in 1904 by Abdullah Abdurahman. It was composed mostly of artisans and professionals; Abdurahman himself was a physician. The APO supported the residential segregation of Africans from Coloreds, and Abdurahman even favored the exclusion of Africans from his group, notwithstanding its name.[53] In 1924, Abdurahman called for the replacement of African dockworkers in Cape Town by Coloreds.[54] This policy was eventually adopted by the NP, decades later.[55] The "Colored Labor Preference Policy," however, proved economically disadvantageous to virtually everyone; Africans were forced out of menial jobs in favor of Coloreds, whose previous better-paying jobs were taken over by Europeans.

Meanwhile, European farmers in the Western Cape began complaining "that their liveli-hood was threatened by the controls, for they relied on unskilled African labor."[56] The pol-icy did, however, succeed in driving a wedge between Coloreds and Africans.

New Colored political organizations appeared in the post–1948 period, including the Colored People's Congress (CPC), allied to the ANC. There was also a collaborationist Fed-eral Colored People's Party, which supported a distinct Colored identity, apartheid, and Christianity; it had relatively little support. The Labor Party, founded in 1966, took a more ambiguous stand; while it rejected apartheid, it was nonetheless willing to participate in the structures set up at the local and national levels by the NP, and strongly opposed the leftist leanings of the ANC and its Colored ally.[57] After the end of apartheid, a few Labor Party leaders joined the ANC, but many others went with the NP.[58]

The Non-European Unity Movement (NEUM) took a position completely opposed to the Labor Party. Extreme left in its rhetoric, but cautious in strategy, the NEUM never supported any anti-government action other than boycotts of government-sponsored insti-tutions.[59] Its radicalism came from its association with Trotskyists, opposed to the pro–Soviet orientation of the ANC and the South African Communist Party; its caution derived from the fact that its leaders were teachers, fearful of losing their government jobs.[60] Although the NEUM was officially committed to the unity of Coloreds and Africans, its support came exclusively from the former. It functioned in practice as a communalist organization, playing a divisive role much like that of Inkatha.

Unlike the NEUM, the CPC was allied with the ANC, the South African Indian Con-gress, and the White leftist Congress of Democrats in the Congress Alliance. But the CPC was the weakest link in this alliance.[61] Its problem was that Coloreds were not always will-ing to join an organization that identified them as a distinct community. A Cape Malay leader, Farid Esack, commented:

> The Colored People's Congress is never mentioned: now that's very significant. We have a sense of embarrassment about it. We really feel uncomfortable about the fact that there was actually a time when the Colored people called themselves "Colored," and we're ashamed of it. Politically, ideologically, we ought to be supporting that idea for that time, but no, we gloss over the idea that our people did actually organize as a separate com-munity.[62]

In 1966, several CPC members defected to the Pan-Africanist Congress (PAC), the main nationalist rival of the ANC.[63] "The PAC offered to the non–Communist CPC men what the ANC did not: full membership and responsibility in an African organization...."[64] But these activists later left the PAC in a bitter split.

Like the Zulus, the Coloreds displayed a basic conservatism that kept many from iden-tifying fully with the anti-apartheid movement. In the first non-racial elections in the coun-try, in 1994, 60 percent of the Colored voters in the Western Cape, where most Coloreds lived, supported the NP, while only 7 percent voted for the ANC (although this increased to 33 percent in the following year's local elections).[65] In the neighboring Northern Cape, in 1998, a Colored voter explained: "We want things to carry on the way they are. Every-thing comes from white people. I've never suffered hunger."[66] And a Colored NP organ-izer, apparently a Malay, stated: "We speak Afrikaans, we live as conservatives, attend church and raise our children on traditional values. Hence we are National.... The ANC with its black profile and Communist cloak repels us."[67]

While Indians were often found in the leadership of the Congress Alliance, there were scarcely any Coloreds. At the same time, the Coloreds played a major role in founding the UDF, which was originally formed to fight the tricameral parliament in which each racial group (other than Africans) would supposedly manage its own affairs, but real power would remain with the Europeans. In its ANC/Congress Alliance form, the anti-apartheid movement could appeal to Zulus but not so much to Coloreds. In its UDF incarnation, however, the same movement could mobilize Coloreds — especially among the more educated youth — while alienating many Zulus. This was hardly a question of economic interest, or even of social conservatism, but of identity. The Zulus were trying to maintain their distinct identity, while the Coloreds were intent on denying that they had one.

The Colored community had no place in the apartheid scheme. Yet due to the psychological process of identification with the aggressor, the majority of them avoided involvement with the liberation movement, and voted for their former oppressors once full-fledged democracy was established.

South Africa's Indians: Accommodation Without Identification

Except for a small number of Chinese, South Africans classified as "Asian" under apartheid were Indian. About 3 percent of the population, they are heavily concentrated in Natal, with most of the remainder living in Transvaal; the Orange Free State prohibited them from living or even visiting there. Indians are more prosperous than other non–White groups. In 1980, their per capita income was 30 percent that of the Europeans; comparable figures for the Coloreds and Africans were 21 and 10 percent.[68] Most are descended from indentured servants from southern India, but about 40 percent are from the northern part, and came over as paid passengers; the social, cultural, and economic distinctions between the two groups are still significant. About a fifth of the Indians are Muslims, nearly all from among the northerners; the remainder are mostly Hindu, but a minority have converted to Christianity.[69]

Under apartheid, the position of the Indians was roughly equal to that of the Coloreds. They could not vote, until they were granted their own separate chamber in parliament with authority only over their own affairs. They could join unions, but the unions were segregated. Like Africans, they were forbidden from purchasing alcohol, and there were only a few places where they could own land — areas where they had purchased it in the years before apartheid. For a long time, South Africa's official policy was to encourage the Indians to return to India, but this had little effect given the extreme poverty in the old country. "They Prefer to Stay in South Africa," declared a government brochure:

> Few Indians in South Africa have taken advantage of assisted repatriation schemes in the last 40 years in spite of allegations that the Indian population is oppressed and persecuted by unjust laws.... The South African Government ... increased the repatriation bonus ... from £20 to £40 ... but only 290 ... took advantage of the Government's offer.[70]

Before World War II, the Indians were led by a conservative Muslim faction which accepted racial separation. The more numerous Hindus were still politically quiescent. The existing leadership was first challenged by Dr. Yussuf Dadoo, a physician from Transvaal, who played a major role in the South African Indian Congress (SAIC) and ultimately became general secretary of the Communist Party. Some Indians were reluctant to support rights for Africans, but Dadoo argued effectively that equality must be for all.[71] Indians were a major force in the UDF, which may have alienated some Zulus. It should be kept in mind that Indians in South Africa — and in East Africa as well — have played a role similar to that of the Chinese in Southeast Asia, or the Jews in Eastern Europe, and that this creates problems between them and the majority. In 1949, there were violent anti–Indian riots by Africans in Durban. Europeans were seen cheering on the Africans as they attacked the Indians.[72] And the ANC's willingness to cooperate with the SAIC "had been the catalyst that had led some comrades in 1958 to break away and form the PAC."[73]

Curiously, once majority rule had been achieved, the Indians drifted away from their alliance with the ANC; in 1999, only a paltry 7 percent of the Indian vote went to the ANC, compared to 36 percent for the National Party, and 25 percent for the Minority Front, an Indian grouping.[74] South African political scientist Tom Lodge argues that some of this support for the very party that had disfranchised them previously was based on "the repressive character of the Indian family structure with its anti-permissive ethos and its deference to age and hierarchy."[75] At the same time, the fact that many Indians were economically successful certainly played a part in their post-apartheid conservatism, as did the modest but genuine benefits both Indians and Coloreds received from the tricameral parliamentary system during the 1980s.[76]

Black Consciousness

Several factors began undermining apartheid during the 1970s. The first was the victory of African nationalist groups in neighboring Angola, Mozambique, and Zimbabwe. The second was the emergence of independent African labor unions, culminating in the formation of COSATU. The third was the Black Consciousness Movement (BC), which began among the students but soon evoked a response among the entire African population.

At the beginning, BC was less a political movement than an attempt to heal the psychological damage done by apartheid. The 1973 Policy Manifesto of the South African Students Organization (SASO), a leading BC group, stated:

> SASO is a black student organization working for the liberation of the black man, first from psychological oppression by themselves through inferiority complex, and secondly from the physical one accruing out of living in a white racist society.[77]

The inferiority complex SASO refers to here is the basis for identification with the aggressor. While undoubtedly a serious consequence of White rule, the apartheid government never considered it an essential element in its strategy of control. Apartheid's ideologists had no problem with separate African institutions as long as Europeans retained ultimate control, and the racial groups did not mix. Consequently, the South African government originally tolerated the rise of BC, even considering co-opting it into the framework of apartheid.[78]

At first, BC activists were not particularly influenced by either the ANC or its rival, the PAC, since both had been virtually stamped out inside the country. While confronting the same issues as the two older movements, the BC advocates approached them from a different direction. Instead of placing the blame for Black people's problems on apartheid and leaving it at that, SASO promoted self-help projects such as "literacy campaigns, health projects ... the building of schools and community centres ... cooperative bulk buying ... [and] black theatre...."[79] Whereas the ANC and PAC would have promoted political action as the means of overcoming Black alienation and feelings of helplessness, BC emphasized, in the words of one of its founders, Drake Kota, "the road of *self-discovery*."[80] (Emphasis in the original.) Much of the BC program "sounded like a course in group psychotherapy, and not like a political programme...."[81] In fact, BC leader Saths Cooper, later president of the BC–oriented Azanian People's Organization (AZAPO), was a clinical psychologist.[82]

Some of BC's early political alliances were surprising. Its Black Community Program had Inkatha members on the Board of Directors[83]; and in 1971, SASO met with the Association for the Educational and Cultural Advancement of Africans, a group started by a conservative faction expelled during the 1950s from the ANC.[84] As BC grew, however, it became more ideologically diverse. Some of its followers were ultimately drawn to the ANC, others to the PAC, and some rejected both older groups and formed AZAPO. That, in turn, helped establish the National Forum, a broad coalition that competed with the ANC–oriented UDF. Simplifying the differences between the three camps, the ANC considered all racial differences as irrelevant, favored secularism, and leaned toward the Soviet Union in foreign policy; the PAC regarded Africans and Coloreds (but not Indians) as Black, favored traditional religion as authentically African, and at one point leaned toward China; and AZAPO counted Indians as Black along with Coloreds and Africans, sympathized with liberation theology,[85] and dismissed both the Soviet Union and China as reactionary.

In one important sense, BC was a failure. Robert Fatton notes that this movement,

> ...with its emphasis on black culture, identity and self-love, could not by itself destroy the system of entrenched white privilege. While psychological emancipation from white supremacy was a fundamental and necessary stage for political action, it tended to become an end in itself and to develop into a poor substitute for revolutionary strategy.[86]

It should also be kept in mind that feelings of inferiority do not begin when one first discovers one's low status in society, but rather in childhood, at the hands of overly demanding and strict parents. This would include children growing up in European, many Colored, and most Indian families in South Africa, as well as African children in either traditional rural or stable urban families. It would not have included urban working-class African families where the breadwinners had to work long hours and commute great distances, leaving them little time to supervise their children; and it would not have included families deported to the Bantustans, where the fathers typically worked in the White areas, and saw their children only on rare vacations. Children in these situations made up the core of the anti-apartheid movement from Sharpeville on, but overcoming authoritarian upbringing was hardly their main priority. They supported BC mostly for want of any alternative.

These activists were fated to develop either in an explicitly political direction, as happened with the large majority of activists who joined the ANC, or drift into political isolation and irrelevance, as happened with those who joined AZAPO, or to a lesser degree the PAC. Despite its radical rhetoric, AZAPO did almost nothing except to clash with the ANC, to the delight of apartheid's supporters. At one point, AZAPO even commemorated the deaths of South African troops who died in Mozambique fighting against ANC guerrillas. Its only demonstration was against apartheid foe Senator Edward Kennedy when he visited South Africa. In practice, like the NEUM among the Coloreds, AZAPO was identifying with the aggressor, its self-help program, at least among the Africans, an obvious treatment failure. In the 1999 elections, after having boycotted the polls in 1994, AZAPO received just a fraction of one percent of the vote.

Nonetheless, the emergence of BC did represent a step forward for the liberation movement, certainly the most important since the post–1948 radicalization of the ANC. First, BC did manage to mobilize enormous numbers of young Africans, students and non-students alike, and this ultimately revived the ANC. Second, BC overcame the effects of tribalism, particularly in the Transvaal, where the African population is particularly diverse. And third, BC mobilized the younger generation of Coloreds for the first time. Its effect among this group, writes Allister Sparks,

> was enormous and lasting. Gone is the shame at the dark side of their parentage. Gone, too, is the fawning desire to be patronized by whites. Instead there is a positive, almost vehement, rejection of the white community and a growing identification with the black cause.[87]

The Downfall of Apartheid

From the mid–1970s on, the Europeans responded in a variety of ways to the gradual erosion of their authority. First, a number of younger Whites began to identify with the liberation movement, particularly with the avowedly non-racial ANC and UDF, as well as the COSATU union federation. In an era of greater creature comforts and worldwide flow of information, it became increasingly difficult to impose narrow conceptions of ethnic loyalty on the youth, or to persuade them to blindly follow the dictates of established authority. When the UDF and COSATU held their mass demonstrations, some White faces could be seen in their ranks, and this had an effect on the rest of the European minority.

Second, the NP made efforts to neutralize the Coloreds and Asians, with some degree of success. The divide and rule policy also led to the creation of more "independent" Bantustans.

Third, partly in response to the concessions to the Asians and Coloreds, new political formations emerged to the right of the NP, calling for a return to the days of Verwoerd and Malan. The largest of these was the Conservative Party, which was strong in Transvaal. The Reconstituted National Party was another extremist group, whose slogan was "Shoot; don't think."[88] The Afrikaner Resistance Movement (AWB in Afrikaans) was even more fanatical. Led by Eugene TerreBlanche, the AWB's members dressed in Nazi-style uniforms and carried flags featuring a swastika-like symbol made up of three 7's, and sometimes displayed the original Nazi flag as well. The AWB called for the creation of a purely Afrikaner state in northern and central South Africa, leaving the rest of the country to the Africans, English, and other "inferior" races. One extremist offshoot, the Boer Republican Army, set off bombs in Johannesburg; little was heard of this group afterwards, indicating that it may have been an alternate name for another organization.

A fourth response was the emergence of religious paranoia, a reaction to the Europeans' perceived helplessness in relation to the West. Charismatic Christianity started to spread among the European minority, particularly in Cape Province (where it was more religiously diverse to begin with), and there was a parallel growth of Hasidism among the Jews.[89] Religion always played a major role in shoring up White supremacy in South Africa. In a message placed in Bibles distributed to South African troops, Prime Minister P.W. Botha said: "This Bible is an important part of your calling to duty. When you are over-whelmed with doubt, pain, or when you find yourself wavering, you must turn to this won-derful book for answers.... Of all the weapons you carry, this is the greatest because it is the Weapon of God."[90]

John Birch–style conspiracy theories about "the Illuminati" plotting to take over the world abounded, as it gradually sank in that the Western powers were increasingly prepared to accept majority rule. Paradoxically, the collapse of the Soviet Union was a devastating blow to the apartheid government, since it eliminated the only threat that might have con-vinced the West to come to their aid. The lame but often-repeated argument that the West's vital "sea routes" to Asia required a stable (read White supremacist) government in South Africa overlooked the existence of the Suez Canal. More important, given the admitted fact that Middle East conflicts have occasionally closed the Suez Canal for periods of time, it ignored the detail that the world is *round*, and that cars from Japan or wool from Australia could reach England via the Panama Canal just as easily as by way of the Cape of Good Hope. But the notion of a round earth is "just a theory," according to the most fundamen-talist of the Dutch Reformed Afrikaners, so the apartheid government was unwilling to spark a controversy by bringing it up.

Prime Minister F.W. de Klerk's response to the growing anti-apartheid movement was to attempt to buy time, split non–White ranks, and persuade the West not to impose sanc-tions. Until the early 1990s, de Klerk does not appear to have been considering any one person, one vote solution, but his concessions began to develop a momentum of their own. NP politicians were proposing all sorts of elaborate constitutional arrangements, from com-plete partition of the country to a limited African majority rule in which the Europeans would retain "group rights." But finally, after more than 300 years of European domina-tion, de Klerk agreed to fully democratic elections, and Nelson Mandela was elected pres-ident of a country where he could not have even voted a few years earlier.

A number of factors combined to bring about this unlikely development. The massive struggle of the UDF to "make South Africa ungovernable" was crucial, as was the armed struggle of Umkhonto we Sizwe, the ANC military wing — although the bombing cam-paign liberated no territory, and it was the threat of escalating violence in the future that had the desired effect. Sanctions by the West were effective, not so much by hurting the South African economy, as by convincing the European minority that their cause was no longer acceptable to the world. Sanctions, in fact, actually helped the South African econ-omy by forcing the country to produce items at home which could no longer be imported. This fostered development, which meant more and better jobs for Africans.[91] On the other hand, wealthy businessmen were not thrilled about substituting South African–made Chevrolets for their imported Porsches.

Another major factor in persuading the European minority to surrender its monopoly of power was the UDF's boycott of their stores.[92] This became more effective as African purchasing power grew, thanks to the rising level of development. It is a paradox that even under a highly repressive White supremacist regime, the wages of the oppressed groups continued to grow. "In 1969 Whites earned eleven times more than Coloureds, who in turn earned 20 percent more than Africans," writes Courtney Jung. "By 1988 Whites earned only three times as much as Coloureds, who then earned twice as much as Africans."[93] Her figures indicate that African wages increased from about 7 percent of those of Europeans to roughly 17 percent. This represents a measurable if modest move toward economic equality; but such a development represents the *failure* of apartheid, not its success.

Apartheid's strategy of promoting dissociation among the Africans failed for several reasons. First, there were no homelands set aside for the Coloreds and Asians, who together formed about an eighth of the population. Also left out were minor tribal groups, detribalized Africans, and those whose race or tribe had not been determined.

Second, dissociation is not the typical defense mechanism of most people. They generally prefer identification with the aggressor; but a strategy of co-opting non–White elites would have endangered Afrikaner domination over the country.

Third, and most ironic, the policy of promoting tribalism among the Africans undermined the effects of centuries of indoctrination aimed at persuading the Africans that they were inferior to Europeans. When African youths witnessed Bantustan leaders being treated as equals by their European rulers, what mattered most was the *image* of the two races meeting on equal terms, not the reality of the Bantustans' dependence on "White South Africa." True, the Bantustans were still subsidized by the South African government, and their legislatures were largely filled with South African–appointed chiefs. It was no more real than what the audience sees in a movie theater: shadows cast on a screen by a light shining through a series of photographs of paid actors pretending to be imaginary people. Yet the movie still has the desired effect on the audience.

Just as the ANC and UDF drew strength from the Black Consciousness Movement, so the latter drew its strength from the existence of African cabinet ministers, bureaucrats and generals in Transkei and the other tribal ministates. If Africans could govern themselves, however poorly, under the circumstances that existed in the Bantustans, one could argue that they could do so elsewhere. The Bantustan leaders — stooges and collaborators by any definition — became the unlikely inspiration for a generation of young African revolutionaries who finally brought about an end to apartheid.

One wonders why Dr. Hendrik F. Verwoerd, with his Ph.D. in behavioral psychology, did not foresee it.

16

Conclusion

Psychohistory Looks Ahead

Psychohistory has not had an easy row to hoe since its beginnings early in the twentieth century, with the biography of President Woodrow Wilson coauthored by Sigmund Freud and William Bullitt. Conventional historians and political scientists fear that psychohistory's success may come at their own expense. Psychotherapists, on the other hand, worry that it may involve them in controversial issues. My response is that the role of psychohistory is to *assist* the social sciences, not to replace any of them; and any psychotherapist who seeks to avoid controversy is probably in the wrong line of work.

What we have seen in the foregoing chapters indicates that there are a variety of factors involved in the emergence of tyranny and genocide. Arthur Janov pointed out in his writings that a given neurotic symptom — say, obesity — might stem from the patient being raised in a home where food was in short supply; equally likely, it could derive from a home where food was the *only* thing that was adequate, becoming a symbolic substitute for love. This concept diverges from the Freudian medical model, where Neurotic Symptom X stems from Family Condition Y, just as a particular medical syndrome indicates the presence of a specific disease.

Hitler's anti–Jewish Holocaust had its roots in the humiliation of boys by their teachers and fathers; Theoneste Bagosora's anti–Tutsi genocide also had its roots in humiliation, but of Hutus by Tutsis during the colonial period, not in the family dynamic. Islamic fanaticism flourished in Algeria because of the falling standard of living under the FLN; but in Iran, it flourished largely because of the *rising* standard of living caused by the oil boom. The weak family structure in Argentina contributed to the violence of the "Dirty War." Across the South Atlantic, similar violence by the forces of apartheid against the movement for justice and equality stemmed from the *strong* family structure of a number of groups.

If there is any one factor that is most responsible for the political madness of the current era, it is probably the rapid rate of change since approximately the turn of the twentieth century, involving everything from the downfall of colonialism to the rise of the internet. Change creates stress, stress produces pain, and pain in turn promotes irrational responses: pollution fantasies, purity crusades, cults of personality, territorial expansionism, paranoia, terrorism, war, and genocide. Yet it would be hopeless to try to prevent further change, especially since most of it over the last hundred years has been positive; the alternative is to make people more amenable to it by reducing the degree of trauma in their childhood and infancy.

Making Childhood Less Traumatic

Reducing the pain of childhood has to start at birth. Natural childbirth has generally been helpful, although there may have been some exceptions. On the other hand, Caesarean delivery has often proven traumatic — although, again, there are cases where it has been less painful than the normal method. Excessive use of anesthesia in childbirth has been shown to be harmful, but there is also the mother's suffering to be considered. Slapping the newborn to start it breathing might be reconsidered; after all, other species manage to produce live offspring without any such action. Placing newborns on rigid feeding schedules should be regarded as a form of child abuse. And no effort should be spared to provide adequate pre-natal care for mothers-to-be.

Post-natal assistance to mothers — especially first-time mothers — is also essential, as is the assurance that infants get adequate food and medical care. Needless to say, this is going to be a difficult undertaking in impoverished countries where there still isn't enough food to go around, in part precisely because of the endless wars that have roots in traumatic childhood. It is a vicious circle, but it can be broken.

Centers to educate new parents in how to raise their children are useful, and the late Robert McFarland, a psychohistorian, pioneered this approach with considerable success in Boulder, Colorado; a similar program has already been started in Tadjikistan. Of course, parents need to be free of serious neurosis in order to benefit from this kind of program.

Essential to any healthy society is the liberation of women, by which I do not mean the incessant denigration of the male sex so popular in post–Vietnam American culture, or the compulsive obliteration of all differences between the two genders. Four decades of this kind of misguidance have left many American women less comfortable than ever with heterosexual relationships, while at the same time their representation in the political leadership remains far lower than in Western European nations. They continue to be sexually repressed, only now the sexual repression is enforced by other women instead of male clergy. And sexually repressed mothers, who cannot give in to their feelings, produce traumatized infants, who then — as in Fascist Italy in particular — express their perinatal traumas in their adult life. The best kind of liberation for women would be to encourage them to experience their sexuality as normal; and they must also learn to feel their anger, especially — but not exclusively — their anger toward their childhood caretakers. Similarly, men should be allowed to feel their fear; it would make them less prone to counter-phobic behavior such as engaging in war, violent crime, and even high-risk "extreme" sports.

Education plays a major role in socialization, and bad education — oversized classes, learning by rote, physical punishment, emotional abuse, emphasis on ideological indoctrination — leads to bad politics in the next generation. Germany, from reunification to the rise of Hitler, is a prime example of this. The madrassas of the Middle East and Pakistan are currently following the same path, producing frustrated fanatics eager to kill infidels. And scholars have overlooked the role of the "Christian Academies," set up throughout the American South to sidestep the integration of the public schools during the 1950s and 1960s, in the emergence of the mindless fundamentalism that ultimately helped put President George W. Bush in the White House.

Demilitarization is essential for a healthy society, although the world is clearly a long way from the point where it could engage in total and universal disarmament. And it is not my belief that powerful armies, by themselves, are the cause of wars; in many cases, their existence prevents them. But countries where fathers have typically been traumatized by their experience in the military are prone to falling prey to radical-right demagogues

It is important, we constantly hear, to keep drugs away from kids. But how can this be done when every instance of troublesome behavior by a schoolchild is treated with Ritalin instead of love and understanding? Schools, too, have to learn to "Say 'No' to drugs." And, at the same time, we might want to take a closer look at the role of legitimate drugs in maintaining what passes for normality in our society. How many adults depend on caffeine, nicotine, alcohol, sedatives, or stimulants on a daily basis to get through their stressful lives? And what are the consequences? The Chinese smoke so much tobacco that they are largely unaware of the serious air and water pollution in their major population centers; Brazilians drink so much coffee — an average of twenty cups a day — that many of them become "wired" from the caffeine and have delusions about flying saucers; and domestic violence in Germany and Ireland is fueled by excessive consumption of alcohol.

Look at Everything

Political madness is only one expression of pain; there are others as well, and examining them gives us an idea of what has been going wrong in a society. Popular songs and national anthems, films, novels, plays, and works of art all reflect the same feelings that underlie irrational political movements. The emotional subtext of the "Hansel and Gretel" fairy tale — children are bad because they need too much — is echoed in a Nazi propaganda film calling on affluent Germans to have more children because kids *don't* need all that much, and comically illustrated by a shot of a hefty, well-dressed chap walking his tiny daschhund.

The Khmer Rouge's anthem was filled with rage and images of blood; Hutu extremists sang of wanting to terrify unspecified others; Italian art of the Fascist era overflowed with birth symbolism; Argentine literature during the Dirty War was in denial about domestic disorder, a problem which Eva Perón sought to address, even if only in a symbolic manner; Duvalierist violence reflected the rage of the Voudou Petro cult dating from slavery times; and the Sinhalese-Tamil conflict in Sri Lanka was foreshadowed in legends going back centuries.

Conventional social scientists often ignore culture, and particularly its pathological expressions, while students of popular culture usually fail to connect their subjects to political developments. America's response to its unexpected defeat in the Vietnam War in 1975 can be seen, over the following quarter century, in the rise of the "Right to Life" movement, as Catholics and conservative Protestants worked out their guilt over having supported the government's anti–Communist crusade in Southeast Asia. Right-to-Lifers are saying, "*I'm* not responsible for killing innocent babies in Vietnam. It's those cursed *liberals* who are killing them right here in America!"

Another response to the defeat can be seen in the current popularity of body-building, personal trainers, magazines devoted to photographs of muscle-bound men (and women), and the careers of brawny film stars like Sylvester Stallone and Arnold Schwarzenegger whose acting abilities may fall a bit short of Sir Lawrence Olivier. They are all expressions of the repressed feeling of "I am afraid of being weak," inculcated into our young boys by our national obsession with competitive sports, and then triggered by America's defeat in Vietnam.

The End of Reductionism

It is clear that we need to get away from simplistic, one-level explanations of political events. "It's all about oil" gets us virtually nowhere as an explanation of the Iraq War. Rather, that conflict should be seen as America's way of dealing with the feeling of "I am afraid of being weak," along with George W. Bush's own neurotic need to prove he was tougher than his father, the kind of struggle that inevitably ends in failure. This point was made by Oliver Stone in his movie "W." Yet there is no doubt that Saddam Hussein's hopes of acquiring weapons of mass destruction represented a genuine threat. And had the United States waited until after Iraq had its WMD arsenal, it would have been too late to act, since Saddam would obviously have used them against the American troops. How curious that no one in the United States even raised this point when Vice President Dick Cheney declared that we were absolutely certain that Baghdad had WMDs even as our troops were being sent to northern Kuwait, where they would have been sitting ducks.

By the same token, Nazi persecution of the Jews should not be explained as simply a way for corrupt German officials to enrich themselves with Jewish wealth — although certainly a number of them did. The German feeling of inferiority toward the Jews, stemming from their overly strict childhoods, and triggered by the defeat in World War I, was a major factor in the Holocaust. So was the neurotic fear of change, such as that brought about by the incomplete revolution of 1918, for which Jews were seen as a catalyst. In Klaus Theweleit's classic two-volume psychohistorical work *Male Fantasies*, the emphasis is placed on male fear of assertive women. Of course, there were comparable fears of the assertiveness of other groups regarded as naturally inferior: workers, Jews, Slavs, non–Europeans. Kevin McDonald's *The Culture of Critique* is a pseudo-scientific defense of Nazi anti–Semitism in the name of "evolutionary psychology"; but it makes the valid point that people who prefer to live in rigid, hierarchical societies are going to regard Jews as somewhat of a threat; Jews are a minority, they are intellectual overachievers, and they prefer to live in societies where one's status is based more on individual achievement than on membership in an ascriptive group. Where McDonald goes wrong is that he regards the preference for hierarchal societies as caused by "Aryan genes," rather than authoritarian upbringing.

The Italian Fascists were able to recruit intellectuals from across the ideological spectrum precisely because they had no ideology of their own, a point that some historians have found hard to grasp. Mussolini retained a hard core of support throughout his regime, even though he never tackled any of the serious social problems besetting his country — unemployment, economic inequality, regional disparity, widespread illiteracy, or oppression of women and ethnic minorities. His followers were little more than a gang of uniformed thugs, but they appealed to Italians because they played on their repressed birth memories. By evoking feelings of "I need to break out," the Fascists were able to stay in power while delivering few benefits to the bulk of the population. But in a different political culture, the United States, the same unfelt feeling of "I need to break out," stemming from the trauma of World War I, led to nothing more than the popularity of escape artists, of whom Harry Houdini was the best-known example.

Repressed feelings are at the core of political madness, whether in Europe, America, or elsewhere. But they do not exist in a vacuum. Conditions on the historical level — political, social, and economic — determine whether these feelings are expressed in the form of a violent dictatorship, an irrational movement that fails to take power, or a harmless if curious fad.

Psychohistory and Neurobiology

Finally, psychohistory needs to integrate the science of neurobiology into its theories, a task which is barely in its preliminary stages. It is now widely believed that emotional and mental illnesses are caused by "chemical imbalances" in the brain, and this assumption is used to discredit the notion that bad parenting in childhood is responsible for most of our problems as adults. But how did the chemical imbalances get there in the first place? Arthur Janov's research indicates that the chemical imbalances are themselves *caused by early traumas*, which continue as reverberating circuits in the brain. Reliving the original trauma can connect the circuits to the conscious part of the brain, relieve the chemical imbalance, and eliminate the symptoms.

Much of what we are depends on our neurotransmitters — particularly endorphin and serotonin. Although this is speculative, it would seem that very early events in our lives — things like breast feeding or toilet training — produce these neurotransmitters, which are then mopped up, as it were, by receptors. These receptors remain in our brains, creating a physical need for more of the transmitters. As adults, we seek to produce these transmitters by our behavior, or else dull the need with various pain-killing drugs, particularly alcohol. Joining a religion or a cult may create a sensation of being loved by the universe (personified as "God"), which is actually the endorphin acting on our brains. Acquiring knowledge, being applauded by a crowd, or exercising power over other people, may activate the cells that produce serotonin; this will give us a sensation of being worthwhile. Some of us are so addicted to these neurotransmitters that we may sacrifice our freedom or commit mass murder in order to get them.

Are there social movements, parties, religious groups, and even entire cultures which are based on one particular neurotransmitter as opposed to another? Are there differences in this regard between men and women? Was the connection between urbanization and the rise of nationalism based less on economics than on the stricter kind of child-rearing practices necessary in cities, and the increased amount of serotonin receptors that resulted? Cities, after all, tend to be cosmopolitan; traditional folk culture is typically lost; and their inhabitants interact with suppliers and customers all over the world. Urbanization should have made people *less* nationalistic, rather than more, if economics were the primary consideration.

We may soon be at the point where the recent advances in brain science can help us explain the extremes of political madness so manifest in the twentieth century. Best of all, with the explanation may come the means of prevention.

Chapter Notes

Chapter 1

1. Arthur Janov, *The Primal Scream* (New York: Perigee, 1980), *passim*.
2. Neil J. Kressel, *Mass Hate* (New York: Westview, 2002), 145 ff.
3. See Chapter 7, below.
4. Gérard Prunier, *Darfur: The Ambiguous Genocide* (Ithaca, New York: Cornell University Press, 2005), *passim*.
5. Sanjib Baruah, *India Against Itself* (Philadelphia: University of Pennsylvania Press, 1999), *passim*.

Chapter 2

1. Peter Fischer, *Fantasy and Politics* (Madison, Wisconsin: University of Wisconsin Press, 1991), 43.
2. Robert G.L. Waite, *The Psychopathic God: Adolf Hitler* (New York: Da Capo Press, 1993), 140 n.
3. Joachim Fest, *Hitler* (New York: Harcourt, Brace & Jovanovich, 1973), 203.
4. Max Domarus (ed.), *The Essential Hitler* (Wauconda, Illinois: Bolchazy-Carducci Publishers, 2007), 56.
5. Dusty Sklar, *The Nazis and the Occult* (New York: Dorset Press, 1977), 79.
6. Woodruff D. Smith, *The Ideological Origins of Nazi Imperialism* (New York: Oxford University Press, 1986), 18–19.
7. Domarus, 186.
8. Richard Grunberger, *The 12-Year Reich* (New York: Ballantine, 1971), 157.
9. Fest, 378.
10. John Laffin, *Jackboot* (New York: Barnes & Noble, 1965), 165.
11. Klaus Fischer, *Nazi Germany: A New History* (New York: Continuum, 1995), 286.
12. H.W. Koch, *A History of Prussia* (New York: Barnes & Noble, 1978), 7.

13. Ibid., 39.
14. Laffin, 7.
15. Heather Pringle, *The Master Plan: Himmler's Scholars and the Holocaust* (New York: Hyperion, 2006), 228–229.
16. Grunberger, 140.
17. Ibid., 140.
18. Ibid., 100.
19. Laffin, 10.
20. Ibid., 94.
21. Richard Evans, *The Coming of the Third Reich* (New York: Penguin, 2003), 9.
22. Laffin, 7.
23. Waite, 254–255.
24. S. William Halperin, *Germany Tried Democracy* (New York: Norton, 1946), 4.
25. Laffin, 151.
26. Ibid., 158.
27. Koch, 286.
28. Grunberger, 310.
29. Laffin, 151.
30. Halperin, 145.
31. Grunberger, 24.
32. Fischer, 313.
33. Grunberger, 66.
34. Ibid., 170
35. Domarus, 452.
36. Fest, 114.
37. Ibid., 127
38. Waite, p 262–263.
39. Ibid, 109.
40. Grunberger, 515.
41. Evans, 23.
42. Waite, 287.
43. Sarah Gordon, *Hitler, Germans and the "Jewish Question"* (Princeton, New Jersey: Princeton University Press, 1984), 32–33.
44. Nicholas Goodrich Clarke, *The Occult Roots of Nazism* (New York: New York University Press, 1985), 124.
45. Rudy Koshar, *Social Life, Local Politics and Nazism* (Chapel Hill, North Carolina: University of North Carolina Press, 1986), 79–80.
46. Evans, 425.

47. Sklar, 85.
48. Fest, 15.
49. Randall L. Bytwerk, *Julius Streicher* (New York: Dorset Press, 1983), 67.
50. S. Edred Flowers, *Fire and Ice: Magical Teachings of Germany's Greatest Secret Occult Order* (St. Paul, Minnesota: Llewellyn, 1990), 133.
51. Peter Padfield, *Himmler* (New York: Henry Holt, 1990), 32.
52. Sklar, 16.
53. Evans, 37.
54. Fest, 36.
55. Fischer, 38.
56. Waite, 95–96.
57. Clarke, 63.
58. Ibid., 177.
59. Fest, 269.
60. Evans, 61.
61. Fischer, 24 ff.
62. Fest, 271.
63. Peter H. Merkl, *Political Violence Under the Swastika* (Princeton, New Jersey: Princeton University Press, 1975), 562.
64. William Sheridan Allen, *The Nazi Seizure of Power* (New York: New Viewpoints, 1973), 69.
65. Waite, 137.
66. Domarus, 465.
67. Bytwerk, 40–41.
68. Ralf Georg Reuth, *Goebbels* (New York: Harcourt, Brace & Co., 1993), 13.
69. Padfield, 24.
70. Charles Bracelen Flood, *Hitler: The Path to Power* (Boston: Houghton Mifflin, 1989), 330.
71. Ibid., 330.
72. Waite, 318.
73. Grunberger, 339.
74. Fritz Redlich, *Hitler: Diagnosis of a Destructive Prophet* (New York: Oxford University Press, 1999), 14–15.
75. Quoted in Ron Rosenbaum, *Explaining Hitler* (New York: HarperCollins, 1999), 385.

Chapter 3

1. Geoffrey Bell, *The Protestants of Ulster* (London: Pluto Press, 1978), 8.

2. Padraig O'Malley, *The Uncivil Wars* (Boston: Houghton Mifflin, 1983), 128.

3. Gerry Adams, *The Politics of Irish Freedom* (Dingle, Ireland: Brandon, 1986), 124.

4. Ken Heskin, *Northern Ireland: A Psychological Analysis* (New York: Columbia University Press, 1980), 49.

5. Sarah Nelson, *Ulster's Uncertain Defenders* (Syracuse, New York: Syracuse University Press, 1984), 12.

6. Ed Moloney and Andy Pollak, *Paisley* (Dublin, Ireland: Poolbeg, 1986), 218.

7. Bell, 141.

8. Michael Farrell, *Northern Ireland: The Orange State* (London: Pluto Press, 1980), 314.

9. Donald S. Connery, *The Irish* (New York: Simon and Schuster, 1968), 22.

10. Edmund Curtis, *A History of Ireland* (London: Methuen, 1936), 175.

11. Ibid., 230–231.

12. Ibid., 209–210.

13. Moloney and Pollak, 382–383.

14. Curtis, 231.

15. R.F. Foster, *Modern Ireland* (New York: Penguin, 1988), 85.

16. Curtis, 245.

17. Ibid., 285.

18. Foster, 74–75.

19. Ibid., 115–116.

20. Ibid., 602.

21. Kevin Kelley, *The Longest War* (New York: Lawrence Hill, 1982), 10.

22. Foster, 317.

23. Rona Fields, *Northern Ireland: Society Under Siege* (Philadelphia, Pennsylvania: Temple University Press, 1980), 6–7.

24. Foster, 467–468.

25. Curtis, 404.

26. Foster, 399–400.

27. Ibid., 465.

28. Farrell, viii.

29. Ibid., 25–26 and 82–83.

30. Moloney and Pollak, 143.

31. Ibid., 97.

32. Farrell, 221.

33. Bell, 55–56.

34 Kevin Toolis, *Rebel Hearts* (New York: St. Martins, 1995), 37.

35. Bell, 56.

36. Connery, 278.

37. Farrell, 92.

38. Connery, 278.

39. Liam O'Dowd, "Shaping and Reshaping the Orange State," in

Liam O'Dowd, Bill Rolston and Mike Tomlinson, *Northern Ireland: Between Civil Rights and Civil War* (London: CSE Books, 1980), 15.

40. John Darby, "Historical Background," in John Darby (ed.), *Northern Ireland: The Background to the Conflict* (Belfast: Appletree Press, 1983), 21.

41. Foster, 529.

42. Farrell, 35.

43. Moloney and Pollak, 28.

44. Connery, 250.

45. Bell, 61.

46. Robin Bryans, *Ulster: A Journey Through the Six Counties* (Belfast: Blackstaff, 1964), 51.

47. Sally Belfrage, *Living With War* (New York: Viking, 1987), 55.

48. Ibid., 116.

49. Ibid., 175.

50. Henry J. Abraham, *The Judicial Process* (New York: Oxford University Press, 1986), 257.

51. Farrell, p 84–85.

52. Ibid., 94.

53. Ibid., 202.

54. Adams, p 21–22.

55. Farrell, 50.

56. Ibid., p. 90–91.

57. Kelley, 63.

58. Farrell, 140.

59. Bell, p 10–11.

60. Farrell, 256.

61. Bell, 10.

62. Steven Howe, *Ireland and Empire* (New York: Oxford University Press, 2000), 194, quoting John Taylor.

63. Bell, 144.

64. O'Malley, 175.

65. Connery, 257.

66. Heskin, 46.

67. William F. Kelleher, Jr., *The Troubles in Ballybogoin* (Ann Arbor: University of Michigan Press, 2003), 51.

68. Farrell, 116.

69. O'Malley, 119.

70. Kelley, 76.

71. Chris Ryder and Vincent Kearney, *Drumcree: The Orange Order's Last Stand* (London: Methuen, 2001), 42.

72. Connery, 272.

73. Steve Bruce, *God Save Ulster* (Oxford: Oxford University Press, 1989), 259.

74. Farrell, 291.

75. Nelson, 109.

76. Farrell, 292.

77. Ibid., 296.

78. Nelson, 95.

79. Ibid., p 166–167.

80. O'Malley, 344.

81. Ibid., 293.

82. *Paisley, the Man and His Message*, 158, quoted in Bruce, 9.

83. Moloney and Pollak, 12–14.

84. Ibid., 17.

85. Ibid., 18.

86. Ibid., 255–256.

87. Ibid., 2–3.

88. Bruce, 101–102.

89. Farrell, 362.

90. Moloney and Pollak, 123.

91. Ryder and Kearney, 44.

92. Mairtin O'Mulleoir, *Belfast's Dome of Delight* (Belfast: Beyond the Pale, 1999), 213–214.

93. Ryder and Kearney, 333.

94. Gerry Adams, *A Farther Shore* (New York: Random House, 2005), 311.

95. Martin Dillon, *The Shankill Butchers* (New York: Routledge, 1999), 37.

96. Quoted in Howe, 240.

Chapter 4

1. Lenard J. Cohen, *Broken Bonds: The Disintegration of Yugoslavia* (Boulder: Westview, 1993), 24.

2. Stjepan G. Meštrović, *The Balkanization of the West* (London: Routledge, 1994), 77.

3. Misha Glenny, *The Fall of Yugoslavia: The Third Balkan War* (London: Penguin, 1992), 34.

4. Mihailo Crnobrnja, *The Yugoslav Drama* (Montreal: McGill-Queens University Press, 1994), 255.

5. R.G.D. Laffan, *The Serbs: Guardians of the Gate* (New York: Dorset Press, 1989), 23–24.

6. S.S. Juka, *Kosova* (New York: Waldon Press, 1989), 29.

7. Tim Judah, *The Serbs* (New Haven: Yale University Press, 1997), 31.

8. Stephen Gazi, *A History of Croatia* (New York: Barnes & Noble Books, 1973), 16.

9. Pavle D. Ostović, *The Truth About Yugoslavia* (New York: Roy Press, 1952), 267–268.

10. Barbara Jelavich, *History of the Balkans, Vol. 1* (Cambridge: Cambridge University Press, 1983), 24.

11. Robert Donia and John Fine, *Bosnia and Hercegovina: A Tradition Betrayed* (New York: Columbia University Press, 1994), 87.

12. Branka Magaš, *The Destruction of Yugoslavia* (London: Verso, 1993), 304.

13. Juka, 15.

14. John Wilkes, *The Illyrians* (Oxford: Blackwell, 1992), 243.

15. Ibid., 243.

16. Ibid., 237.

17. Alenka Puhar, "On Childhood Origins of Violence in Yu-

goslavia: II, The Zadruga," *The Journal of Psychohistory*, Fall, 1983, passim.

18. Ibid., 176–177.
19. Ibid., 177–178.
20. Miranda Vickers, *Between Serb and Albanian* (New York: Columbia University Press, 1998), 110–111.
21. Gazi, 113.
22. Rebecca West, *Black Lamb and Grey Falcon* (New York: Penguin, 1940), 52.
23. Noel Malcolm, *Bosnia: A Short History* (New York: New York University Press, 1994), 5.
24. Jelavich, Vol. 1, 316.
25. Gazi, 148.
26. Marcus Tanner, *Croatia: A Nation Forged in War* (New Haven: Yale University Press, 1997), 89.
27. Judah (1997), 87–88.
28. Jelavich, Vol. 1, 91–92.
29. John Lampe, *Yugoslavia as History* (Cambridge: Cambridge University Press, 1996), 107.
30. Ibid., 106–107.
31. Judah (1997), 97–98.
32. Laffan, 196.
33. Ostović, 125.
34. Ivo Banac, *The National Question in Yugoslavia* (Ithaca, New York: Cornell University Press, 1984), 388.
35. Jelavich, Vol. 2, 152.
36. Jovo Tomasevich, *The Chetniks* (Stanford, California: Stanford University Press, 1975), 119.
37. Ostović, 174.
38. Alex N. Dragnich, *Serbs and Croats* (San Diego, California: Harcourt Brace, 1992), 78.
39. Gazi, map section, endpapers.
40. Ibid., 328; Crnobrnja, 61.
41. Jelavich, Vol. 2, 236.
42. Tomasevich, 46.
43. Ibid., 50; Jelavich, Vol. 2, 236.
44. Tomasevich, 106.
45. Dragnich, 102–103.
46. Wolfgang Hoepken, "Yugoslavia's Communists and the Bosnian Muslims," in *Muslim Communities Reemerge*, Andreas Kappler, Gerhard Simon and Georg Brunner (eds.) (Durham, North Carolina: Duke University Press, 1994), 223–224.
47. Malcolm (1994), 189–190.
48. Stjepan G. Meštrović, *Habits of the Balkan Heart* (College Station, Texas: Texas A&M University Press, 1993), 39.
49. Tomasevich, 106.
50. Christopher Simpson, *Blowback: America's Recruitment of Nazis and Its Effects on the Cold War* (New York: Weidenfeld and Nicolson, 1988), 179 and 185.

51. Tomasevich, 148.
52. Malcolm (1994), 178–179.
53. Tomasevich, 261.
54. Ibid., 458 ff.
55. Crnobrnja, 83.
56. Dragnich, 121.
57. Ibid., 121.
58. Meštrović (1993), vii–viii.
59. Sabrina Ramet, *Nationalism and Federalism in Yugoslavia* (Bloomington, Indiana: Indiana University Press, 1992), 37.
60. Vickers, xiv.
61. Tim Judah, *Kosovo: War and Revenge* (New Haven: Yale University Press, 2000), 28–29.
62. Jelavich, Vol. 2, 275.
63. Judah (2000), 29.
64. Vickers, xiv.
65. Malcolm (1994), 205.
66. Ibid., 205.
67. Ramet, 20.
68. Louis Sell, *Slobodan Milosevic and the Destruction of Yugoslavia* (Durham, North Carolina: Duke University Press, 2002), 76.
69. Crnobrnja, 76.
70. Magaš, 4.
71. Hugh Poulton, *The Balkans: Minorities and States in Conflict* (London: Minority Rights Group, 1993), 153 ff.
72. Robert D. Kaplan, *Balkan Ghosts* (New York: Vintage, 1994), 41.
73. Ramet, 193.
74. Julie Mertus, *Kosovo* (Berkeley: University of California Press, 1999), 34.
75. Poulton, 17.
76. Sell, 79.
77. Judah (2000), 46–47.
78. Crnobrnja, 97.
79. Ibid., 98.
80. Ramet, 225–227.
81. Magaš, 331.
82. Ramet, 231.
83. Crnobrnja, 97.
84. Cohen, 126.
85. Poulton, 36.
86. Cohen, 121.
87. Ibid., 122.
88. Ibid., 110–114.
89. Ibid., 100.
90. Glenny, 12.
91. Ibid., 12.
92. Crnobrnja, 151.
93. Donia and Fine, 223; Glenny, 77 and 103.
94. Glenny, 105.
95. Crnobrnja, 166.
96. Ibid., 145.
97. Ramet, 267–268.
98. Cohen, 93.
99. Magaš, 254.
100. Cohen, 91.
101. Magaš, 254.
102. Cohen, 280.
103. Anthony Lewis, "Fanatical

and Ruthless," *New York Times*, March 10, 1995.
104. Crnobrnja, 22.
105. Ibid., 177.
106. Florence H. Levinsohn, *Belgrade: Among the Serbs* (Chicago: Ivan R. Dee, 1994), 97–98.
107. Ibid., 14–15.
108. Cohen, 240.
109. Levinsohn, 203.
110. Åsne Seierstad, *With Their Backs to the World* (New York: Basic Books, 2005), 322–323.
111. Francine Friedman, *The Bosnian Muslims: Denial of a Nation* (Boulder, Colorado: Westview, 1996), 122.
112. Ramet, 111.
113. Levinsohn, 246–247.
114. Raoul Hilberg, *The Destruction of the European Jews* (New York: Harper, 1961), 435 ff.
115. Richard West, *Tito and the Rise and Fall of Yugoslavia* (New York: Carroll and Graf, 1994), 385.
116. Sell, 214.
117. West, 376–377.
118. Meštrović (1993), 108.

Chapter 5

1. Jared Diamond, *Collapse* (New York: Viking, 2005), 325.
2. Fergal Keane, *Season of Blood* (New York: Penguin, 1996), 22.
3. Stephen Kinzer, *A Thousand Hills* (Hoboken, New Jersey: John Wiley and Sons, 2008), 23.
4. Mahmood Mamdani, *When Victims Become Killers* (Princeton, New Jersey: Princeton University Press, 2001), 52.
5. Quoted in Scott Peterson, *Me Against My Brother* (New York: Routledge, 2001), 258.
6. Gérard Prunier, *The Rwanda Crisis* (New York: Columbia University Press, 1995), 7–8.
7. Peterson, 259.
8. Mamdani, 90.
9. Keane, 15.
10. Alison Des Forges, *Leave None to Tell the Story* (New York: Human Rights Watch, 1999), 74–75.
11. Michael Mann, *The Dark Side of Democracy* (Cambridge: Cambridge University Press, 2005), 431.
12. Mamdani, 54.
13. Ibid., 47.
14. Des Forges, 32.
15. Ibid., 35.
16. Ibid., 30.
17. Joan Kakwenzire and Dixon Kamukama, "The Development and Consolidation of Extremist Forces in Rwanda 1990–1994," in Howard

Adelman and Astri Suhrke (eds.), *The Path of a Genocide* (New Brunswick, New Jersey: Transaction, 2000), 74.

18. Philip Gourevitch, *We Wish to Inform You That Tomorrow We Will Be Killed with Our Families* (New York: Picador, 1998), 334.

19. Des Forges, 31.

20. Keane, 17.

21. Des Forges, 33.

22. Prunier, 47.

23. Keane, 16–17.

24. Mamdani, 97.

25. Peterson, 274.

26. Ogenga Otunnu, "Rwandese Refugees and Immigrants in Uganda," in Howard Adelman and Astri Suhrke (eds.), 25 n. 6.

27. Prunier, 48.

28. Ibid., 47.

29. Mamdani, 121.

30. Rosamund Halsey Carr, with Ann Howard Halsey, *Land of a Thousand Hills* (New York: Plume, 2000), 118–119.

31. Mamdani, 247.

32. Ibid., 123.

33. Gourevitch, 58–59.

34. Keane, 18.

35. Carr, 140.

36. Prunier, 50.

37. Ibid., 58.

38. Mamdani, 124.

39. Prunier, 53.

40. Mamdani, 128.

41. Prunier, 56.

42. Ibid., 58.

43. Ibid., 51.

44. Gourevitch, 66.

45. Ibid., 66.

46. Kinzer, 35–36.

47. Mamdani, 136–137.

48. Linda Melvern, *Conspiracy to Murder: The Rwandan Genocide* (London: Verso, 2004), 11–12.

49. Mamdani, 37.

50. Jean Hatzfeld, *Machete Season* (New York: Farrar, Strauss, and Giroux, 2005), 54.

51. Prunier, 76.

52. Mamdani, 141.

53. Dina Temple-Raston, *Justice on the Grass* (New York: Free Press, 2005), 24.

54. Ibid., 94.

55. Bill Berkeley, *The Graves Are Not Yet Full* (New York: Basic Books, 2001), 256.

56. Prunier, 168.

57. Des Forges, 44.

58. Melvern, 15.

59. Prunier, 84–87.

60. Ibid., 84–85.

61. Michael Barnett, *Eyewitness to a Genocide* (Ithaca, New York: Cornell University Press, 2002), 56.

62. Temple-Raston, 26.

63. Kakwenzire and Kamukama, in Adelman and Suhrke (eds.), 83.

64. Prunier, 100.

65. Keane, 26.

66. Prunier, 167.

67. Peterson, 271–272.

68. Frank Chalk, "Hate Radio in Rwanda," in Adelman and Suhrke (eds.), 98.

69. Mamdani, 162 ff.

70. Gourevitch, 219.

71. Bruce D. Jones, "Civil War, the Peace Process, and Genocide in Rwanda," in Taisier M. Ali and Robert O. Matthews, *Civil Wars in Africa* (Montreal: McGill-Queens University Press, 1999), 59.

72. Melvern, 16.

73. Prunier, 96.

74. Gourevitch, 79.

75. Des Forges, 49.

76. Barnett, 55.

77. Des Forges, 49.

78. Kinzer, 77–78.

79. Carr, 201.

80. Prunier, 96.

81. Melvern, 33.

82. Ibid., 51.

83. Kinzer, 101.

84. Des Forges, 87.

85. Ibid., 141.

86. Barnett, 57.

87. Melvern, 59.

88. Temple-Raston, 165.

89. Peterson, 271.

90. Prunier, 173–174.

91. Peterson, 261.

92. Romeo Dallaire, *Shake Hands with the Devil* (New York: Carroll and Graf, 2003), 129.

93. Melvern, 71–72.

94. Ibid., 72.

95. Gourevitch, 100.

96. Keane, 23.

97. Diamond, 315–316.

98. Jones, in Ali and Matthews (eds.), 85 n.

99. Melvern, 22.

100. Des Forges, 194.

101. Prunier, 229.

102. Mann, 447.

103. Melvern, 162.

104. Peterson, 272.

105. Dallaire, 198.

106. Immaculée Ilibagiza, *Left to Tell* (Carlsbad, California: Hay House, 2006), 39.

107. Melvern, 156.

108. Ibid., 139.

109. Des Forges, 192.

110. Ibid., 196.

111. Ibid., 613; Prunier, 235.

112. Diamond, 318.

113. Keane, 163.

114. Prunier, 231.

115. Diamond, 328.

116. Nicola Graydon, "The Rwandan Schindler," in Terry George

(ed.), *Hotel Rwanda* (New York: Newmarket Press, 2005), 39.

117. Hatzfeld, 117.

118. Prunier, 246.

119. Des Forges, 226.

120. Ibid., 384.

121. Martin Meredith, *The Fate of Africa* (New York: Public Affairs, 2005), 515–516.

122. Melvern, 118.

123. Mamdani, 212.

124. Gourevitch, 91–92.

125. Mann, 446.

126. Prunier, 142.

127. Des Forges, 215.

128. Prunier, 292 n.

129. Gourevitch, 156–157.

130. Kinzer, 183.

131. Tom Odom, *Journey Into Darkness* (College Station, Texas: Texas A&M University Press, 2005), 165.

132. Hatzfeld, 114.

133. Ibid., 121.

134. Ibid., 48.

135. Graydon, 34.

Chapter 6

1. Satchi Ponnambalam, *Sri Lanka: The National Question and the Tamil Liberation Struggle* (London: Zed Press, 1983), 18–19.

2. Steven Kemper, *The Presence of the Past: Chronicles, Politics and Culture in Sinhala Life* (Ithaca, New York: Cornell University Press, 1991), 121.

3. Tessa J. Bartholomeusz, "Buddhist Burghers and Sinhala-Buddhist Fundamentalism," in Tessa J. Bartholomeusz and Chandra R. De Silva (eds.), *Buddhist Fundamentalism and Minority Identities in Sri Lanka* (New York: State University of New York Press, 1998), 173.

4. Kemper, 54 ff.

5. Ibid., 56.

6. Ibid., 60 ff.

7. Ibid., 132–133.

8. Personal communication, Hannah Lessinger of the South Asia Program at Columbia University, 1987.

9. Nur Yalman, *Under the Bo Tree* (Berkeley: University of California Press, 1971), 316.

10. A. Sivanandan, *Communities of Resistance* (London: Verso, 1990), 200–201.

11. S.J. Tambiah, *Sri Lanka: Ethnic Fratricide and the Dismantling of Democracy* (Chicago: University of Chicago Press, 1986), 103.

12. Ibid., 99.

13. Ponnambalam, 26.

14. Ibid., 20.

15. Ibid., 21.

16. Sivanandan, 232.

17. Bruce Kapferer, *A Celebration of Demons: Exorcism and the Aesthetics of Healing in Sri Lanka* (Washington, DC: Smithsonian Institution Press, 1983), 231.

18. R.L. Sirrat, "Catholic Identity and Global Forces in Sinhala Sri Lanka," in Bartholomeusz and De Silva (eds.), 158.

19. Yalman, 27.

20. Ibid., 58 ff.

21. Robert N. Kearney, "The Marxist Parties of Ceylon," in *Radical Politics in South Asia*, Paul Brass and Marcus Franda (eds.), MIT Press, Cambridge, MA, 1973, 409; Bryce Ryan, *Caste in Modern Ceylon* (New Brunswick, New Jersey: Rutgers University Press, 1953), 278.

22. Sadham Mukherjee, *Ceylon: Island That Changed* (New Delhi: People's Publishing House, 1971), 35.

23. Yalman, 108.

24. Personal communication, Robert N. Kearney, Syracuse University, 1974.

25. Ryan, 117.

26. Yalman, 94–95.

27. Ibid., 94–95.

28. Ibid., 137.

29. Ponnambalam, 24.

30. Yalman, 272.

31. Ibid., 205.

32. Personal communication from Fred Mackey, former police detective in Sri Lanka during the British colonial period, Santa Ana, CA, 1972.

33. Gananath Obeysekere, "Depression, Buddhism, and the Work of Culture in Sri Lanka," in Arthur Kleinman and Byron Good (eds.), *Culture and Depression* (Berkeley, California: University of California Press, 1985), 141.

34. Ibid., 141–143.

35. Judith Hooper and Dick Teresi, *The 3-Pound Universe* (New York: Dell, 1980), 88.

36. Arthur Janov, *Prisoners of Pain* (Garden City, New York: Anchor Press, 1980), 88.

37. Hooper and Teresi, 170–171.

38. Jayasumana Obeysekara, "Revolutionary Movements in Ceylon," in Kathleen Gough and Hari Sharma (eds.), *Imperialism and Revolution in South Asia* (New York: Monthly Review Press, 1973), 377.

39. Calvin A. Woodward, *The Growth of a Party System in Ceylon* (Providence, Rhode Island: Brown University Press, 1969), 4; Ponnambalam, 26.

40. Woodward, 263.

41. Tambiah, 103.

42. Sinnahpah Arasaratnam, *Ceylon* (Englewood Cliffs, New Jersey: Prentice-Hall, 1964), 8–9.

43. Ibid., 21–22.

44. Tambiah, 132.

45. Ibid., 133.

46. Donald E. Smith, "The Political Monks and Monastic Reform," in Donald E. Smith (ed.), *South Asian Politics and Religion* (Princeton, New Jersey: Princeton University Press, 1966), 492.

47. Woodward, 104.

48. Smith, 495 ff.

49. Donald L. Horowitz, *Ethnic Groups in Conflict* (Berkeley, California: University of California Press, 1985), 393.

50. Tambiah, 106–107.

51. Ponnambalam, 174.

52. Ibid, 194.

53. Ibid., xii ff.

54. Donald K. Swearer, "Fundamentalist Movements in Theravada Buddhism," in Martin E. Marty and R. Scott Appleby (eds.), *Fundamentalisms Observed* (Chicago: University of Chicago Press, 1991), 644.

55. Robert N. Kearney, *Communalism and Language in the Politics of Ceylon* (Durham, North Carolina: Duke University Press, 1967), 114.

56. Tambiah, 24, quoting a member of the Liberation Tigers.

57. Swearer, 644.

58. L. Piyadasa, *Sri Lanka: The Holocaust and After* (London: Marram Books, 1984), 100.

59. "Sri Lanka: Racism and the Authoritarian State," special issue of *Race and Class*, Summer, 1984 (London), 129–130.

60. Ibid., 132.

61. Ibid., 133.

62. Piyadasa, 101–102.

63. Anonymous, "1971— The Year of the Revolution," *Journal of Contemporary Asia*, Vol. 1, No. 4 (London), 95.

64. Obeysekara, 390 and 393.

65. Ponnambalam, 156; Kearney, in Brass and Franda (eds.), 207.

66. James Sterba, "Ceylon's Economy is Seen as Stagnating a Year After Youth Revolt," *New York Times*, April 9, 1972.

67. Nagalingam Sanmugathasan, "Sri Lanka: The Story of the Holocaust," *Race and Class*, Summer, 1984, 74.

68. Sumantra Bose, *Contested Lands* (Cambridge, Massachusetts: Harvard University Press, 2007), 6.

69. Ibid., 33–34.

70. Anita Pratap, *Island of Blood* (New York: Penguin, 2001), 63.

71. Ibid., 88.

72. Bose, 32.

73. Ibid, 35.

Chapter 7

1. Charles Twining, "The Economy," in Karl Jackson (ed.), *Cambodia, 1975–1978: Rendezvous with Death*, Princeton University Press, Princeton, NJ, 1989, 150; Grant Evans and Kevin Rowley, *Red Brotherhood at War* (London: Verso, 1984), 179.

2. Michael Coe, *Angkor and the Khmer Civilization* (New York: Thames and Hudson, 2003), 97.

3. Evan Gottesman, *Cambodia After the Khmer Rouge* (New Haven: Yale University Press, 2003), 14.

4. Philip Short, *Pol Pot* (New York: Henry Holt, 2004), 443.

5. Milton Osborne, *Before Kampuchea* (North Sydney, Australia: George Allen & Unwin, 1979), 191.

6. Karl Jackson, "The Ideology of Total Revolution," in Jackson (ed.), 68.

7. Wilfred Burchett, *The China-Cambodia-Vietnam Triangle* (Chicago: Vanguard Books, 1981), 19.

8. Michael Vickery, *Cambodia, 1975–1982* (Boston: South End Press, 1984), 3.

9. Ibid., 1–2.

10. Quoted by Kenneth Quinn, "The Pattern and Scope of Violence," in Jackson (ed.), 237.

11. Ben Kiernan, *How Pol Pot Came to Power* (London: Verso, 1985), 119–120; Elizabeth Becker, *When the War Was Over* (New York: Simon and Schuster, 1986), 63.

12. Becker, 190–191.

13. Joan Criddle and Teeda Butt Mam, *To Destroy You Is No Loss* (New York: Doubleday, 1987), 76.

14. Jackson, in Jackson (ed.), 72.

15. Sarom Prak, "The Unfortunate Cambodia," in *Children of the Killing Fields*, compiled by Dith Pran (New Haven, Connecticut: Yale University Press, 1997), 70; Ben Kiernan, *The Pol Pot Regime* (New Haven, Connecticut: Yale University Press, 1996), 211.

16. Osborne, 42–43.

17. Haing Ngor, *A Cambodian Odyssey* (New York: Warner Books, 1987), 19.

18. Francois Ponchaud, "Social Change in the Vortex of Revolution," in Jackson (ed.), 165–166.

19. David Steinberg, *Cambodia: Its People, Its Society, Its Culture* (New Haven, Connecticut: HRAF Press, 1957), 79–80.

20. Ibid., 82.

21. Short, 18–19.

22. Steinberg, 80.

23. Maslyn Williams, *The Land in Between* (Sydney, Australia: Collins, 1969), 154.

24. Ngor, 293.
25. Ibid., 26.
26. Ibid., 384.
27. Becker, 84.
28. Vickery, 19.
29. Osborne, 167.
30. Kiernan (1985), xiv-xv.
31. David Chandler, *The Tragedy of Cambodian History* (New Haven, Connecticut: Yale University Press, 1991), 242–243.
32. Malcolm Caldwell and Lek Tan, *Cambodia in the Southeast Asian War* (New York: Monthly Review Press, 1973), 204.
33. Kiernan (1985), xii-xiv.
34. Burchett, 21–22.
35. Evans and Rowley, 17.
36. Becker, 63.
37. Chandler (1991), 41.
38. Kiernan (1985), 229.
39. Michael Vickery, "Looking Back at Cambodia, 1942–1976," in Ben Kiernan and Chanthou Boua (eds.), *Peasants and Politics in Kampuchea, 1942–1981* (London: Zed Press, 1982), 96; Burchett, 19.
40. Chandler (1991), 37.
41. Kiernan (1985), 229.
42. Osborne, 61; Kiernan (1985), 305; Williams, 110–113.
43. David Chandler, *Brother Number One: A Political Biography of Pol Pot* (Boulder, Colorado: Westview, 1999), 77.
44. Becker, 97; Kiernan (1985), 174.
45. Kiernan (1985), 197–198.
46. Burchett, 55.
47. Kiernan (1985), 280.
48. Caldwell and Tan, 228.
49. Williams, 110–113.
50. Kiernan (1985), 284.
51. Chandler (1991), 174–175.
52. Ngor, 61.
53. Kiernan (1985), 121.
54. Becker, 135.
55. Pin Yathay, "*Stay Alive, My Son*," (New York: Simon and Schuster, 1988), 58.
56. Kiernan (1985), 248.
57. Evans and Rowley, 112.
58. Kiernan, in Kiernan and Boua (eds.), 235–237.
59. François Bizot, *The Gate* (New York: Knopf, 2003), 108.
60. Short, 210–211.
61. Ervin Staub, *The Roots of Evil* (Cambridge: Cambridge University Press, 1989), 190.
62. Becker, 169.
63. Ibid., 169; Criddle and Mam, 71.
64. Burchett, 60.
65. Evans and Rowley, 251.
66. Chandler (1999), 114.
67. Ngor, 154.
68. Becker, 167.

69. Criddle and Mam, 63.
70. Yathay, 119.
71. Molyda Szymusiak, *The Stones Cry Out* (New York: Hill and Wang, 1986), 20.
72. Vickery, 178.
73. Chandler (1991), 285.
74. Becker, 43.
75. Ngor, 276–277.
76. Szymusiak, 136.
77. Yathay, 170.
78. Kiernan, in Kiernan and Boua (eds.), 295.
79. Twining, in Jackson (ed.), 141.
80. Chandler (1991), 242–243.
81. Criddle and Mam, 92.
82. Jackson, in Jackson (ed.), 72–73.
83. Ngor, 140.
84. Jackson, in Jackson (ed.), 72.
85. Kiernan, "Orphans of Genocide," *Bulletin of Concerned Asia Scholars*, Vol. 20, No. 4, 1988, 25–26.
86. Ibid., 32.
87. Ibid., 14–15.
88. Ibid., 30.
89. Vickery, 181.
90. See Kiernan (1996), 252–288, *passim*.
91. Ibid., 300.
92. Ibid., 300–301.
93. Ibid., 301–302.
94. Vickery, 125 and 129.
95. Kiernan (1996), 302–303.
96. Vickery, 136.
97. Becker, 255.
98. Gottesman, 73.
99. Becker, 186.
100. Chandler (1991), 51.
101. Kiernan (1985), 3.
102. Ibid., 25–27.
103. Short, 27.
104. Vickery, 152.
105. Becker, 431.
106. Ibid., 203.
107. Ibid., 250; Vickery, 86 and 136.
108. Kiernan (1996), 379.
109. Evans and Rowley, 113.
110. Short, 387.
111. Nic Dunlop, *The Lost Executioner* (New York: Walker and Co., 2005), 16.
112. Kiernan (1996), 390.
113. Burchett, 201–209.
114. Evans and Rowley, 172.
115. Chandler (1999), 178–188.
116. Dunlop, 42.
117. Short, 342.

Chapter 8

1. Jonathan Spence, *The Search for Modern China* (New York: Norton, 1990), 601.

2. Lynn T. White III, *Politics of Chaos* (Princeton, New Jersey: Princeton University Press, 1989), 7; Maurice Meisner, *Mao's China and After* (3rd ed.) (New York: Free Press, 1999), 354
3. Michael Schoenhals (ed.), *China's Cultural Revolution* (Armonk, New York: M.E. Sharpe, 1996), 244.
4. Zhai Zhenhua, *Red Flower of China* (New York: Soho, 1982), 231.
5. Maria Antonietta Macciocchi, *Daily Life in Revolutionary China* (New York: Monthly Review Press, 1972), 456.
6. Roderick MacFarquhar and Michael Schoenhals, *Mao's Last Revolution* (Cambridge, Massachusetts: Belknap Press, 2006), 1.
7. Hans Grandqvist, *The Red Guard* (London: Pall Mall Press, 1967), 154.
8. Philip Short, *Mao: A Life* (New York: Henry Holt, 1999), 356–357.
9. Lowell Dittmer, *Liu Shao-chi and the Chinese Cultural Revolution* (Berkeley: University of California Press, 1974), 59.
10. Anne F. Thurston, *Enemies of the People* (Cambridge, Massachusetts: Harvard University Press, 1988), 179.
11. Meisner, 254–255.
12. Richard Baum and Louise Bennett (eds.), *China in Ferment* (Englewood Cliffs, New Jersey: Prentice-Hall, 1971), 50–51.
13. MacFarquhar and Schoenhals, 9.
14. Anita Chan, *Children of Mao* (Seattle: University of Washington Press, 1985), 130.
15. MacFarquhar and Schoenhals, 30.
16. Fulang Lo, *Morning Breeze* (San Francisco: China Books, 1989), 19.
17. Li Zhisui, *The Private Life of Chairman Mao* (New York: Random House, 1994), 234.
18. Spence, 520.
19. Meisner, 316.
20. Chan, 12.
21. Ibid., 118.
22. Ibid., 128.
23. Ibid., 140.
24. Mao Zedong (ed.), *Socialist Upsurge in China's Countryside* (Beijing: Foreign Languages Press, 1957), *passim*.
25. Jin Qiu, *The Culture of Power* (Stanford, California: Stanford University Press, 1999), 25.
26. Roderick MacFarquhar, *The Origins of the Cultural Revolution (Vol. II)* (New York: Columbia University Press, 1983), 195–196.
27. Li, 282–283.

28. Dittmer, 42.
29. Lo, 170.
30. Richard Evans, *Deng Xiaoping and the Making of Modern China* (New York: Penguin, 1993), 140.
31. Meisner, 211.
32. Baum and Bennett (eds.), 14.
33. Jean Daubier, *A History of the Chinese Cultural Revolution* (New York: Vintage, 1974), 136.
34. Gordon Bennett and Ronald Montaperto, *Red Guard* (Garden City, New York: Anchor, 1972), 224.
35. Hong Yung Lee, *The Politics of the Chinese Cultural Revolution* (Berkeley: University of California Press, 1978), 303.
36. Daubier, 71.
37. William Hinton, *Hundred-Day War*, special issue of *Monthly Review*, New York July-Aug. 1972, 19.
38. Zhai, 116–117.
39. Ross Terrill, *Madame Mao: The White-Boned Demon* (New York: Touchstone, 1992), 154.
40. Ibid., 246–247.
41. Ibid., 254.
42. Evans, 159.
43. Stanley Karnow, *Mao and China* (New York: Viking, 1972), 164.
44. Terrill, 125.
45. Spence, 599.
46. Christopher Andrew and Vasili Mitrokhin, *The World Was Going Our Way* (New York: Basic Books, 2005), 4.
47. Evans, 94–95.
48. Roderick MacFarquhar, *The Origins of the Cultural Revolution (Vol. I)* (New York: Columbia University Press), 148.
49. Terrill, 152–153.
50. Li, 397.
51. Bennett and Montaperto, 126–127.
52. Dittmer, 139.
53. Bennett and Montaperto, 126–127.
54. Daubier, 103.
55. Dittmer, 139.
56. Hinton, 61–62.
57. Bennett and Montaperto, 125.
58. Chan, 4.
59. Joan Robinson, *The Cultural Revolution in China* (Harmondsworth, United Kingdom: Pelican, 1969), 55.
60. Anne F. Thurston, *Enemies of the People* (Cambridge, Massachusetts: Harvard University Press, 1988), 101–102.
61. Chan, 139.
62. Bennett and Montaperto, 125.
63. Karnow, 233–234.
64. White, 244–245.
65. Li, 493.
66. MacFarquhar and Schoenhals, 100–101.

67. Zhai, 141.
68. Macciocchi, 50.
69. Schoenhals, 119.
70. Gao Yuan, *Born Red* (Stanford, California: Stanford University Press, 1987), 39–40.
71. Neale Hunter, *Shanghai Journal* (Hong Kong: Oxford University Press, 1988), 174–175.
72. Hinton, 193.
73. Gao, 96–97.
74. Karnow, 7.
75. MacFarquhar and Schoenhals, 155.
76. White, 244.
77. Hinton, 132.
78. White, 40.
79. Daubier, 198.
80. Hunter, 151.
81. Elizabeth Perry and Li Xun, *Proletarian Power* (Boulder, Colorado: Westview, 1997), 8.
82. MacFarquhar and Schoenhals, 162.
83. Perry and Xun, 67.
84. Ibid., 135–136.
85. Ken Ling, *The Revenge of Heaven* (New York: Ballantine, 1972), 243–244.
86. Karnow, 434 ff.
87. White, 14.
88. Ling, 14.
89. Hinton, 107.
90. Kerry Brown, *The Purge of the Inner Mongolian People's Party in the Chinese Cultural Revolution, 1967–69* (Folkestone, United Kingdom: Global Oriental, 2006), 26.
91. Paul Hyer and William Heaton, "The Cultural Revolution in Inner Mongolia," *China Quarterly*, #36 (Oct.-Dec. 1968), 117.
92. Ibid., 116.
93. Ibid., 116.
94. Ibid., 120.
95. Ibid., 124.
96. Brown, 63.
97. Ibid., 67.
98. Hyer and Heaton, 125.
99. Ibid., 124.
100. Brown, 94.
101. Ibid., 62.
102. Ibid., 49–50.
103. Ibid., 72–73.
104. Ibid., 3.
105. Ibid., 121.
106. MacFarquhar and Schoenhals, 257–258.
107. Brown, 119.
108. MacFarquhar and Schoenhals, 221–222.
109. Ibid., 233.
110. Hinton, 129.
111. Qiu, 108–109.
112. Ibid., 123 ff.
113. Ibid., 126.
114. Ibid., 99.
115. Ibid., 8–9.

116. Ibid., 131.
117. Ibid., 179.
118. Ibid., 9.
119. Ibid., photo section following 106.
120. Thurston, 23.
121. Ibid., 25.
122. Macciocchi, 227.
123. Meisner, 254–255.

Chapter 9

1. Brian Steidle, *The Devil Came on Horseback* (New York: Public Affairs, 2007), 141.
2. Robert Collins, *A History of the Sudan* (Cambridge: Cambridge University Press, 2008), 199.
3. Bill Berkeley, *The Graves Are Not Yet Full* (New York: Basic Books, 2001), 204.
4. Awad Abdelrahim Abdelgadir with Linda Boxberger, "Memories of a Nubian Boyhood: Growing up in a Sudanese Nile Village," in Elizabeth Warnock Fernea, *Remembering Childhood in the Middle East* (Austin, Texas: University of Texas Press, 2002), 245.
5. Jok Madut Jok, *Sudan: Race, Religion and Violence* (Oxford: Oneworld, 2007), 119.
6. Julie Flint and Alex de Waal, *Darfur: A Short History of a Long War* (London: Zed, 2005), 17–18.
7. Collins, 42–43.
8. Francis Bok with Edward Tivnan, *Escape from Slavery* (New York: St. Martins Griffin, 2003), 233.
9. Jok Madut Jok, *War and Slavery in the Sudan* (Philadelphia: University of Pennsylvania Press, 2001), 49.
10. Brian Steidle and Gretchen Steidle Wallace, *The Devil Came on Horseback* (New York: Public Affairs, 2007), 20.
11. Judith Miller, *God Has Ninety-Nine Names* (New York: Touchstone, 1997), 131.
12. Collins, 238.
13. T. Abdou Maliqalim Simone, *In Whose Image?* (Chicago: University of Chicago Press, 1994), 72–73.
14. Jok (2001), 107.
15. Ibid., 110.
16. Jok, 110–111; Simone, 67–68.
17. Gerard Prunier, *Darfur: The Ambiguous Genocide* (Ithaca, New York: Cornell University Press), 15–16.
18. M.W. Daly, *Darfur's Sorrow* (New York: Cambridge University Press, 2007), 57.
19. Scott Peterson, *Me Against*

My Brother (New York: Routledge, 2001), 178.

20. Daly, 63.

21. Alan Moorehead, *The White Nile* (New York: HarperCollins, 1960), 233.

22. Peterson, 177.

23. Miller, 131–132.

24. Moorehead, 231.

25. Ibid., 307–308.

26. Miller, 132.

27. Prunier, 20.

28. John Markakis, *National and Class Conflict in the Horn of Africa* (London: Zed, 1990), 146.

29. Ibid., 148.

30. Daly, 134.

31. Markakis, 51.

32. Martin Meredith, *The Fate of Africa* (New York: Public Affairs, 2005), 344–345.

33. Daly, 116.

34. Don Petterson, *Inside Sudan* (Boulder, Colorado: Westview, 2003), 180.

35. Markakis, 81.

36. Ibid., 83.

37. Flint and de Waal, 20.

38. Simone, 183.

39. Ibid., 115.

40. Meredith, 346.

41. Collins, 146.

42. Meredith, 588.

43. Miller, 128.

44. Collins, 191.

45. Ibid., 196.

46. Jok (2007), 74.

47. Peterson, 181.

48. Simone, 64.

49. Collins, 227–228.

50. Ibid., 147–149.

51. Jok (2001), 133–134.

52. Ibid., 10.

53. Flint and de Waal, 41.

54. Collins, 279.

55. Mende Nazer and Damien Lewis, *Slave: My True Story* (New York: Public Affairs, 2003), 79

56. Ibid., 106.

57. Miller, 128.

58. Markakis, 215.

59. Daly, 247.

60. Benson Deng, in Benson Deng, Alephonsion Deng, and Benjamin Ajak, *They Poured Fire on Us from the Sky* (New York: Public Affairs, 2005), 46.

61. Benjamin Ajak, ibid., 213.

62. Peterson, 217 ff.

63. Collins, 248–249.

64. Benson Deng, in Deng, Deng and Ajak, 136.

65. Berkeley, 223.

66. Petterson, 232.

67. Ibid., 243.

68. Prunier, 161.

69. Flint and de Waal, 114.

70. Collins, 289.

71. Ibid., 73.

72. Daly, 268.

73. Petterson, 69.

74. Jok (2001), 227.

75. Simone, 87.

76. Ibid., 149.

77. Ibid., 230.

Chapter 10

1. Bernard Lewis, *The Emergence of Modern Turkey*, 3rd edition (New York: Oxford University Press, 2002), 356.

2. Taner Akçam, *A Shameful Act* (New York: Metropolitan Books, 2006), 86–87.

3. G.J. Meyer, *A World Undone* (New York: Delta, 2006), 88–89.

4. Andrew Mango, *Atatürk* (Woodstock, New York: Overlook Press, 2002), 8.

5. Ibid., 368.

6. Peter Balakian, *The Burning Tigris* (New York: HarperCollins, 2002), 36.

7. Stephen Kinzer, *Crescent and Star* (New York: Farrar, Straus and Giroux, 2001), 233.

8. Mango, 381.

9. Christopher Houston, *Islam, Kurds, and the Turkish Nation-State* (Oxford: Berg, 2001), 99.

10. Ibid., 78 n.

11. Lewis, 359.

12. Ibid., 206.

13. Ibid., 216.

14. Quoted in Akçam, 69.

15. Ibid., 44.

16. Ibid, 94–95.

17. Ibid., 125.

18. Mango, 415.

19. Akçam, 5–6.

20. Christophe Jaffrelot (ed.), *A History of Pakistan and Its Origins* (London: Anthem Press, 2002), 228–229.

21. Ibid., 241.

22. Ramachandra Guha, *India After Gandhi* (New York: Harper, 2007), 93–94.

23. Damodar Singhal, *Pakistan* (Englewood Cliffs, New Jersey: Prentice-Hall, 1972), 81.

24. Jaffrelot, 241.

25. Khalid B. Sayid, *The Political System of Pakistan* (Boston: Houghton Mifflin, 1967), 179–180.

26. Jaffrelot, 70.

27. Nasim Ahmed Jawed, *Islam's Political Culture* (Austin, Texas: University of Texas Press, 1999), 62–63.

28. Owen Bennett Jones, *Pakistan: Eye of the Storm* (New Haven: Yale University Press, 2002), 62–63.

29. Sayid, 179–180.

30. Singhal, 81–82.

31. Jaffrelot, 245.

32. Ibid., 230.

33. Ibid., 231.

34. Syed Rashid Ali, "Post Anti Qadiani Ordinance of 1984," Internet document, dated 1/13/00.

35. Ibid.

36. Ibid.

37. Ibid.

38. Ibid.

39. John Ruedy, *Modern Algeria* (Bloomington, Indiana: Indiana University Press, 1992), 50–51.

40. Ibid., 75–76.

41. Alistair Horne, *A Savage War of Peace* (New York: New York Review of Books, 2006), 221–223.

42. Milton Viorst, *In the Shadow of the Prophet* (Boulder, Colorado: Westview, 2001), 240.

43. Reinhard Schulze, *A Modern History of the Islamic World* (New York: New York University Press, 2002), 161.

44. Ruedy, 102.

45. Michael Willis, *The Islamist Challenge in Algeria* (New York: New York University Press, 1996), 17.

46. Ruedy, 192–194.

47. Miller, 176; Hugh Roberts, *The Battlefield: Algeria, 1988–2002* (London: Verso, 2003), 11–12.

48. Willis, 67.

49. Roberts, 13 ff.

50. Willis, 49–50.

51. Ruedy, 226.

52. Roberts, 20.

53. Viorst, 265–266.

54. John Entelis, "Introduction," in Luis Martinez, *The Algerian Civil War: 1990–1998* (New York: Columbia University Press, 2000), xi-xii.

55. Roberts, 83.

56. Willis, 193–194.

57. Roberts, 84.

58. Ibid., 273.

59. Willis, 134–136.

60. Ibid., 193–194.

61. Miller, 180.

62. Fouad Ajami, *The Arab Predicament* (Cambridge: Cambridge University Press, 1992), 248–249.

63. Willis, 199.

64. Roberts, 153.

65. Miller, 181–182.

66. Ibid., 184.

67. Martinez, 197–198.

68. Giles Kepel, *Jihad: The Trail of Political Islam* (Cambridge, Massachusetts: Belknap Press, 2002), 262.

69. Martinez., 74–75.

70. Willis, 285.

71. Horne, 213–214.

72. Martinez, 116.

73. Willis, 367–368.

74. Martin Meredith, *The Fate of Africa* (New York: Public Affairs, 2005), 460.

Chapter 11

1. Setarrah Farma Farmaian, *Daughter of Persia* (New York: Anchor, 1992), page 23.
2. Hooman Majd, *The Ayatollah Begs to Differ* (New York: Doubleday, 2008), 51.
3. Elaine Sciolino, *Persian Mirrors* (New York: Free Press, 2005), 342.
4. Ibid., 338.
5. Mehrzad Boroujerdi, *Iranian Intellectuals and the West* (Syracuse, New York: Syracuse University Press, 1996), 36.
6. Dilip Hiro, *The Iranian Labyrinth* (New York: Nation Books, 2005), 99.
7. Ervand Abrahamian, *Iran Between Two Revolutions* (Princeton, New Jersey: Princeton University Press, 1982), 97–99.
8. Eqbal Ahmad, "The Iranian Revolution: A Landmark for the Future," *Race and Class*, Summer, 1979, 6.
9. William Forbis, *Fall of the Peacock Throne* (New York: McGraw-Hill, 1981), 265.
10. Nikki Keddie, *Roots of Revolution: An Interpretive History of Modern Iran* (New Haven, Connecticut: Yale University Press, 1981), 81–88.
11. Abrahamian, 382.
12. Ibid, 487.
13. Baqer Moin, *Khomeini: Life of the Ayatollah* (New York: St. Martin's, 1999), 252.
14. Reza Baraheni, *The Crowned Cannibals* (New York: Vintage, 1977), 34–35.
15. Hiro, 152.
16. Sciolini, 97.
17. Farmaian, 58.
18. Ibid., 12.
19. Ibid., 69.
20. Ibid., 251.
21. Robin Wright, *The Last Great Revolution: Turmoil and Transformation in Iran* (New York: Vintage, 2000), 54.
22. Sandra Mackey, *The Iranians: Persia, Islam, and the Soul of a Nation* (New York: Plume, 1998), 24–25.
23. Moin, 62.
24. Abolqasem Ferdowsi, *Shahnameh* (translated by Dick Davis) (New York: Penguin, 2006), 452.
25. Ibid., 724.
26. Moin, 15–16.
27. Mackey, 55.
28. See Peter Chelkowski and Hamid Dabashi, *Staging a Revolution: The Art of Persuasion in the Islamic Republic of Iran* (New York: New York University Press, 1999), 172–173.

29. Ibid., 59.
30. Moin, 311.
31. Chelkowski and Dabashi, 78.
32. Mackey, 85.
33. Moin, 294.
34. Mohammad Mohaddessin, *Islamic Fundamentalism* (Washington, DC: Seven Locks Press, 2001), 8.
35. Mackey, 169.
36. Afshin Molavi, *The Soul of Iran* (New York: W.W. Norton, 2002), 13.
37. Mackey, 170.
38. Ibid., 78.
39. Ibid., 274.
40. Touraj Atabaki, *Azerbaijan* (London: I.B. Tauris, 2000), 58.
41. Molavi, 246–247.
42. Hiro, 119.
43. Mackey, 190.
44. Farmaian, 192–194.
45. Boroujerdi, 96.
46. Farmaian, 233.
47. Robert Graham, *Iran: The Illusion of Power* (New York: St. Martin's, 1979), 17.
48. Cheryl Benard and Zalmay Khalilzad, *The Government of God: Iran's Islamic Republic* (New York: Columbia University Press, 1984), 12.
49. Abrahamian, 473–474.
50. Assef Bayat, *Workers and Revolution in Iran* (London: Zed, 1987), 42.
51. Azar Tabari, "The Role of the Clergy in Modern Iranian Politics," in Nikki Keddie (ed.), *Religion and Politics in Iran* (New Haven: Yale University Press, 1983), 70.
52. See Abrahamian, 347 ff.
53. Molavi, 23.
54. Bayat, 23.
55. Fred Halliday, *Iran: Dictatorship and Development* (Middlesex, United Kingdom: Penguin, 1979), 12.
56. Boroujerdi, 29.
57. Tabari, in Keddie (ed.), 70; Michael M.J. Fischer, *Iran: From Religious Dispute to Revolution* (Cambridge, Massachusetts: Harvard University Press, 1980), 189.
58. Graham, 18.
59. Donald Wilber, *Iran: Past and Present* (Princeton, New Jersey: Princeton University Press, 1981), 206.
60. Keddie (1981), 127.
61. Wilber, 206.
62. Fischer, 37.
63. Graham, 211–212.
64. Barry Rubin, *Paved with Good Intentions* (Middlesex, United Kingdom: Penguin, 1980), 150.
65. Forbis, 178.
66. Majd, 69.
67. Ibid., 71.
68. Roger T. Olson, "Persian Gulf Trade and the Agricultural Economy of Southern Iran in the Nineteenth

Century," in Michael Bonine and Nikki Keddie (eds.), *Continuity and Change in Modern Iran* (Albany: State University of New York Press, 1981), 143.
69. Forbis, 178.
70. Keddie (1981), 28.
71. Forbis, 178–179.
72. Majd, 69.
73. Forbis, 179.
74. Sciolini, 320.
75. Fischer, 106.
76. MERIP Report #40, quoted in Baraheni, 43.
77. Azar Tabari and Nahid Yeganeh (eds.), *In the Shadow of Islam: The Women's Movement in Iran* (London: Zed, 1982), 190.
78. E. Michael Holden, "The Sensory Window and Access to Primal Pain," in Arthur Janov and E. Michael Holden, *Primal Man: The New Consciousness* (New York: Crowell, 1975), 158–159.
79. Sciolino, 44–45.
80. Keddie (1981), 150.
81. Abrahamian, 420.
82. Halliday, 46–47.
83. Surhoosh Irfani, *Revolutionary Islam in Iran: Popular Liberation or Religious Dictatorship?* (London: Zed, 1983), 81–83.
84. Molavi, 250.
85. Halliday, 47.
86. Abrahamian, 433.
87. Ibid., 446.
88. Graham, 58–59.
89. Chelkowski and Dabashi, 128–129.
90. Graham, 193.
91. Fischer, 193.
92. Roy Mottahedeh, *The Mantle of the Prophet* (New York: Pantheon, 1985), 371–373.
93. Ervand Abrahamian, "The Strengths and Weaknesses of the Labor Movement in Iran," in Bonine and Keddie (eds.), 201.
94. Hamid Algar, "Introduction," in Ayatollah Ruhollah Khomeini, *Islam and Revolution* (London: KPI, 1981), 13.
95. Ibid., 13.
96. Ibid., 15.
97. Abrahamian, 426 and 473–479.
98. Khomeini (1981), 56.
99. Ibid., 96.
100. Irfani, 80.
101. Khomeini (1981), 52.
102. Ibid., 385.
103. Ibid., 330.
104. Wilber, 342–343.
105. Michael M.J. Fischer and Mehdi Abedi, "Foreword," in Ayatollah Ruhollah Khomeini, *A Clarification of Questions* (Boulder, Colorado: Westview, 1984), xiv.

106. Sciolino, 55.
107. Moin, 184.
108. Ibid., 216.
109. Wright, 5.
110. Ibid., 230.
111. Chelkowski and Dabashi, 83.
112. Moin, 269.
113. Robin Wright, *In the Name of God* (New York: Simon and Schuster, 1989), 190.
114. Hiro, 336.
115. Sciolino, 194.
116. Ibid., 199.
117. Mohaddessin, 63.
118. Mackey, 323; Moin, 249.
119. Chelkowski and Dabashi, 235.
120. Wright (2000), 15.
121. Behzad Yaghmaian, *Social Change in Iran* (New York: State University of New York Press, 2002), 212.
122. Atabaki, 40.
123. See Vali Nasr, *The Shia Revival* (New York: Norton, 2007), 136.
124. Mohaddessin, xxxvi.
125. Khasra Naji, *Ahmadinejad* (Berkeley: University of California Press, 2008), 48.
126. Ibid., 88.
127. Ibid., 181.
128. Ibid., 109.
129. Hiro, 124–125.
130. Wright (2000), 284.
131. Ibid., 156.
132. Chelkowski and Dabashi, 252.
133. David McDowall, *A Modern History of the Kurds* (London: I.B. Tauris, 1996), 279.
134. Judith Miller, *God Has Ninety-Nine Names* (New York: Touchstone, 1996), 450.
135. McDowall, 261–262.
136. Ibid., 276.
137. Yaghmaian, 143.
138. Sciolino, 170.
139. Ibid., 366.
140. Farmaian, 346.
141. Mackey, 349.
142. Nasr, 135.
143. Ibid., 58.
144. Daniel Pipes, *The Hidden Hand: Middle East Fears of Conspiracy* (New York: St. Martins Griffin, 1996), 344.
145. Molavi, 100–101.
146. Yaghmaian, 170–171.
147. Wright (2000), 258.
148. Ibid., 28.
149. Chelkowski and Dabashi, 247.

Chapter 12

1. Quoted in Emilio Gentile, *The Sacralization of Politics in Fascist Italy* (Cambridge, Massachusetts: Harvard University Press, 1996), 59–60.
2. Barbara Spackman, *Fascist Virilities* (Minneapolis: University of Minnesota Press, 1996), 125.
3. Denis Mack Smith, *Mussolini* (New York: Vintage, 1983), 263.
4. Ibid., 138.
5. John Pollard, *The Fascist Experience in Italy* (London: Routledge, 1998), 120.
6. Joseph La Palombara, "Italy: Fragmentation, Isolation, Alienation," in Lucien Pye and Sydney Verba (eds.), *Political Culture and Political Development* (Princeton, New Jersey: Princeton University Press, 1965), 318–319.
7. Ibid., 318–319.
8. Alexander De Grand, *Italian Fascism* (Lincoln, Nebraska: University of Nebraska Press, 1982), 126.
9. Luigi Barzini, *The Italians* (New York: Atheneum, 1964), 203.
10. Nicholas Farrell, *Mussolini: A New Life* (London: Phoenix, 2004), 19.
11. Ibid., 8.
12. Ibid., 19.
13. Ibid., 19 and 21.
14. Laura Fermi, *Mussolini* (Chicago: University of Chicago Press, 2003), 70.
15. R.J.B. Bosworth, *Mussolini's Italy* (New York: Penguin, 2006), 147.
16. Fermi, 39.
17. Ibid., 120–121.
18. Farrell, 217.
19. Fermi, 286–288.
20. Bosworth, 315.
21. Ibid., 353.
22. Ibid., 9.
23. Farrell, 115.
24. Fermi, 193.
25. Farrell, 24.
26. Denis Mack Smith, *Italy and Its Monarchy* (New Haven: Yale University Press, 1989), 63.
27. Ibid., 129.
28. Adrian Lyttleton, *The Seizure of Power: Fascism in Italy, 1919–1929* (Princeton, New Jersey: Princeton University Press, 1973), 16.
29. Ibid., 16; also, Armando Borghi, *Mussolini: Red and Black* (New York: Haskell House, 1974), 93.
30. Alessandra Piontelli, *From Fetus to Child* (London: Routledge, 1992), 64.
31. Gentile, 151.
32. Ibid., 147–148.
33. Farrell, 175.
34. Bosworth, 399.
35. Marco Palla, *Mussolini and Fascism* (New York: Interlink, 2000), 22.
36. Bosworth, 463–464.
37. Farrell, 334.
38. F.L. Carsten, *The Rise of Fascism* (Berkeley: University of California Press, 1971), 19.
39. Gentile, 14.
40. Smith (1989), 185.
41. Fermi, 54.
42. Bosworth, 48.
43. Ibid., 112.
44. Ibid., 23.
45. Gaetano Salvemini, *The Origins of Fascism in Italy* (New York: Harper, 1973), 125.
46. Bosworth, 22.
47. Bruno Mantura et al. (eds.), *Futurism in Flight* (Rome: De Luca Edizioni D'Arte, 1990), 186.
48. Spackman, 53–54.
49. Lyttleton, 371.
50. Caroline Tisdall and Angelo Bozzolla, *Futurism* (New York: Oxford University Press, 1978), 196.
51. David Forgacs (ed.), *Rethinking Italian Fascism* (Lincoln, Nebraska: University of Nebraska, Press, 1982), 165.
52. Lyttleton, 368.
53. Fermi, 30.
54. Lyttleton, 368.
55. Salvemini, 125.
56. Marjorie Perloff, *The Futurist Moment* (Chicago: University of Chicago Press, 2003), 86–87.
57. Smith (1989), 186.
58. Bosworth, 39.
59. Borghi, 40–41.
60. Smith (1989), 197.
61. Ibid., 212.
62. Salvemini, 7.
63. Jasper Ridley, *Mussolini* (New York: Cooper Square Press, 1998), 84.
64. Smith (1989) 233.
65. Fermi, 152.
66. Ibid., 54–55.
67. Bosworth, 180.
68. Harry Fornari, *Mussolini's Gadfly: Roberto Farinacci* (Nashville, Tennessee: Vanderbilt University Press, 1971), 27.
69. Farrell, 81.
70. Bosworth, 167.
71. Benito Mussolini, *My Rise and Fall*, Vol. I (New York: Da Capo, 1998), 70.
72. Carsten, 51.
73. Fornari, 39.
74. Carsten, 55–56.
75. Smith (1989), 248.
76. Ibid., 250–251.
77. Salvemini, 387.
78. Farrell, 133.
79. Bosworth, 192–193.
80. Farrell, 145.
81. Bosworth, 213–214.
82. Ibid., 232.
83. Ibid., 212.

84. Smith (1983), 112.
85. Barzini, 136.
86. Farrell, 40.
87. Salvemini, 259.
88. Tracy H. Koon, *Believe, Obey, Fight: Political Socialization of Youth in Fascist Italy, 1922–1943* (Chapel Hill, North Carolina: University of North Carolina Press, 1985), 3.
89. Lyttleton, 303.
90. Robert Casillo, "Fascists of the Final Hour," in Richard J. Golsan (ed.), *Fascism, Aesthetics, and Culture* (Hanover, New Hampshire: University Press of New England, 1992), 104.
91. Meir Michaelis, *Mussolini and the Jews* (Oxford: Clarendon, 1978), 215.
92. De Grand, 93.
93. Koon, 77.
94. De Grand, 43.
95. Smith (1983), 210.
96. Bosworth, 198.
97. Smith, 151.
98. Ruth Ben-Ghiat, *Fascist Modernities* (Berkeley: University of California Press, 2001), 177.
99. MacGregor Knox, *Mussolini Unleashed, 1939–1941* (Cambridge, United Kingdom: Cambridge University Press, 1982), 76.
100. Smith (1983), 161.
101. Bosworth, 215.
102. A. James Gregor, *Mussolini's Intellectuals* (Princeton, New Jersey: Princeton University Press, 2005), 86.
103. Farrell, 359.
104. Bosworth, 1. See also Farrell, 99.
105. Farrell, 140.
106. Bosworth, 381.
107. Palla, 57.
108. Bosworth, 188.
109. Farrell, 236.
110. Valerie Warrior, *Roman Religion* (Cambridge, United Kingdom: Cambridge University Press, 2006), 82.
111. Ibid., 89–91.
112. Gentile, 86.
113. Farrell, 275.
114. Ibid., 269.
115. Bosworth, 367.
116. Alberto Sbacchi, *Ethiopia Under Mussolini* (London: Zed, 1985), 167–168.
117. Ibid., 169.
118. Susan Zuccotti, *The Italians and the Holocaust* (New York: Basic Books, 1987), 58–59
119. Bosworth, 415
120. Gregor, 215, n. 104.
121. Bosworth., 400.
122. Gentile, 103–104.
123. Farrell, 309–310.

124. Koon, 241.
125. Zuccotti, 39.
126. Bosworth, 411.
127. Fermi, 300–301.
128. Palla, 35–36.
129. Bosworth, 566.
130. Gentile, 112.
131. Palla, 117–118.
132. Fermi, 415.
133. Bosworth, 445.
134. Ibid., 446.
135. Ibid., 443–444.
136. Farrell, 335.
137. Bosworth, 466.
138. Ibid., 458–459.
139. Palla, 124.
140. Farrell, 376.
141. Max Ascoli, "Preface: The Mussolini Story," in Mussolini, *My Rise and Fall*, Vol. II, 15.
142. Farrell, 450.
143. Bosworth, 525.
144. Ibid., 527.
145. Fermi, 442.
146. Bosworth, 510–511.
147. Farrell, 430; and F.W. Deakin, *The Brutal Friendship* (London: Phoenix Press, 1962), 796–797.
148. Bosworth, 552–553.
149. Ibid., 519.
150. Gregor, 219.
151. Quoted in Berezin, 18–19.
152. Berezin, 7.
153. Spackman, 116.
154. Perloff, 80.

Chapter 13

1. Quoted in Robert Crassweller, *Perón and the Enigmas of Argentina* (New York: Norton, 1987), 7.
2. Gabriela Nouzeilles and Graciela Montaldo (eds.), *The Argentina Reader* (Durham, North Carolina: Duke University Press, 2002), 5.
3. Crassweller, 19.
4. Julia Rodriguez, *Civilizing Argentina* (Chapel Hill, North Carolina: University of North Carolina Press, 2006), 14.
5. Roberto Aizcorbe, *Argentina: The Perónist Myth* (Hicksville, New York: Exposition Press, 1975), 14.
6. Maria Flores, *The Woman with the Whip* (Garden City, New York: Doubleday, 1952), 50.
7. David Rock, *Argentina, 1516–1987* (Berkeley: University of California Press, 1987), 7.
8. Martin Edwin Andersen, *Dossier Secreto* (Boulder, Colorado: Westview, 1993), 127.
9. Nouzeilles and Montaldo, 16.

10. John A. Crow, *The Epic of Latin America* (4th ed.) (Berkeley: University of California Press, 1992), 34.
11. Ibid., 456–457.
12. Jonathan Brown, *A Brief History of Argentina* (New York: Checkmark Books, 2004), 107.
13. David Viñas, "The Foundation of the National State," in Nouzeilles and Montaldo (eds.), 162–163.
14. Charles Darwin, "Wars of Extermination," in Nouzeilles and Montaldo (eds.), 117.
15. Rock (1987), 123.
16. *Argentina* (London: Insight Guides, 2006), *passim*.
17. Rock (1987), 23.
18. Ibid., 14.
19. Ibid., 58–59.
20. Brown, 120.
21. Crow, 191–208, *passim*.
22. Brown, 38.
23. Ibid., 39.
24. Crassweller, 58.
25. Ibid., 64.
26. Crow, 565.
27. See Domingo Faustino Sarmiento, *Facundo: Civilization and Barbarism*, translated by Kathleen Ross (Berkeley, California: University of California Press, 2003), *passim*.
28. Crow, 135.
29. Daniel James, *Resistance and Integration* (Cambridge: Cambridge University Press, 1988), 31.
30. David Rock, "Argentina, 1930–1946," in Leslie Bethell (ed.), *Argentina Since Independence* (Cambridge: Cambridge University Press, 1993), 206.
31. Aizcorbe, 14.
32. Crow, 568; Nouzeillo and Montaldo, 159.
33. John Lynch, "From Independence to National Organization," in Bethell (ed.), 15.
34. Brown, 122.
35. Crassweller, 29.
36. Lynch, in Bethell (ed.), 14–15.
37. Judith L. Elkin, *The Jews of Latin America* (New York: Holmes and Meier, 1998), 58.
38. Crassweller, 53.
39. Ibid., 48.
40. Rodriguez, 243.
41. Nouzeilles and Montaldo, 157.
42. Crassweller, 45–46.
43. Roberto Cortés Conde, "The Growth of the Argentine Economy," in Bethell (ed.), 55.
44. Ezequiel Gallo, "Society and Politics, 1880–1916," Ibid., 88.
45. Brown, 167.
46. See David Beisel, "French

Group-Fantasies and the Origins of the Second World War," *The Journal of Psychohistory*, Winter, 2008, 287–304, *passim*.

47. Rodriguez, 108.
48. Ibid., 107–108.
49. Rock (1987), 176.
50. Rodriguez, 132.
51. Crassweller, 81.
52. Quoted in Ibid., 81.
53. James, 26–27.
54. Crow, 584.
55. Brown, 129–130.
56. Sarmiento, 221.
57. Ibid., 226.
58. Crow, 588.
59. Lynch in Bethell (ed.), 27.
60. Diana Taylor, *Disappearing Acts* (Durham, North Carolina: Duke University Press, 1997), 231.
61. Lynch, in Bethell (ed.), 22.
62. Crassweller, 38.
63. Andersen, 188.
64. Pablo T. Spiller and Mariano Tommasi, "The Institutional Foundations of Public Policy: A Transaction Cost Approach and Its Application to Argentina," in Steven Levitsky and Maria Victoria Murillo (eds.), *Argentine Democracy* (University Park, Pennsylvania: Pennsylvania State University Press, 2005), 46.
65. Juan Carlos Torre and Liliana de Riz, "Argentina Since 1946," in Bethell (ed.), 350.
66. David Rock, *Authoritarian Argentina* (Berkeley: University of California Press, 1993), 7–8.
67. Taylor, 37.
68. Rock (1993), xvii.
69. Rock, in Bethell (ed.), 202.
70. Rock (1993), 1.
71. Rock (1987), 143.
72. Rock (1993), 65–66.
73. Brown, 176–177.
74. Elkin, 98.
75. Rock (1993), 67.
76. Ibid., 23.
77. Elkin, 260.
78. Rock (1987), 244.
79. Rock (1993), xix.
80. James, 14.
81. Rock (1987), 216.
82. Brown, 188–189.
83. Crassweller, 74.
84. Crow, 841.
85. Rock (1993), 133.
86. Crassweller, 102.
87. Ibid., 110.
88. Rock (1987), 249–250.
89. Patricia Marchak, *God's Assassins* (Montreal: McGill-Queens University Press, 1999), 47.
90. Crassweller, 152–153.
91. Mariano Ben Plotkin, *Mañana es San Perón: A Cultural History of Perón's Argentina* (Wilmington, Delaware: Scholarly Resources, 2003), ix.

92. Ibid., 196.
93. Crassweller, 227–228.
94. Plotkin, 24.
95. Crassweller., 228.
96. Flores, 46.
97. James, 23.
98. Rock (1993), 126.
99. James W. McGuire, *Peronism Without Perón* (Stanford, California: Stanford University Press, 1997), 60–61.
100. Crassweller, 176.
101. James, 32–33.
102. Taylor, 44.
103. John Barnes, *Evita: First Lady* (New York: Grove Press, 1978), 76.
104. Tomás Eloy Martinez, "Saint Evita," in Nouzeilles and Montaldo (eds.), 298.
105. Crassweller, 210; Barnes, 115–116.
106. Barnes, 68.
107. Flores, 180–190.
108. Crassweller, 206–207.
109. Ibid., 247.
110. Ibid., 215.
111. Quoted in Aizcorbe, 50.
112. Plotkin, 165.
113. Ibid., 109.
114. Flores, 242.
115. Crassweller, 133.
116. Barnes, 171.
117. Crassweller, 273–274.
118. Ibid., 274.
119. McGuire, 50.
120. James, 13.
121. Brown, 209–210.
122. McGuire, 57.
123. Daniel James, "Perón and the People," in Nouzeilles and Montaldo (eds.), 275.
124. Crassweller, 118.
125. Flores, 232.
126. Rock (1987), 302–303.
127. James, 34; Rock (1987), 265.
128. James, 69.
129. McGuire, 76–77.
130. Marguerite Feitlowitz, *A Lexicon of Terror* (New York: Oxford University Press, 1988), 124.
131. Rock (1987), 312.
132. Marchak, 57–58.
133. Crassweller, 203.
134. Brown, 214.
135. Ibid., 214; Rock (1993), 165.
136. Marchak, 57.
137. Crassweller, 272; Brown, 214.
138. Andersen, 31.
139. Brown, 214.
140. Plotkin, 164.
141. Rock (1987), 305–306.
142. Andersen, 185.
143. Ibid., 70–71.
144. James, 206–207.
145. McGuire, 160–161.
146. Ibid., 126–127.

147. Ibid., 146–147.
148. Ibid., 140.
149. James, 207.
150. Marchak, 182.
151. Ibid., 342.
152. Ibid., 100.
153. Richard Gillespie, "Montoneros: Soldiers of Perón," in Nouzeilles and Montaldo (eds.), 381.
154. Rock (1987), 352–355.
155. McGuire, 163.
156. Brown, 234.
157. Marie Langer, *From Vienna to Managua* (London: Free Association Books, 1989), 127–128.
158. Marchak, 113.
159. Andersen, 83.
160. Ibid., 50.
161. Ibid., 83.
162. Ibid., 151–152.
163. McGuire, 158.
164. Naomi Klein, *The Shock Doctrine* (New York: Metropolitan Books, 2007), 97.
165. Andersen, 13.
166. John Dinges, *The Condor Years* (New York: The New Press, 2004), 82.
167. Marchak, 305.
168. Dinges, 205.
169. Rock (1993), 227.
170. Klein, 96.
171. Marchak, 228.
172. Taylor, 11.
173. Crow, 850–851.
174. Brown, 240.
175. Taylor, 130.
176. Feitlowitz, 159.
177. Anthony Pereira, *Political (In)justice* (Pittsburgh, Pennsylvania: University of Pittsburgh Press, 2005), 133.
178. Taylor, 183.
179. Feitlowitz, 27–28.
180. Andersen, 196.
181. Feitlowitz, 106.
182. Andersen, 242.
183. Ibid., 145.
184. Marchak, 302–303.
185. Dinges, 225–226.
186. Langer, 153.
187. Rock (1993), 116–117.
188. Rock (1987), 370.
189. Crow, 849.
190. Marchak, 148.
191. Taylor, 13.
192. Feitlowitz, 212.

Chapter 14

1. Mark Kurlansky, *A Continent of Islands* (Cambridge, Massachusetts: Perseus Publishing, 1992), 178–179.
2. Ibid., 162.
3. Peter Hallward, *Damming the Flood* (London: Verso, 2007), 1–2.

4. Kurlansky, 34.
5. Elizabeth Abbott, *Haiti: An Insider's History of the Rise and Fall of the Duvaliers* (New York: Touchstone, 1988), 276.
6. Hyppolite Pierre, *Haiti: Rising Flames from Burning Ashes* (Lanham, Maryland: University Press of America, 2006), 328.
7. Ibid., 328; Hallward, 7.
8. Michel-Rolph Trouillot, "Haiti's Nightmare and the Lessons of History," in North American Congress on Latin America (NACLA) (ed.), *Haiti: Dangerous Crossroads* (Boston: South End Press, 1995), 121–122.
9. Lloyd de Mause, "The Childhood Origins of World War II and the Holocaust," *The Journal of Psychohistory*, Summer 2008, Vol. 36 No. 1, 14.
10. Doris Garraway, *The Libertine Colony* (Durham, North Carolina: Duke University Press, 2005), 8; Paul Farmer, *The Uses of Haiti* (Monroe, Maine: Common Courage Press, 2006), 55.
11. Garraway, 127.
12. Ibid., 128.
13. Laurent Dubois, *Avengers of the New World* (Cambridge, Massachusetts: Belknap Press, 2004), 39.
14. Kurlansky, 46.
15. Garraway, 241.
16. Ibid., 240.
17. Kurlansky, 46.
18. Dubois, 42–43.
19. David Nicholls, *From Dessalines to Duvalier* (New Brunswick, New Jersey: Rutgers University Press, 1996), 20
20. C.L.R. James, *The Black Jacobins* (New York: Vintage, 1989), 41.
21. Dubois, 62.
22. Ibid., 64.
23. Ibid., 54–55.
24. James, 19.
25. Wade Davis, *The Serpent and the Rainbow* (New York: Touchstone, 1997), 193–194.
26. Jeremy Popkin, *Facing Racial Revolution* (Chicago: University of Chicago Press, 2007), 278.
27. James, 32.
28. Garraway, 28.
29. Davis, 66; James Ferguson, *Papa Doc, Baby Doc* (Oxford: Basil Blackwell, 1987), 16.
30. Dubois, 302.
31. James, ix.
32. Ibid., 42–43.
33. Pierre, 39.
34. Maya Deren, *Divine Horsemen: The Living Gods of Haiti* (Kingston, New York: McPherson and Co., 2004), 272.
35. Madison Smartt Bell, *Toussaint L'Ouverture* (New York: Vintage, 2007), 174.
36. Joan Dayan, *Haiti, History and the Gods* (Berkeley: University of California Press, 1995), 16–17.
37. Nicholls, 33.
38. Ferguson, 13.
39. Michel-Rolph Trouillot, *Haiti: State Against Nation* (New York: Monthly Review Press, 1990), 48.
40. Pierre, 24.
41. Trouillot (1990), 217.
42. Kim Ives, "The Lavalas Alliance Propels Aristide to Power," in NACLA (ed.), 42.
43. Sidney Mintz, *Caribbean Transformations* (New York: Columbia University Press, 1989), 273.
44. Kurlansky, 52.
45. Dubois, 244.
46. Kurlansky, 78–79.
47. Nicholls, 132–133.
48. Deren, 179.
49. Mintz, 301.
50. Nicholls, 60.
51. Catherine Orenstein, "An Interview with Ben Dupuy," in NACLA (ed.), 95–96.
52. Hallward, 4.
53. Trouillot (1990), 127.
54. Dayan, 15.
55. Michael Deibert, *Notes from the Last Testament* (New York: Seven Stories Press, 2005), 12–13.
56. Nicholls, 64–65.
57. Dayan, 10.
58. Bernard Diederich and Al Burt, *Papa Doc and the Tontons Macoutes* (Princeton, New Jersey: Marcus Weiner, 2005), 347.
59. Bell, 203–204.
60. Dubois, 239.
61. Randall Robinson, *An Unbroken Agony* (New York: Basic Books, 2007), 38–39.
62. Ferguson, 15.
63. Trouillot in NACLA (ed.), 124.
64. Irwin Stotsky, *Silencing the Guns in Haiti* (Chicago: University of Chicago Press, 1997), 20.
65. Dubois, 248.
66. Abbott, 28.
67. Diederich and Burt, 30.
68. Kathie Klarreich, *Madame Dread* (New York: Nation Books, 2005), 69–70.
69. Abbott, 256.
70. Robinson, 122.
71. Abbott, 190.
72. Deren, 43 n.
73. Davis, 80.
74. Ibid., 116.
75. Pierre, 310–311.
76. Max-G. Beauvoir, "Herbs and Energy: The Holistic Medical System of the Haitian People," in Patrick Bellegarde-Smith and Claudine Michel (eds.), *Haitian Voudou* (Bloomington, Indiana: Indiana University Press, 2006), 129.
77. Dubois, 102.
78. Deibert, 202.
79. Deren, 61.
80. Ibid., 62–63.
81. Davis, 172.
82. Deren, 115.
83. Ibid., 95.
84. Beauvoir in Bellegarde-Smith and Michel (eds.), 127–129.
85. Trouillot (1990), 13–14.
86. Max Boot, *The Savage Wars of Peace* (New York: Basic Books, 2002), 157.
87. Nicholls, 108.
88. Farmer, 67.
89. Robinson, 20–22.
90. Farmer, 73.
91. Nicholls, 143.
92. Farmer, 77–78.
93. Nicholls, 146.
94. Trouillot, 129.
95. Nicholls, 142.
96. Farmer, 83–84.
97. Dayan, 87.
98. Farmer, 82–83.
99. Abbott, 43
100. Ibid., 49–50.
101. Michelle Wucker, *Why the Cocks Fight* (New York: Hill and Wang, 1999), 46*ff* and 102.
102. Diedrich and Burt, 47–48.
103. Quoted in Kurlansky, 50.
104. Nicholls, 166–167.
105. Dayan, 30.
106. Diederich and Burt, 102–103.
107. Ferguson, 33.
108. Ibid., 34.
109. Nicholls, 191–192.
110. Pierre, 93–94.
111. Mintz, 288.
112. Diederich and Burt, 61.
113. Abbott, 57.
114. Diederich and Burt, 13.
115. Trouillot, 136; Farmer, 91–92.
116. Abbott, 55.
117. Diederich and Burt, 42.
118. Nicholls, 150–151.
119. Abbott, 51.
120. Ferguson, 38.
121. Ibid., 39.
122. Abbott, 101–102.
123. Ibid., 142.
124. Ibid., 137.
125. Diederich and Burt, 368.
126. Nicholls, 172.
127. Diederich and Burt, 174.
128. Ibid., 225.
129. Nicholls, 237.
130. Diederich and Burt, 115*ff*.
131. Abbott, 96–97.
132. Diederich and Burt, 169; Abbott, 103.

133. Pierre, 107.
134. Diederich and Burt, 276.
135. Ibid., 279.
136. Ferguson, 58.
137. Abbott, 302
138. Trouillot, 190.
139. Diederich and Burt, 224.
140. Ibid., 173.
141. Farmer, 142.
142. Davis, 257.
143. Abbott, 87.
144. Ibid., 118.
145. Farmer, 95.
146. Trouillot, 168.
147. Hallward, 155.
148. Diederich and Burt, 269.
149. Nicholls, 246–247.
150. Diederich and Burt, 349.
151. Pierre, 106.
152. Diederich and Burt, 345.
153. Trouillot, 16–17.
154. Davis, 250.
155. See Abbott, following 244.
156. Ibid., 61.
157. Ibid., 96 and 144.
158. Diederich and Burt, 396–397.
159. Trouillot, 207.
160. Deibert, 24.
161. Wucker, 115.
162. Abbott, 250.
163. Ibid., 172–173.
164. Ibid., 219.
165. Ferguson, 72.
166. Hallward, 15.
167. Kurlansky, 288.
168. Farmer, 193.
169. Ferguson, 82.
170. Deibert, 24.
171. Abbott, 324–325.
172. Trouillot, 222.
173. Stotzky, 190–191.
174. Hallward, 28.
175. Wucker, 118.
176. Deibert, 25.
177. Stotzky, 161.
178. Pierre, 122–123.
179. Farmer, 381.
180. Hallward, 32.
181. *Country Studies: Dominican Republic and Haiti* (Washington, DC: Federal Research Division, Library of Congress, 2001), 302–303.
182. Farmer, 134–135.
183. Anne-Christine D'Adesky, "Père Lebrun in Context," in NACLA (ed.), 176.
184. Greg Chamberlain, "Haiti's Second Independence: Aristide's Nine Months in Office," in NACLA (ed.), 55.
185. Federal Research Division, 304.
186. Hallward, 35.
187. Ibid., 40–41.
188. Farmer, 183.
189. Pierre, 132.
190. Robinson, 180.
191. Catherine Orenstein, "What

Do Haitians Want from the United States?" in NACLA (ed.), 90–91.
192. Hallward, 42
193. Farmer, 321.
194. Deibert, 41.
195. Farmer, 221.
196. Hallward, 44.
197. Nicholls, xxxi.
198. Hallward, 53.
199. Stotzky, 157–158.
200. Hallward, 44.
201. Deibert, 128.
202. Hallward, 80–81.
203. Ibid., 132.
204. Robinson, 148–149.
205. Hallward, 261.
206. Ibid., 252.
207. Deibert, 128 and 131.
208. Ibid., 357.
209. Hallward, 124.
210. Deibert, 369.
211. Ibid., 141–142.
212. Jonathan Kozol, "Foreword," in Farmer, 12.
213. Klarreich, 320.
214. Deibert, 367.
215. Hallward, 157–158.
216. Stotzky, 202.
217. Deibert, 2–3.
218. Ibid., 355.
219. Ibid., 292.
220. Ibid., 290.
221. Ibid., 395.
222. Hallward, 66.
223. Robinson, 43–45.
224. Farmer, 398–399.
225. Deibert, 395.
226. Robinson, 194.
227. Hallward, 206.
228. Deibert, 416.
229. Hallward, 257–258.
230. Robinson, 254–255.
231. Ibid., 257.
232. Pierre, 250.
233. Hallward, 261.
234. Robinson, 148–149.
235. Larry Birns and Jessica Leight, "Afterword," in Farmer, 403–404.
236. Deibert, 429.
237. Robinson, 253.
238. Ibid., 253.
239. Ibid., 254–255.
240. Jean Jean-Pierre, "The 10th Department," in NACLA (ed.), 195.
241. Abbott, 145.
242. Robinson, 117.
243. Diederich and Burt, 21.

Chapter 15

1. John Allen, *Desmond Tutu: Rabble Rouser for Peace* (Chicago: Lawrence Hill Books, 2008), 11.
2. Padraig O'Malley, *Shades of Difference* (New York: Penguin, 2007), 27.

3. Allen, 12.
4. Ibid., 18.
5. Leonard Thompson and Andrew Prior, *South African Politics* (New Haven: Yale University Press, 1982), 173–174.
6. Joseph Lelyveld, *Move Your Shadow* (New York: Random House, 1985), 15.
7. Peter Lambley, *The Psychology of Apartheid* (Athens, Georgia: University of Georgia Press, 1980), 30.
8. Brian Bunting, *The Rise of the South African Reich* (Harmondsworth, United Kingdom: Penguin, 1964), 83.
9. Conor Cruise O'Brien, *Passion and Cunning* (New York: Touchstone, 1989), 153.
10. State Information Office, *The South African Indian, 1956*, Pretoria, n.d., 4.
11. The *Progress of the Bantu Peoples Toward Nationhood, Vol. 1: Self-Government* (Johannesburg: Union of South Africa Government Information Service, 1960), 12.
12. Heribert Adam and Kogila Moodley, *South Africa Without Apartheid* (Berkeley, California: University of California Press, 1986), 158.
13. Courtney Jung, *Then I Was Black* (New Haven: Yale University Press, 2000), 202.
14. Antjie Krog, *The Country of My Skull* (New York: Three Rivers Press, 2000), 289.
15. Lelyveld, 156.
16. O'Malley, 94.
17. Jeremy Seekings, *The UDF* (Athens, Ohio: Ohio University Press, 2000), 4.
18. Jung, 42.
19. O'Malley, 62.
20. Jung, 43.
21. O'Malley, 63.
22. Tudor Parfitt, *Journey to the Vanished City* (New York: Vintage, 1992), *passim*.
23. Stephen Taylor, *Shaka's Children: A History of the Zulu People* (New York: HarperCollins, 1995), 75 and 319.
24. Bill Berkeley, *The Graves Are Not Yet Full* (New York: Basic Books, 2001), 157.
25. Mzala, *Gatsha Buthelezi: Chief with a Double Agenda* (New York: St. Martin's Press, 1988), 9.
26. Ibid., 15–16.
27. Ibid., 120.
28. Andrew Reynolds, "The Results," in Andrew Reynolds (ed.), *Election '99 South Africa* (New York: St. Martin's Press, 1999), 197.
29. Martin Murray, *South Africa:*

Time of Agony, Time of Destiny (London Verso, 1987), 285.

30. Mzala, 133–134.
31. Murray, 120.
32. Mzala, 116–117.
33. Taylor, 68.
34. Jung, 104.
35. J.B. Peires, *The House of Phalo* (Berkeley: University of California Press, 1981), 40.
36. Michael Cross and Linda Chisholm, "The Roots of Segregated Schooling in Twentieth Century South Africa," in Mokubung Nkomo (ed.), *Pedagogy of Domination* (Trenton, New Jersey: Africa World Press, 1990), 124.
37. Mzala, 52–53.
38. Allister Sparks, *The Mind of South Africa* (New York: Ballantine Books, 1990), 274.
39. Jung, 97.
40. Ibid., 4–6.
41. Allen, 332.
42. Ibid., 325.
43. Berkeley, 144.
44. Ibid., 147.
45. Ibid., 149.
46. Pierre Van den Berghe, *South Africa: A Study in Conflict* (Berkeley, California: University of California Press, 1967), 297.
47. Bunting, 40–41.
48. Ian Goldin, *Making Race* (Cape Town: Maskew Miller Longman, 1987), 133–134.
49. Murray, 59–60.
50. Allen, 337.
51. Jung, 208.
52. Van den Berghe, 65.
53. Goldin, 32 ff.
54. Ibid., 63.
55. Baruch Hirson, *Year of Fire, Year of Ash* (London: Zed Press, 1979), 216–217.
56. Goldin, 103–104.
57. Jung, 172.
58. Ibid., 199–200.
59. Goldin, 58–59.
60. Jung, 172.
61. Van den Berghe, 177.
62. Julie Fredrikse, *The Unbreakable Thread* (Bloomington: University of Indiana Press, 1990), 188.
63. Tom Lodge, *Black Politics in South Africa Since 1945* (London: Longman, 1983), 301.
64. Ibid., 34.
65. Tom Lodge, *Consolidating Democracy* (Johannesburg: Witwatersrand University Press, 1999), 141–142.
66. Ibid., 148.
67. Lodge (1999), 8.
68. Adam and Moodley, 171.
69. Van den Berghe, 297.
70. *The South African Indian, 1956*, 10.
71. H.J. and R.E. Simons, *Class and Colour in South Africa* (Baltimore: Penguin, 1969), 505–507.
72. O'Malley, 44.
73. Ibid., 215.
74. Lodge (1999), 72–73.
75. Ibid., 16.
76. Jung, 175.
77. Frederikse, 108.
78. Hirson, 7.
79. Ibid., 84.
80. Ibid., 291.
81. Ibid., 297.
82. Sparks, 267.
83. Hirson, 305.
84. Ibid., 77.
85. Robert Fatton, Jr., *Black Consciousness in South Africa* (Albany, New York: State University of New York Press, 1986), 66–67.
86. Ibid., 56–57.
87. Sparks, 74–75.
88. Adam and Moodley, 60–61.
89. Vincent Crapanzano, *Waiting: The Whites of South Africa* (New York: Random House, 1985), 209–210.
90. Pumla Gobodo-Madikizela, *A Human Being Died That Night* (Boston: Houghton-Mifflin, 2003), 53.
91. Jung, 123.
92. Gobodo-Madikizela, 147.
93. Jung, 184.

Bibliography

Abbot, Elizabeth. *Haiti: An Insider's History of the Rise and Fall of the Duvaliers.* New York: Touchstone, 1988.

Abrahamian, Ervand. *Iran Between Two Revolutions.* Princeton, New Jersey: Princeton University Press, 1982.

Adam, Heribert, and Kogila Moodley. *South Africa Without Apartheid.* Berkeley, California: University of California Press, 1986.

Adams, Gerry. *A Farther Shore.* New York: Random House, 2005.

_____. *The Politics of Irish Freedom.* Dingle, Ireland: Brandon, 1986.

Adelman, Howard, and Astri Suhrke (eds.). *The Path of a Genocide.* New Brunswick, New Jersey: Transaction, 2000.

Aizcorbe, Roberto. *Argentina: The Perónist Myth.* Hicksville, New York: Exposition Press, 1975.

Ajami, Fouad. *The Arab Predicament.* Cambridge, United Kingdom: Cambridge University Press, 1992.

Akçam, Taner. *A Shameful Act.* New York: Metropolitan Books, 2006.

Ali, Taisier, and Robert O. Matthews. *Civil Wars in Africa.* Montreal: McGill-Queens University Press, 1999.

Allen, John. *Desmond Tutu: Rabble-Rouser for Peace.* Chicago: Lawrence Hill Books, 2008.

Allen, William Sheridan. *The Nazi Seizure of Power.* New York: New Viewpoints, 1973.

Andersen, Martin Edwin. *Dossier Secreto.* Boulder, Colorado: Westview, 1993.

Andrew, Christopher, and Vasili Mitrokhin. *The World Was Going Our Way.* New York: Basic Books, 2005.

Arasaratnam, Sinnahpah. *Ceylon.* Englewood Cliffs, New Jersey: Prentice-Hall, 1964.

Atabaki, Touraj. *Azerbaijan.* London: I.B. Tauris, 2000.

Balakian, Peter. *The Burning Tigris.* New York: HarperCollins, 2002.

Banac, Ivo. *The National Question in Yugoslavia.* Ithaca, New York: Cornell University Press, 1984.

Baraheni, Reza. *The Crowned Cannibals.* New York: Vintage, 1977.

Barnes, John. *Evita: First Lady.* New York: Grove Press, 1978.

Barnett, Michael. *Eyewitness to a Genocide.* Ithaca, New York: Cornell University Press, 2002.

Bartholomeusz, Tessa J., and Chandra R. De Silva (eds.). *Buddhist Fundamentalism and Minority Identities in Sri Lanka.* New York: State University of New York Press, 1998.

Baruah, Sanjib. *India Against Itself.* Philadelphia: University of Pennsylvania Press, 1999.

Barzini, Luigi. *The Italians.* New York: Atheneum, 1964.

Baum, Richard, and Louise Bennett (eds.). *China in Ferment.* Englewood Cliffs, New Jersey: Prentice-Hall, 1971.

Bayat, Assef. *Workers and Revolution in Iran.* London: Zed, 1987.

Becker, Elizabeth. *When the War Was Over.* New York: Simon and Schuster, 1986.

Belfrage, Sally. *Living with War.* New York: Viking, 1987.

Bell, Geoffrey. *The Protestants of Ulster.* London: Pluto Press, 1978.

Bell, Madison Smartt. *Toussaint L'Ouverture.* New York: Vintage, 2007.

Bellegarde-Smith, Patrick, and Claudine Michel (eds.). *Haitian Voudou.* Bloomington, Indiana: Indiana University Press, 2006.

Benard, Cheryl, and Zalmay Khalilzad. *The Government of God: Iran's Islamic Republic.* New York: Columbia University Press, 1984.

Ben-Ghiat, Ruth. *Fascist Modernities.* Berkeley, California: University of California Press, 2001.

Bennett, Gordon, and Ronald Montaperto. *Red Guard.* Garden City, New York: Anchor, 1974.

Berkeley, Bill. *The Graves Are Not Yet Full.* New York: Basic Books, 2001.

Bethell, Leslie (ed.). *Argentina Since Independence.* Cambridge, United Kingdom: Cambridge University Press, 1993.

Bizot, François. *The Gate.* New York: Knopf, 2003.

Bok, Francis, with Edward Tivnan. *Escape From Slavery.* New York: St. Martins Griffin, 2003.

Bonine, Michael, and Nikki Keddie (eds.). *Continuity and Change in Modern Iran.* Albany: State University of New York Press, 1981.

Boot, Max. *The Savage Wars of Peace.* New York: Basic Books, 2002.

Borghi, Armando. *Mussolini: Red and Black*. New York: Haskell House, 1974.

Boroujerdi, Mehrzad. *Iranian Intellectuals and the West*. Syracuse, New York: Syracuse University Press, 1996.

Bose, Sumantra. *Contested Lands*. Cambridge, Massachusetts: Harvard University Press, 2007.

Bosworth, R.J.B. *Mussolini's Italy*. New York: Penguin, 2006.

Brass, Paul, and Marcus Franda (eds.). *Radical Politics in South Asia*. Cambridge, Massachusetts: MIT Press, 1973.

Brown, Jonathan. *A Brief History of Argentina*. New York: Checkmark Books, 2004.

Brown, Kerry. *The Purge of the Inner Mongolian People's Party in the Chinese Cultural Revolution, 1967–69*. Folkestone, United Kingdom: Global Oriental, 2006.

Bruce, Steve. *God Save Ulster*. Oxford, United Kingdom: Oxford University Press, 1989.

Bryans, Robin. *Ulster: A Journey Through Six Counties*. Belfast: Blackstaff, 1964.

Bunting, Brian. *The Rise of the South African Reich*. Harmondsworth, United Kingdom: Penguin, 1964.

Burchett, Wilfred. *The China-Cambodia-Vietnam Triangle*. Chicago: Vanguard Books, 1981.

Bytwerk, Randall L. *Julius Streicher*. New York: Dorset Press, 1983.

Caldwell, Malcolm, and Lek Tan. *Cambodia in the Southeast Asian War*. New York: Monthly Review Press, 1973.

Carr, Rosamund Halsey, with Ann Howard Halsey. *Land of a Thousand Hills*. New York: Plume, 2000.

Carsten, F.L. *The Rise of Fascism*. Berkeley, California: University of California Press, 1971.

Chan, Anita. *Children of Mao*. Seattle: University of Washington Press, 1985.

Chandler, David. *Brother Number One: A Political Biography of Pol Pot*. Boulder, Colorado: Westview, 1999.

_____. *The Tragedy of Cambodian History*. New Haven, Connecticut: Yale University Press, 1991.

Chelkowski, Peter, and Hamid Dabashi. *Staging a Revolution: The Art of Persuasion in the Islamic Republic of Iran*. New York: New York University Press, 1999.

Clarke, Nicholas Goodrich. *The Occult Roots of Nazism*. New York: New York University Press, 1985.

Coe, Michael. *Angkor and the Khmer Civilization*. New York: Thames and Hudson, 2003.

Cohen, Lenard J. *Broken Bonds: The Disintegration of Yugoslavia*. Boulder, Colorado: Westview, 1993.

Collins, Robert. *A History of the Sudan*. Cambridge, United Kingdom: Cambridge University Press, 2008.

Connery, Donald S. *The Irish*. New York: Simon and Schuster, 1968.

Crapanzano, Vincent. *Waiting: The Whites of South Africa*. New York: Random House, 1985.

Crassweller, Robert. *Perón and the Enigmas of Argentina*. New York: Norton, 1987.

Criddle, Joan, and Teeda Butt Mam. *To Destroy You Is No Loss*. New York: Doubleday, 1987.

Crnobrnja, Mihailo. *The Yugoslav Drama*. Montreal: McGill-Queens University Press, 1994.

Crow, John A. *The Epic of Latin America*. Berkeley: University of California Press, 1992.

Curtis, Edmund. *A History of Ireland*. London: Methuen, 1936.

Dallaire, Romeo. *Shake Hands with the Devil*. New York: Carroll and Graf, 2003.

Daly, M.W. *Darfur's Sorrow*. New York: Cambridge University Press, 2007.

Darby, John (ed.). *Northern Ireland: The Background to the Conflict*. Belfast: Appletree Press, 1983.

Daubier, Jean. *A History of the Chinese Cultural Revolution*. New York: Vintage, 1974.

Davis, Wade. *The Serpent and the Rainbow*. New York: Touchstone, 1997.

Dayan, Joan. *Haiti, History and the Gods*. Berkeley: University of California Press, 1995.

Deakin, F.W. *The Brutal Friendship*. London: Phoenix Press, 1962.

De Grand, Alexander. *Italian Fascism*. Lincoln, Nebraska: University of Nebraska Press, 1982.

Deibert, Michael. *Notes From the Last Testament*. New York: Seven Stories Press, 2005.

DeMause, Lloyd. *Foundations of Psychohistory*. New York: Creative Roots, 1982.

Deng, Benson, Alephonsion Deng, and Benjamin Ajak. *They Poured Fire on Us from the Sky*. New York: Public Affairs, 2005.

Deren, Maya. *Divine Horsemen: The Living Gods of Haiti*. New York: McPherson and Co., Kingston, 2004.

Des Forges, Alison. *Leave None to Tell the Story*. New York: Human Rights Watch, 1999.

Diamond, Jared. *Collapse*. New York: Viking, 2005.

Diederich, Bernard, and Al Burt. *Papa Doc and the Tontons Macoutes*. Princeton, New Jersey: Marcus Weiner, 2005.

Dillon, Martin. *The Shankill Butchers*. New York: Routledge, 1999.

Dinges, John. *The Condor Years*. New York: The New Press, 2004.

Dittmer, Lowell. *Liu Shao-chi and the Chinese Cultural Revolution*. Berkeley: University of California Press, 1974.

Domarus, Max (ed.). *The Essential Hitler*. Wauconda, Illinois: Bolchazy-Carducci Publishers, 2007.

Donia, Robert, and John Fine. *Bosnia and Hercegovina: A Tradition Betrayed*. New York: Columbia University Press, 1994.

Dragnich, Alex N. *Serbs and Croats*. San Diego, California: Harcourt Brace, 1992.

Dubois, Laurent. *Avengers of the New World*. Cambridge, Massachusetts: Belknap Press, 2004.

Dunlop, Nic. *The Lost Executioner*. New York: Walker and Co., 2005.

Elkin, Judith L. *The Jews of Latin America*. New York: Holmes and Meier, 1998.

Evans, Grant, and Kevin Rowley. *Red Brotherhood at War*. London: Verso, 1984.

Evans, Richard. *The Coming of the Third Reich.* New York: Penguin, 2003.

_____. *Deng Xiaoping and the Making of Modern China.* New York: Penguin, 1993.

Farmaian, Setarrah Farma. *Daughter of Persia.* New York: Anchor, 1992.

Farmer, Paul. *The Uses of Haiti.* Monroe, Maine: Common Courage Press, 2006.

Farrell, Michael. *Northern Ireland: The Orange State.* London: Pluto Press, 1980.

Farrell, Nicholas. *Mussolini: A New Life.* London: Phoenix, 2004.

Fatton, Robert, Jr. *Black Consciousness in South Africa.* Albany, New York: State University of New York Press, 1986.

Federal Research Division, Library of Congress. *Country Studies: Dominican Republic and Haiti.* Washington, DC: 2001.

Feitlowitz, Marguerite. *A Lexicon of Terror.* New York: Oxford University Press, 1988.

Ferdowsi, Abolqasem. *Shahnameh* (translated by Dick Davis). New York: Penguin, 2006.

Ferguson, James. *Papa Doc, Baby Doc.* Oxford, United Kingdom: Basil Blackwell, 1987.

Fermi, Laura. *Mussolini.* Chicago: University of Chicago Press, 2003.

Fernea, Elizabeth Warnock. *Remembering Childhood in the Middle East.* Austin, Texas: University of Texas Press, 2002.

Fest, Joachim. *Hitler.* New York: Harcourt, Brace & Jovanovich, 1973.

Fields, Rona. *Northern Ireland: Society Under Siege.* Philadelphia: Temple University Press, 1980.

Fischer, Klaus P. *Nazi Germany: A New History.* New York: Continuum, 1995.

Fischer, Michael M.J. *Iran: From Religious Dispute to Revolution.* Cambridge, Massachusetts: Harvard University Press, 1980, p. 189.

Fischer, Peter. *Fantasy and Politics.* Madison, Wisconsin: University of Wisconsin Press, 1991.

Flint, Julie, and Alex de Waal. *Darfur: A Short History of a Long War.* London: Zed, 2005.

Flood, Charles Bracelen. *Hitler: The Path to Power.* Boston: Houghton Mifflin, 1989.

Flores, Maria. *The Woman with the Whip.* Garden City, New York: Doubleday, 1952.

Flowers, S. Edred. *Fire and Ice: Magical Teachings of Germany's Greatest Secret Occult Order.* St. Paul, Minnesota: Llewellyn, 1990.

Forbis, William. *Fall of the Peacock Throne.* New York: McGraw-Hill, 1981.

Forgacs, David (ed.). *Rethinking Italian Fascism.* Lincoln, Nebraska: University of Nebraska Press, 1982.

Fornari, Harry. *Mussolini's Gadfly: Roberto Farinacci.* Nashville, Tennessee: Vanderbilt University Press, 1971.

Foster, R.F. *Modern Ireland.* New York: Penguin, 1988.

Fredrikse, Julie. *The Unbreakable Thread.* Bloomington, Indiana: University of Indiana Press, 1990.

Friedman, Francine. *The Bosnian Muslims: Denial of a Nation.* Boulder, Colorado: Westview, 1996.

Fulang Lo. *Morning Breeze.* San Francisco, California: China Books, 1989.

Gao Yuan. *Born Red.* Stanford, California: Stanford University Press, 1987.

Garraway, Doris. *The Libertine Colony.* Durham, North Carolina Duke University Press, 2005.

Gazi, Stephen. *A History of Croatia.* New York: Barnes & Noble Books, 1973.

Gentile, Emilio. *The Sacralization of Politics in Fascist Italy.* Cambridge, Massachusetts: Harvard University Press, 1996.

George, Terry (ed.). *Hotel Rwanda.* New York: Newmarket Press, 2005.

Glenny, Misha. *The Fall of Yugoslavia: The Third Balkan War.* London: Penguin, 1992.

Gobodo-Madikizela, Pumla. *A Human Being Died that Night.* Boston: Houghton-Mifflin, 2003.

Goldin, Ian. *Making Race.* Cape Town: Maskew Miller Longman, 1987.

Golsan, Richard J. (ed.). *Fascism, Aesthetics, and Culture.* Hanover, New Hampshire: University Press of New England, 1992.

Gordon, Sarah. *Hitler, Germans and the "Jewish Question."* Princeton, New Jersey: Princeton University Press, 1984.

Gottesman, Evan. *Cambodia After the Khmer Rouge.* New Haven, Connecticut: Yale University Press, 2003.

Gough, Kathleen, and Hari P. Sharma (eds.). *Imperialism and Revolution in South Asia.* New York: Monthly Review Press, 1973.

Gourevitch, Philip. *We Wish to Inform You That Tomorrow We Will Be Killed with Our Families.* New York: Picador, 1998.

Graham, Robert. *Iran: The Illusion of Power.* New York: St. Martin's, 1979.

Grandqvist, Hans. *The Red Guard.* London: Pall Mall Press, 1967.

Gregor, A. James. *Mussolini's Intellectuals.* Princeton, New Jersey: Princeton University Press, 2005.

Grunberger, Richard. *The 12-Year Reich.* New York: Ballantine, 1971.

Guha, Ramachandra. *India After Gandhi.* New York: Harper, 2007.

Halliday, Fred. *Iran: Dictatorship and Development.* Middlesex, United Kingdom: Penguin, 1979.

Hallward, Peter. *Damming the Flood.* London: Verso, 2007.

Halperin, S. William. *Germany Tried Democracy.* New York: Norton, 1946.

Hatzfeld, Jean. *Machete Season.* New York: Farrar, Strauss, and Giroux, 2005.

Heskin, Ken. *Northern Ireland: A Psychological Analysis.* New York: Columbia University Press, 1984.

Hilberg, Raoul. *The Destruction of the European Jews.* New York: Harper, 1961.

Hinton, William. *Hundred-Day War,* special issue of *Monthly Review,* New York, 1972.

Hiro, Dilip. *The Iranian Labyrinth.* New York: Nation Books, 2005.

Hirson, Baruch. *Year of Fire, Year of Ash.* London: Zed Press, 1979.

Hooper, Judith, and Dick Teresi. *The 3-Pound Universe*. New York: Dell, 1980.

Hong Yung Lee. *The Politics of the Chinese Cultural Revolution*. Berkeley: University of California Press, 1978.

Horne, Alastair. *A Savage War of Peace*. New York: New York Review of Books, 2006.

Horowitz, Donald L. *Ethnic Groups in Conflict*. Berkeley, California: University of California Press, 1985.

Houston, Christopher. *Islam, Kurds, and the Turkish Nation-State*. Oxford, United Kingdom: Berg, 2001.

Howe, Steven. *Ireland and Empire*. New York: Oxford University Press, 2000.

Hunter, Neale. *Shanghai Journal*. Hong Kong: Oxford University Press, 1988.

Ilibagiza, Immaculée. *Left to Tell*. Carlsbad, California: Hay House, 2006.

Irfani, Surhoosh. *Revolutionary Islam in Iran: Popular Liberation or Religious Dictatorship?* London: Zed, 1983.

Jackson, Karl (ed.). *Cambodia, 1975–1978: Rendezvous with Death*. Princeton, New Jersey: Princeton University Press, 1989.

Jaffrelot, Christophe (ed.). *A History of Pakistan and Its Origins*. London: Anthem Press, 2002.

James, C.L.R. *The Black Jacobins*. New York: Vintage, 1989.

James, Daniel. *Resistance and Integration*. Cambridge, United Kingdom: Cambridge University Press, 1988.

Janov, Arthur. *The Anatomy of Mental Illness*. New York: Berkley, 1971.

_____. *The Biology of Love*. Amherst, New York: Prometheus, 2000.

_____. *The Feeling Child*. New York: Touchstone, 1973.

_____. *Imprints: The Lifelong Effects of the Birth Experience*. New York: Coward-McCann, 1983.

_____. *The New Primal Scream*. Wilmington, Delaware: Enterprise, 1991.

_____. *The Primal Scream*. New York: Perigee, 1980.

_____. *Prisoners of Pain*. New York: Anchor Press, 1980.

_____, with E. Michael Holden. *Primal Man: The New Consciousness*. New York: Crowell, 1975.

Jaweed, Nasim Ahmed. *Islam's Political Culture*. Austin, Texas: University of Texas Press, 1999.

Jelavich, Barbara. *History of the Balkans, Vol. 1*. Cambridge, United Kingdom: Cambridge University Press, 1983.

Jin Qiu. *The Culture of Power*. Stanford, California: Stanford University Press, 1999.

Jok, Jok Maduk. *Sudan: Race, Religion and Violence*. Oxford, United Kingdom: Oneworld, 2007.

_____. *War and Slavery in the Sudan*. Philadelphia: University of Pennsylvania Press, 2001.

Jones, Owen Bennett. *Pakistan: Eye of the Storm*. New Haven, Connecticut: Yale University Press, 2002.

Judah, Tim. *Kosovo: War and Revenge*. New Haven: Yale University Press, 2000.

_____. *The Serbs*. New Haven: Yale University Press, 1997.

Juka, S.S. *Kosova*. New York: Waldon Press, 1989.

Jung, Courtney. *Then I Was Black*. New Haven, Connecticut: Yale University Press, 2000.

Kapferer, Bruce. *A Celebration of Demons: Exorcism and the Aesthetics of Healing in Sri Lanka*. Washington, DC: Smithsonian Institution Press, 1983.

Kaplan, Robert D. *Balkan Ghosts*. New York: Vintage, 1994.

Kappler, Andreas, Gerhard Simon and Georg Brunner (eds.). *Muslim Communities Reemerge*. Durham, North Carolina: Duke University Press, 1994.

Karnow, Stanley. *Mao and China*. New York: Viking, 1972.

Keane, Fergal. *Season of Blood*. New York: Penguin, 1996.

Kearney, Robert N. *Communalism and Language in the Politics of Ceylon*. Durham, North Carolina: Duke University Press, 1967.

Keddie, Nikki. *Roots of Revolution: An Interpretative History of Modern Iran*. New Haven, Connecticut: Yale University Press, 1981.

_____ (ed.). *Religion and Politics in Iran*. New Haven, Connecticut: Yale University Press, 1983.

Kelleher, William F., Jr. *The Troubles in Ballybogoin*. Ann Arbor, Michigan: University of Michigan Press, 2003.

Kelley, Kevin. *The Longest War*. New York: Lawrence Hill, 1982.

Kemper, Steven. *The Presence of the Past: Chronicles, Politics and Culture in Sinhala Life*. Ithaca, New York: Cornell University Press, 1991.

Keppel, Giles. *Jihad: The Trail of Political Islam*. Cambridge, Massachusetts: Belknap Press, 2002.

Kiernan, Ben, and Chanthou Boua (eds.). *Peasants and Politics in Kampuchea, 1942–1981*. London: Zed Press, 1982.

Kiernan, Ben. *How Pol Pot Came to Power*. London: Verso, 1985.

_____. *The Pol Pot Regime*. New Haven, Connecticut: Yale University Press, 1996.

Kinzer, Stephen. *Crescent and Star*. New York: Farrar, Strauss and Giroux, 2001.

_____. *A Thousand Hills*. Hoboken, New Jersey: John Wiley and Sons, 2008.

Klarreich, Kathie. *Madame Dread*. New York: Nation Books, 2005.

Klein, Naomi. *The Shock Doctrine*. New York: Metropolitan Books, 2007.

Kleinman, Arthur, and Byron Good (eds.). *Culture and Depression*. Berkeley, California: University of California Press, 1985.

Knox, MacGregor. *Mussolini Unleashed, 1939–1941*. Cambridge, United Kingdom: Cambridge University Press, 1982.

Koch, H.W. *A History of Prussia*. New York: Barnes & Noble, 1978.

Koon, Tracy. *Believe, Obey, Fight: Political Socialization of Youth in Fascist Italy, 1922–1943*. Chapel

Hill, North Carolina: University of North Carolina Press, 1985.

Koshar, Rudy. *Social Life, Local Politics and Nazism*. Chapel Hill, North Carolina: University of North Carolina Press, 1986.

Kressel, Neil. *Mass Hate*. New York: Westview, 2002.

Krog, Antjie. *The Country of My Skull*. New York: Three Rivers Press, 2000.

Kurlansky, Mark. *A Continent of Islands*. Cambridge, Massachusetts: Perseus Publishing, 1992.

Laffan, R.G.D. *The Serbs: Guardians of the Gate*. New York: Dorset Press, 1989.

Laffin, John. *Jackboot*. New York: Barnes & Noble, 1965.

Lambley, Peter. *The Psychology of Apartheid*. Athens, Georgia: University of Georgia Press, 1980.

Langer, Marie. *From Vienna to Managua*. London: Free Association Books, 1989.

Lelyveld, Joseph. *Move Your Shadow*. New York: Random House, 1985.

Levitsky, Steven, and Maria Victoria Murillo (eds.). *Argentine Democracy*. University Park, Pennsylvania: Pennsylvania State University Press, 2005.

Lewis, Bernard. *The Emergence of Modern Turkey*. New York: Oxford University Press, 2002.

Li Zhisui. *The Private Life of Chairman Mao*. New York: Random House, 1994.

Ling, Ken. *The Revenge of Heaven*. New York: Ballantine, 1972.

Lodge, Tom. *Black Politics in South Africa Since 1943*. London: Longman, 1983.

_____. *Consolidating Democracy*. Johannesburg: Witwatersrand University Press, 1999.

Lyttleton, Adrian. *The Seizure of Power: Fascism in Italy, 1919–1929*. Princeton, New Jersey: Princeton University Press, 1973.

Macciocchi, Maria Antonietta. *Daily Life in Revolutionary China*. New York: Monthly Review Press, 1972.

MacFarquhar, Roderick. *The Origins of the Cultural Revolution (Vols. I and II)*. New York: Columbia University Press, 1983.

_____, and Michael Schoenhals. *Mao's Last Revolution*. Cambridge, Massachusetts: Belknap Press, 2006.

Mackey, Sandra. *The Iranians: Persia, Islam, and the Soul of a Nation*. New York: Plume, 1998.

Magaš, Branka. *The Destruction of Yugoslavia*. London: Verso, 1993.

Majd, Hooman. *The Ayatollah Begs to Differ*. New York: Doubleday, 2005.

Malcolm, Noel. *Bosnia: A Short History*. New York: New York University Press, 1994.

Mamdani, Mahmood. *When Victims Become Killers*. Princeton, New Jersey: Princeton University Press, 2001.

Mango, Andrew. *Atatürk*. Woodstock, New York: Overlook Press, 2002.

Mann, Michael. *The Dark Side of Democracy*. Cambridge, United Kingdom: Cambridge University Press, 2005.

Mantura, Bruno et al. (eds). *Futurism in Flight*. Rome: De Luca Edizioni D'Arte, 1990.

Mao Zedong (ed.). *Socialist Upsurge in China's Countryside*. Beijing: Foreign Languages Press, 1957.

Marchak, Patricia. *God's Assassins*. Montreal: McGill-Queens University Press, 1999.

Markakis, John. *National and Class Conflict in the Horn of Africa*. London: Zed, 1990.

Martinez, Luis. *The Algerian Civil War: 1990–1998*. New York: Columbia University Press, 2000.

Marty, Martin E., and R. Scott Appleby (eds.). *Fundamentalisms Observed*. Chicago: University of Chicago Press, 1991.

McDowall, David. *A Modern History of the Kurds*. London: I.B. Tauris, 1996.

McGuire, James W. *Peronism Without Perón*. Stanford, California: Stanford University Press, 1997.

Meisner, Maurice. *Mao's China and After*. New York: Free Press, 1999.

Melvern, Linda. *Conspiracy to Murder: The Rwandan Genocide*. London: Verso, 2004.

Meredith, Martin. *The Fate of Africa*. New York: Public Affairs, 2005.

Merkl, Peter H. *Political Violence Under the Swastika*. Princeton, New Jersey: Princeton University Press, 1975.

Mertus, Julie. *Kosovo*. Berkeley: University of California Press, 1999.

Meštrović, Stjepan G. *The Balkanization of the West*. London: Routledge, 1994.

_____, with Slaven Letica and Miroslav Goreta. *Habits of the Balkan Heart: Social Character and the Fall of Communism*. College Station, Texas: Texas A&M University Press, 1993.

Meyer, G.J. *A World Undone*. New York: Delta, 2006.

Michaelis, Meir. *Mussolini and the Jews*. Oxford, United Kingdom: Clarendon, 1978.

Miller, Judith. *God Has Ninety-Nine Names*. New York: Touchstone, 1997.

Mintz, Sidney. *Caribbean Transformations*. New York: Columbia University Press, 1989.

Mohaddessin, Mohammad. *Islamic Fundamentalism*. Washington, DC: Seven Locks Press, 2001.

Moin, Baqer. *Khomeini: Life of the Ayatollah*. New York: St. Martin's Press, 1999.

Molavi, Afshin. *The Soul of Iran*. New York: Norton, 2002.

Moloney, Ed, and Andy Pollak. *Paisley*. Dublin, Ireland: Poolbeg, 1986.

Moorehead, Alan. *The White Nile*. New York: Harper-Collins, 1960.

Mottahedeh, Roy. *The Mantle of the Prophet*. New York: Pantheon, 1985.

Mukherjee, Sadham. *Ceylon: Island That Changed*. New Delhi: People's Publishing House, 1971.

Murray, Martin. *South Africa: Time of Agony, Time of Destiny*. London: Verso, 1987.

Mussolini, Benito. *My Rise and Fall*. New York: Da Capo, 1998.

Mzala. *Gatsha Buthulezi: Chief with a Double Agenda*. New York: St. Martin's Press, 1988.

Naji, Khasra. *Ahmedinejad*. Berkeley: University of California Press, 2008.

Nasar, Vali. *The Shia Revival*. New York: Norton, 2007.

Nazer, Mende, and Damien Lewis. *Slave: My True Story*. New York: Public Affairs, 2003.

Nelson, Sarah. *Ulster's Uncertain Defenders*. Syracuse, New York: Syracuse University Press, 1984.

Ngor, Haing. *A Cambodian Odyssey*. New York: Warner Books, 1987.

Nicholls, David. *From Dessalines to Duvalier*. New Brunswick, New Jersey: Rutgers University Press, 1996.

Nkomo, Mokubung (ed.). *Pedagogy of Domination*. Trenton, New Jersey: Africa World Press, 1990.

North American Congress on Latin America (NACLA) (ed.). *Haiti: Dangerous Crossroads*. Boston: South End Press, 1995.

Nouzeilles, Gabriela, and Graciela Montaldo (eds.). *The Argentina Reader*. Durham, North Carolina: Duke University Press, 2002.

O'Brien, Conor Cruise. *Passion and Cunning*. New York: Touchstone, 1989.

Odom, Tom. *Journey Into Darkness*. College Station, Texas: Texas A&M University Press, 2005.

O'Dowd, Liam, Bill Rolston, and Mike Tomlinson. *Northern Ireland: Between Civil Rights and Civil War*. London: CSE Books, 1980.

O'Malley, Padraig. *Shades of Difference*. New York: Penguin, 2007.

_____. *The Uncivil Wars*. Boston: Houghton Mifflin, 1983.

O'Mulleoir, Martin. *Belfast's Dome of Delight*. Belfast: Beyond the Pale, 1999.

Osborne, Milton. *Before Kampuchea*. North Sydney, Australia: George Allen & Unwin, 1979.

Ostović, Pavle D. *The Truth About Yugoslavia*. New York: Roy Press, 1952.

Padfield, Peter. *Himmler*. New York: Henry Holt, 1990.

Palla, Marco. *Mussolini and Fascism*. New York: Interlink, 2000.

Parfitt, Tudor. *Journey to the Vanished City*. New York: Vintage, 1992.

Peires, J.B. *The House of Phalo*. Berkeley, California: University of California Press, 1981.

Pereira, Anthony. *Political (In)justice*. Pittsburgh, Pennsylvania: University of Pittsburgh Press, 2005.

Perloff, Marjorie. *The Futurist Moment*. Chicago: University of Chicago Press, 2003.

Perry, Elizabeth, and Li Xun. *Proletarian Power*. Boulder, Colorado: Westview, 1997.

Peterson, Scott. *Me Against My Brother*. New York: Routledge, 2001.

Petterson, Don. *Inside Sudan*. Boulder, Colorado: Westview, 2003.

Pierre, Hyppolite. *Haiti: Rising Flames from Burning Ashes*. Lanham, Maryland: University Press of America, 2006.

Pipes, Daniel. *The Hidden Hand: Middle East Fears of Conspiracy*. New York: St. Martins Griffin, 1996.

Piontelli, Alessandra. *From Fetus to Child*. London: Routledge, 1992.

Piyadasa, L. *Sri Lanka: The Holocaust and After*. London: Marram Books, 1984.

Plotkin, Mariano Ben. *Mañana es San Perón: A Cultural History of Perón's Argentina*. Wilmington, Delaware: Scholarly Resources, 2003.

Pollard, John. *The Fascist Experience in Italy*. London: Routledge, 1998.

Ponnambalam, Satchi. *Sri Lanka: The National Question and the Tamil Liberation Struggle*. London: Zed Press, 1983.

Popkin, Jeremy. *Facing Racial Revolution*. Chicago: University of Chicago Press, 2007.

Poulton, Hugh. *The Balkans: Minorities and States in Conflict*. London: Minority Rights Group, 1993.

Pran, Dith (ed.). *Children of the Killing Fields*. New Haven, Connecticut: Yale University Press, 1997.

Pratap, Anita. *Island of Blood*. New York: Penguin, 2001.

Pringle, Heather. *The Master Plan: Himmler's Scholars and the Holocaust*. New York: Hyperion, 2006.

Prunier, Gérard. *Darfur: The Ambiguous Genocide*. Ithaca, New York: Cornell University Press, 2005.

_____. *The Rwanda Crisis*. New York: Columbia University Press, 1995.

Pye, Lucien, and Sydney Verba (eds.). *Political Culture and Political Development*. Princeton, New Jersey: Princeton University Press, 1965.

Ramet, Sabrina P. *Nationalism and Federalism in Yugoslavia*. Bloomington, Indiana: Indiana University Press, 1992.

Redlich, Fritz. *Hitler: Diagnosis of a Destructive Prophet*. New York: Oxford University Press, 1999.

Reuth, Ralf Georg. *Goebbels*. New York: Harcourt, Brace & Co., 1993.

Reynolds, Andrew (ed.). *Election '99 South Africa*. New York: St. Martin's Press, 1999.

Ridley, Jasper. *Mussolini*. New York: Cooper Square Press, 1998.

Roberts, Hugh. *The Battlefield: Algeria, 1988–2000*. London: Verso, 2003.

Robinson, Joan. *The Cultural Revolution in China*. Harmondsworth, United Kingdom: Pelican, 1969.

Robinson, Randall. *An Unbroken Agony*. New York: Basic Books, 2007.

Rock, David. *Argentina, 1516–1987*. Berkeley, California: University of California Press, 1987.

_____. *Authoritarian Argentina*. Berkeley, California: University of California Press, 1993.

Rodriguez, Julia. *Civilizing Argentina*. Chapel Hill, North Carolina: University of North Carolina Press, 1975.

Rosenbaum, Ron. *Explaining Hitler*. New York: HarperCollins, 1999.

Rubin, Barry. *Paved with Good Intentions*. Middlesex, United Kingdom: Penguin, 1980.

Ruedy, John. *Modern Algeria*. Bloomington, Indiana: Indiana University Press, 1992.

Ryan, Bryce. *Caste in Modern Ceylon*. New Brunswick, New Jersey: Rutgers University Press, 1953.

Ryder, Chris, and Vincent Kearney. *Drumcree:*

The Orange Order's Last Stand. London: Metheun, 2001.

Salvemini, Gaetano. *The Origins of Fascism in Italy.* New York: Harper, 1973.

Sayid, Khalid B. *The Political System of Pakistan.* Boston: Houghton Mifflin, 1967.

Sbacchi, Alberto. *Ethiopia Under Mussolini.* London: Zed, 1985.

Schoenhals, Michael (ed.). *China's Cultural Revolution.* Armonk, New York: M.E. Sharpe, 1996.

Schulze, Reinhard. *A Modern History of the Islamic World.* New York: New York University Press, 2002.

Sciolino, Elaine. *Persian Mirrors.* New York: Free Press, 2005.

Seekings, Jeremy. *The UDF.* Athens, Ohio: Ohio University Press, 2000.

Seierstad, Åsne. *With Their Backs to the World.* New York: Basic Books, 2005.

Sell, Louis. *Slobodan Milosevic and the Destruction of Yugoslavia.* Durham, North Carolina: Duke University Press, 2002.

Short, Philip. *Mao: A Life.* New York: Henry Holt, 1999.

_____. *Pol Pot.* New York: Henry Holt, 2004.

Simone, T. Abdou Maliqalim. *In Whose Image?* Chicago: University of Chicago Press, 1994.

Simons, H.J., and R.E. Simons. *Class and Colour in South Africa.* Baltimore: Penguin, 1969.

Simpson, Christopher. *Blowback: America's Recruitment of Nazis and Its Effects on the Cold War.* New York: Weidenfeld and Nicolson, 1988.

Singhal, Damodar P. *Pakistan.* Englewood Cliffs, New Jersey: Prentice-Hall, 1972.

Sivanandan, A. *Communities of Resistance.* London: Verso, 1990.

Sklar, Dusty. *The Nazis and the Occult.* New York: Dorset Press, 1977.

Smith, Denis Mack. *Italy and Its Monarchy.* New Haven, Connecticut: Yale University Press, 1989.

_____. *Mussolini.* New York: Vintage, 1983.

Smith, Donald E. (ed.). *South Asian Politics and Religion.* Princeton, New Jersey: Princeton University Press, 1966.

Smith, Woodruff D. *The Ideological Origins of Nazi Imperialism.* New York: Oxford University Press, 1986.

Spackman, Barbara. *Fascist Virilities.* Minneapolis: University of Minnesota Press, 1996.

Sparks, Allister. *The Mind of South Africa.* New York: Ballantine, 1990.

Spence, Jonathan. *The Search for Modern China.* New York: Norton, 1990.

Staub, Ervin. *The Roots of Evil.* Cambridge, United Kingdom: Cambridge University Press, 1989.

Steidle, Brian. *The Devil Came on Horseback.* New York: Public Affairs, 2007.

Steinberg, David. *Cambodia: Its People, Its Society, Its Culture.* New Haven, Connecticut: HRAF Press, 1957.

Stotsky, Irwin. *Silencing the Guns in Haiti.* Chicago: University of Chicago Press, 1997.

Szymusiak, Molyda. *The Stones Cry Out.* New York: Hill and Wang, 1986.

Tabari, Azar, and Nahid Yeganeh (eds.). *In the Shadow of Islam: The Women's Movement in Iran.* London: Zed, 1982.

Tambiah, S.J. *Sri Lanka: Ethnic Fratricide and the Dismantling of Democracy.* Chicago: University of Chicago Press, 1986.

Tanner, Marcus. *Croatia: A Nation Forged in War.* New Haven: Yale University Press, 1997.

Taylor, Diana. *Disappearing Acts.* Durham, North Carolina: Duke University Press, 1997.

Taylor, Stephen. *Shaka's Children: A History of the Zulu People.* New York: HarperCollins, 1995.

Temple-Raston, Dina. *Justice on the Grass.* New York: Free Press, 2005.

Terrill, Ross. *Madame Mao: The White-Boned Demon.* New York: Touchstone, 1992.

Theweleit, Klaus. *Male Fantasies.* Vols I and II. Minneapolis: University of Minnesota Press, 2001 and 2002.

Thompson, Leonard, and Andrew Prior. *South African Politics.* New Haven, Connecticut: Yale University Press, 1982.

Thurston, Anne F. *Enemies of the People.* Cambridge, Massachusetts: Harvard University Press, 1988.

Tomasevich, Jovo. *The Chetniks.* Stanford, California: Stanford University Press, 1975.

Toolis, Kevin. *Rebel Hearts.* New York: St. Martins, 1995.

Trouillot, Michel-Rolph. *Haiti: State Against Nation.* New York: Monthly Review Press, 1990.

Van den Berghe, Pierre. *South Africa: A Study in Conflict.* Berkeley, California: University of California Press, 1967.

Vickers, Miranda. *Between Serb and Albanian.* New York: Columbia University Press, 1998.

Vickery, Michael. *Cambodia, 1975–1982.* Boston: South End Press, 1984.

Viorst, Milton. *In the Shadow of the Prophet.* Boulder, Colorado: Westview, 2001.

Waite, Robert G.L. *The Psychopathic God: Adolf Hitler.* New York: Da Capo Press, 1993.

Warrior, Valerie. *Roman Religion.* Cambridge, United Kingdom: Cambridge University Press, 2006.

West, Rebecca. *Black Lamb and Grey Falcon.* New York: Penguin, 1940.

West, Richard. *Tito and the Rise and Fall of Yugoslavia.* New York: Carroll and Graf, 1994.

White, Lynn T. III. *Politics of Chaos.* Princeton, New Jersey: Princeton University Press, 1989.

Wilber, Donald. *Iran: Past and Present.* Princeton, New Jersey: Princeton University Press, 1981.

Wilkes, John. *The Illyrians.* Oxford, United Kingdom: Blackwell, 1992.

Williams, Maslyn. *The Land In Between.* Sydney, Australia: Collins, 1969.

Willis, Michael. *The Islamist Challenge in Algeria.* New York: New York University Press, 1996.

Woodward, Calvin A. *The Growth of a Party System in*

Ceylon. Providence, Rhode Island: Brown University Press, 1969.

Wright, Robin. *In the Name of God*. New York: Simon and Schuster, 1989.

_____. *The Last Great Revolution: Turmoil and Transformation in Iran*. New York: Vintage, 2000.

Wucker, Michelle. *Why the Cocks Fight*. New York: Hill and Wang, 1999.

Yaghmaian, Behzad. *Social Change in Iran*. New York: State University of New York Press, 2002.

Yalman, Nur. *Under the Bo Tree*. Berkeley: University of California Press, 1971.

Yathay, Pin. *"Stay Alive, My Son."* New York: Simon and Schuster, 1988.

Zhai Zhenhua. *Red Flower of China*. New York: Soho, 1982.

Zuccotti, Susan. *The Italians and the Holocaust*. New York: Basic Books, 1987.

Index

Fermanagh County 38
Fermi, Laura 156
Fest, Joachim 22–23
Firmenich, Mario 183
Fiume 162
The Flame (Gabriele D'Annunzio) 159
Fon 188
Formosa province (Argentina) 172
Fort Hare College 209
Foster, R.F. 37
Foundations of Psychohistory (Lloyd de Mause) 3
Fourcaud, Dr. Jacques 196
France: in Algeria 131; revolution in 189; in Rwanda 68
Franco, Francisco 153
Franz Ferdinand, Archduke 160
Free Presbyterian Church 54
Free Radio and Television of the Thousand Hills (RTLM) 68, 71
Freud, Sigmund 2, 79
Fromm, Erich 7, 19
Frondizi, Arturo 183
Front for the Advancement and Progress of Haiti (FRAPH) 200–202
Fur 123
Futurists 159

Gaelic language 36, 41
Galtieri, Gen. Leopoldo 186
Gang of Four 102, 111, 113–115
ganja 80
Garang, John 122–123
Garraway, Doris 189
gauchos 173–174
General Workers Confederation (CGT) (Argentina) 179, 182
Gentile, Giovanni 158, 160
German Democratic Party (DDP) 25
German National People's Party (DNVP) 25
German People's Party (DVP) 25
Germany: assassinations in 21; childhood in 10; colonial empire of 22, 24; Drang Nach Osten in 26; educational system in 20, 21, 30; entitlement fantasy in 13, 21; fairy tales of 24–25; fear of Communism in 29; Great Depression in 28; Gypsies in 27; Jews in 12, 15, 25ff., 31, 32; masochism in 23; Masons in 27; and Slavs 26–27; *sonderweg* in 19; starvation fantasy in 26; war guilt in 10, 18, 31, 32–33
Gilan province 138
Giovinezza (Italian Fascist Anthem) 159, 164
Gisenyi 67
Gitera, Joseph 65
Giuliano, Balbino 153
Goa 11
God-stealing 166
Goebbels, Josef 29–30
golondrinas 174

Göring, Hermann 29–30
Gourevitch, Philip 64
Gourgue, Gerard 201
Goyigamas 79, 81, 84
grand blancs 188–189
Grandqvist, Hans 102
Great Britain: in South Africa 206
Great Leap Forward 105–106
Great Trek 206
Greece: Italian invasion of 158, 165, 168
Gregor, A. James 170
Grimm Brothers 24–25
group fantasies 8
Guangdong province 106

Habyarimana, Agathe Kanziga 68
Habyarimana, Juvenal 64, 66–67, 69, 72; assassination of 70–71
Hai Jui Dismissed from Office 107
Haider, Jorg 33
Haing Ngor 89, 96
Haiti: foreign intervention in 193–194; homosexuality in 192; Hurricane Hazel in 187; malnutrition in 187; maroons in 189; mulattoes in 188–190; overpopulation of 187; partition of (1807) 190; peasants in 191; population of 187; slavery in 188; soil exhaustion in 187
Hallward, Peter 190
Hatzfeld, Jean 74
Haughey, Charles 36
Heng Samrin 99
hero culture 48
Herzog, J.B.M. 212
Hilberg, Raoul 60
Himmler, Heinrich 22, 26, 29
Hitler, Adolf 19, 20, 21, 29–30, 31
Hitler Youth 23
Hitler's Willing Executioners (Daniel Jonah Goldhagen) 19, 32
Hittites 127
holistic thought 17
hollow Earth theory 20
holocaust 6, 31
Homey, Karen 2
Hong Yung Lee 106
Horrors of War (Franjo Tudjman) 57
Hou Yuon 93
houngans 197–198
How to Be a Good Communist (Liu Shaoqi) 104
Hoxha, Enver 55
Hsuan Tsang 76
Hu Nim 93
Hun Sen 99
Hungary 50
Hussein 139–140
Hussein, Saddam 148
hypnosis 156

Ibn Abdallah, Mohammed Ahmad 118
L'Idea Nazionale 158
identification with the aggressor 11

Ieng Sary 89
Illia, Arturo 183
Illyrians, Illyrian movement 49–50
immigrants, in Argentina 174–175
Impuzamugambe 69, 72
Incas 172
India 88, 109, 129; war with China 11
Indians, in Argentina 172, 173
inferiority complex 14
Inkatha Freedom Party 209ff.
Inner Mongolia 111ff.
interactionism 17–18
Interahamwe 69, 71–72
International Psychohistorical Association 3
Inyenzi 66
Iran: drug problem in 144–145; dyarchy in 149; economic growth in 143; ethnic groups in 138; family life in 139; paranoia in 137; Shi'ite Islam in 141; suicide rate in 152
Iran Air flight #655 148
Iraq, 2003 invasion of 18
Irish-Americans 37
Irish Independence Party 43
Irish Republican Army (IRA) 43, 44, 46
Irish War of Independence 38
Islamic Salvation Front (FIS) 134–135
Island in Reverse (Joaquín Balaguer) 194
Issaraks 91, 92
Italian Social Movement 170
Italian Social Republic 169
Italy: anti–Semitism in 166–168; birth trauma in 157–158; colonial expansion of 156–157; defeat of in Battle of Adowa 15–16; family life in 154; Nazi occupation of 168; reunification of 156; wars of 165; in World War I 160–161; in World War II 168–169; xenophobia in 168
Izetbegovich, Alija 59

Jaffrelot, Christophe 130
Jamaica 187
James, C.L.R. 189
James, Daniel 181
Janata Vimukhti Peramuna (JVP) 84, 85
janjaweed 121
Janov, Arthur 2, 9, 220, 224
Japanese invasion of China 33
Jasenovac 57
Jatika Sevaka Sangamaya (JSS) 83
Jawed, Nasim Ahmed 129
Jayawardena, Junius Richard 83
Jelachic, Baron Josip 50
Jellinek, Walter 25
Jeremie 190
Jews: in Algeria 131–132; in Argentina 178, 185; in Italy 167–168, 170
Jiang Qing 102, 105, 107–108, 113–114